RULED BY RACE

RULED BY RACE

Black/White Relations in Arkansas from Slavery to the Present

GRIF STOCKLEY

The University of Arkansas Press
Fayetteville
2009

Manufactured in the United States of America

ISBN-10: 1-55728-885-2
ISBN-13: 978-1-55728-885-1

13 12 11 10 09 1 2 3 4 5

Designed by Liz Lester

♾ The paper used in this publication meets the minimum requirements of the American National Standard for Permanence of Paper for Printed Library Materials Z39.48-1984.

LIBRARY OF CONGRESS CATALOGING-IN-PUBLICATION DATA

Stockley, Grif.
Ruled by race : Black/White relations in Arkansas from slavery to the present / Grif Stockley.
p. cm.
Includes bibliographical references and index.
ISBN-13: 978-1-55728-885-1 (cloth : alk. paper)
ISBN-10: 1-55728-885-2 (cloth : alk. paper)
1. Arkansas—Race relations. 2. African Americans—Arkansas—History. 3. African Americans—Arkansas—Social conditions. 4. African Americans—Civil rights—Arkansas. I. Title.
E185.93.A8S768 2009
305.896'0730767—dc22

2008031017

To my granddaughter, Emily Catherine Tulk

CONTENTS

ILLUSTRATIONS

Following page 250

ACKNOWLEDGMENTS

In 1976 I first began working on a book whose subject was a history of Arkansas race relations between African Americans and whites. Thanks to a number of Arkansans and Arkansas institutions, I have been able to return to this project. In 2007 the Butler Center for Arkansas Studies published *Race Relations in the Natural State,* which has been approved by the Arkansas Department of Education for high school students. That book is intended to supplement Arkansas history texts. Although it does not contain a chapter on Hispanic immigrants, *Ruled by Race: Black/White Relations in Arkansas from Slavery to the Present* is a much more comprehensive version of *Race Relations in the Natural* State. It is intended to be a documented survey of the history of race relations between blacks and whites in Arkansas and does not concentrate specifically on the African American experience. Though it relies heavily on the work—published and unpublished of others—it contains original research, particularly beginning with the fire at the Negro Boys Industrial School in 1959. Though research by many excellent scholars in the last fifty years or so has transformed our understanding of Arkansas racial history between blacks and whites, clearly we have only begun to explore this subject.

To begin, I must express my deepest gratitude to Dr. Bobby Roberts and Dr. David Stricklin who, with the aid of generous donors, are creating an environment for the study of Arkansas history second to none. The Arkansas Studies Institute across the street from the main library in the River Market in Little Rock will be a treasured resource for generations of Arkansans to come.

Dr. Roberts made it possible for me in 2006 to continue

to research and write this book through a fellowship named in honor of the great Arkansas historian Dee Brown. A timely grant from the Darragh Foundation allowed me to continue through June 2007. I must also acknowledge the generous support of the Winthrop Rockefeller Foundation for the Butler Center's Ruled by Race Project, which is allowing the center to make available to Arkansas history teachers lessons plans and other materials on race relations for the purpose of supplementing existing history texts.

Dr. David Stricklin, head of the Butler Center for Arkansas Studies and an academic historian, patiently, ever so patiently, served as editor for *Race Relations in the Natural State* as well as *Ruled by Race* and cheerfully saw them both to completion. Constantly busy with other duties, he performed this chore with expertise and tact, and I am enormously in his debt.

I have been aided throughout by my colleagues both at the Butler Center and the *Encyclopedia of Arkansas*. I thank Kay Bland, Stephanie Bayless, Jajuan Johnson, Holly Mathisen, Brian Robertson, Charles Rodgers, Rhonda Stewart, Shirley Schuette, Anna Morshedi, Nathania Sawyer, Guy Lancaster, Anna Lancaster, Mike Polston, and Michael Keckhaver. A special thanks for compiling the index to Butler Center staff Chris Stewart and Sara Thompson. I am indebted to Bob Razer and to all the librarians and employees at the Central Arkansas Library System who have made my stay a pleasure and particularly to the youth services staff that has graciously shared its space.

At the Arkansas History Commission, I have continued to receive wonderful service from Wendy Richter, Russell P. Baker, Linda McDowell, Carolyn Hervey, and Lynn Ewbank.

I thank the staff at the University of Arkansas at Little Rock, Ottenheimer Library, Archives and Special Collections. Similarly, I am indebted to the special collections staffs at the University of Arkansas at Fayetteville, University of Central Arkansas, Arkansas State University, the Wisconsin State Historical Society, and the Library of Congress.

I am also indebted to the following historians: Jayme

Stone, Randy Finley, Johanna Miller Lewis, Jeannie Whayne, Elizabeth Jacoway, Fred Williams, Nan Woodruff, John Kirk, Story Machen-Rawn, Tom DeBlack, Blake Wintory, Gene Vinzant, Holly McGee, Michael Dougan, S. Charles Bolton, Carl Moneyhon, Vincent Vinikas, Kenneth Barnes, Mark Christ, Caroline Proctor, Sondra Gordy, George Lankford, Todd Lewis, Elizabeth Payne, John Graves, Laura Miller, Ethel Simpson, Ben Johnson III, Judith Kilpatrick, Ronnie Nichols, Richard Cortner, Williard Gatewood, Brent Riffel, Jessica Hayes, and Geoffery Stark.

I would be remiss in not expressing my appreciation to historian Tom Dillard, who from the very beginning of my career as a writer has encouraged and assisted me with each project involving Arkansas racial history. Now at the University of Arkansas at Fayetteville, Tom's expertise in black history has been shared with many historians.

Thank you also to Lynn Pence, Annie Abrams, Walter Nunn, Barrie Olson, Joanna Edwards, Kathryn Fitzhugh, Ernie Dumas, Dr. Cal Ledbetter, Brady Banta, Starr Mitchell, J. E. Bush IV, Constance Sarto, Dan Tulk, Dr. Gordon Morgan, Dr. Jay Barth, Roy Reed, Jim Porter, Tim Nutt, Terrence Roberts, Minnijean Brown, Elizabeth Eckford, Thelma Mothershed, Ernest Green, and Sarah Ziegenbein.

Finally, I heartily express my gratitude to the University of Arkansas Press; to its editor and director, Larry Malley; to Julie Watkins, Tom Lavoie, and Brian King; and to D. S. Cunningham, who copyedited this book. All errors and omissions are mine alone.

INTRODUCTION

We are ruled by race in Arkansas. For almost 150 continuous years, interrupted in part and only briefly by the politics of Reconstruction, white Arkansans since territorial days used whatever means necessary to control and dominate black persons. Generation upon generation of white Arkansans, with some notable exceptions, chose slavery, murder, rape, torture, beatings, intimidation, fraud, theft, discrimination, harassment, and humiliation as the instruments of control and domination of black Arkansans. Beginning with slavery white Arkansans justified this domination through their insistence that blacks were not only intellectually and emotionally undeserving of democracy and equality but were inherently dangerous. This repeated justification of white supremacy was ultimately no more than a rationalization to excuse economic exploitation and continued domination. At the same time white Arkansans insisted that their treatment of African Americans fell squarely within the most revered traditions of Southern paternalism and was absolutely necessary under the circumstances.

It was not until the modern civil rights movement in the 1960s that this power began to be seriously curbed by the federal government and by black people themselves. Simultaneously, with the arrival of farm mechanization and other technological innovations that made a large black labor force superfluous, some influential members of the white power structure recognized that the stability and growth of their communities in Arkansas were better served by a grudging and often token acceptance of the changes demanded by blacks and the law and imposed by the federal government.[1]

Despite this legacy of relentless white supremacy, at no point did black Arkansans remain passive in the teeth of such an onslaught. As we shall see, beginning with the slave era and continuing through the 1960s, black Arkansans attempted various strategies to carve out an existence that allowed them to live with dignity and autonomy. In Steven Hahn's Pulitzer Prize–winning book, *A Nation Under Our Feet: Black Political Struggles in the Rural South from Slavery to the Great Migration,* he describes the struggles of Southern rural blacks and in so doing captures much of the flavor of the Arkansas experience. He writes

> about extraordinary people who did extraordinary things under the most difficult of circumstances and, in the process, transformed themselves and the world in which they lived. . . . It is . . . about how African Americans in the rural South conducted politics and engaged in political struggle as slaves and as freedpeople, about how they constituted themselves as political actors in a society that tried to refuse them that part, and thus how they gave powerful direction to America's revolutionary experience of disunion, emancipation, and nation-building.[2]

For all Arkansans of the time Hahn describes, geography, of course, was destiny within the context of the Southern experience. Numerous Arkansas historians have pointed out the frontier qualities that made Arkansas unique as part of the Old South.[3] It is enough here to acknowledge that as, a frontier state of the Old South, timing, of course, was everything. As we shall see, when the nation burst apart in 1861, Arkansas was just beginning the process of becoming a major slave state. Its distinct geography, divided diagonally into fertile lowlands and highlands, made the state like and at the same time quite unlike, for example, Mississippi. When war came, Arkansas's location in the west made the state, much to its leaders' chagrin, an afterthought instead of a major player in the Civil War. As important as the Reconstruction era was in giving opportunities to blacks within the state—an unsurpassed record twenty blacks were elected in 1873 to serve in the legislature—their leadership roles were limited in comparison, for example, to Mississippi, which sent two African Americans to the U.S. Senate.[4] Relatively soon after the war ended, once again geography dictated the state's racial composition, for blacks from the older cotton states such as Georgia, Alabama, and Mississippi, lured by labor contractors, poured into the state seeking greater freedom and opportunities. By the 1890s lynching was on the rise, and Arkansas soon joined the rest of the Old South in passing Jim Crow legislation and measures to disfranchise its black citizens. For most of the first half of the twentieth century, the state's commitment to white supremacy in many ways made it little different from the rest of the Old South. By the late 1940s, however, Arkansas distinguished itself from other Old South states by admitting a few blacks into graduate schools without litigation, welcoming blacks into the Democratic Party (with litigation), and even voluntarily desegregating some facilities in the capital city of Little Rock. These progressive events appeared to make all the more unlikely the 1957 Central High School desegregation crisis, an event which briefly captured the entire world's attention. The attention given to Arkansas was soon overshadowed by events in other Deep South states with much larger black populations and governors more determined than Orval E. Faubus to make a career of defying the federal government. Though the Student Non-violent Coordinating Committee (SNCC) established itself in Arkansas in the 1960s, the nation's attention was turned to more violent locales like Philadelphia, Mississippi, and Birmingham. By 1966 Arkansas seemed to be leading the way to the New South with the election of Republican Winthrop Rockefeller, a genuine progressive on the issue of race. However, the murder of Martin Luther King Jr. in 1968 appeared to reignite the civil rights movement in the Arkansas Delta, and towns like Forrest City and Marianna experienced violence and bitter boycotts that were reminiscent of an earlier phase of the civil rights movement. Since then, Arkansas has been much like other Southern states in trying to cope with white flight and school desegregation issues.

Why should white and black Arkansans read this book? The short answer is that the human condition drives them to seek answers about their behavior and values as individuals and as a society. As they take stock of their lives, they cannot avoid noticing at the end of the day after school and work the physical and emotional separation between most blacks and whites in Arkansas. These questions of why they are so isolated from each other are worth pondering if only because they sense the answers will tell them something about themselves that their study of Arkansas history has not revealed. They sense that clues to their present behavior have to do with the past but have been provided no convincing narrative of a comprehensive racial history that begins with the slave era and ends in the present.

A consequence of white supremacy has been the historical fact of black racism and black self-hatred. Beginning with slavery, in Arkansas, for example, African Americans learned at every turn from their masters that a lighter skin color meant advantages that nothing else could provide. With the inevitable consequence of the sexual domination and exploitation by white males of black women during slavery, a racial pecking order based on white ancestry, skin color, and class arose that would profoundly affect not only race relations between whites and blacks but those among blacks themselves.[5] As today's historians and political scientists acknowledge, the cost of maintaining white supremacy in Arkansas was immeasurable in many ways, not only to the generations of people it affected but also to the very institutions of state government.

Ruled by Race

Now, where Arkansans live, send their children to school, work, travel, shop, spend leisure time, worship, and are buried and whom they choose as friends and life partners are guided by considerations of race. As documented by the media, racial tension exists in every part of the state. The contempt and rage that exist between many blacks and whites in Arkansas run beneath the surface like underground streams that occasionally boil out of the ground with a suddenness and a fury that compel the nation's attention. Taken as a whole, the examples sketched below suggest deeply rooted anger and pent-up frustration on the part of both blacks and whites. I shall review these incidents in more detail in the last chapter. In 2003 in the southern Arkansas town of Fordyce, the prosecuting attorney charged two black female nurse's aides with murder and conspiracy to commit murder for the beating death with brass knuckles by one of them of an elderly white female resident in a nursing home. Ominously, the motive for beating to death this helpless woman, who suffered from dementia, was racial: she had "disrespected" the aide charged with murder.[6]

In 2004 in central Arkansas, which has often considered itself a model for race relations for the rest of the state, the Little Rock School Board split along strictly racial lines in a five-to-two vote to close the small, mostly black Mitchell Academy. Angry that the school board did not hire as superintendent of the Little Rock School District Morris Holmes, a former principal of Central High School, and interim superintendent Leon Modeste, a member of a group called Concerned Citizens United, confronted the school board:

> It is becoming quite apparent what majority white board members were seeking in a superintendent. It would seem they wanted a person of black complexion but of white mentality like themselves. One who would do their bidding and mirror their insensitivity, indifference and callousness to parents and the community.[7]

The majority white board had selected Roy Brooks, a black educator from out of state who had convinced them that his primary goal would be to try to equalize test scores. The white majority of the board was thought by many in the black community to have given little consideration to the application of Morris Holmes who had been widely trusted and respected by many black patrons of the school district. In 2007 black members of the board, now constituting a majority after recent elections, voted to buy out Brooks's contract, alleging as one of their reasons that he failed to consult with black members on the board.

In 2004 at the state capitol in Little Rock, black leaders rallied on the steps of the capitol protesting the incontestable fact that 45 percent of Arkansas's prison population is black while only about 15 percent of the state's population is African American. Blacks wanted comparison data on plea bargains and probation. "African-Americans are not inherently criminal people," state senator Hank Wilkins told the crowd.[8]

Though former University of Arkansas at Fayetteville basketball coach Nolan Richardson was not successful in 2004 in a racial discrimination lawsuit against his former employers for wrongful termination of his contract and violation of his constitutional rights, federal judge Bill Wilson found:

> There was troubling testimony from witnesses about racism in the higher ranks of UAF. A former member of the Board of Trustees and former board chair, and a current board member admitted, during examination by Plaintiff's counsel, that they still use the word "nigger" and tell racial and ethnic jokes. Most troubling to me was that neither of these witnesses seemed abashed by their admissions.[9]

In the Arkansas Delta in towns such as Helena–West Helena, blacks and whites battled for control. In 2005 black attorney Dion Wilson told the *Arkansas Times,* "I come from a place where *race* is the order of the day. Every move you make in Phillips County is *that.*"[10] In the summer of 2007 a white West Memphis policeman shot and killed unarmed twelve-year-old DeAunta Farrow, touching off a racial confrontation in that city that has continued into 2008.

Fairly or unfairly, blacks simply avoid northwest Arkansas. "The reputation within the state is that the area is racist," said Shanna Ammons in her Rogers home. "We knew Harrison was the headquarters for the Ku Klux Klan. No one wanted to come here for college, because this area of the state always had bad connotations."[11]

The Burden of Arkansas History

Though today's racial flare-ups in the state play out in the glare of media attention, the official telling of Arkansas's racial past was put in the service of white supremacy for much of the state's existence. Until it becomes a routine matter for students of Arkansas history to acknowledge this reality, readers will continue to puzzle over the absence of much of the state's racial history. In his 2005 book, *The Southern Past: A Clash of Race and Memory,* W. Fitzhugh Brundage observes,

> When the North Carolina and Arkansas history commissions made their first forays into marking and preserving historic "shrines," as they were charged to do by their charters, they inevitably focused on sites hallowed by whites. To the extent that the history of African Americans was preserved, it was through official documents and slaveholders' records. Black newspapers, institutional records, and private correspondence went uncollected. The void in the collections of the South impeded opportunities to understand the southern racial order from any perspective other than that of its architects. Moreover, it twisted and constrained all subsequent historical research on African Americans in the region, effectively erasing black historical agency.[12]

Arkansas State University history professor Dr. Calvin Smith, who graduated from Robert R. Moton High School in the heart of the Arkansas Delta in Marianna in Lee County in 1961, remembers, "The books that we got from Futrall [the white high school] had nothing on black history. To read them was to reinforce your nonexistence."[13]

Worse than that, for generations when they did appear in Arkansas history books, African Americans were variously portrayed as happy but limited children to be guided, mindless Sambos to be worked, sexual beasts to be controlled, and devious and treacherous pawns of evil whites, never as self-directed adults.

None of this was by accident. As Brundage contends, "At its most fundamental level, the project of public history in the early twentieth century South was the archiving of white civilization."[14] The consequences have been enormous to the general understanding of the past. Brundage writes, "In ways obvious and subtle, public history in the South explained white racial privilege as the inevitable and proper consequence of history."[15]

Thus, the value of a book on race relations in Arkansas is compromised not only by what both races do not know about the actions and motivation of African Americans in the past but also often by what whites, in particular, have said and done in order to justify the present.

Morality and History

I have three goals in writing this book: (1) to understand what has happened between whites and blacks from the time Arkansas became a territory and coming forward to the present era, (2) to understand why race relations have followed the course they have, and (3) to explore in the present the moral significance, if any, of race relations in light of the state's past.[16]

Historians know well that any inquiry into the past that touches on the morality of any era is a tricky proposition. The temptation is to judge the past in light of present day standards of morality. Thus, my goal is not to judge Arkansans of the past but to understand why they believed what they did and why they behaved as they did.

As it must, this book begins with slavery, an institution that proved irresistible to the white Arkansan who needed and could afford slaves. It conferred status, provided leisure from unwanted and difficult tasks, allowed some to escape from subsistence and others to become wealthy, and provided a source of pleasure for white males. The reader is asked to be mindful that the purpose is not to give a complete picture of the institution in Arkansas but to point out those features that affected the relationship between blacks and whites.

RULED BY RACE

CHAPTER 1

Voices of Slavery

The forty-six years of slavery in Arkansas (1819–1865) have to be understood in human terms to appreciate their power and influence over the *telling* of the state's history for so many generations. Until we begin to appreciate the profound grip slavery had on the state of Arkansas and its institutions, we will not be able to understand the ineffable bitterness that came when it ended.

Let us begin with the voices of former slaves who were living in Arkansas toward the very end of the slave era or, in some cases, with their memories of what their parents told them about the institution. A "New Deal" creation of the Works Progress Administration (WPA) during the Great Depression, the Federal Writers Project hired unemployed writers to write about each state. As part of one of the projects, writers were hired to interview former slaves about their experiences. Fortunately, almost all of these interviews with individuals who had been slaves in Arkansas have now been collected into a single book by George Lankford.[1]

Scholars of slavery have been reluctant to rely on these slave narratives as stand-alone information about slavery because of the advanced ages of the interviewees and the impossibility of verifying their accounts of often brutal treatment. Of the 186 interviews collected by Lankford, approximately one-third relate an episode of violence against an Arkansas slave. What safeguards are in place to guard against exaggeration or outright falsehood from a bitter survivor of the slave era? In fact, one might begin by consulting the written accounts of Freedmen's Bureau personnel in Arkansas after slavery ended during the period known as Reconstruction (set out in detail in Chapter 4) to understand that whipping of blacks was still a regular event on and off the plantation. The head of the Freedmen's Bureau for Arkansas, General John Sprague, reported in September 1866 that although there were a few planters who did not abuse freedmen most were of the opinion that "the only way to manage niggers is to whip them and make them *know their* places."[2] The brutality was mind boggling. Randy Finley has documented that "pregnant women at Hamburg and Camden received such severe beatings that they miscarried their unborn children."[3]

"Discipline"

The following except is from Sallie Crane, estimated to be over ninety years old. Crane said she was born in Hempstead County and had never been out of the state in her entire life.

> I have worn a buck and gag in my mouth for three days for trying to run away. I couldn't eat nor drink—couldn't even catch the slobber that fell from my mouth and run down my chest till the flies settled on it and blowed it. 'Scuse me but jus' look at these places (She pulled open her waist and showed scars where the maggots had eaten in. . . .) They kept a bowl filled with vinegar and salt and pepper settin' nearby, and when they had whipped me till the blood come, they would take the mop and sponge the cuts with this stuff so it would hurt more. They would whip me with the cowhide part of the time and with birch sprouts the other part. There were splinters long as my finger left in my back. . . . They jus' whipped me 'cause they could —'cause they had the privilege. It wasn't nothing' I done; they just whipped me. My married young master, Joe and his wife, Jennie, they was the ones that did the whipping. But I belonged to Miss Evelyn.[4]

In matter-of-fact terms, the former slave T. W. Cotton, age eighty, remembered being a small boy in Phillips County "when the Civil War broke out." His mother was a cook for the master, Ed Cotton. "We lived in part of their house. Walter (white) and me slept together." Without warning, the narrative reads,

> Aunt Ruthie was a field hand. Aunt Adeline must have been a field hand, too. She hung herself on a black jack tree on the other side of the pool. . . . She hung herself to keep from getting a whooping. Mother raised (reared) her boy. She told mother she would kill herself before she would be whooped. . . . She took a rope and tied it to a limb and to her neck and then jumped. Her toes barely touched the ground. They buried her in the cemetery on the old Ed Cotton place.[5]

Adrianna Kerns, eighty-five, who was born in Tulip in Dallas County, said she

> had three aunts in the field. They could handle a plow and roll logs as well as any man. Trees would blow down and trees would have to be carried to a heap and burned. I been whipped many a time by my mistress and overseer. I'd be behind with my work and he would come by and give me a lick with his bull whip he carried with him.[6]

Kerns continued:

> When we [Viney and I] got larger we worked in the field picking cotton and pulling corn as high as we could reach. You had to pull the fodder first before you could pull the corn. When we had to come out of the field on account of the rain, we would go to the corn crib and shuck corn if we didn't have some weaving to do. We got so we could weave and spin. When master caught us playing, he would set us to cutting jackets. He would give us each two or three switches and we would stand up and whip each other. I would go easy on Viney but she would try to cut me to pieces. She hit me so hard I

> would say, "Yes suh, massa." And she would say, "Why you sayin' 'Yes suh, massa,' to me? I ain't doing nothin' to you."[7]

Peter Brown, age eighty-six, who was born on the "Woodlawn Place" outside of Pine Bluff, gave the following account:

> My remembrance of slavery is not atall favorable. I heard the master and overseers whooping the slaves b'fore day. They had stakes fixed in the ground and tied them down on their stomachs stretched out and they beat them with a bull whip (cowhide woven). They would break their blisters on them with white oak paddles that had holes in it so that it would suck. . . . I heard that going on when I was a child morning after morning.[8]

Joe Ray, age eighty-three, told his interviewer that he was born in Fulton, Arkansas, in 1855.

> Dere was two overseers on the place and dey carried a bull whip all the time. They didn't whip the girls; the old master pinch their ears if dey get mean and not mind. But I saw a slave man whipped until his shirt was cut to pieces! Dey whipped dem like horses, but the master didn't want dem beat to death. If dey whip dem too hard the old master shake his head and say, "Dat's too much money to kill!"[9]

Mollie Barber, seventy-nine, said she was born on the plantation of Nat Turner four miles north of Helena two years before the Civil War broke out. "Dey had a white overseer to run things. He picked out de biggest slave man on de place and made him de 'whip-man.' When de overseer or de Master figured out a slave was due a beating dey call in de whip man and he lay on de lash."[10]

Katie Rowe, eighty-eight, recalled her experiences while living on a plantation near Washington in Hempstead County.

> Old man Saunders was de hardest overseer of anybody. He would git mad and give a whipping some time and de slave wouldn't even know what it was about. My

uncle Sandy was de lead row nigger, and he was a good nigger and never would tech a drap of likker. One night some de niggers get hold of some likker somehow, and dey leave de jug half full on de step of Sandy's cabin. Next morning old man Saunders come out in de field so mad he was pale. He jus go to de lead row and tell Sandy to go wid him, and start toward de woods along Bois d'Arc Creek wid Sandy following behind. De overseer always carry a big heavy stick, but we didn't know he was so mad, and dey just went off in de woods. Purty soon we hear Sandy hollering and we knew old overseer pouring it on, den de overseer come back by his self and go on up to de house. Come late evening he come and see what we done in de day's work, and go back to de quarters wid us all. When he git to mammy's cabin, whar grandmammy live too, he say to grandmammy, "I sent Sandy down in de woods to hunt a hoss, he gwine come in hungry purty soon. You better make him an extra hoe cake," and he kind of laugh and go on to his house. Jest soon as he gone we all tell grandmammy we think he got a whipping, and so 'nuff he didn't come in. De next day some white boys find uncle Sandy what dat overseer done killed him and thowed him in a little pond and dey never done nothing to old man Saunders at all![11]

When he go to whip a nigger he makes him strip to de waist, and he take a cat-o-nine tails and bring de blisters, and den bust the blisters wid a wide strap of leather fastened to a stick handle. I seen de blood running out'n many a back, all de way from de neck to de waist! Many de time a nigger git blistered and cut up so dat we have to git a sheet and grease it wid lard and wrap 'em up in it, and dey have to wear a greasy cloth wrapped around dey body under de shirt for three-four days afer dey git a big whipping![12]

Horatio W. Williams, age eighty-three, was born on July 2, 1854. He was a slave of Woodruff Norsworthy in Pine Bluff. He remembered the following, after a slave stole the shirt of a guest.

> When de boss finds it out he takes dat nigger down in de bottom and I crawls through de bresh and watches. Dey tie he foots together over de limb and let he head hang down and beat him till de blood run down on de roots of dat tree. When dey takes him down he back look like raw meat and he nearly die.[13]

Maggie Wesmoland, eighty-five, described in tragic detail the relationship among herself, her young white mistress, "Miss Betty," and her middle-aged husband, a man named Cargo near Des Arc in White County.

> I had a hard time. I was awfully abused by the old man that married Miss Betty. She was my young mistress. He was poor and hated Negroes. He said they didn't have no feeling. He drunk all the time. He never had been used to Negroes and he didn't like em. He was a middle age man but Miss Betty Holland was in her teens. . . . Nothing Miss Betty ever told him did a bit of good. . . . I was scared to death of him—he beat me so I'm scarred up all over now where he lashed me. He would strip me start naked and tie my hands crossed and whoop me till the blood ooze out and drip on the ground when I walked. The flies blowed me time and again. Miss Betty catch him gone, would grease my places and pat turpentine on them to kill the places blowed. He kept a bundle of hickory switches at the house all the time. Miss Betty was good to me. She would cry and beg him to be good to me.[14]

O. W. Green, seventy-eight, Bradley County:

> My old masta was good, but when he found you shoutin' he burnt your hand. My grandmother said he burnt her hand several times. Masta wouldn't let de cullud folks have meetin,' but dey would go out in the woods in secret to pray and preach and shout.[15]

Resistance by Slaves

Lucindy Allison, Poinsett County, said that an aunt had told her about a slave woman who was pregnant and working in the fields.

> She didn't keep up. Said the riding boss got down, dug a hole with the hoe to lay her in it 'cause she was so big in front. Her mother told him if he had put her daughter there in that hole she'd cop him up in pieces with her hoe. He found he had two to conquer and he let her be. But he had to leave 'cause he couldn't whoop the niggers.[16]
>
> My mother had Indian in her. She would fight. She was the pet of the people. When she was out, the pateroles [Arkansas law permitted designated whites to whip blacks who were found off the plantation without permission] would whip her because she didn't have a pass. She has showed me scars that were on her even till the day that she died. She was whipped because she was out without a pass. She could have had a pass any time for the asking, but she was too proud to ask. She never wanted to do things by permission.
>
> My pappy killed an overseer who tried to lash him; they sent him off to another plantation for a while. Dat's all the punishment he got.[17]

Peter Brown, age eighty-six, Helena, said,

> Ma had to go to work when she wasn't able. Papa stole her out and one night a small panther smelled them and come on a log up over where they slept in a canebrake. Pa killed it with a bowie knife. Ma had a baby out there in the canebrake. Pa stole her out. They went back and they never made her work no more. She was a fast breeder; she had three sets of twins. They told him if he would stay out of the woods they wouldn't make her work no more, take care of her children. They prized fast breeders.[18]

Lewis Chase, about ninety, Prairie County, said,

> I was sold. Yes mam I sho was. Jes put up on a platform and auctioned off. Sold rite here in Des Arc. Nom taint right. . . . One man I sho was glad didn't get me cause he whoop me. No'om he didn't get me. I heard him putting up the prices and I sho hope he didn't get me. . . . My old mistress [Mrs. Snibley] whoop me till I run off and they took me back when they found out where I lef from. I stayed way bout two weeks.[19]

Charlie McClendon, seventy-seven, Jefferson County, said,

> My father run off and stay in the woods one or two months. Old master say, "Now, Jordan, why you run off? Now I'm goin' to give you a light brushin' and don't you run off again." But he'd run off again after awhile. . . . He had one man named Miles Johnson just stayed in the woods so he put him on the block and sold him.[20]

Sex

Augustus Robertson, seventy-eight, said that he was born in Calhoun County in 1860 but was sold.

> My daddy was a white man, my master. His wife was so mean to me that my master sold me to keep her from beating me and kicking me and knocking me around. She would have killed me if she could have got the chance.[21]

Apparently to get him out of harm's way, Robertson said his father sold him to a preacher who raised him as his own son.

> Whenever he sat down to the table to eat, I sat down. He made no difference at all. He raised me in El Dorado, Arkansas. His name was James Godwin. He sent me to school too.[22]

Anthony Taylor, approximately seventy-eight, was born on a vast plantation between Malvern and Arkadelphia in Clark County.

I heard that if the boss man wanted to be with women that they had, the women would be scared not to be with him for fear he would whip them. And when they started whipping them for that they kept on till they got what they wanted. They would take them 'way off and have dealings with them. That is where so much of that yellow and half-white comes from.[23]

Katie Rye, eighty-two, Faulkner County, said,

We lived in Greenbrier, Faulkner County, Arkansas. All staid at home and got along very well. We had enough to eat and wear. Mistress was awful mean to us but we staid with them until after the war. . . . They awful good to us, but mistress was so high tempered she would get mad and whip some of the slaves but she never whipped any of us. We had two white grand pas and grand mas. We colored children called them grandpa and ma and uncle and aunt like the white children did and we didn't know the difference.[24]

Jeff Davis, age seventy-eight, remembered the following:

There was several white mens dat I knowed in dis part of de county what raised nigger fambles, but there wasn't so many at dat. I will say this for them mens though. While it wasn't right for dem to do like dat, dem what did have em a nigger woman what they had chillum by sure took care of de whole gang. I riccolect one white man in particular, an' I knows you is heered of him too. How-some-ever, I won't call no names. He lived down on de ribber on de island. The white man, he was a overseer for a sidder woman what lived in Helena an' what owned de big place dat dis man over-seer was on. Dis white man, he hab him dis nigger woman for de longest. She have five chillum by him, three boys an' two girls.

After a while dis man, he got him a place up close to Marvell, where he moved to. He brought his nigger fambly with him. He built dem a good house on his farm where he kept them. He give dat woman an' dem chillum dey livin' till de chillum done grown an' de

> woman she dead. Then he married him a nice white woman after he moved close to Marvell. . . . De most of de chillum of dis man is livin' in this county right now.[25]

Food

Mary Estes Peters, seventy-eight, whose mother came from Missouri to Phillips County and was sent into the fields, remembered,

> My mother said that they used to pour the food into troughs and give it to the slaves. They'd give them an old wooden spoon or something and they all eat of the same dish or trough. They wouldn't let the slaves eat out of the things they et out of. Fed them just like they would hogs.[26]

Oscar Felix Junell, sixty, said about his father:

> His masters was good to him. . . . Old man Junell was rich and had lots of slaves. When he went to feed his slaves, he would feed them jus like hogs. He had a great long trough and he would have bread crumpled up in it and gallons of milk poured over the bread and the slaves would get round it and eat. Sometimes they would get to fighting over it. You know, just like hogs! They would be eatin' and sometimes one person would find somethin' and get holt of it and another one would want to take it, and they would get to fightin' over it. Sometimes blood would get in the trough, but they would eat right on and pay no 'tention to it. I don't know whether they fed the old ones that way or not. I just heered my father tell me how he et out of the trough hisself.[27]

As was typical in slave states, the Arkansas narratives leave the familiar impression that treatment in the "big house" was much better than in the fields. Those who worked in the master's house inevitably ate better than the other slaves. Early Arkansas history books picture slaves eating in their cabins. More than one Arkansas narrative has the slaves who worked in the fields eating in far different conditions. Sallie Crane, ninety, Hempstead County: "Mush and milk. Cedar trough and long-handled spoons. Didn't know what meat was. Never got a taste of egg. Oo-ee! Weren't allowed to look at a biscuit."[28]

Scott Bond, eighty-four, Cross County, who became one of the wealthiest men in Arkansas, recalled,

> I didn't live with my mammy because she worked all the time, and us children all stayed in one house. It was a little one room log cabin, chinked and daubed, and you couldn't stir us with a stick. When we went to eat we had a big pan and all ate out of it. One what ate the fastest got the most.[29]

Families Split

Katie Rowe, eighty-eight, who lived on a plantation near Washington in southern Arkansas, remembered,

> Before old Master died he sold off a whole lot of hosses and cattle, and some niggers too. He had de sales on de plantation, and white men from around dar come to bid, and some traders come. He had a big stump what he made de niggers stand while dey was being sold, and dem men and boys had to strip off to de waist to show dey muscle and iffen dey had any scars or hurt places, but de women and gals didn't have to strip to de waist. The white men come up, and look in de slave's mouth jest lak he was a mule or hoss. . . . I seen chillum sold off and de mammy not sold and a little baby kept on de place and give to another woman to raise. Dem white folks didn't care nothing 'bout how de slaves grieved when dey tore up a family.[30]
>
> The other thing clear to my memory is when my uncle Tom was sold. Another day when mother was washing at the wellhouse and I was laying around, two

> white men came with a big, broad-shouldered colored man between them. Mother put her arms around him and cried and kissed him goodbye.[31]

Soloman Lambert, eighty-nine, said,

> The worst thing I ever seen in slavery was when we went to Texas we camped close to Camden. Camden, Arkansas! On the way down there we passed by a big house, some kind. I seen mighty little of it but a big yard was pailened [?] in. It was tall and fixed so they couldn't get out. They opened the gate and let us see. It was full of darkies. All sizes. All ages. That was a *Nigger Trader Yard* the worst thing I ever seen or heard tell of in my life. . . . I nearly fell out with slavery then.[32]

Katie Rowe told what slavery was like on a plantation near old Washington.

> Old master allus kind of techy 'bout old Mistress having niggers he can't trade or sell. . . . He makes grandmammy and mammy and me stand to one side and den he say to the other niggers, "Dese niggers belong to my wife but you belong to me, and I'm de only one you is to call Master. Dis is Tom, and Bryan, and Bob, and Miss Betty, and you is to call 'em dat, and don't you ever call one of 'em Young Master or Young Mistress, cuss fire to your black hearts!" All de other white folks look kind of funny, and old Mistress looked 'shamed of old Master.[33]

One of the most poignant stories in the Arkansas narratives came from Lucretia Alexander, Chicot County, eighty-nine.

> I'll bet the grandest moment in the life of Sister Alexander's mother when her mistress said, "Agnes, will you follow me if I buy your husband?" Fifteen hundred dollars to buy a rebellious slave in order to unite a slave couple? It's epic.[34]

Laura Hart, eighty-five, Pine Bluff, remembered,

> My father's mother was a white woman from the North and my father was a colored man. Her folks run her here to Arkansas and she stayed with her brother till my father was nine months old and then she went back North and my papa stayed with his uncle.
>
> When his uncle died he willed my papa his place. He had it recorded at the cotehouse in Little Rock that my papa was a free man. But he couldn't stay in Arkansas free [an Arkansas law required freed slaves to leave the state] so he just rambled till he found old man Carson and my mother. He offered to buy my mother but old master wouldn't sell her so he stayed with old man Carson till they was all free.[35]

Work

Louis Young, eighty-eight, a slave of Hampton Atkinson on a small farm in Phillips County told how when he was twelve he was sold to a master in Texas.

> Yes, suh, I starts to work when eight on dat plantation where I'm born. Dat in Arkansaw, and Massa Hampton own me and my mammy and eight other niggers. . . . Us all work from light to dark and Sunday, too. I don't know what Sunday am till us come to Texas, and dances and good things, I don't know nothin' bout dem till us come to Texas. Massa Hampton, he am long on de work and short on de rations, what he measure out for de week. Seven pounds meat and one peck meal and one quart 'lasses, and no more for de week. If us run out, us am out, dat's all.[36]

The legendary Little Rock school teacher Charlotte Stephens, eighty-three, said,

> Few of the trade workers were white. Brick maker and brick layers, stone masons, lathers, plasters,—all types of builders were of the freed men. You must remember that slaves were the only ones who did this work.[37]

John A. Holt, ninety-one, born in Fayetteville, was living with his mother on the farm of Polly Warmack who hired him out. "My slave mama use' to come over and collect five dollars in gold for my work, every month."[38]

R. C. Smith, age ninety-six, remembered his father talking about life in Fayetteville:

> My father was half Cherokee Indian. His father was bought by an Indian woman and she took him for her husband. His father was bought by Presley Smith. Pappy learned the stone mason's trade and old Master let him hire out and he let him keep the money he made.[39] Old Master's children went to school and they would come home and try to learn us everything they learned at school. I couldn't be still long enough to learn anything but my pappy and mammy both learned to read and write. . . . He had nine slaves besides our family and they worked the farm. . . . He never allowed his grown slaves to be whupped and when they went away from home he didn't write them no passes either. The patrollers didn't pay them no mind for they knowed Smith took care of his own niggers. We all was known as "Smith's free niggers." . . . My father and a lot more of the slaves of the neighbors around Fayetteville had slipped away and joined the northern army in Kansas. They belonged to the first and second Kansas regiment. They heard his family was treated differently because his family had saved his master's life.[40]

Paternalism

From the Cotton interview: "I would say anything to the Yankees and hang and hide in Miss Fannie's dress. She wore long big skirts. I hung about her. Grandma raised me on a bottle so mother could nurse Walter [white]."[41]

Solomon Lambert remembered,

> When I was small I minded the calves when they milk, pick up chips to dry to start fires, then I picked up nuts,

> helped feed the stock, learned all I could how to do things 'bout the place. We thought we owned the place. I was happy as a bird. I didn't know no better than it was mine. All the home I ever knowed. I tell you it was a good home. Good as ever had since. It was thiser way yo mama's home is your home. Well my moster's home was my home like dat.[42] None of us worked very hard except mother. I think back and I don't hardly remember ever seeing her setting down unless she was sewing or weaving.[43]

Matilda Hatchett, Yell County, ninety-nine: she recalled receiving a whipping only once as a child and only because she was endangering herself by riding a horse backwards. "But I would have cried for my ole master though because I really loved him."[44]

Eva Strayhorn, seventy-nine, who lived in Johnson County, remembered,

> After peace was made old Master called us all to him and told dat we was free now, jus as free as he was, and dat he had some things dat he wanted to tell us. He talked to us jest like we was his own children wid tears running down his cheeks. He said, "Cindy, I've raised you from a baby and you, Henry, since you was a young man. I've tried to be good to you and take care of you in return for de good work you have always done for me. I want you to go out in the worl' now and make good citizens. Be honest and respectable and don't turn against the good raisin' you have had and remember dat me and my wife loves you all."[45]

Jane Osbrook, ninety, said,

> I was borned within three miles of Camden but I wasn't raised there. We moved to Saline County directly after peace was declared. . . . My old master was Adkinson Billingsley. My old mistress treated us just like her own children. She said we had feelin's and tastes. I visited her long after the war. Went there and stayed there all night. . . . Some of the folks said they never

seed a biscuit from Christmas to Christmas, but we had 'em every day. . . . I come up in the way of obedience. Any time I wanted to go, had to go to old mistress and she say, "Don't let the sun go down on you." And when we come home the sun was in the trees. If you seed the sun was goin' down on you, you run.[46]

Hannah Jameson, eighty-six, Howard County remembered,

Ole Mistress girls and boys all had them a little Nigger. Miss Ella was my young Mistress. She divide her bread and meat with me and take her book and give me my A B Cs. The white boy and the Nigger et bread and meat together, played together and if old Master or Mistress started to whip him, he would say, "This is my Nigger, don't thrash him."[47]

Nelsen Densen, ninety, Ashley County, said,

Most of the slaves was happy, the ones I knowed. They figgers the white man fightin' for some principal [*sic*] but lots of them didn't care nothin' 'bout bein' free. I s'pose some was with bad white folks, but not round us. We had more to eat and now I'm so old I wouldn't feel bad if I had old mares to look after me 'gain.

Julia White, seventy-nine, remembered,

One of my mother's babies died and Master went to Little Rock on a horse and carried back a little coffin under his arm. The mistress had brought mother a big washing. She was working under the cover of the well-house and tears was running down her face. When master came back, he said: "How come you are working today, Angeline, when your baby is dead?" She showed him the big pile of clothes she had to wash, as mistress said. He said: "There is plenty of help on this place what can wash. You come on in and sit by your little baby, and don't do no more work till after the funeral." He took up the little dead body and laid it in the coffin with his own hands. I'm telling you this for what happened later on. A long time after peace, one evening mother heard a tapping at the door. When she went, there was her old master, James Moore. "Angeline," he said, "you remember me, don't you?" Course she did. Then he told her he was hungry and homeless. Mother took him in and fed him for two or three days till he was rested.[48]

Family Relationships among Slaves

Adrianna Kerns, eighty-five, Pulaski County, said,

> I have heard my mother tell many a time that there was a slave man who used to take his own dinner and carry it three or four miles to his wife. His wife belonged to a mean white man who wouldn't give them what they needed to eat. He done without his dinner in order that she might have enough. Where would you find a man to do that now? Nowadays they are taking the bread away from their wives and children and carrying it to some other woman.[49]

Solomon Lambert, age eighty-nine, Holly Grove:

> My parents' name was Fannie and Ben Lambert. They had eight children. How did they marry? They say they jump the broomstick together! But they had brush brooms so I reckon that what they jumped. Think the moster and mistress jes havin' a little fun outen it then. . . . Some got passes go see their wife and family 'bout every Sunday and some other times like Fourth of July.[50]

The Sambo Myth

In summary, if one begins with the Arkansas narratives, men, women, and children begin to emerge as complex psychological beings instead of the caricatures painted by generations of white Arkansans to justify slavery. And, as well, white Arkansans come across as extremely conflicted individuals. Given what the institution of slavery involved, how could they not? The excerpts above reveal that in the administration of slavery white Arkansans experienced a range of emotions including jealousy, hatred, lust, shame, guilt, paternalism, and love. Nothing is more apparent from the Arkansas narratives than that white Arkansans, like other Southerners, could not avoid *experiencing* slaves as human beings who were no different in their "feelins and tastes" than themselves.

And when the narratives are taken as a whole, slaves do not appear as simply passive victims of a culture and political system dominated by white supremacy but as active participants in a never-ending struggle to retain control over as much of their lives as possible. What also emerges from the Arkansas narratives is a numbing description of the brutality of slavery inflicted by members of the master class. Despite the abuse, the narratives reveal that some members of both races in the slave-master relationship, especially slaves who worked in the "big house" or who had skills, developed deep emotional relationships, depending on the personality and circumstances of those involved.

Nineteenth-Century School Histories of Slavery

The narratives stand in direct contradiction to the overwhelming majority of Arkansas school history books that portrayed typical stereotypes of slaves until well after the middle of the twentieth century. In elementary textbooks slaves were depicted as happy and well treated. As only one example, in an elementary textbook entitled *Makers of Arkansas History* published in 1905, John Hugh Reynolds, a University of Arkansas historian who is credited with "guiding" the Arkansas History Commission in its early years, had this to say about the slaves:

> These simple-minded people went to their work cheerfully. They were fond of joking and playing pranks, and

> frequently they tried to outstrip one another in hoeing and picking cotton, humming some tune as they worked. . . . Knowing that he would be provided for, he was happy and care-free. . . . It is true that once in a while a master was cruel to his darkies; but, for the most part, he was kind and lenient to them. They in turn loved their master.[51]

Insofar as they touched on slavery, these histories went beyond simply telling the story of the past. They also served to advance the cause of white supremacy. In other words, they were political documents in service to the white power structure and its preferred self-image. Not until after the modern civil rights movement in the 1960s did Arkansan historians significantly begin to change the way they wrote racial history.

In no small part, from these documents we learn that much more than an institution that white Arkansans accepted as simply the fabric of every day life, slave owners *experienced* slavery in ways they surely could not have anticipated. They often behaved in ways that proved Lord Acton's maxim: "Power tends to corrupt and absolute power corrupts absolutely." Along with the brutality, the stories told by Arkansas slaves demonstrate the emotions of jealousy, competitiveness, and possessiveness but also the love and concern felt by both races.

Slavery Reinterpreted

Present-day historians of race in Arkansas have corrected the absurdities found in the early histories, and slaves emerge as actors in their own lives. The challenge for the Arkansas historian has been in documenting the methods and motivation of slave behavior. Carl Moneyhon offers illustrations of how slaves negotiated terms of the master-slave relationship.

> The most common tool used by slaves to extract concessions from their owners was to stop work. As a group,

> slaves could sabotage the plantation routine by carefully exploiting white managers. . . . Ultimately, the only ways that slaves could force accommodations were by withholding labor, running away, or gaining skills essential to the plantation or local economy.[52]

Though from the narratives and other sources it is clear that overseers often went beyond their authority to punish slaves, a crippled slave or one beaten so severely that he or she was unable to work was obviously a liability, except as an example. Moneyhon quotes from the diary of John Brown who blamed his overseer for "not being firm enough." John Brown observed, "Mr. Bankston . . . has much yet to learn respecting his new undertaking & the Negroes are not slow to discern it."[53]

Traditionally, however, Arkansas whites interpreted the behavior of blacks as evidence of laziness, stupidity, or perverseness, but much of what occurred on the plantation was a type of low-level guerrilla warfare. Lawrence W. Levine in *Black Culture and Black Consciousness* has found evidence from narratives in other states that demonstrate that many blacks had no intention of accepting conventional white thinking as to their responsibilities toward their owners. A North Carolina slave remembered,

> They fed the animals better. They give the mules the roughage and such, to chaw on all night. But they didn't give us nothing to chaw on. Learned us to steal, that's what they done. Why, we would take anything we could lay our hands on. Then they'd whip us for lying when we say we don't know anything about it. But it was easier to stand when the stomach was full.

Levine, writing in the 1970s, said, "Thus, it was possible for slaves to rationalize their need to lie, cheat, and steal without holding these actions up as models to be followed in all instances."[54]

Other slaves found it expedient to behave in ways that won them favor. A recent history of Arkansas race relations during the slave era documents that slaves did not accept their status as passive work animals but indirectly conducted negotiations with their owners for improved conditions. Donald McNeilly has written: "The annals of the Arkansas slave experience are replete with stories of the success of skilled and resourceful slaves who built their worlds of semi-autonomy."[55] Slaves got themselves out of the cotton fields by acquiring specific skills. McNeilly quotes a slave owner from Desha County. "Caleb & Elijah & Rubin are with the workmen [white carpenters] as hired hands. I never saw a more constant worker than Rubin in my life. He is a very valuable negro. Elijah is equally so and Caleb is hard to beat."[56]

As much as slaves tried and sometimes were successful in influencing their treatment through their own behavior, slavery was ultimately in the hands of whites. In the next chapter we will examine the institution more from the point of view of the Arkansas whites who owned slaves and the white power structure generally.

CHAPTER 2

Owning Slaves

While slavery was for a time as American as apple pie, it had its roots in the old countries. Slavery was a part of the Arkansas experience beginning with a group that arrived with settlers sent from New Orleans in 1721 to found a colony, but the official story truly starts with the Louisiana Purchase in 1803. Seventeen years later, and one year after Arkansas had achieved territorial status, the 1820 census determined there were 1,617 slaves out of a total population of 14,273. By 1860 the number of slaves had climbed to over 114,000. By then, one out of every four Arkansans was a slave.[1]

It is already understood that whites in positions of authority in Arkansas claimed slavery was a moral institution, ordained by God and administered for the benefit of both slave and master. A decision by the Arkansas Supreme Court in 1859 clearly articulated the justification:

> There is a striking difference between the *black* and *white* man, in intellect, feelings and principles. In the order of providence, the former was made inferior to the latter; and hence the bondage of the other to the other. For government and protection, the one race is dependent on the other. It is upon this principle alone that slavery can be maintained as an institution.[2]

Obviously, one might accept the premises set out in the first sentence of the above quotation and believe that slavery was immoral and could not be justified on the grounds of racial inferiority. Indeed, in a debate with Stephen A.

Douglas in 1858, the future "Great Emancipator," Abraham Lincoln, who opposed slavery, had opined:

> There is a physical difference between the white and black races which I believe will forever forbid the two races living together on terms of social and political quality. And inasmuch as they cannot so live, while they do remain together there must be the position of superior and inferior, and I as much as any other man am in favor of having the superior position assigned to the white race.[3]

Slavery was legal, however, in Arkansas, and white Arkansans, arguing racial inferiority and divine intervention, took upon themselves the responsibility of administering a system where slaves were supposed to be protected and treated humanely. Though the Arkansas slave narratives suggest that slavery was often brutal and that certain aspects of the experience were troubling to their masters, we must also look at slavery from the perspective of the power structure that administered it. Was the overall system of slavery administered morally and humanely by the men who held power in Arkansas through the judiciary, legislative, and administrative branches of government? Additionally, and leaving aside the evidence found in the slave narratives for the moment, we must ask what slavery was like as *experienced* by Arkansas whites. Does the evidence show that Arkansas whites generally, with some exceptions, held to a genuine paternalism that took into account the welfare of slaves? And, if not, did the white power structure through its system of government hold accountable its citizens and make an effort to protect slaves from abuse? Finally, was it true that the whites in power felt strongly that slavery had been ordained by God? Or was this belief a convenient rationalization by whites for continuing a system that held great promise of enriching it?

Arkansas Government and Slavery

In an exposition of the legal trappings of the Arkansas slave experience, legal scholar L. Scott Stafford has thoroughly examined not only the constitutional and statutory edifice of slavery in Arkansas but also has rigorously and meticulously analyzed the basis for the decisions of the Arkansas Supreme Court regarding slavery. In the 1836 state constitution, which legalized slavery, the framers authorized future lawmakers to pass laws to protect slaves, specifically to enact legislation that obligated slave owners "to treat them with humanity."[4] As Stafford documents, lawmakers in Arkansas, unlike legislators in some of the other states in the South, ignored this provision. Stafford explains,

> The absence of standards in Arkansas made it extremely difficult to prosecute a white person for using excessive physical force against a slave and may explain why Arkansas was one of the few slave states in which there is no appellate record of such prosecutions.[5]

The Arkansas Supreme Court developed a hierarchy of legal values vis-à-vis slavery. At the top was the maintenance of the system itself. To kill or injure someone's slave was a destruction of valuable property and was taken very seriously, but it gave way to the "right of any white person to overcome a slave's rebellion against lawful authority."[6] As a consequence, though in theory a white could be prosecuted for committing a crime against a slave, "the appellate record suggests that in Arkansas such crimes were seldom prosecuted."[7]

Slaves had no right to sue for injuries to themselves. Their masters did have a legal right, however, but only if they could show "economic injury." The reason, the court said, was that

> it would encourage slaves, of their own propensity, or by the sufferance of their masters, to be insolent by word or demeanor. The elevation of the white race, and the happiness of the slave, vitally depend upon maintaining the ascendancy of one and the submission of

> the other. The rights of individuals must yield to the necessity of preserving the distinction between races.[8]

In other words, a happy slave was one who acted happy to be a slave. This rationalization legally justified some force against slaves for almost any display of displeasure so long as it did not result in economic loss.

The Arkansas Supreme Court, composed of men who were often slave owners themselves, took with absolute seriousness their role to protect the institution of slavery as opposed to interpreting the law in ways that would make the institution more humane. Thus, historians in the past presumed that Southern slave owners, overseers, and drivers would not mistreat slaves out of their own self-interest since they would not want to kill or maim valuable property. In fact, violence against slaves was officially tolerated to some degree because it kept slaves in check. Stafford writes, "Many of the court's decisions clearly and frankly reflect its perceived need to maintain the white racial dominance that underpinned slavery."[9]

No decision epitomizes the hierarchy of values articulated by the Arkansas Supreme Court more than the infamous case of *Pyeatt v. Spencer* decided in 1842. The Arkansas Supreme Court considered the case of a slave, Sophia, who had been beaten for running away to try to visit her children from whom she had been sold away. The buyer, Spencer, sued the seller, Pyeatt, alleging that Pyeatt had sold him a slave who was mentally ill and had been aware of it at the time he sold her. The jury agreed with Spencer and awarded him $716 in damages. Pyeatt appealed to the Arkansas Supreme Court, and the court found the following facts had been established.

> A few days after Spencer bought the slave, he was found whipping her. He had her stripped, and staked down on the ground; her hands and feet extended, and fastened to stakes; and her face downward. He . . . was whipping her at intervals; using a cowhide, with a

> plaited buckskin last about fifteen inches long. . . . Spencer had drawn some blood, but not a great deal. He took salt and a cob, and salted her back. The witness stated that he thought her deranged. He had never seen her before, but has often seen her since, and she is deranged and valueless.[10]

Stafford notes that the court did nothing to alleviate her condition even though it took note of the cruelty of her new owner. The remedy imposed by the court was to send the case back for a new trial to determine whether the slave had been, in fact, mentally ill before the sale.[11]

Treating slaves with "humanity" in no way meant treating them equally before the law. A "Negro or mulatto" automatically received the death penalty for attempted rape of a white woman; a white male who was convicted of attempted rape of a white woman received a prison sentence. As far as the Arkansas criminal code went, white males were legally free to rape black woman since slaves were considered property.[12]

Legal scholar Robert Shafer has also concluded:

> When confronted with the real-world facts of [two Arkansas] cases, the supreme court could not provide a reasoned justification for the slave system it governed, nor even a consistent approach to reaching judicial results.[13]

As Stafford suggests, the members of the Arkansas Supreme Court felt within the state's "repressive political climate enormous pressure . . . to defend slavery as a legal institution when addressing slave-related issues."[14]

Fear and Slavery

It is fear that has guided so much of race relations in Arkansas, and we must bear in mind during this era Michael Dougan's comment that "white Arkansans lived in fear of slave uprisings."[15] White Arkansans could not admit that slaves might have good reason to revolt for it would call into question their own behavior and cause them anxiety and fear, but it was impossible to ignore what had happened in Virginia beginning in August 1831. A list of the fifty-nine whites savagely murdered by Nat Turner and his band appeared in the *Arkansas Gazette.* While these murders would have sent chills down the back of any slave owner, Dougan documents that "Arkansas experienced two waves of hysteria, the first in 1835 and a second in the late 1850's."[16]

Rumors of slave uprisings sent white Arkansans into a frenzy: slaves were lynched, but so were whites who were allegedly their supporters. Dougan writes that before the Civil War, in Prairie County

> three slaves and a white man were lynched on the basis of testimony extracted through torture. Another [supposed abolitionist] Methodist minister was hung at Oil Trough in northeastern Arkansas, and all southern Arkansas was tense.

In fact, there were no slave uprisings in Arkansas, but the fear caused white Arkansas to react accordingly. By 1858 it was a crime, as was common elsewhere in the South, for a free person "by speaking or writing [to] maintain that owners have not right of property in their slaves."

This surrendering of First Amendment rights to free speech in this regard obviously seemed a small price to pay for imagined security. As the looming sectional crisis over slavery approached, other like measures, discussed below, would be taken.

The Reality of Slavery

Though the evidence suggests that slave owners and their allies were not concerned with treating slaves humanely before the law, we must look to the actual experience of Arkansas whites themselves. To begin, it is helpful to keep in mind the observation of Carl Moneyhon that

> paternalism was never more than the ideal. In the face of an economic or other crisis in the life of the slave owner, the ideal could be abandoned for the expedient. Maintenance of family life, kindness, adequate food and clothing, religious education and restraint in punishment were all easily forgotten in the face of necessity.[17]

But what was the necessity for abandoning the belief that slaves must be cared for and treated humanely? It appears that the very nature of the work itself in the Delta prevented a paternalistic attitude from being a reality. In *The Old South Frontier: Cotton Plantations and the Formation of Arkansas Society, 1819–1861* published in 2000, Donald McNeilly notes the

> fertile Arkansas lowlands, the fountain of wealth for planters and bestower of independence on lesser farmers, were a malarial inferno for slaves forced to move here. . . . Freedom and prosperity for whites came to rest on the agony of blacks.[18]

The work was not merely agonizing; it was deadly. In comparing the death and birth rates for blacks and whites in Arkansas in 1859 and 1860, Orville Taylor concluded that "it is equally obvious that slaves had both a higher death rate and a lower birth rate than the whites," which he found consistent with the data in other states.[19]

Slaves were an expensive proposition. A single slave could be worth as much as eighty acres of land, and anecdotal evidence suggests that Arkansas owners had no choice but to see slavery in terms of their financial worth. Dead or sick slaves were no use. According to Taylor,

> Another indication of the mercenary concerns of owners for the health of their slaves was the frequency with which they expressed disappointment or disgust for the loss of their services of the slaves because of injury or loss.[20]

Taylor notes that paternalistic feelings were often expressed.

> The constant concern for the health of the slaves was not caused entirely by mercernary feelings, however. In many instances the relationship between the master and the slave was so close that quite naturally the master felt genuine concern and regret when the slave fell ill. Practically all slaveowners—and more especially those with relatively few slaves—habitually referred to their slaves as members of the family, and expressed the same feelings for ill slaves as for ill children of their own.[21]

Despite expressions of concern that exhibited compassion for the suffering of their slaves, however, white Arkansans returned again and again to the fact that their profit was at stake.

Taylor writes, "John Brown, who in general was very considerate of the welfare of his slaves, wrote in his diary of 1856, 'Thom got his ankle hurt with Arrington and Vaughan house moving and is of no service to me now.'" Of another valued slave he wrote, "Steven is better but it seems difficult to get him up to be fit to work again. He has not worked a day for three or four months." A few days later: "Steven is slowly recovering from his illness, but cannot do any work and I fear will not shortly—This shortens my cash income rather inconveniently." The same attitude prevailed even toward childbirth among the slaves; Brown once commented laconically, "After much suffering, a stillborn child is born, so goes my luck with negroes."[22]

Even those whites who considered blacks "family members" could turn testy after months of their illness. "Our black family have been quite sick," wrote Amanda Trulock five weeks after their arrival in Jefferson County in the winter of 1845. Nine months later, she wrote, "Our black ones have all been sick and nothing doing but a heavy expence [*sic*] on our hands."[23]

The real issue was often how hard one was willing to be to run a profitable operation. Taylor gives the example of the planter John Brown of Princeton who left his plantation in the hands of an overseer in 1854 and moved into Camden. He had been able to do so because of success the previous year. According to Taylor, 1854 offered as much chance for financial success as the previous year, but a sadder but wiser John Brown noted the following:

> Went through Princeton to my farm. Found all well and the crop almost lost. It will make it very difficult to get along, a sad misfortune at present but the thing is done and what can't be cured must be endured. My negroes do badly and I ought to have employed a strict overseer who would have pulled them up. They have not worked.[24]

As many commentators have noted, including Donald McNeilly, slavery was less onerous in those situations where owners and their families had no choice but to share in the work alongside their slaves, and in the early years of slavery in Arkansas, many did. He writes,

> But over the course of three decades, as lowland Arkansas emerged from frontier to settled farming country to plantation district, these bonds of intimacy lessened and vanished. The frontier slave experience slowly gave way to a more regimented and socially distant slave society. Over time, slaves worked harder and under more restrictive rules of conduct in every sphere of their lives.[25]

Urban Slavery

There were regional variations of Arkansas slavery. While in the Delta life for slaves was increasingly in lockstep as the 1850s wound down, in Little Rock, however, a very different picture of slave life emerges, one that openly mocked the rationalization that slaves were basically children in adult bodies. One of the first clues was a lament in the Little Rock *Arkansas Democrat* in 1859 that the city's slave patrol was not doing its job. Blacks were noted to "traverse the streets at all hours of the night free from hindrance" and were "permitted to carry knives and pistols."[26] As S. Charles Bolton notes, this opinion was inspired by the growing paranoia, but clearly what was occurring in Little Rock—home to black artisans, free blacks, and runaway slaves—meant a different type of relationship, particularly in urban areas as the WPA interview with Charlotte Stephens confirms and bears repeating in part.

> Brick makers and brick layers, stone masons, lathers, plasters,—all types of builders were of the freed men. You must remember that slaves were the only ones who did this work. Their masters had used their labor as their means of income. Not all slaves were in the cotton fields, as some suppose. The slave owners in towns and villages had their slaves learn skill trade occupations and made a great deal of money by their earnings.[27]

At the same time, slaves who worked for hire might be permitted to keep at least some of their earnings, which translated into a measure of the most precious commodity of all. Bolton observes, "Slaves and free blacks made up a large segment of the urban working class and enjoyed much more freedom than elsewhere in the state."[28] Those artisans had the least difficulty making the future transition to freedom.

Free Black Arkansans in the Slave Era

The possibilities of freedom for the slave caused Arkansas whites to take whatever steps they thought necessary to secure themselves and their property. Like other Southern states, Arkansas discouraged the presence of free persons of color, having passed legislation that prohibited free blacks from entering the state after March 1, 1843 and requiring those who already lived there to post a five-hundred-dollar bond to guarantee their "good behavior."[29] Such legislation hardly seems to have been required. Orville Taylor reports finding before the Civil War "only three criminal convictions of free Negroes," and two of those convictions were for harboring free blacks (their own wives).[30] The evidence, in fact, suggests that the few free blacks who lived in Arkansas stayed on good terms with whites. In Little Rock, Nathan "Nace" Warren, who had been a slave of Robert Crittenden, was given his freedom in 1838. Working as a barber, all-around handyman, carriage driver, and cook, he soon made himself indispensable as what appears to be the state's first confectioner. Two Little Rock society matrons used his services often:

> Uncle Nace Warren was the first confectioner we remember in Little Rock. He was a free Negro, but had married Mr. Ashley's cook, so, of course, he was adopted by the community as kinfolks. He was an expert in making cakes and was patronized by the best people in town. He was smart enough to keep the secret of his success in his own possession, saying, "If I lets you white ladies have my receipts, I gives away my trade."[31]

Warren was always ready to supply his cakes on short notice. Obviously, Warren knew exactly what was required not only to survive but to flourish in a society where slavery was the norm.

Just as blacks adapted survival techniques during the Jim Crow era, former slaves obviously understood that it made no sense as free persons of color who were virtually powerless to bring the wrath of whites down upon them. In *A Stranger and a Sojourner: Peter Caulder, Free Black Frontiersman in Antebellum Arkansas* Billy D. Higgins documents that for three decades before the Civil War a small community of free blacks prospered in harmony in northern Arkansas alongside their white neighbors. Higgins shows that whites in Marion County on the Missouri border ignored the law prohibiting blacks from entering Arkansas. By 1850 free blacks in Marion County composed nineteen households totaling 129 members. For decades beginning in 1819 when David Hall, a free mulatto, brought his sons and their families to settle on the White River, the community was a model of Arkansas pioneer enterprise and stability as they "cleared trees, planted crops, raised livestock, and patented their lands."[32] A native of South Carolina, Peter Caulder, the main subject of Higgins's work, following the War of 1812 found himself stationed in the Arkansas Territory as a private in the U.S. Army at what is now Fort Smith. Though earning the respect of his commanding officer, there was little future for blacks in the army, and like many soldiers at the time, black or white, Caulder eventually walked away from his enlistment. He made his way in 1824 to what is now Marion County and married Hall's daughter Eliza six years later. Over time, they would raise seven children in this remote area of the state that paid little notice to racial distinctions.

In September 1851 an event occurred that sorely tested relationships between the free blacks of Marion County and their neighbors. After a fight, James Hall was charged with the murder of John H. Tolbert, a white man. Despite the fact that Arkansas law prevented free blacks from testifying in court against whites, an all-white Marion County jury acquitted Hall, a mulatto, who had hired two white lawyers to defend him. Higgins has inferred that the acquittal, remarkable as it was, resulted in an increase in racial tension in Marion County. He documents that the extended Hall family that included Peter Caulder temporarily disappeared from the tax roles of Marion County. Higgins assumes the Hall home place was sold to pay attorneys' fees. In any event, six of the Halls appeared again on the tax roles by 1855. The name of Peter Caulder resurfaced on the rolls in 1859, but it would be the last year he would pay taxes in Arkansas.

Lest one think that peaceful relationships between free blacks and whites were solely confined to an area near the Missouri border, Higgins briefly discusses a small settlement of free blacks in the river town of Napoleon in Desha County in the heart of the Delta. Higgins documents that "at least ten free black families plus several mixed households resided near Napoleon," a town that no longer exists because of a channel change in the Mississippi. Rather astonishingly, "a town ordinance allowed black men to serve on slave patrols," giving lie to the "oft-repeated argument of anti-black Southerners that free blacks by nature and by habit conspired with slaves against whites."[33]

It can be seen, then, that the experience of whites did not match up with their stated reason for their behavior when it came to dealing with blacks. In fact, the evidence was that free blacks in Arkansas were actually productive members of society. It would have been an acknowledgement of this fact that would have caused real anxiety to whites. If blacks could survive as free beings and be productive citizens, the rationale that they were inferior beings who must be treated like children stopped working. Rather than confront the anxiety that came with the acceptance of the knowledge that their only real reason for owning slaves was to exploit them financially, Arkansas whites convinced themselves upon no meaningful evidence that free blacks were a drain on society. In fact, they were a threat to their consciences, but as the years went by, white Arkansans increasingly shut out the voices that nagged at them. By February 1859, helped by the decision of the U.S. Supreme Court that blacks were not citizens of the United States, influential whites got the state legislature to pass a law requiring free blacks to leave Arkansas by January 1, 1860. Higgins writes,

> Expelling the free mulattoes as required by state law may have been slowed by local indifference, but that changed with the action of John Brown at Harper's Ferry in October 1859. Opinions about Brown's violence and the threat of insurrection spewed from tens of thousand of tongues.[34]

In the same year, building on opposition to emancipation of slaves that had been gathering since the 1840s, the legislature outlawed "any further emancipation of slaves."[35] With restriction upon restriction, with regard to slavery, Arkansas was becoming a police state.

God and Slavery in a Frontier State

The sincerity of whites in claiming that God had decreed that blacks must be slaves must be put in historical context. Many claimed that God had ordained slavery, but not all white Arkansans agreed. One who did not and who opposed slavery was Jesse Haile, a fiery abolitionist Methodist preacher during Arkansas's territorial days from 1825 to 1829. Haile was credited with persuading fellow minister Thomas Tennant into giving up his slave though young Tennant soon regretted it, saying he had been "reduced to a condition of want and suffering."[36] Haile was so adamant on the evils of slavery that to avoid him but to remain Christians, a number of his flock transferred to the Cumberland Presbyterian Church, which had no problem with the institution. Ultimately, in 1830 Haile met the fate of Methodist ministers who upset their flock and was transferred to Illinois. One can assume that once the word got around that Methodist ministers were being martyred for their beliefs that owning slaves was sinful, some reconsidered their advocacy. In fact, the condemnation of slavery by Christian ministers was an extremely rare position in Arkansas at any time. Plantation owners were interested in the message of obedience, and most ministers were happy to oblige. A Saline County former slave remembered the message of the white preacher who managed to minister to both white and black congregations at once. After speaking to the whites, the minister would lean his head out the window and exhort the blacks:

> You cullud people out dar—lissen at me! De way ter make good slaves, is ter obey yo' Massa an' Missis! Obey 'em constant—'Den he stick his haid back in, and preach till he had some mo' words fo' us-all.[37]

In fact, Arkansas preachers of the gospel knew firsthand of what they were expounding because a number of them owned slaves. Walter Vernon identifies twenty-four Methodist ministers in 1850 as owning slaves, including a William Moores, who owned fifteen.[38]

The conflict with northern white churches over the issue of slavery, of course, mirrored the conflict in the larger society. Now that slavery was no longer considered economically feasible in the north, the view of many northern churches that slavery was a sin was easier to hold, a fact not lost on Southerners. As views hardened, white Southerners found it easier to split off from the northern churches than to endure their criticism. A resolution voted by the Arkansas Annual Conference

> declare[d] our solemn preference for, and our determination strictly to adhere to the Methodist Episcopal Church, *South,* in conformity to the plan of separation adopted by the General Conference of the Methodist Episcopal Church in 1844.[39]

Indeed, Horace Jewell, the first historian of the Methodist denomination in Arkansas, candidly acknowledged that the separation relieved "the preachers being released [by the split] from a cause of embarrassment."[40]

The biblical justification for slavery, which appears in accounts in older and more settled states of the South, apparently was in Arkansas a doctrine more assumed than argued. Truly a frontier state, Arkansas had no educational institutions such as the University of Virginia founded in 1826 and therefore no theologians to develop religious arguments. Though ultimately it made no difference, supporters of slavery probably had less support in Arkansas from religious leaders than commonly believed because, as Donald McNeilly points out, Arkansas was still a frontier state and religious institutions were few and far between. He quotes Methodist bishop Lay in 1863 after the occupation of Little Rock: "It seems as if scarce one in a hundred of this western population has any practical sense of religious obligation, the stupendous irreligious[ness] of the country appals [*sic*] one and tempt to unbelief and despondency."[41] Based on the general lack of interest in religion throughout the state, it is frankly difficult to imagine that in Arkansas, before or at the time of the Civil War, many persons other than politicians and judges cared one way or another about the arguments for or against slavery from theologians, newspaper editors, and political theorists.

The Growing Importance of Slavery and Secession

In 1857 an Arkansan wrote, "Ere long, Arkansas will be the cotton state of the union. If cotton will only hold present prices for five years, Arkansas planters will be as rich as cream a foot thick."[42] Thomas A. DeBlack has observed only once before 1860 did the price of cotton drop below eleven cents per pound. By 1861 Arkansas was on her way to becoming a rival of the cotton kingdoms of the Old South. Twenty million pounds of the fiber had been produced in 1850. Ten years later the amount of cotton taken from the state had skyrocketed to 150 million pounds. And in a matter of a decade "the cash value of Arkansas farms increased from $15,265,245 in 1850 to $91,649,773."[43] For the only time in its history, by 1860 Arkansas was not a poor state in terms of relative wealth. Slaves and cotton put it in the top half of the country in per capita income. And the wealthiest part was in the Delta where slaves commanded prices that were among the highest in the South. Already by 1850, 70 percent of the slave population in the state was in the Delta. But it was not only material wealth derived from slavery that white Arkansans craved. It was status, too. As Lucy Drucker, whose husband was a yeoman farmer in Phillips County, wrote her brother, "The best society is those that live on plantations. . . . Wealth here is estimated by the number of slaves they work."[44]

After all other questions about race have been put to rest, however, the question that continues to haunt is this: how and why did Arkansas, where most whites did not own slaves, attempt to take itself out of the United States in order to protect the rights of those who did? Or as Kenneth Barnes puts it, "One of the great questions that still remains is why landless white farmers would go to war to defend a system that did not benefit them?"[45] A partial answer is that the political power exercised by Arkansas slaveholders was dramatically disproportionate to their actual number. Ralph Wooster has analyzed the holdings of the men who were elected on February 18, 1861, as delegates to Arkansas's secession convention and found that "forty-seven of the seventy-seven man convention (or 61.1 percent) were slaveholders."[46] While this statistic says volumes about the influence of slaveholders in Arkansas society by 1860, it is merely one indication of their political power. One understood that slave owners in the Delta would wield such influence, but recent scholarship involving two upcountry counties (Johnson and Pope) documents the political and economic importance of owning slaves, wherever one lived in Arkansas. Though the actual number of slaves and slave owners in the upcountry of Arkansas were far fewer than in the Delta in the 1840s and 1850s, there was no disapproval of the institution itself. In fact, slave owners in these two counties on the other side of the state dominated political life far beyond what their numbers would suggest their influence would be. Gary Battershell shows that, for example, 59 percent of those holding the offices of judge, sheriff, surveyor, clerk, and coroner in Johnson County between 1840 and 1860 were slaveholders. He has made the point that "had there been animosity between the slaveholders and the much more numerous non-slaveholders, it is unlikely that the latter would have been so willing to cast their votes for the former."[47] One can go further and make the statement that in fact owning slaves anywhere in Arkansas was a mark in one's favor, a sign of success.

In order to sustain the cotton kingdom it continued to be an article of faith that white men were physically incapable of withstanding the kind of work necessary in the climate of states like Arkansas; only black people could. Indeed, Henry Rector's written message dated March 2, 1861, to the seventy-four white men who had been elected to attend a convention to consider secession claimed as much. According to the governor, "The productive portion of the soil of Arkansas is so geographically circumstanced as to preclude the idea that it can be successfully cultivated by white labor."[48] There in one sentence was the unvarnished justification for slavery. White men did not have the physical constitution to do the kind of work necessary in the South; blacks did. Of course, instead of acknowledging that blacks were physically superior to whites, they claimed this ability was proof of their near animal-like status. But an admission of relative weakness could hardly support the justification for secession, and so Rector then offered up what the South had now been saying for years:

> God in his omnipotent wisdom, I believe, created the cotton plant—the African slave—and the lower Mississippi valley, to clothe and feed the world, and, a gallant race of men and women produced upon its soil, to defend it, and execute that decree.

Confident of the reaction to what he was about to say, Rector offered a simple choice to the delegates.

> But if, upon the other hand, we are prepared to admit the argument that slavery is a sin—that the melioration of the white and black races requires us to abolish it, we shall keep in the true line of policy marked out by the incoming President.

Rector then reminded the delegates that though Abraham Lincoln was now promising not to end slavery in those states where it already existed, he had once said that the country "cannot exist half slave and half free." Previously, the nation had limped along with one compromise after another. Each had eventually self-destructed through internal stress, but for over three decades as the country grew, Congress had maintained a rough balance of power between free and slave states. Despite efforts on both sides to avert a showdown, that kind of arrangement was no longer deemed acceptable to many on both sides. Though Lincoln had hoped to appeal to Southerners by campaigning for the limited goal of prohibiting slavery in the western territories, he had not carried a single Southern state and had not even been on the ballot in Arkansas and in eight other Southern states.

Though the vote was 27,412 to 15,826 to hold such a convention and debate the issue, there was no rush to secede. In fact, those who declared themselves as unionists received 23,626 votes to 17,927 for self-proclaimed secessionists. Though Unionists such as convention president David Walker from Washington County in northwest Arkansas rejected, for the time being, the idea of immediate secession, the delegates did go on record as "strongly opposing northern aggression against the six southern states that had already left the Union."[49]

Arkansas historians of the Civil War appear to assume that even if the question of secession had been referred to the people, the outcome would have been the same, for after the attack on Fort Sumter, the issue for most white male Arkansans suddenly was solidarity with people in those states that had seceded. It came with a cost that few imagined.

Why Arkansas Chose Secession

White Arkansans did not choose to attempt to secede from the United States in order to vindicate the rights of statehood. Indeed, no one put the issue more clearly than Governor Rector in his message to the secession convention. The issue was slavery and what it meant to the prosperity of the white people who made up Arkansas at the time. Cotton meant wealth, but white people were helpless to cultivate and extract it without the institution of slavery. That white Arkansans would choose to go to war in order to maintain an institution as manifestly destructive of freedom and human values as slavery should have been a sobering commentary on the human condition. Instead of taking stock and coming to terms with the fearful arrogance of white supremacy and perhaps devising ways to keep it in check, white Arkansans, like their brethren, chose to maintain it at a cost that still has not been counted.

CHAPTER 3

The Civil War in Arkansas and the Refashioning of Black Identity

For virtually everyone in the state, the decision to join the Confederacy was a disaster from the very beginning. Thomas A. DeBlack puts it,

> The Civil War was the most divisive and destructive event in Arkansas history. . . . [Arkansans] shared a romanticized view of war that would quickly be shattered by the boredom and disease of camp life and the horrors of the battlefield. What began with parades and stirring speeches in 1861 would end in injury and death for thousands of young Arkansas men and unimaginable hardships for those parents, sweethearts, wives, and children who remained at home.[1]

Despite its high strategic importance as a base of operations for holding onto the crucial slave state of Missouri, the Confederate high command in Virginia "viewed Arkansas primarily as a source of men and material for the fighting east of the Mississippi and as a dumping ground for incompetent generals from the eastern theater."[2] An officer sent to evaluate the abilities of the state to wage armed conflict reported back to the secretary of war for the Confederacy, "Arkansas has less the appearance of a military organization than any people I ever yet knew."[3]

With the defeat at Pea Ridge in northern Arkansas in March 1862 ending any hope that Missouri could be won by the Confederacy and with the Battle of Prairie Grove in

December 1862, which cost both sides over 1,250 casualties as well as substantial desertions for the Southern army, Union forces established a presence in northwest Arkansas. The Mississippi River town of Helena had been taken without a fight in July. Guerilla tactics helped to prevent Little Rock from falling into Union hands, but a decision by the Confederate army brass to withdraw forces from Arkansas made defeat only a matter of time. The surrender of 4,793 men at Arkansas Post in January 1863 signaled the desperation of the Confederates in the state. An effort to retake Helena in July ended in devastating defeat, and Little Rock was in Union hands by September.

The Price of Freedom

If the Civil War proved anything to white Arkansans about their slaves, it was that men and women who had never once risen up against them in a mass rebellion would desert them given the first opportunity. White Arkansans often expressed surprise that their slaves would run away. In November 1862 Mary Eskridge wrote, "Those I *trusted most* deceived me most."[4] This expression of outrage was typical of white Arkansans who told themselves (and others) that they had treated their slaves with kindness and that these slaves had no reason to desert them, but flee their slaves did when Union armies approached. As Carl Moneyhon notes, "well-treated slaves left as quickly as others."[5] When Union ships in 1862 began dominating the rivers in Arkansas, slaves "merely had to run to the Union boats and camps, and this they did in droves."[6]

With the invasion of Union general Samuel R. Curtis in the spring, slaves by the thousands abandoned their owners and followed Curtis's army as it moved down the White River. Elsewhere the same phenomenon occurred as the state was overrun by Union troops. Boston Blackwell from Jefferson County expressed every slave's goal: "Iffen you could get to the Yankee's camp you was free right now."[7] By November

1862 Arkansas blacks were being employed to "help man the many new boats coming into service" in support roles as seamen, firemen, and coal heavers. Though efforts were made to prepare for the number of slaves coming over to the Union side, the initial response was woefully insufficient. "Some blacks headed back home after finding little food, poor shelter, and no work in Helena's overcrowded Camp Ethiopia."[8] "Well, Uncle," Mary Breckenridge, a nurse stationed on a federal hospital boat, asked a slave waiting on the levee, "how do you like being free?" He replied, "I haint seen no freedom, yet, missis, I'se a gwine home again."[9] Other Delta blacks made it to Memphis. The Union army housed them in camps named Camp Dixie and New Africa. Camps at Little Rock, Fort Smith, Van Buren, Camden, and De Valls Bluff were simply overrun with former slaves, but most stuck it out despite the hardships.

If Arkansas blacks thought they had suffered as slaves, they had no idea what was coming in their first few months of freedom. Death stalked them at every turn, and with a vengeance. Commenting on the rate of deaths in the spring and summer of 1864, David Todd, an American Missionary Association agent in Pine Bluff, wrote, "The mortality here in the Freedmen's Camp is astonishing." In May 1864 there were fifty-four deaths and in June sixty-three. The diseases of whooping cough, measles, mumps, pneumonia, and dysentery swept the camps, leaving more than 10 percent dead in the summer of 1864. In a later two-month period 117 of 650 died, as well. The causes were primarily "privation, exposure, and malnutrition."[10]

Conditions were worse than hideous. One army officer described the Little Rock camp as "really in fact nothing more nor less than one vast hospital, strictly speaking it is a grave yard rather than the residence of human beings. There is scarcely one family in camp that can boast of all its members being well."[11] From Camden the report was that freedmen were "hungry, naked, and destitute," while at the De Valls Bluff camp smallpox was everywhere. In the first few weeks mortality ran as high as 25 percent. The U.S. Army had prepared to fight but not to heal. There were no medicines, no surgeons, and no basic supplies to deal with the tragedies unfolding on a daily basis.

The emphasis of the army was on getting the former slaves back to work. In wartime there was no point in the black refugees sitting idle. Thousands toiled as "teamsters, cart drivers, herders of cattle and horses, cooks, servants for commissioned officers, nurses for hospitals, laundresses and laborers."[12] By October 1863 Adjutant General Lorenzo Thomas, who had been sent to the Mississippi valley to recruit troops and develop a labor policy, announced a plan that would allow abandoned plantations to be leased and freedmen to be employed, but it was March 1864 before he had authority to implement it. In an experiment that was a harbinger of the future, Arkansas freedmen were encouraged to sign labor contracts to work on abandoned plantations. These lands were leased primarily to white northerners, but according to Carl Moneyhon, many of the lessees in Arkansas were the original owners. By the end of 1864 former slaves were working on at least a hundred plantations, probably mostly in Phillips, Chicot, and Arkansas counties. Though the overall goals were to help the freedmen adjust to a totally new of life, in fact, they were seldom met in this experiment because of the lack of adequate supervision "to insure that the freedmen were not cheated in their contractual relationships or to insure that the freedmen received the educational goals intended."[13]

To expect that northern U.S. military personnel would evenhandedly administer labor arrangements between Arkansas plantation owners and former slaves was clearly an overly optimistic assessment of the situation as it existed in the South. Though as conquerors, military officers had the authority and means to implement their decisions, their beliefs about the capacity of the former slaves to engage in what they considered constructive behavior were likely not a great deal different than the beliefs of their Southern counterparts. In any event, for the most part, military personnel in charge of the plantations assumed that blacks had to be coerced into working and acted accordingly. Instead of being given the opportunity to select their own employers, the former slaves had no choice in the matter and were assigned to a plantation. Nor did they have a choice about their wages or any terms of employment. As during slavery, they worked in gangs under overseers. Instead of being paid in cash, they were often given supplies and overcharged, anticipating the labor arrangement known as peonage that extended well into the twentieth century.[14]

Plantation Resistance by Former Slaves

There is evidence that Delta blacks sometimes tried to resist the domination of the plantation owners even as the war was ending in the Arkansas Delta. Watt McKinney interviewed former slaves for the WPA slave narrative collection and in the course of an interview of Henry Turner of Phillips County recounted the labor organizing of Bryant Singfield, a former slave.

> After leaving the Turner plantation Singfield became active as a leader and agitator among the former slaves who remained with their masters and who had entered into contracts to work their crops on a share basis, and in these activities he was in a large measure encouraged and assisted by the commanders of the Federal soldiers who were garrisoned at Helena for many months after the close of the war. . . . Singfield was successful in inducing large numbers of ex-slaves to desert their former owners and join in a colony that he had established midways [*sic*] between Trenton and Helena. Even those Negroes who did not join Singfield's group became restless and dissatisfied with their lot and a general discontent prevailed among them due to his disturbing influence and the landowners were faced with a serious labor shortage and a very serious Negro question that threatened the peace and welfare of the county.[15]

No sympathizer of black labor activists, McKinney states with obvious satisfaction that it was the "general opinion" that whites led by Bart Turner, later sheriff of Phillips County, went to the homes of Singfield and his supporters and murdered them.[16]

Black Arkansans Fighting in the Civil War

Despite victories, Union generals were running out of soldiers, but President Lincoln's Emancipation Proclamation effective January 1, 1863, not only freed slaves in the rebellious states but made them eligible to become soldiers. In 1863 the number of male slaves of military age in Arkansas totaled 23,088. It is estimated that planters had taken as many as a hundred thousand slaves to Texas from Arkansas and surrounding states in an attempt to avoid giving up their property. By November 7, 1864, Arkansas had equipped seven black troop regiments to fight for the Union cause. According to Ronnie Nichols, 5,526 black men were recruited from Arkansas. Another 5,000 African Americans "served in Arkansas between 1863–1866. . . . They comprised . . . every branch of service (Infantry, Cavalry, Artillery—Light, Artillery—Heavy as well as sailors)."[17] Nothing would bring into question the basis of slavery after it was determined that these men would fight. Accustomed to former slaves made to appear docile by the whips of their masters, some commanders assumed that blacks now dressed in Yankee blue would simply quake with fear during battle and allow themselves to be led back into bondage. Knowing they were about to battle black troops, the Confederate 29th Texas Cavalry Regiment brought "some 500 pairs of shackles . . . which were designed to be placed upon the limbs of our negro soldiers when Fort Gibson was captured."[18] Confederate troops learned to their extreme discomfort at the Battle of Honey Springs in present-day Oklahoma on July 17, 1863, that the kind of behavior slaves exhibited on the plantation did not manifest itself on the battlefield. The 1st Kansas Colored

Volunteer Infantry Regiment "participated with great gallantry in the fight and grinned from ear to ear at the sight of their old companions the *shackles,"* wrote eyewitness Colonel Thomas Moonlight, army chief of staff under Major General James G. Blunt, who himself gave special praise to only one regiment in his official report: "The First Kansas (colored) particularly distinguished itself; they fought like veterans. . . . Their coolness and bravery I have never seen surpassed." Significantly, for these same adversaries would fight again in nine months at the Battle of Poison Spring, Colonel Moonlight also noted,

> Be it said to the memory of the 1st Kansas Colored they behaved with marked humanity and kindness to the wounded, who but a few hours before had [worked] to place the yoke of slavery for ever on their necks.[19]

Historians have noted that Confederates themselves in their own accounts of the Battle of Honey Springs did not mention any misbehavior on the part of the 1st Kansas Colored. For purposes of future discussion, three thousand Arkansas cavalrymen under the command of Brigadier General William Cabell were part of the Confederate forces who arrived to provide reinforcements the evening of the Battle of Honey Springs; however, commanding officer Douglas H. Cooper chose not to continue the fight. White Arkansans learned, not for the first time, that as an increasingly important part of the Union army (eventually black soldiers would compose 10 percent of the Union army) blacks had nothing to be ashamed of in battle. As a Confederate soldier confided by letter to his wife, "We have had a fight with the enemy and they whipped us bad. They are too strong for us . . . and good fighters. I know it for I have tried them and they are as good as we are, better drilled and better armed."[20]

Black troops had already performed well on the expedition to Little Rock, supporting artillery positions during the Union army's expedition to the state capital and engaging in limited combat. The soldiers were said to have "behaved with admirable coolness." Black troops also fought in the Battle of Helena. In one battle near Helena, the regimental report read, "The Colored troops fought like veterans; none flinched."[21]

The Poison Spring Massacre

It was the Battle of Poison Spring (sometimes referred as Poison Springs) on April 18, 1864, that has drawn the attention of historians assessing Arkansas race relations during the Civil War. In a symposium held in Little Rock on January 26, 2002, six historians evaluated the Battle of Poison Spring from a number of perspectives in order to clarify what has become one of the enduring controversies in Arkansas history. Their work has resulted in a book entitled *All Cut to Pieces and Gone to Hell: The Civil War, Race Relations, and the Battle of Poison Spring*. Edited by Mark K. Christ, the book tells the story of 438 officers and men from the 1st Kansas Colored Infantry who were assigned to provide protection for a forage train of 198 wagons that was taking five thousand bushels of corn for Union troops in Camden. Texas was the ultimate destination of the commander of the Union forces, Major General Frederick Steele, who was leading a force of nine thousand men from Little Rock to Shreveport, Louisiana, to join Major General Nathaniel Banks. Food was a problem, and the hungry invaders had already taken what they could find from the horrified and terrified residents of Camden. On their way back to Camden the troops encountered "lead elements of 3,621 Confederate cavalry and horse artillery who were converging on Poison Spring as quick as their mounts could carry them."[22] What occurred next—the deliberate slaughter and mutilation by Confederate troops including Arkansans of African Americans who had surrendered—is indisputable. Poison Spring was a military disaster for the federal troops who were outsmarted by Confederates who anticipated their foraging efforts. Cut off from the larger federal force at Camden, the train escort of 438 officers and men from the

1st Kansas Colored Infantry and 197 troopers from other units had the help of a 501-man relief column but were no match for 3,621 Confederate cavalry and horse artillery. It took three assaults before the 1st Kansas Colored collapsed under the weight of four Confederate brigades. Why General Steele, who could hear the artillery fire from Poison Spring, never sent reinforcements from Camden has never been answered. A massacre of hideous proportions was soon under way as Confederate "execution squads from the Twenty-ninth Texas Cavalry roamed the battlefield to finish off the First Kansas Colored's wounded."[23] The Texans were said to chant as they murdered their victims, "Where is the First Kansas Nigger now?" The answer would come back: "All cut to pieces and gone to hell by bad management." Fighting for the Southern command, Choctaw Indians stripped and scalped their victims, and according to the *Washington Telegraph,* added the following twist under the heading Choctaw Humor: after the battle "the Choctaws buried a Yankee in an ordinary grave. For a headstone they put up a stiff Negro buried to the waist. For a footstone another negro reversed out from the waist to the heels."[24] Arkansas troops under General Cabell were assigned to drive off the captured wagons. "Each Arkansan vied to see if he could crush the most 'nigger heads' under his wagon wheels."[25] In all the Confederates killed 117 men of the 1st Kansas Colored. They took no black prisoners. In all, 125 white federal prisoners were taken. A few days later Confederates attacked another wagon train three miles out of Camden at Marks' Mills. Once more, William Cabell led Arkansas troops, and "again reports surfaced of the murder of blacks."

The question is no longer whether such horrendous war crimes occurred, but why. The actions of the Confederates went far beyond the rules of engagement they observed for much of the war. The standard answer from Southerners of this period was that they saw blacks as

> inherently savage and had to be kept in bondage to lead orderly and productive lives. Remove their shackles,

> and blacks would revert into murderous beasts intent on slaying all whites regardless of sex or age.[26]

Thus, given this reasoning, it was possible for the editor of the *Washington Telegraph,* John R. Eakin, the de facto voice of Confederate Arkansas after the fall of Little Rock, to compare Lincoln's act of issuing the Emancipation Proclamation "and seducing our slaves into the ranks of his army" to "those stupendous wrongs against humanity, shocking to the moral sense of the world." As a consequence, "we *cannot* treat negroes taken in arms as prisoners of war, without a destruction of the social system for which we contend."

Retaliation by Blacks

Whites were not alone in perpetrating racial violence. The officers of General Steele's other black regiment, the 2nd Kansas Colored Infantry, took a solemn vow that "the regiment would take no prisoners so long as the Rebels continued to murder our men."[27] In a battle on April 30 south of the Saline River at Jenkins' Ferry, blacks from the 2nd Kansas took their revenge. "The Second Kansas leveled its bayonets and raced forward, the men shouting, 'Poison Springs!' The blacks overran their objective in a matter of seconds, plunging their bayonets into every Confederate they could catch, including three artillerists who tried to surrender."[28] Gregory J. Urwin provides document after document that confirms a massacre nearly as grisly as one that whites committed at Poison Spring.

> We found that many of our wounded had been mutilated in many ways. Some with ears cut off, throats cut, knife stabs, etc. My brother . . . was shot through the body, had his throat cut through the windpipe and lived several days. . . . I saw several who were treated in the same way. One officer . . . wrote on a piece of paper that his lower jaw and tongue were shot off after the battle was over.[29]

If the officers of the 2nd Kansas thought that retaliation would end the massacre of their black soldiers, they were mistaken. A Confederate soldier dressed as a Union officer sneaked into a store room at Princeton where wounded blacks lay. Surgeon William L. Nicholson of the 29th Iowa recalled later that he "saw a Confederate soldier emerge with a smoking revolver in each hand." "I went over at once," Nicholson wrote, "and found all the Negroes shot through the head."[30]

Both races paid a price in lives lost during the Civil War. The number of white Arkansans fighting for the Confederacy who either died in battle or disease has been estimated at 6,862. White Arkansans who died fighting for the Union numbered 1,713. Over 1,500 Arkansas black males died fighting for the Union cause. But there were many, many Arkansans, both white and black, who simply had left the state. Though it is impossible to confirm the number of blacks who left Arkansas and never returned (many were taken to Texas), Carl Moneyhon accepts the estimate of Governor Murphy that as many as 50,000 left the state by 1865. As noted, Arkansas had begun the decade with 111,000 slaves. The white population had also shrunk by 50 percent.

The Political Landscape

While the war was going badly for the Confederacy, the administration of Abraham Lincoln was eager to establish relationships with white Southerners who could claim loyalty to a national government. In an election conceded to be "very irregular," Union supporters mustered the necessary 10 percent of eligible voters in Arkansas and received presidential recognition of their government. Isaac Murphy, who had been the only delegate in the final vote to oppose secession, was sworn in as governor in April 1864. The legislature in 1865 ratified the Thirteenth Amendment to the U.S. Constitution, officially ending slavery in the state, but did little else for blacks. In fact, the constitution of 1864 declared that unless a black person was already living in Arkansas, he or she could not establish residence in the state without permission of the United States government. Slaves, of course, were still being held mostly in the southwestern part of the state by Confederate troops. The Unionist government's domination of the state was to be quite temporary. Historians of the period agree that despite the dislocation and the costs of the War that

> in 1865 the state's antebellum elite—the very people who had directed its destiny before the war, the wealthy, the large landowners—were still on top, in position to control the economic and political reconstruction of the state. . . . The leaders of the Old South were the ones who took the state into Reconstruction, the New South, and beyond.[31]

In 1865 Congress created the Freedmen's Bureau (Bureau of Refugees, Freedmen, and Abandoned Lands), which in part was the creation of Senator Charles Sumner of Massachusetts, a bulldog of an abolitionist and scourge of the South on the subject of slavery. Sumner kept Congress's attention fixed on the plight of black Southerners who he feared would be coerced back into virtual slavery. "There must be no slavery under another alia[s]," Sumner told his Senate colleagues.[32] Following a fact-finding mission to the South, a Congressional committee in May 1864 recommended the creation of the Freedmen's Bureau. Congress approved it in March 1865, after finally agreeing that the bureau would be administered by the War Department, surely a necessary decision in light of the attitude of embittered Southerners who had no intention of cooperating with a plan to help the freedmen. In part, the bureau's mission was humanitarian: agents were to dole out provisions, clothing, and fuel. But they also would have wide authority to maintain order and oversee labor contracts between planters and freedmen. When the Freedmen's Bureau came into being, the federal government had already begun efforts to help freedmen by leasing or selling land to them. In a few cases this idea had proved successful. Bobby Lovett notes that in 1864 black farmers near Helena had made forty thousand dollars. [33]

White Unionist Arkansans who had fought for their lives against Confederate Arkansans undoubtedly gave little thought to the problems blacks encountered as they made the transition to becoming free, nor could they easily have anticipated that one day soon they would ally themselves with blacks politically and militarily in their fight for survival and control. In any event these bitter encounters among white Arkansans did not end with the North's victory in 1865. Kenneth Barnes has identified Conway County as a "microcosm" of Arkansas with planters along the Arkansas River and small farmers in the mountains and hills to the north.[34] He depicts the entire spectrum of the conflicts waged during this period in Conway County, when "the use of political violence was central to the fashioning and streamlining of patterns historians call the New South: the single-party system, black disfranchisement, and segregation by law."[35] It is enough now to note that during the Civil War Conway County and "neighboring counties of the Arkansas Ozarks" experienced "the earliest known organized resistance to secession in Arkansas."[36] By the last two years of the Civil War, Barnes reminds the reader that the "county, like most of northern Arkansas, experienced a vicious local civil war between Union and rebel guerrillas."[37] In fact, the citizens of Conway County waged war on each other for decades after the Civil War. The black citizens of Conway County suffered the most.

Refashioning of Black Identity after the Civil War

Despite the hardships during the Civil War a whole new world was opening to slaves, and they desperately required an evenhanded approach from federal authorities employed by the Freedmen's Bureau whose job it was to assist them. Randy Finley explains that instead, "Bureau officials often perceived themselves as surrogate planters, white patriarchs taking care of infantile Sambos." He quotes agent E. G. Barker of Marion, who said to a friend in the north that "colored people having been suddenly changed from slaves to that of citizens of the U.S. are but *children* in their new position, and easily led astray."[38]

While the freedmen needed all the help they could get, it is not true that they were always led by stronger whites. Finley contends that freedmen created their own identities. Freedom meant for former slaves that they had the power to choose identities for themselves in ways unlike what they had ever experienced. Finley acknowledges that

> it is a daunting task to attempt to ponder the identities of others. Even though it is impossible to *know* the freedpersons or their former masters, the processes they used to reconstruct themselves may be glimpsed. There are further complications in a study of self: Were these new identities which freedpersons in 1865 and 1866 so openly displayed the same selves which had been camouflaged under slavery? Or were these new identities devised by blacks to test the boundaries of freedom? Or were they not masks at all, but rather the genuine African American, revealed at last?[39]

For former slaves, the creation of identities first meant names and family. Finley quotes Sallie Crane, who told her WPA interviewer that as slaves, "We hardly knowed our names. . . . We never heard our names scarcely at all."[40] The emotional catharsis of fully realizing that one may choose a first and last name is a liberating experience. Though Arkansas whites, like Southerners everywhere, had no choice but to acknowledge legally whatever names blacks gave themselves, for almost a hundred years they would deny blacks the dignity of addressing them by the courtesy titles of *Mr.* and *Mrs.* and would simply call adult blacks by their first names as if they were still slaves. Besides one's name the notion of family was crucial in fashioning identity for the freedmen. Even superficial acquaintances with Arkansas blacks today alert one to the overwhelming importance of family. Losing family members to the slave markets brought home the preciousness of family connections, but even this seemingly innocuous task proved initially problematic: Finley notes that "former masters reluctantly recognized blacks' kinship rights," and he quotes Freedmen's Bureau agent Lewis Carhart of Camden who ordered a Ouachita County planter to "allow the bearer Sam [to] have his family. Wife and five children now on your place." Even as late as 1867 bureau agents were having to intervene on behalf of blacks to take family members from the control of planters. "The bearer Bean Brown (a freeman) claims you have a minor Son belonging to him in your possession. He has a right to control and you will deliver the boy Isaiah to him upon receipt of this order."[41]

Blacks constantly used the Freedmen's Bureau to search for lost relatives. Lula Taylor of Brinkley told a WPA interviewer that upon her emancipation "we kept writing till we got in tech [touch] with [her grandmother]. We finally got granny with us on the Jeffries place at Clarendon."[42] In forging their own identities, the strong bond with family did not equate in the freedperson's mind with Victorian notions of sexual morality. Finley writes,

> Enslaved African Americans had developed their own values and mores regarding sexuality and marriage. Rejecting Calvinistic sentiments of a tainted and sinful body, slaves engaged in premarital sexual intercourse as a natural, biological instinct.[43]

An entire class of Arkansas mulatto leaders emerged from the unions of blacks and whites during slavery. With slavery a relic of the past, at least in theory, sex as a political issue came to the forefront. In typical fashion whites who composed the "conservative" wing at the constitutional convention of 1868 tried to make the issue of miscegenation a part of the state constitution. Generations of white Southerners had remained in denial about interracial sex during slavery with the result that they risked appearing as laughable hypocrites at the convention. Black delegate William H. Grey dryly reminded the delegates that "the purity of blood . . . has already been somewhat interfered with" and then proposed to laughter and applause that should intermarriage be prohibited in the new constitution "any white man shall be found cohabiting with a negro woman, the penalty shall be death."[44] Miscegenation became a dead issue at the convention though it would be prohibited by state law when the legislature came into session.

A Passion for Learning

Many Arkansas blacks coming out of slavery wanted learning. Not until 1868 did white Arkansans systematically begin to provide freedpersons with education, but that did not prevent interested northerners, the federal government, and a few Arkansas whites from setting up schools and supporting black education. At the behest of the military, Quakers and members of the American Missionary Association made their way to Arkansas to begin teaching even before the war was over, and freedpersons were clearly overjoyed. Teacher Carrie Moffatt wrote in 1864 from Little Rock that black students came up "with tears coursing down their cheeks" and told her "how long they have prayed for and *expected* this time to come."[45] Finley quotes Joel Grant, Little Rock Freedmen's Bureau agent in 1865: "The desire of the free people for education is unabated, and is so strong as to be deemed by some excessive, amounting almost to a passion."[46] Henry Sweeney, the Freedmen's Bureau agent in Helena reported, "It is extraordinary to see with what avidity the little ones pursue knowledge and how rapidly they learn."[47] In 1867 August Strickland who taught at a freedmen's school in Jefferson County wrote a friend, "I never saw people learn so fast. It generally took me three months to teach what they learn in ten or fifteen days. But I am satisfied the difference is caused by more intense application."[48]

It was one thing to want education, another to get it.

Certainly, many whites were not getting an education. The 1860 census showed that there were more than 23,000 illiterate white adults in the state. Still, in that year 42,271 whites attended some kind of school.[49] In a state that never saw the need to pass a law prohibiting blacks from learning to read as did other states in the Confederacy, the reaction of more prosperous Arkansas whites to blacks' hunger for education was relatively positive. In 1866 James Tibbets, who had once practiced law, noticed upon his return to the state that the former slaves were "anxious to learn." Blacks themselves donated what they could. Finley records that a freedman from Phillips County bought a lot for three hundred dollars to be used for a school. "I'll do it myself if I never get a cent for it; I want to see my people educated."[50] Yet at the same time, Finley notes that "bureau agents from all over the state used language such as 'unsafe, indifferent, unfriendly, bitterness and opposed' to describe the antipathy toward black schools generally among whites in their locales."[51] White Arkansans need not have worried. Despite the assignment in January 1865 of Joel Grant, an army officer and Freedmen's Bureau agent, to the responsibility of developing educational opportunities for the freedmen in Arkansas for that year, there were never more than twenty-two teachers and only about a thousand students.[52] Assuming there were fifty thousand uneducated freedmen in the state by 1865, black education was a drop in the bucket but certainly significant for those who got to benefit from it, and for none more so than Charlotte Andrews, once a slave of the rich and famous Chester Ashley. A student at the Union school in Little Rock established in 1867 by the Quakers but taken over by the Little Rock School Board in 1868, she got her chance to teach when she was asked to take the place of a white teacher (there were no black teachers at the school then) who had become ill in the spring of 1869. Obviously a superior student, she was admitted to Oberlin College and came back to teach in the segregated Little Rock school system until her retirement in 1939, teaching Latin, science, and English among other subjects. Though she was called Little Rock's first black teacher, she gave that honor to her father, William Wallace Andrews, who upon being freed by General Steele in 1863 opened a school for black children at the Negro Methodist Church where he served as minister.[53]

The Black Church after Slavery

At the same time some blacks were discovering that doors to self-discovery were opened through education, many more explored and expanded their identities through the black church. As Finley says,

> No collective institution nourished black personal growth and quickened quests for identity more than did African-American religion. Churches became literal sanctuaries for freedpersons and provided spaces that black could totally control. All of the critical questions of the day about politics, economics, education, social standing, gender and identity were debated, and answers were formulated, at the local church. Yet, the religious content, remained after the war ended, the same. Lawrence W. Levine comments that "much about post-bellum black religion and religious song remained familiar. The war and emancipation . . . initially tended to reaffirm the validity of the slaves' religion."[54]

In addition to the church, one can detect other indications that some blacks early on saw racial separation as the best way to create their own identities: Arkansas Freedmen's Bureau agent Francis Springer noted with dismay "an inclination [by freedmen] to take children from white families merely because of color."[55] In separating from whites, Arkansas blacks at the same time began to identify with Africans worldwide. In Little Rock and Batesville blacks held parades and dinners to celebrate the emancipation of Caribbean slaves each year in August.[56]

The Rocky Road to Black Citizenship

The Arkansas political process was where freed blacks would demonstrate how essential it was to their identities to participate as citizens, but any efforts to shape their own destinies could not occur merely with the war's end in 1865. As the planter class and its allies began their bid to return to power, blacks surely wondered if freedom meant only that they were no longer slaves.[57] Indeed, as freedmen, they made convenient political targets for the Conservatives. Carl Moneyhon notes that "an appeal to white racism was . . . an important part of the Conservative campaign during the October 1865 election for Congress. The party identified Unionism with abolition and asserted that a Unionist victory would cause a full-scale race war and the collapse of society." Besides opposing any civil rights for blacks, the idea that blacks might get the vote drove Conservatives into a fury. In appealing for the poor white vote that was also courted by the Unionists who sought to make the issue a class one, Conservatives trumped them by playing the race card. The *Washington Telegraph* called for "the defeat of the wild visionary and oppressive theories of those who, not satisfied with the freedom of the negro, would make slaves and menials of the working men of the South."[58] With so few persons voting, Congress refused to seat anyone, but the Conservatives were heartened the fact that their candidate Lorenzo Gibson, who could not swear allegiance to the United States, had received a majority of the votes cast in the second district.

Again in political races in 1866, the Conservatives sounded the alarm that a Unionist victory meant black suffrage as well as black equality. By the fall of 1866 they were back in full control of the state though Murphy was still governor.[59] Viewing the return of the old order throughout the South with undisguised disgust, many national Republicans felt the time was ripe for congressional reconstruction of the South. Race relations in Arkansas were about to take a radical turn.

CHAPTER 4

Reconstruction

With the Civil War over and Arkansas occupied by federal troops in 1865, blacks might have hoped that slavery and the violence associated with it would have by now been eliminated, but not so. The first bitter pill freedmen had to swallow was the knowledge that almost none of them would be given land to farm when new president Andrew Johnson took office and soon thereafter ordered that lands be returned to white Southerners who could prove ownership. Without their own land former slaves would be at the mercy of people who had convinced themselves that blacks were owed nothing for their labor except what they chose to give them. As one former slave told a Union officer in Fort Smith, "I cannot help myself unless I get some land; then I can take care of myself and family; otherwise, I cannot do it." E. W. Gantt, once a staunch Arkansas Confederate but now an agent for the newly formed Freedmen's Bureau, predicted the future with deadly accuracy. If agents could not do their job, he wrote his supervisor in December 1865, former slaves faced being "starved, murdered, or forced into a condition more horrible than the worst stage of slavery." As an agent, Gantt's job was to serve as a kind of administrative referee between planters and freedmen. Though in theory he was not to interfere with the contractual relationship that was to serve as the basis for the planter-tenant relationship, if required, an agent had authority to "administer justice," which allowed him to reform the contract or insure that the freedmen got paid. As a white Arkansan Gantt understood only too well the basis for the rage that would be visited upon the freedmen if it were not contained. "I say this sorrowfully of our people, but I know it is but too true. Their wrath over defeat would be poured upon the hands of the helpless ones once their slaves."[1]

Violence against "the Helpless Ones"

The documented violence against Arkansas freedpersons after the war ended is numbing. Lewisburg bureau agent William Morgan in January 8, 1867, wrote, "Attacks upon and murders of freedmen are of frequent occurrence and the peaceably disposed citizens both white and colored are in a constant state of alarm for their lives and property."[2] In 1865 Captain J. M. McCain, agent for the Freedmen's Bureau, observed in the Camden area, "Many [freedpersons] are whipped as formerly."[3] When freedman Smart McCoy "accidentally tripped a white man while in a Hamburg store," his "punishment consisted of an hour-long beating, his attackers using a bailing rope and a belt; the snow outside where he was beaten reddened with his blood."[4] Albert Coons, a white man from Lewisville, tied freed woman America Anderson "to the limb of a tree by the thumbs and otherwise treated her cruelly."[5] There was more than just rage at work. A message was being sent to the former slaves when "some whites in Lafayette County tied down an elderly Lewisville black man and, after drenching his feet and legs with turpentine, set him afire."[6] J. L. Thorpe, Camden agent, reported in 1867 that freedpersons were complaining to him that their lives were in "constant danger." Whites threatened them with death and then threatened retribution if they reported it.[7] Besides acts of violence committed against freedpersons by ordinary white Arkansans, blacks also had much to fear from outlaws. The Cullen Baker gang, a group of fifteen former Rebel soldiers, "robbed, whipped, and killed scores of blacks in both Arkansas and Texas."[8]

Where was the army and why wasn't it more active in preventing and dealing with these racial outrages? Freedmen's Bureau agents asked for help, but it was not forthcoming. Responding in March 1867 as others had before him, General Ord wrote Agent Gantt, "I have just ten men to the thousand square miles, and not more than one of these is mounted."[9] A sufficient number of troops, including blacks, would have obviously served as a statewide deterrent to mistreatment. A Jefferson County planter was reported as saying that "if ever we get clear of the negro troops [we would] . . . be able to get them [black workers] a little under discipline."[10] Federal troops, however, were too few and ill equipped. The adage "out of sight, out of mind" proved only too true.

The two races in the state understood different things about what freedom meant for the former bondsmen. "As their own masters," Otis Hackett, an Episcopal priest in Helena said, as much for others of his race as for himself, "they [the freedmen] are restless, shiftless, and idle. They are slow to learn that can be any connection between liberty and labor."[11] National historian Eric Foner has made the point that freedom to someone who has always been free means something quite different to someone who has been deprived of freedom and then gains it. According to Foner,

> For the newly freed African-American freedom seemed an open-ended ideal; white southerners clung to the antebellum view that freedom meant mastery and hierarchy; it was a privilege, not a universal right, a juridical status, not a promise of equality.[12]

On the plantations the whip had never disappeared. A sense of fatalism about the new system set in eventually for those whose duty it was to administer the new system. William Stuart, an agent at Arkadelphia in Clark County, reported, "Every day's observation shows that the great panacea of the South would be to place a whip in the white man's hand, with the privilege of using it on the 'trifling niggers.'"[13] Arkansas planters saw no reason to change from the past. Rather, they saw whipping as an absolute necessity. "I will keep my niggers if I can whip them, and make them mind," an Arkadelphia planter told a bureau agent in the summer of 1865.[14]

These actions by planters were not merely occasional outbursts. Randy Finley writes, "Freedmen's Bureau agents from 1865 to 1869 continually reported cases of planters who flogged freedpersons."[15]

A Contractual Relationship and the Advent of the Share System

For some freedmen, it may have been difficult to tell the difference between freedom and slavery. Carl Moneyhon quotes a planter as saying, "Let everything proceed as formerly, the contractual relation being substituted for that of master and slave."[16] And the person drawing up the contract was, of course, the planter. The system of planters formally contracting with freedmen that had been developed by the military during the war years was continued under the supervision of the Freedmen's Bureau in Arkansas and "proved to be the chief means that helped landowners restore a measure of control over the freedmen."[17] Initially the army and the Freedmen's Bureau convinced themselves that the process of planters' paying wages to freedpersons to work on a contractual basis might work, for after all a top hand in some places was receiving wages of twenty-five dollars a month, a place to live, food, medicine, and medical treatment, which was comparable to that being received by white laborers. With the labor shortage that existed, bureaucrats allowed themselves to believe that planters would not take advantage of the freedmen. "In practice," according to Moneyhon, "bureau agents often favored planters and farmers over laborers."[18]

> When times were bad economically as they were in 1866, many employers endeavored to deprive their laborers of their wages or their share of the crops. Some drove their workers from the farms, charging that they

> had failed to honor their contracts. Other refused to pay their laborers, citing a variety of reasons for not complying with the agreements.

Moneyhon states that General Sprague guessed that as much as one third of what was owed to freedmen was not paid. Sprague wrote, "Men who profess to be honest and honorable cannot understand that there is any moral wrong in *robbing and cheating* a Negro."[19]

The share system was in place throughout Arkansas by 1867. The optimistic tone of some bureau agents who thought it might work turned sour as they realized the share system could be easily manipulated to cheat freedmen. Moneyhon cites the reports of agent A. E. Habicht of Arkadelphia who admitted that "employers attempted to defraud the tenants in every way possible when they settled with them on the cost of supplies."[20] In one area planters seemed willing to accommodate freedmen. General Sprague in January 1866 wrote that at the request of the freedmen many planters actually established schools on their plantations. Officials at the Freedmen's Bureau observed that schools resulted in more workers, so it was a benefit for the planters to provide this new feature, however brief, of plantation life. It went without saying that under this arrangement planters controlled what was taught in the schools.

The WPA narratives give eloquent testimony to the despair felt by blacks in their dealings with white landowners. Anthony Taylor, who had labored after slavery for a white man in Clark County, said the following:

> He was a pretty good man. Of course, you never seen a white man that wouldn't cheat a little. He'd cheat you out of a little cotton. He would have the cotton carried to the gin. He would take half the corn and give us five or six shoats. After he got the cotton all picked and sold, the cotton it would go to him for what you owed him for furnishing you. You never saw how much cotton was ginned, nor how much he got for it, nor how much it was worth nor nothing. They would just tell you you

> wasn't due nothing. They did that to hold you for another year. You got nothing to move on so you stayed there and take what he gives you.[21]

Carl Moneyhon notes,

> The freedmen understood what was happening. No matter what system of labor was used, they would be cheated and nothing could be done to prevent it. Distrust of whites became a part of their view of the postwar view.

Bureau agents were aware that African Americans had few illusions about the labor system. "Freedmen in many places are still *freedmen* not *freemen,"* wrote the Arkansas bureau chief in August 1867. "The white man still arrogates the rights and powers of masters while the freedmen half acknowledge them."[22] Significantly, patterns of behavior were set in 1867 that continued well into the next century.

President Lincoln's plan had been to end the war and slavery with as little sectional bitterness as possible. One can only speculate what arrangements he ultimately would have made with the white power structure of the South if he had lived. The war had changed him but to what degree is simply unknown. Eric Foner notes that four days before Lincoln was assassinated he cautiously embraced at least limited suffrage for blacks ("the very intelligent" and "those who serve our cause as soldiers"), but his assassination in April 1865 dramatically changed the political landscape. Vice President Andrew Johnson of Tennessee had neither the stature nor temperament to work with Congress, and very nearly was removed from office after articles of impeachment were filed against him. Johnson's plan, announced at the end of May, was to restore "property rights except for slaves, to all southern whites except Confederate leaders and wealthy planters (and most of those subsequently received individual pardons)."[23] According to Eric Foner, Johnson did not anticipate that the South would elect the same structure that had been in place at the moment of secession. Apparently, he assumed that a whole new breed of yeomen farmers would now lead the South. If that was his expectation, he was sorely disappointed.

Congressional Reconstruction

The Radical Republicans and their supporters who had such influence in Congress, in part because of President Johnson's inept stubbornness, showed themselves to be a unified group of politicians who blended a stew of idealism and self-interest into a legislative program that would forever change America by the passage of two amendments to the Constitution and a civil rights statute.[24] Constitutional amendments granting all persons due process and equal protection of the laws, and giving freedmen as citizens of the United States the right to vote, had significant consequences for whites, as well. Events in the South since the war's end had demonstrated to the Radical Republicans that nothing would be accomplished until, as Foner suggests, they turned the "political clock" back to Lee's surrender. Thus, over the president's veto again, they passed the Reconstruction Acts in 1867, which imposed military rule on the South.

The South was now carved into five military districts. Arkansas and Mississippi were placed under the jurisdiction of General E. O. C. Ord, who knew Arkansas well, having been a former assistant commissioner of the Freedmen's Bureau. Laws passed by the previous Arkansas legislature were declared to be in legal limbo, and Ord called off the legislative session set for July 1867. If the rebellious states wished to escape military rule, they were now required to pass the Fourteenth Amendment. Additionally, they would have to enact new state constitutions that gave adult black males the vote. On and on the legislation went, even intruding on the jurisdiction of the state judicial system, particularly when litigation involving race was at issue. Additional measures relating to voter registration plainly stacked the deck against those who had been loyal to the Confederacy, but this was precisely the point. The price of rejoining the country would mean major changes would have to take place, and those changes could not happen if those who had left the country could now vote unimpeded and if those who had never voted could not now exercise the franchise.

As intended, the Reconstruction Acts breathed new life into Arkansas Unionists who now organized the state's first Republican Party and held their first convention in April 1867. With new life came new blood: newcomers from the north joined the Arkansas Republican Party. More liberal than their counterparts from Arkansas, they would soon play a significant role in state government. One of those was former general Powell Clayton, who had been a commander at Pine Bluff where he married an Arkansas woman and became a plantation owner. As Republican governor, Clayton became perhaps the most controversial governor in the state's history. Though the Republican Party would ultimately depend for its survival on black votes, only three blacks participated at this first convention, but one of them, John Peyton who had come to Little Rock as a slave in 1832, served on the state central committee. Becoming a minister after slavery, Peyton used his oratorical skills "before a crowd of freedmen on the Convention's first day," urging them to loud cheering to "rightly use the freedom" they now enjoyed.[25]

Freedmen and the Political Process

Knowing how desperately it needed black support, Republicans began to organize the Union League, originally a province of the middle-class North during the Civil War. By 1867 it had become a primary vehicle though which blacks participated in Arkansas politics. Beginning in May, 21, 696 blacks ultimately registered to vote in Arkansas as a result of the implementation of the federal Reconstruction Acts. Tom DeBlack writes,

> Many freedpersons found the combination of political education and the organization's mysterious rituals extremely appealing, and membership in the league

> skyrocketed. Over two thousand blacks attended a league rally at Helena in May of 1867, while the Little Rock chapter raised almost eighteen hundred dollars for the coming election.[26]

Randy Finley notes that while Republicans "effectively used political clubs and rallies to mobilize freedpersons' support; so, too, did Democrats woo adherents." Democratic clubs consisting of Arkansas blacks sprouted in Hamburg, Marion, Jonesboro, Pine Bluff, and Searcy. Finley contends that it would be an error to conclude that blacks were necessarily duped into joining with the Democrats. Besides the hope for patronage positions, "there also was a strain of black conservatism which sincerely believed the Freedmen's Bureau and Republican promises would reenslave blacks just as Southern white planters had done."[27]

Inevitably, given the process, it was the Republicans who carried the day. In November 1876, 25,576 Arkansans voted to hold a constitutional convention to take place in January 1868. Black Arkansans, fresh out of the gate, had participated in their first victory and, with eight delegates to participate in the convention, were sky high with hope for the future, but Arkansas whites were not going to make it easy. Conservatives set about to organize the Arkansas Democratic Party in December. The Little Rock *Daily Arkansas Gazette* announced that the organization's purpose would be to save "the country from negro supremacy in any of the states in the union."

In late 1867 Ku Klux Klan (KKK) activity began in the state as a political terrorist organization. How the KKK was linked, if indeed it was, to the Democratic Party has never been determined. As a secret organization formed by Confederate general Nathaniel Bedford Forrest, the Klan had already been active in other Confederate states. In Arkansas its self-proclaimed leader (or "wizard") was Colonel Robert G. Shaver, former commander of the 38th Arkansas Infantry, who boasted the Klan had dens all over the southwest part of the state with fifteen thousand members.[28] The Klan was an equal-opportunity band of terrorists, attacking blacks, Freedmen's Bureau officials, state officials, and even the military, but it would not gear up fully in the state until after the constitutional convention of 1868 met in January.

Blacks and the Constitutional Convention of 1868

The convention, which began on January 7, was historic for several reasons, first and foremost because almost two out of every three of the seventy delegates were Republicans. So-called "carpetbaggers," men who had entered Arkansas after 1860, numbered seventeen. Called political opportunists by Conservatives, some had come south to make their fortunes, and in so doing assisted in transforming Arkansas, in many respects, into an economic system that resembled the North. Others who carried this label were agents of the Freedmen's Bureau, missionaries, or teachers.[29] It was these seventeen men who dominated the convention and influenced the twenty-three so-called "Scalawags," those white Arkansans who had either been Unionists from the beginning or had come over to the Union side during the war. Far from having brought their belongings to Arkansas on their back, the seventeen carpetbaggers had superior educations, past leadership experience, and a strong sense of cohesiveness, which according to John Graves

> gave them a tremendously disproportionate influence. With three physicians, seven lawyers, a merchant, a manufacturer, an engineer, three farmers and a minister, their backgrounds had better prepared them for leadership than their less affluent white allies. Thomas Bowen, who was elected President of the Convention, quickly saw to it that his group of 17 received 78 of 184 committee assignments.[30]

Finally, among the Republicans were eight black delegates whose independence and abilities have long been debated by historians. Thomas Staples, who had studied under the influential historian of Reconstruction William A. Dunning at

Columbia, wrote in 1923 that the eight blacks at the Arkansas convention were "ignorant and deluded negroes," implying there were sycophants of the Radical Republicans.[31] As far as the group as a whole, the *Arkansas Gazette* said at the time of the convention the Republicans were a "bastard collection whose putridity stinks in the nostrils of all decency."[32] Nothing, of course, threatened and incensed the planter class and its supporters so much as seeing their former slaves and their enemies in positions to make the promises of equality before the law a reality. Given how they had treated slaves before the war, freedmen soldiers during the war, and laborers afterwards, they understandably expected the worst. But in his study of the Arkansas black delegates to the constitutional convention of 1868, Joseph St. Hilaire paints a different portrait of the black delegates. The "typical" black delegate "spoke eight or nine times and for the most part, routinely defended enfranchisement of blacks and continuation of the Freedmen's Bureau." According to St. Hilaire, "Evidence shows . . . that they were capable of grasping the intricacies of political problems of the day. Basically, they were successful in their efforts to defend the newly-gained political rights of their black constituents."[33] Indeed, the written record of the debates leaves no doubt of the ability and independence of some of the black delegates, particularly William H. Grey, a minister who had never been a slave and at one time as a servant of Virginia governor Henry Wise had been allowed to attend sessions of Congress. By 1863 he was living in Helena with his wife Henrietta and five children and, as made obvious by his remarks at the convention, was quite well educated. As leader of the black delegation, Grey took on Jesse N. Cypert, a Confederate veteran from White County, who on January 13 introduced a measure to adopt the 1864 state constitution, which, of course, had no provision for black suffrage. Grey told the convention that blacks

> have stood by the Government and the old flag in times of trouble. . . . From this and other considerations we are here not to ask for charity . . . but to receive . . . the

> apportionment of our rights, as assigned by the Reconstruction Acts of Congress.

He pointed out that freedmen could vote just as intelligently as illiterate whites and then recited the history of voting by blacks in other parts of the country.[34]

When Conservatives attempted to divide the Republicans by inserting a clause in the proposed constitution prohibiting marriage between a white person and "a person of African descent," James White, the only member of the black delegation who was not from the South (Indiana) and who had not been a slave, told the delegates before the debate was over what all of them knew but in language local blacks did not dare use in public venues:

> The white men of the South have been for years indulging in illicit intercourse with colored women, and in the dark days of slavery this intercourse was in a great majority of cases forced upon the innocent victims.[35]

St. Hilaire points out that not all the black delegates were equally able or aggressive as Grey and White. Given the hostility they faced and their understandable lack of political experience and sophistication, their participation was all the more remarkable. It made sense that they would take direction, as did the Scalawags, from more experienced allies. For purposes of Arkansas history, perhaps the most fascinating African American delegate was James W. Mason, who was the son of Chicot County's Elisha Washington, the largest slave holder in the state. Elisha Washington arranged for Mason to study at Oberlin College and then at St. Cyr, a prestigious military school in France. Fluent in French, Mason returned to the United States in 1865. Perhaps not surprisingly, Mason appeared on some occasions to identify with the Conservatives and according to St. Hilaire "voted thirteen times in opposition to the majority of its Negro members."[36]

To the lasting bitterness of most white Arkansans, the constitution of 1868 was approved by a healthy majority of delegates who supported "Negro Suffrage." Besides the right to vote, the document approved by the Republican majority gave blacks the right to serve on juries, hold office, and serve in the militia. Finally, it gave Arkansans of both races free public schools and provided for the creation of a state university. Outside the convention, white Arkansans had no intention of retreating from the doctrine of white supremacy, which in no way made them unique. John Graves points out that by 1860 just five of sixteen states in the north allowed blacks to vote, and Massachusetts alone permitted blacks to serve on juries. As Graves notes, "Southerners, however, failed to appreciate the extent to which the Civil War and the struggle for emancipation had begun to alter Northern attitudes."[37] The election for ratification of the new constitution was set for two weeks in the middle of March. With the election machinery entirely in the hands of Arkansas Republicans and no meaningful opposition, the passage was a foregone conclusion. There was only one real issue—whether blacks would achieve political equality—but Conservatives/Democrats saw the proposed constitution as no more than a way to ensure Republican dominance. To them the campaign was simple: a vote against the constitution meant maintaining, as a newspapers blared, "a WHITE MAN'S GOVERNMENT IN A WHITE MAN'S COUNTRY."[38] Had all white males in Arkansas been allowed to vote, Arkansas would have remained in the hands of the Conservatives and their allies. As it was, the constitution of 1868 was narrowly ratified by 25,600 to 22,994 with voting having begun in March.

The Ku Klux Klan and Powell Clayton

On April 2, 1868, a historic day for the freedmen, the Arkansas legislature unanimously ratified the Fourteenth Amendment. All over the South, the same result was reached: all states that had seceded seven years earlier now ratified the Fourteenth Amendment and reentered the Union. Arkansas was allowed to do so upon Congressional approval on June 22, 1868. Resistance to the new order was continued by other means: by the spring of 1868 there were Klan chapters in Little Rock, Fort Smith, Searcy, Batesville, Pine Bluff, Monticello, Camden, El Dorado, Arkadelphia, and in other places in Arkansas. White Arkansans were determined not to allow blacks and their allies to cast votes in the presidential election of 1868. "I was as scared of the Ku Klux Klan as rattlesnakes," Henry Walker of Hazen told his WPA interviewer.[39] Warnings were left at the homes of many persons who had something to do with the coming election. Jackson County sheriff-elect Riley Kinman received the following:

> We have come! We are here! Beware! Take heed! Speak in whispers and we hear you. Dream as you sleep in the inmost recesses of your house, and, hovering over your beds, we gather your sleeping thoughts, while our daggers are at your throat. Ravishers of liberties for the people for whom we died and yet live, begone ere it is too late. Unholy blacks, cursed of God, take warning and fly.[40]

The day after his inauguration as governor on July 2, 1868, Powell Clayton moved to create a force to deal with the disturbances. The legislature at Clayton's request passed into law an act creating a state militia, which was limited to eligible voters. On August 27 Clayton proclaimed he had the right to organize a state guard. Otis Singletary notes, "This proclamation was issued in defiance of the existing Congressional prohibition, and since the troops were openly recruited, Washington presumably gave tacit approval."[41] Meanwhile, the "disturbances" were continuing. The Lafayette County chairman of the voter registration board got word to the governor that he had been given no choice but to flee for his life.

> There was an organization formed of from one to two hundred men, for the avowed object of killing Union men, of both colors, who would not join democratic clubs and vote their ticket. Some ten to fifteen colored

> men were shot down for this cause, and I had reliable information that if I attempted to register [any voters] I would be assassinated.[42]

In August a member of the legislature from Columbia County informed Governor Clayton that "ten black men had been murdered in a period of twenty days."[43] Klansmen took a deputy sheriff from his house in Monticello one night during October and tied him to a rope whose other end encircled the neck of a local black man. They shot them and arranged their dead bodies in an embrace where they were left for forty-eight hours. In November two black preachers who were also local leaders of the Republican Party in Monticello were taken out and whipped. Historians have documented a long litany of acts of intimidation and violence too numerous to mention here. Present-day Arkansas histories accept historian Allen Trelease's estimate that "over two hundred Arkansans were murdered on the eve of the election."[44] The brazen quality of the attacks reached a crescendo in October when U.S. congressman James M. Hinds and another prominent Republican, Joseph Brooks, were ambushed while campaigning for Ulysses Grant in Monroe County. Hinds died from his wound though Brooks recovered. Who shot them would never be known. Hinds received the dubious distinction of being the "highest-ranking government official to be killed in any state during Reconstruction."[45]

The day after the presidential election Powell Clayton moved against the Klan and his other enemies by issuing a declaration of martial law that eventually applied to fourteen counties. His proclamation noted that "in many of these counties a perfect reign of terror exists," and the civil authorities were unable to maintain even a semblance of law and order.[46] Clayton also nullified voter registration in twelve counties, nor was there registration allowed in Lawrence County, and from Fulton County there were no returns. It was hardly a coincidence that in April only two of these counties had recorded majorities for the constitution.

Black Militia during Reconstruction

Blacks got in on the action, as well. Kenneth Barnes writes, "In Conway County, the Klan itself was terrorized by armed black militiamen, a feat seldom seen in the South."[47] As an example during the most vicious cycle of violence, Barnes has uncovered an incident of retaliation by black militia for the murder of Wash Lewis, who was killed by six disguised Klansmen on November 30, 1868. During this period someone set fire to downtown Lewisburg. Finally, Clayton ended martial law in Conway County on December 8.

These violent acts by blacks were not confined to Conway County. A black militia man was alleged to have raped a white woman in present day Howard County in southern Arkansas while four others stole property from her house. Though the military commander in charge ordered arrests and trials that resulted in the execution of the alleged rapist by a firing squad composed exclusively of blacks, there were numerous reports of brutality and theft from the southwest region of the state. Otis Singletary writes that

> cases of rape or attempted rape implicating Negro troopers were also reported. . . . While the colored troops were charged with many crimes and atrocities of which they were wholly innocent, they did engage in many discreditable pursuits.[48]

He cites evidence of extortion "in connection with militia prisoners." Additionally, "'Protection papers' and 'safeguards' were issued to citizens in exchange for specified sums of money." Clearly, given their attitudes about blacks, whites were outraged by most anything involving a black soldier.[49]

Three companies composed of black militia men arrested a member of the KKK in Monticello in southeast Arkansas who was alleged to have killed a local freedman along with a Drew County deputy sheriff. A delegation of prominent citizens prevailed upon the governor to withdraw the troops and convicted and executed the murderer. Other Klan members fled. In another instance a detachment of black militia was nearly slaughtered at the county courthouse in Marion in Crittenden County. They were saved by a former Union officer named William Monks who commanded six hundred Missouri troops who engaged the KKK in battles from Fulton to Crittenden County.[50] By March 1869 the Klan had been largely subdued, and Powell Clayton, according to historian Allen Trelease, "accomplished more than any other Southern governor in suppressing the Ku Klux conspiracy."[51] Neither race would forget the cost.

Kenneth Barnes has summarized this period as follows,

> The last half of 1868 had been a second civil war for Arkansas. Conway County, in particular, was a battleground between former Confederates calling themselves the Ku Klux Klan and the alliance of former slaves and former Unionists from the northern hills who temporarily wielded power. Democrats showed they were willing to use violence to regain power taken from them by Congressional Reconstruction. The alliance of white and black Republicans met violence with violence. Governor Clayton's use of military force throughout Arkansas had broken the Klan and restored order.[52]

A Record Number

Politically and as designed, blacks benefited dramatically during Reconstruction. By 1873 there were four black senators and sixteen black representatives serving in the Arkansas legislature, a feat that has not been matched since.[53] Besides the legislature, blacks occupied some county government offices, primarily in the Delta, where in some instances they far outnumbered whites numerically but also in the number of registered voters. For example by November 1867 blacks in Phillips County had 2,681 registered voters; white registered voters numbered 955. In Jefferson County black registered voters totaled 2,738, whites 1,048. Perhaps no more than one black has ever been elected to the all-important administrative position of county judge.[54] Blake Wintory has shown that H. C. Newsome served as county judge of Chicot County from 1882 to 1884. Blacks served variously during Reconstruction in the positions of sheriff, coroner, assessor, and treasurer in Chicot, Pulaski, Lee, Jefferson, Phillips, Lincoln, and St. Francis counties. Besides political gains, blacks benefited from legislation passed during Reconstruction. On July 14, 1868, Governor Clayton signed into law Act 15, which prohibited racial discrimination on public carriers, steamships, railroads, street cars, and stagecoaches. Other areas included were inns, hotels, and places of entertainment. If convicted, punishment was not less than two hundred dollars nor more than five thousand dollars and a possible jail sentence of twelve months. In 1873 Governor Elisha Baxter signed a similar act, lowering the fines but including a prohibition against discrimination in saloons.[55] In fact blacks only occasionally tested this legislation, knowing that mostly all-white juries would never convict whites, but the fact that discrimination in public accommodations was, in theory, against the law was an important symbol. Also, in 1868 the first legislature after the constitutional convention enacted a law that required segregation in public education. Though nineteen legislators in the house of representatives voted against the measure, which passed unanimously in the Arkansas Senate, John Graves writes that "most Arkansas blacks appear to have soon acquiesced in segregated schooling without sustained protest."[56] In 1868 segregation was not a problem that seemed paramount. Eric Foner has written about the constitutional conventions in the South at this time and has said,

> All southern Republicans favored the establishment of state-supported public school systems. But many whites, and not a few blacks, preferred the establishment of separate schools for the two races. Most black delegates seemed more concerned with securing long-denied education for their children and employment opportunities

> for black teachers (who they believed white parents would never accept) than with integrating schools.[57]

John Graves notes that "by the late 1870s, in fact, some blacks in Little Rock were requesting that only teachers from their own race be employed in the city's black schools."[58]

As important as the subject of education would be, nothing in the nineteenth century matched the idea of owning and cultivating one's own land. Despite a proposal of land for freedmen in the constitutional convention of 1868 by black Phillips County delegate William H. Grey, it was an idea that seemed way too radical for the average Radical at the convention.[59] Thaddeus Stevens of Pennsylvania and some other Radicals in Congress had wanted to confiscate property of the losers and redistribute it to the freedmen, but nothing came of it. And if these ideas were too extreme for a Congress that was doing some truly radical things, they had no chance in Arkansas. The problem was not lack of land but finding the money to buy it. And though the planter class was able to reassert itself after a fashion after the war, one could imagine the difficulties in buying property for an illiterate population that had almost nothing but the clothes on their backs in 1865 when the war finally ceased. Truly, one of the most amazing aspects of Arkansas history is the fact that by 1900 the census showed that there were 11, 766 black farmers in the state who owned all or part of their land. Granted, as John Graves points out, "most of these black yeomen were marginal operators eking out a bare subsistence; 73.3 percent owned homesteads of fifty acres or under."[60] Yet it was this small but hopeful population that joined the black agricultural Wheels to fight for small farmers in the 1880s, and afterwards it was this population in addition to the black elite in the towns that gave lie to the notion that African Americans cared for nothing but living in the moment. And as many historians have pointed out, the groundwork was being laid for two African American economic miracles: in 1917 St. Francis County resident Scott Bond "turned down an offer of two million dollars for his combined properties."[61] In northeast Arkansas in Jackson County, Pickens W. Black farmed an astonishing eight thousand acres.

An Unnatural Death—the End of Reconstruction

Though the removal of federal troops from the South in 1876 signaled the end of Reconstruction in the old Confederacy and the beginning of a hands-off policy, fierce Republican politics in Arkansas that degenerated into armed conflict hastened its slightly premature death in 1874. Though African Americans, for the most part, stayed out of the so-called "Brooks-Baxter War," at one point in the debacle blacks supplied a portion of the militias supporting Republican rivals Joseph Brooks and Elisha Baxter. In skirmishes and accidents that historians estimate may have taken as many as two hundred lives, the dispute over which of the men would sit in the governor's chair finally had to be settled in Washington by no less than President Grant. After a month of dithering, on May 15 Grant ordered the militia formed by Brooks to disband and recognized Baxter as governor.

Reviewing the accomplishments of blacks during Reconstruction, besides the appointment of James T. White as commissioner of public works, William H. Grey served in the state government in the cabinet-level post of commissioner of immigration and state lands from 1872 to 1874. A graduate of Ohio University, Joseph C. Corbin was appointed superintendent of public instruction, a post he held from 1873 to 1874. Though during Reconstruction blacks were not elected to the legislature in proportion to their numbers, afterwards, with white Conservatives again voting, the number of black men would never again come close to the number of twenty in 1873.

It would be in this transition period in 1874 during which some black Republicans began to listen and support men whom one normally would have supposed were unacceptable to them. Todd Lewis writes,

> Black Republicans in several counties followed [James T.] White's lead, forming coalitions with pro-Baxter conservatives and supporting a call for a constitutional convention controlled by Conservatives which would roll back gains they had made.[62]

Despite these alliances of convenience, the vote for a constitutional convention to be held in 1874 must have been hard to swallow for steadfast Republicans, black or white. In fact, 80,259 were said to vote for a convention. Only 8,687 voted not to have one. Obviously, blatant fraud once again carried the day. In Phillips, Lee, and St. Francis counties, the heart of the Delta, the press reported that the call for the convention passed without a single dissenting vote.[63]

It is useful to contrast the constitutional convention of 1868 and that of 1874. Again there were eight black delegates, but in 1874 out of ninety-one delegates "over seventy . . . were Democrats."[64] Yet with the deck stacked against them, on one crucial issue the black delegates were successful. Barely two weeks into the convention, a motion was made requiring a poll tax before one could vote. James T. White, who had been a member of the constitutional convention of 1868 and had argued vehemently for voting rights for black males, now contended, "The rights we acquired in 1868 we expect to maintain. It is a premeditated plan by this convention to take as many of them as they can."[65] Put on the defensive, a number of Democrats argued they had no plan to disfranchise blacks, but their reasons for voting with James White on this issue were not necessarily predicated on justice for black people. Some voted with White to avoid disfranchising poor whites; some feared federal intervention. A future governor, William M. Fishback, called attention to the federal act dealing with Arkansas's readmission to the United States that said that "the Constitution of Arkansas shall never be so amended or changed as to deprive any citizen or class of citizens of the United States of their right to vote who are entitled to vote by the Constitution herein recognized." In addition, John Graves notes that the constitution of 1874 contained an explicit equal protection clause that prohibited any citizen from being "deprived of any right, privilege or immunity . . . on account of race, color, or previous condition."[66]

Besides reducing the term of governor to two years the new state constitution in 1874 sharply limited the powers of the governor and undid much of the work of the framers of the constitution of 1868. One of the more important negative changes for African Americans was to reduce their strength in eastern Arkansas through legislative apportionment. Early historians dismissed Reconstruction in Arkansas (1868–1974) as merely an interim of infighting among Republicans, both white and black, for political spoils, economic exploitation, high taxes, fraud, and waste. Certainly, this brief era was that also, but its significance was much greater than the larger-than-life personality of Powell Clayton and those who battled on his behalf and against him. Quite unexpectedly, out of this era would come an acceptance by white Arkansans of all political stripes of African Americans' right to vote and hold political office for the next twenty years, a truly significant development given what the white majority's attitudes had been in the recent past and would be in the future. In retrospect it was merely a matter of time before the former Confederates regained control of state government in every part of the old Confederacy, but when they returned to power in Arkansas in 1874, in many ways they had accepted the revolutionary changes of the Thirteenth, Fourteenth, and Fifteenth Amendments to the Constitution. John Graves has succinctly summarized this sea change in political behavior:

> By the close of Reconstruction, Democrats as well as Republicans were actively courting the black electorate and were even recruiting and employing black troops

> in support of their cause. In the immediate aftermath of Reconstruction, Democratic leaders, defying criticism from white-supremacist elements in their own party, would continue to reach out to blacks and follow moderate racial policies.[67]

As Graves says, however, one must be careful not to read too much into the gestures of the Democratic leadership during this period as it regained ascendancy. Initially fearful of what the North might do if they clamped down with too harshly, Democrats made a show of evenhandedness toward blacks. This attitude would change over time, and the Democrats would genuinely earn their reputation as "Redeemers."

CHAPTER 5

Redeemers

To outsiders, Augustus H. Garland, a former Confederate senator and a Democrat, would not have seemed to have the kind of credentials of a man who would accept the results of Reconstruction with anything approaching grace, but in his first proclamation in 1874 as governor, he said the following: "Let the people of all parties, races, and colors, come together, be welcomed to our State, and encouraged to bring her up to a position of true greatness."[1] Garland was not merely engaging in rhetorical excess. Campaigning for governor, he had promised blacks that if elected he "would retain the Civil Rights Act of 1873 and protect black citizens' access to the ballot and to free public schools."[2] And it was Augustus Garland, as a Democratic leader, who had traveled to Conway County with Governor Clayton during the violence in 1868 and "scolded whites for disarming freedmen and reminded them that 'the colored man possesses the same rights, privileges, and immunities—civil and political—that the white man possesses.'"[3]

Racial Moderation, White Supremacy

With such a racial moderate, in word and in deed, at the helm of the state, blacks were given hope for the future. It was not that Garland, a staunch Democrat, was an anomaly. In 1878 the Arkansas Democratic platform called on blacks to join them:

> It is the sense of this convention that the colored people of this state are identified in interest with the great Democratic Party of the state, and, fully recognizing the importance of a more harmonious feeling between them, embrace this opportunity of inviting them—the colored people of this state—to an active cooperation with us in furthering our common interests.[4]

And it was not merely convention rhetoric. Garland's successor, William R. Miller, governor from 1877 to 1881, committed his administration in his initial inaugural address to using "the whole power of the state" to guarantee the rights of its black citizens. When several blacks were murdered by "roving bands of marauders" that operated on the Arkansas-Louisiana border, he ordered two companies of militia, one black and one white, to Union County. When some of the ringleaders were captured in Texas, Miller ordered militia from Hempstead County to guard the prisoners to avert a rescue attempt as they proceeded home. John Graves has pointed out how politically courageous this action was since black militias had been so resented during the Reconstruction era. Yet this willingness to recognize the right of blacks to participate in defense of their own citizens did not end with Miller either. Graves relates that Thomas J. Churchill, governor from 1881 to 1883, ordered that a white officer in Pine Bluff to be court-martialed in 1881 after he had willfully disobeyed instructions "to enroll a newly organized black company" and then "dispatched a Little Rock officer to muster in the blacks."[5]

In trying to understand the Redeemer era, Peggy Lloyd makes the point that "the racial climate in post-bellum Arkansas varied markedly between counties and even between communities within the same county."[6] At the same time John Graves has said,

> It would be easy, if misleading to exaggerate the benevolence of Redeemer racial policies. So long as their basic control and Democratic political domination were not in jeopardy, so long as their financial interests were not

> endangered, the Redeemers saw little harm in acknowledging the Negro's formal constitutional rights. The Redeemers were chiefly concerned that they remain free to utilize the state's large pool of cheap labor without hindrance.[7]

While both these statements are true, they do not necessarily contradict each other. Whites in power during the Redeemer era often went considerably beyond the position that all that was needed for racial harmony was to give lip service to the constitutional rights of blacks. In certain areas and under the right circumstances, racial attitudes seemed highly evolved. But when all was said and done, political control by those in power on both a state and local level went hand in hand with exploitation of the black labor supply. Reconstruction in Arkansas ended three years before national politics resulted in the deal made by Republicans after the presidential election of 1877 to end military occupation in the remaining Southern states in exchange for Rutherford B. Hayes becoming president. As Kenneth Barnes notes,

> It was the final federal retreat with President Hayes's southern policy in 1877 that signaled real change. Black citizens understood that their status and rights had been redefined in Arkansas. . . . But the retreat from Reconstruction was more than just black perception. White Democrats in Arkansas counties with large black populations, such as Phillips County, took their cues as well. In the next election, they boldly used force and fraud to take back control of local government in [Phillips, Lee, and Crittenden counties].[8]

Clearly, with such rampant fraud and intimidation, something had to give in the Delta if the political situation were to avoid major conflict.

Fusion Politics

Both sides of the political equation in the heavily black counties in the Delta finally recognized that each had much to lose if some sort of political compromise were not worked out. Desperately needed black labor in the Delta would flee Arkansas for a more hospitable environment unless whites could learn to restrain themselves in these black-majority counties from insisting on exercising complete political domination in such an aggressive manner. There was nothing new in this thought. Unless some power sharing arrangement was agreed upon, the Delta would be continually on the verge of chaos. John Graves notes that Governor Garland had "encouraged Democrats in the predominately black counties of the Delta to share offices with Negroes through the arrangement known as the 'fusion principle.'"[9] This device, while not to anyone's satisfaction, was seen as necessary in the Arkansas Delta where by 1890 there were fifteen counties whose populations were 50 percent black. Six of these counties, all contiguous to the Mississippi and Arkansas rivers, had black populations of approximately 75 percent. Fusion was a way of keeping a relative degree of racial peace. Kenneth Barnes and other historians have shown that as a result "the franchise appears to have returned to African Americans in the 1882 elections throughout most of the Delta, and by 1884, even in stubborn Phillips County."[10]

For a number of years fusion seemed to work as blacks and whites would get together to divide up county and state offices before election day. Historians have tracked the number of black office holders in the state legislature and found that, though the number of blacks elected to the Arkansas legislature never equaled the highest number during the Reconstruction era, beginning in 1874 blacks continued to be elected as representatives and less often as state senators. Blacks served as sheriffs in Chicot, Desha, Lee, and Phillips counties. Other county offices blacks were elected to included circuit clerk, county clerk, treasurer, assessor, and coroner. John Graves has written that "fusion arrangements existed at one time or another in Chicot, Crittenden, Desha, Jefferson, Lee, Lincoln, Monroe, Phillips, and St. Francis counties and perhaps others."[11] In addition, Kenneth Barnes has identified

Lafayette, Hempstead, and Little River counties as jurisdictions that at times embraced the fusion principle.[12]

Earlier local historians in the Arkansas Delta interpreted the willingness of blacks to enter into fusion arrangements as evidence of their passivity and capacity for being manipulated.[13] In fact, scholars know painfully little about the specifics of these arrangements. Historians would like to know much more about the conditions under which these individuals accommodated themselves to the whites who controlled politics in these counties and whose lack of numbers was more than made up for by the control of land, jobs, and other resources. Remaining unknown, as well, are the points of view of local office seekers who with each election cycle made the decision to share offices, to run the risk of violence, and to employ fraud and measures of intimidation to control elections. The complicated saga of W. Hines Furbush—an African American mulatto Republican who initially represented Phillips County in the Arkansas legislature in 1873, served as Lee County's first sheriff, and then later became a Democratic representative—says much about the difficulty of fully understanding the motivation and pressure upon those African American individuals who had a grasp on the levers of power in both black and white worlds in the post-Reconstruction era preceding the imposition of Jim Crow.[14]

If fusion was not popular with anybody, it was still supported by influential whites because they knew that in most counties whites had sufficient control over county governments in the Delta. In 1889 the *Arkansas Gazette* editorialized against tampering with a system that had already broken down in some districts.

> The charge that good government cannot be secured [without disfranchisement] in counties where there is a large colored vote is not true. Jefferson County with an immense Negro majority, has as good a local government as there is in the south. So has Chicot, Phillips and other large Negro counties in this state. They have

> adopted the plan that justice and common sense suggests.[15]

This willingness of the whites in power to permit African Americans to have some political power in the Delta was clearly instrumental in accomplishing the goal of attracting black labor to the state, who migrated in ever increasing numbers. Kenneth Barnes writes that the black population grew faster during the 1880s than in any state in the country except Georgia, increasing by 98,451.

Little Rock—a Different World

Whatever the motives of the *Arkansas Gazette* in 1889 in commenting on the need to retain the principles of political fusion in the Delta, a different system was continuing to emerge in Little Rock. For it was in the capital city that opportunities for African Americans were brightest, and those who were able to take advantage of them achieved results that were, for the times, amazing. John Graves quotes Charles Stewart, a black reporter from Chicago, who observed, "While in Little Rock I have visited the offices of . . . successful negro lawyers and have seen white men go in to consult them. Negro doctors have white patients. Negro merchants have white customers and the like."[16] John Graves, among other historians, has traced the lives of a number of black businessmen who worked hand-in-glove with whites, none more so than the premier black entrepreneur of his day, Mifflin W. Gibbs, who combined a talent for accumulating wealth with political skills that took him far from the California gold rush where he had realized he could make more money by importing fine boots and shoes to San Francisco and selling them to the newly rich than by panning for gold. Gibbs, who had been born free in Philadelphia in 1828 and worked for others' freedom in the Underground Railroad, made money wherever he went, including Victoria, Canada. By 1870 he had graduated from Oberlin Law School and turned his attention to Arkansas after having met William H. Grey and other successful blacks at a convention in Charleston, South Carolina. By 1871 he was in Little Rock, having hitched his political wagon to Powell Clayton. Appointed Pulaski County attorney in 1871, he was elected municipal judge of Little Rock in 1873. As Clayton's "chief black political lieutenant," he was appointed to such plums as federal land registrar and U.S. receiver of public monies and capped it off when in 1897 he became U.S. consul in Madagascar. With the connections he had, networking in the Little Rock business community was second nature to him. By 1889, among other affiliations with whites, he was "a partner in the Little Rock Electric Light Company and a shareholder in other enterprises."[17]

Born in 1856, John E. Bush, whose white features were evident, came to Arkansas from Tennessee at the age of six with his slave mother and her master who was trying to stay a step ahead of federal troops. An orphan by seven, Bush drifted from one place to another and, by his own admission, gained a reputation as a troublemaker. Somehow, after being coerced to attend school Bush turned his life around, he finished high school as an honor student in 1876 and served as principal of two high schools for three years. His marriage to Cora Winfrey whose father was wealthy contractor Solomon Winfrey further helped smooth his way as he became involved with Republican politics. Every business tycoon has his favorite motivational story, and Bush was no exception. One day in 1883 while he was engaged in conversation with a white man, a black woman approached them to ask for money to bury her husband. The white man complained to Bush, "I cannot see or understand your race. When they work they throw their earnings away and whenever a Negro dies or needs help the public must be worried to death by Negro beggars—it is a shame!"[18] The rest would be history, of course, as John Bush and Chester W. Keatts went into business together to create the Mosaic Templars of America, which became fabulously successful selling burial insurance, operating three thousand lodges in twenty-six states and in foreign countries, as well, by 1928. But it had to grow first, and along with it Chester Bush and others of his ilk would become quintessential "race" men. Their model was Booker T. Washington who delighted white America in 1895 with his famous Atlanta speech that signaled his desire that black Americans busy themselves with creating wealth and leave politics and racial equality alone for the foreseeable future while the "race" built itself up. It was the duty of those blacks who had become successful to "uplift" the race. What this meant in theory was that the mass of poor blacks would emulate them and develop habits of thrift and develop practical skills through industrial education that would allow them to become financially secure. In practice it meant that blacks would not attempt to compete with whites through the political process or strive for social equality. Though not every black person agreed, including the brilliant thinker and writer W. E. B. Du Bois who became Washington's arch enemy, his words suited many blacks and whites. Washington's stature as a black leader meant an alliance with a segment of the white community that, at times, reached from the White House to the governor's office in Arkansas. Booker T. Washington, himself entertained at the White House by President Theodore Roosevelt, would make a total of three visits to Arkansas to praise and encourage his Arkansas acolytes, some of whom besides Bush and Gibbs were farmer Scott Bond; ministers E. C. Morris, Joseph P. Robinson, and J. M. Connor; and educators Joseph A. Booker and James Monroe Cox. Before long these men would be joined by Scipio Africanus Jones, a Little Rock attorney, businessman, and Republican who eventually would have the ear of Arkansas governors and claim friendship with one in particular, George Donaghey. All of these men and others, including a number of black physicians, dentists, lawyers, and educators, would constitute a mostly mulatto elite that thrived not only in Little Rock but in small towns and even in rural areas in Arkansas as farmers who owned their own land.

In particular, life for a small but growing group of

"middle-class" blacks in Little Rock definitely had its compensations. With the founding of three black colleges in Pulaski Country before the turn of the twentieth century, Philander Smith College (originally named Walden Seminary), Arkansas Baptist College in Little Rock, and Shorter College in North Little Rock, blacks benefited not only through the opportunity for an education but also employment. Besides educators, this elite group of blacks, most of whom were not elite in any financial sense, was composed of a few doctors, lawyers, businessmen, ministers, landowners, and employees of the post office and railroads. In Little Rock they had a unique opportunity to participate in the political system. While Arkansas itself was the most Democratic of states, Little Rock, because of its distinctly Whiggish merchant class, saw its interests differently even before the Civil War, and as John Graves has said,

> Unlike much of Arkansas, Little Rock maintained something approaching a viable two-party system, and the measure of party competition worked to the advantage of blacks. . . . Periodic election irregularities did not prevent Negroes from remaining a force in local politics; from 1869 through the seventies and eighties, they always had at least one or two of their race on the city council.[19]

This political participation extended to the local school board, as well.

But it was not only the lives of the so-called black elite that were benefiting from the less stratified existence available to blacks in Little Rock. In the capital city there was a genuine high school for blacks that opened in 1873 that offered Latin, French, German, science, and higher math as well as vocal music and drawing. William G. Whipple, who served as Little Rock's mayor from 1887 to 1891 and on the board of visitors, made the following observation after holding a two-hour class in electricity and magnetism at Little Rock's black Union High School in 1880.

> [Blacks] acquitted themselves well and creditably. . . . Scarcely a question was missed. . . . Most of the class seems to have a clear understanding of the reasons and principles of the subject which to the majority of minds is quite abstruse and difficult of comprehension. . . . No class, colored or white, could have done much, if any better.[20]

The importance of a high school education cannot be overestimated for those blacks lucky enough or persistent enough to get one. John Graves points out that only 52 percent of white children and 45 percent of black children were in any kind of school in Arkansas as late as 1895–1896, and as for blacks, 70 percent of them went no further than the fourth grade. Graduating in the class of 1899, William Pickens was truly fortunate to make it to Union High School, since only 4 percent of the entire black enrollment in the state was in grades ten through twelve. He remembered,

> I plunged into that High School work with a zest such as I have seldom experienced before. My never-absent, never-tardy record was maintained, and indeed during the three High School years once was I absent, and then because of an illness that took me for a day in the spring of my last year.[21]

The Blurring of the Color Line

There were more things to do in Little Rock than go to school, and there were areas where the color line especially blurred. First, as John Graves has so clearly documented, though the new suburb of Pulaski Heights was to be advertised as "exclusively for white people" and "while there was a predominantly black neighborhood in the central part of Little Rock, and a tendency for blacks sometimes to cluster together elsewhere," as late as 1900 "in numerous instances blacks and whites lived side by side."[22] Berna J. Love has shown that blacks and whites lived next to each other in Little Rock before World War I. "The areas of Fifth Street to

Twelfth Street east and west of Main, including West Ninth Street, were mixed neighborhoods with whites and blacks living side by side."[23] And there is at least anecdotal evidence that the races in parts of Little Rock got along. Future composer William Grant Still, whose mother moved him to Little Rock in 1896, would remember his own neighborhood where "white and colored lived amicably side by side in nice houses." Still took violin lessons from a "Mr. Price. He may have been German, but I do not know his nationality."[24] Blacks and whites also socialized on occasion, as well. Graves writes that though a saloon or restaurant might be characterized as a "Negro" establishment, in fact, "in some of these businesses, as late as the 1890s, the races mixed freely."[25] One place where the races mixed freely was the club scene. Though there were racially exclusive bars and gambling/lottery dens, a reporter in 1891 wrote of a club just across the river in North Little Rock, then called Argenta. In the back room it consisted of

> a billiard hall and a dance hall in the rear, in which at one end is a raised platform or stage, where the most obscene and revolting orgies are enacted. In the same lot are several cabins occupied by the lowest type of women who have given up their lives to prostitution. Here white and black mingle together, and it is here that toughs and criminal of all classes make their rendezvous.[26]

In spite of some opportunities for upward mobility, the reality in Little Rock was that most blacks were living at the subsistence level in this era. Though in 1896 blacks constituted 46.4 percent of the population, statistics show they paid, exclusive of poll taxes, only $6,609.99 in real and personal property taxes in Pulaski County compared to $275,309.40 to whites.[27]

Of course, it was not just in Little Rock that "white and black mingle[d]" together. Kenneth Barnes has shown that "the testimony of local residents in Conway County revealed that as late as 1888, blacks and whites drank whiskey together in the same saloon and gambled together at dice games in Plumerville." In fact, the night when Powell Clayton's brother, John Clayton, was murdered in Plumerville, blacks and whites were together watching black men play the fiddle and banjo and dancing in a local barbershop.[28]

Some African Americans worked in business with whites and thrived in other towns besides Little Rock in Arkansas, as well. For example ex-slave Wiley Jones prospered in Jefferson County and was believed to be "probably the wealthiest black in the state."[29] Owning real estate that took in a racetrack and fair grounds in Jefferson County, Jones also had a controlling interest in the Pine Bluff streetcar line. But he also bought and sold property as far away as San Francisco. Blacks also had political power in Pine Bluff. At one time three members of the city council were black as well as half of the policemen and a number of justices of the peace.

Debt Slavery instead of Milk and Honey

If Arkansas on the whole seemed too good to be true for most African Americans, especially in rural parts of the state, in fact, it was. The reality was that once most black immigrants got to Arkansas, instead of a land of milk and honey, they were trapped in poverty and debt. Yet the need for black labor on the plantations was continual and incessant. William Pickens, whose family left South Carolina for Arkansas in 1888, said his family was recruited by labor agents who described the state as "a tropical country of soft and balmy air, where cocoanuts, oranges, lemons and bananas grew. Ordinary things like corn and cotton, with little cultivation, grew an enormous yield."[30] The experience for the Pickens family was unfortunately all too familiar. They arrived on January 15, 1889, to snow and ice and already in debt for what they owed for their transportation. With no work initially, they had to depend on credit given to them by their planter-employer. All who could work did, and none of the children went to school that first year, the youngest hoeing and picking cotton. His older sisters drove a plow. Pickens remembered,

> When the first year's settlement came around, and a half hundred bales of cotton had been produced by the family and sold by the planter, Father came home with sad, far-away eyes, having been told that we were deeper in debt than on the day of our arrival. And who could deny it? The white man did all the reckoning. The Negro did all the work.[31]

Doing all the work and getting deeper in debt was one thing; pushing on to somewhere else was quite another because of Arkansas's 1875 landlord's lien law, which helped to insure that planters would be paid for supplies given to the tenant by imposing a lien on what the tenant produced. Making the arrangement a throwback to slavery was the provision that the tenant was prohibited from leaving his tenancy before his contract was up. As John Graves writes, though there were provisions in the act that protected tenants,

> given the nature of Delta society, it was usually the laborers who were prosecuted, fined and jailed; fear of such punishment could virtually bind a hand to the plantation. The Little Rock *Daily Republican* referred to the measure as a "peonage act," which is essentially what it became.[32]

The Pickens family was exhibit A of how the lien law worked in practice. William Pickens, who graduated Phi Beta Kappa at Yale, continues his story.

> The second year the whole family plunged into work, and made a bigger and better crop. But at reckoning time history repeated itself; there was still enough debt to continue the slavery. If the debt could not be paid in fat years, there was the constant danger that lean years would come and make it bigger. But there was the contract—and the law; and the law would not hunt the equity, but would enforce the letter of the contract. . . . There was but one recourse—the way of escape. The

> attempt must be executed with success, or there might be fine and peonage. On some pretext my father excused himself and went to Little Rock. A few miles out of that city he found a landowner who would advance the fares for the family and rent to us a small farm. This looks at first sight like "jumping from the frying-pan into the fire," but a rented farm with a definite loan is a different proposition from a state of debt-slavery, where the creditor sells all the produce and does all the counting. . . . And so one night the young children and some goods were piled into a wagon and the adults went afoot. By morning we were in the town of Augusta, twelve or fifteen miles away, when we caught the first train [to Little Rock].[33]

The Pickens family's situation was replicated over and over again in Arkansas despite occasional efforts on the federal level to stop it. In fact, black Arkansans had been leaving the state for years.

Back to Africa

On November 23, 1877, blacks held the first convention of the Liberian Exodus Arkansas Colony at the Third Baptist Church in Helena. Attendees came from Lee, St. Francis, and Cross counties in addition to Phillips. Blacks considering moving to Africa risked more than simple hostility from whites. B. K. McKeevers from Phillips County wrote the colonization society in February 1879 that

> the Kuklus has begun to talk to Negroes out here and whip them about a week ago they taken out one C. J. Thomas [Clerk of Number 16 Liberia Exodus Colony]. After giving him two heavy blows over the head with a pistol he got away.[34]

In May 1880 two separate expeditions left for Liberia out of New York transporting 136 men, women, and children from Arkansas to Liberia under the auspices of the American Colonization Society. As will be seen, it was the first of a number of attempts by Arkansas blacks to establish a life free of white dominance outside of the state. The poverty and hardships encountered by the group even before they left New York would make national news stories as groups rushed to their aid. Throughout, generally among poorer blacks in Arkansas, there was a continued receptivity to the sentiment begun in 1877 that their lives would be better off if they returned to Africa. Beginning in 1880, with the election of Henry McNeal Turner to serve as bishop in Arkansas (as well as Mississippi and the Indian territory in what is now Oklahoma) of the African American Episcopal Church, rural blacks in the state got a powerful advocate for the back-to-Africa movement. Turner's biographer, Stephen Ward Angell, describes the highly charismatic and influential bishop as "possess[ing] strong support in certain areas such as rural Arkansas."[35] Unlike many of his peers, Turner protested loudly against Jim Crow laws and advocated racial pride as well as immigration. His message and the receptivity to it were an early indication that rural blacks in the state were prime candidates for the separatist message of Marcus Garvey in the 1920s.

The Howard County Riot

The racial complexities of the Redeemer era run deep in Arkansas history. In 1883 the Howard County race riot occurred, a multi-layered event that displayed, in large part, the ambiguities of the era that make generalizations difficult. In some ways the Howard County Riot foreshadowed the Elaine Race Massacres of 1919. Just as in the days of slavery, rumors often swept Arkansas warning of impending "insurrections" by African Americans. Indeed, in southwestern Arkansas during the previous year "news of planned insurrections at Prescott in Nevada County and Hope in Hempstead County" had proven to be nothing more than rumors cooked up in the fevered brains of whites who had feared retribution from blacks as far back as the days of slavery. As would occur in Phillips County in 1919, an influential white, former Confederate general and one-time Ku Klux Klan leader Robert G. Shaver, insisted that "local blacks had already established an organization to kill certain men in the county."[36] As in 1919 no evidence would be adduced of a planned insurrection, but that did not stop the *Arkansas Gazette* from running a front-page story on August 2, 1883, that blacks in the northwest corner of Hempstead County were "on the warpath" and had murdered a white man by the name of Wyatt as he was plowing a field.[37] And as happened in Phillips County in 1919, the response from Little Rock was to send in the troops and put down the trouble. And also as in Phillips County, by the time the trouble was over innocent black men, including a fourteen-year-old boy, had been murdered, black men had been arrested, put on trial and convicted, and no whites were ever held accountable.

But there the similarities mostly end. Two historians have examined in detail the Howard County riot of 1883 as well as the time period involved and have come to different conclusions about the motives of some of the actors surrounding the events. They place much different emphasis on certain aspects of the so-called riot and the implications flowing from it. At the same time both perhaps have a piece of whatever truths can be gleaned from this understudied event in Arkansas racial history. Peggy Lloyd, writing in the *Arkansas Historical Quarterly*, and Helen Hoguet, author of a master's thesis at the University of Wisconsin, agree that in Hempstead County in August 1883 there was a dispute between a black and a white and a possible rape or attempted rape of a black girl by a white man and that a group of offended black men decided to effect a then-lawful citizen's arrest of the alleged perpetrator that ended not in his capture but in his death. The white response was to take into custody forty-three black men (in the process killing four blacks including the boy) and to put them on trial for the murder of a single white. One black man was eventually executed and most of the convicted blacks were eventually pardoned and released. No whites were arrested. From these agreed-upon facts, these two historians emphasize quite different aspects of the events that followed. Lloyd finds it significant that the blacks who were charged received aggressive legal representation from the white legal community in the area. Instead of the brief show trials in which appointed counsel from the Helena bar went through the motions of representation in the Elaine Race Massacres thirty-six years later, the white attorneys, who were mostly from Washington in Howard County, vigorously defended their clients all the way from challenging prospective juror after juror to filing exhaustive appeals and petitions for clemency. In addition, as Lloyd states, "prominent men, both black and white, and of different political persuasions, lobbied the governor to commute the death penalties or pardon the convicted men."[38] Ultimately, one black man, Charles Wright, was hanged, but by 1890 all of the other defendants, with the exception of six who died in the horrible jail, were free. Lloyd offers a number of reasons for this response that was so different from 1919 where it took lawyers in Little Rock, Boston, and New York to free the men. The most persuasive reason Lloyd offers is the following: instead of mostly poor sharecroppers who had joined a union to help themselves, as were the defendants in Elaine, the black defendants in Howard County were mostly men who owned their own farms and thus were respected by landowning whites and who, though conservatives of the old school, appreciated their aspirations. What motive would a successful farmer, albeit a black one, have to go on a rampage? As Lloyd points out, Wright, the one black man who paid the ultimate price, was landless and a relative newcomer to the community and did not have the standing of the other defendants. In any age, even during the darkest days of Jim Crow, blacks who had some money and property enjoyed a somewhat different reception than poor blacks among the richer class of whites. Certainly they were not going to be accorded social equality, but so long as they did not demand it, some whites, those that felt no particular threat, retained the capacity to be indignant at treatment of blacks they could not justify and provided assistance.

In her saga of her family's mixed-race history in Howard County in this same era, Ruth Polk Patterson provides a rich description of the interaction her mulatto landowning grandfather, Spencer Polk, had with whites. Spencer Polk, according to his granddaughter and her informants, thought of himself as more white than black in his tastes and habits. Patterson interprets her grandfather's life-long identification with white culture as a result of his close and warm association as a young man with his white father and his half brothers. As an example of his behavior in this regard, Patterson writes,

> From all indications, Spencer accepted his "Negroness" as an unfortunate badge he and his offspring had to bear. It is alleged that because he considered himself more white than black, he did not allow his children to mingle freely with other dark-skinned blacks. In fact, he frowned upon intermarriage of his children with blacks, and forbade black men to call upon his daughters.[39]

But more than this, "Spencer insisted that his daughters portray the image of the Southern Belle. They dressed in the latest fashions and often attended square dances and parties with the white neighbors, according to the oral tradition."[40] While Spencer Polk represented an extreme mindset, it is an indication that some blacks clearly felt they had much in common with their white neighbors. Patterson's account suggests that in Howard County landowning blacks of this era had little in common with the dirt-poor black sharecropper.[41]

The Importance of Black Land Ownership

Hoguet, who had the benefit of reading Lloyd's article, apparently sees little significance in Lloyd's points about the aggressive representation by white attorneys, for she does not mention them. Rather, she interprets white behavior in this era as a mixture of paternalism and violence in order to assure the continuation of white supremacy. She characterizes the statements of racial cooperation by whites in authority in this era as nothing more than paternalistic and empty gestures. Both historians, however, stress the importance of the fact that most of the blacks who were involved in this incident owned their own land and were not subject to the typical sharecropping arrangements of the time. Hoguet points out that "black landownership fractured the link between economic and social control that white Southerners had relied on since slavery to subordinate black men and women to the greatest extent possible," a fact emphasized by the black *Weekly Mansion*, a newspaper published in Little Rock particularly devoted to racial uplift in rural areas.[42]

In fact, there is little doubt that blacks who owned their own land and businesses were often treated differently and with more respect by whites. Money and wealth, of course, command attention in any age in a capitalist society. Perhaps the biggest lesson to be learned from the so-called Howard County riot of 1883—and it would be one that endured through the 1930s—is that no African Americans living in Arkansas, regardless of their status and wealth, were ever safe from acts of individual or mass violence from whites who, on a moment's notice, could whip themselves into a frenzy of fear and violence even in a relatively tranquil period. With the coming of Jim Crow, the 1870s and 1880s would seem like a paradise.

CHAPTER 6

The Coming of Jim Crow

The year 1891 was a legislative disaster for African Americans like no other in the history of the state. Measures were passed that would soon result in their effective banishment from the political process and segregate them from whites. Kenneth C. Barnes argues that the key to understanding these catastrophic events lies in an analysis of what happened years before in places like Conway County. As already noted, Conway County was the scene of vengeful behavior that far outlasted the Civil War itself, but by 1872 the Democrats were again in control and surely thought their domination would last indefinitely. But from their perspective an unnerving demographic began to occur. From no more than 630 blacks in 1870 the black population shot to 3,206 in 1880, a rate of growth dwarfing the increase of the white population. By 1890 it had doubled again; suddenly blacks composed 39.4 percent of the population of the county. Many blacks came from South Carolina where voter fraud and violence followed the end of Reconstruction, and understandably they hoped the situation would be different in a part of Arkansas where many whites had not wanted to secede from the United States.

The Lure of Populism

Blacks, lured by labor agents to Conway County, made their homes in the fertile bottomlands north of the Arkansas River. Besides blacks came a number of immigrants including Germans, French, Italians, and Polish, many of whom were

Catholic. By September 1884 Republicans, with the aid of black voters in Conway County, were now back in power. But it was not only the Republicans who had come back to life, for in their midst there was a whole new political force now sweeping the country. Farmers who had never cared about politics were now joining something called the Agricultural Wheel in Arkansas. The Wheel and its organizational forerunners stood outside the traditional parties and attracted disgruntled farmers of both races who began seeing their world through a populist lens that counted as enemies merchants and their laws that favored the mortgagor and their economic policies that resulted in low prices for their crops.

Beginning as early as 1882 black farmers in Prairie County in east-central Arkansas were listening to populists voices for help on solving their financial woes, and with the help of the founder, a white man by the name of Milton George from the Northwestern Farmers Alliance, they put together the first local organization in Arkansas.[1] Wheelers and groups like them talked a language farmers could understand. Steven Hahn writes,

> During the early 1880s, blacks in the Arkansas Delta built the Sons of the Agricultural Star to such a size that the state Agricultural Wheel, in 1886, dropped its "whites only" eligibility clause to accept the membership (though in racially separate units). By 1888, two hundred black wheels (as they were called) could be identified in Arkansas, and when the Wheel and Farmers' Alliance merged, resurrecting the policy of racial exclusion, they went on to form the Colored State Agricultural Wheel.[2]

While Kenneth Barnes is unable to trace the nature of any new political alliance in Conway County, whether farmers who identified themselves with the new populism and Republicans joined together or had separate slates, he maintains that "by 1884 Conway County Democrats became well aware of the splintering effects of a third-party vote but argued futilely that a vote for the farmers meant a vote for the Republican Party." With "the highest voter turnout ever seen in Conway County, the farmers and Republicans defeated the Democrats for every County office, with most of the winners appearing to be Republican."[3] Despite having their ballots and poll books stolen in a Republican township, this coalition brought in votes, as well, for the Republican candidate for governor Thomas Bole who beat Democrat Simon P. Hughes by sixty-seven ballots. None of this would have been possible without the support of the county's black population, and the Democrats knew it. Suddenly, populism had become a threat that had the Democrats reeling. In Arkansas the Agricultural Wheel by 1884 had ten thousand members and was growing fast.

Blacks Battle the Klan in Conway County

Barnes has documented that early in 1885 the Ku Klux Klan had reappeared in Conway County and details the violence directed against blacks. Blacks were ordered to leave, and one, J. W. Hawthorne, was called out of his house and shot dead. All through the month of March the Klan rode. With no help coming from local law enforcement, though now it was Republican, by the summer blacks formed their own militia. Conway County again in 1886 went Republican despite evidence of Democratic fraud and even elected a black man, G. E. Trower, as state representative, a fact that obviously galled the hearts of many Conway County whites, for Trower, Barnes determined, was threatened and moved in 1887 to Independence County.[4] Despite Trower's departure from the county, Barnes has documented that blacks continued to migrate to Lick Township in Conway County in February 1888, apparently confident that the former Unionists would stay in control. They were badly mistaken.

Barnes contends that the Conway County Democrats responsible for the fraud had simply underestimated what it would take to win the elections in 1886 but did not make the same mistake in 1888. In that year the agrarian populist challenge to Democratic rule statewide was at its peak. There were twelve black Wheels representing thirteen counties in Arkansas, indicating strong black support. The Agricultural Wheel now claimed over seventy-five thousand members statewide and put out their own newspapers, including one in Conway County. Instead of putting up a candidate themselves, the Republicans supported the Wheel candidate for governor, a one-legged ex-Confederate by the name of C. M. Norwood. Republican John Clayton, brother of Powell Clayton, was on the federal election ballot in November for the U.S. House of Representatives.

In retrospect one could have anticipated what was coming in Conway County, for a seventy-five-man white militia had been drilling for weeks in the streets of Morrilton. On election day at 7:35 in the morning the militia marched to the courthouse as Democrats ordered black Republican election officials to depart and took control of the election. Blacks were not permitted to vote, and when the township votes were counted, they favored the Democrats by a six-to-one margin. Two years earlier Democrats had just narrowly carried Morrilton. In Plumerville where blacks outnumbered whites two to one, much the same occurred. Black election judges who arrived at the polls were told they had been replaced by white judges. Predictably, Plumerville, which had gone Republican by a five-hundred-vote majority two years earlier, went Democratic by seventy-six votes. Conway County, of course, went Democratic. Norwood, who claimed fraud in Conway and other counties, demanded that the legislature investigate. The response was that if Norwood put up forty thousand dollars to pay for the costs, the Democrats would agree. Unable to raise that kind of money, Norwood had no choice but to accept the results.

Though no militia appeared on the streets in the November federal election, the new county sheriff swore in more than a dozen Democrats from Morrilton and Plumerville as deputy sheriffs to "insure a fair election and count."[5] In fact, the deputies were selected to neutralize the appointment by a federal judge of local white Republican

Charles Wahl as a federal supervisor to watch the polling place at Plumerville. Again on election day, as in September, the Republican black election judges were dismissed by Democrats. When they tried to set up an alternative site at a black barbershop, they were followed and told they would be put in jail if they tried to allow voting. The deputies hung around all day, "intimidating black voters." Not taking any chances, the Democrats sent four masked men armed with pistols to Smith's Drugstore where the votes were being counted and simply stole the ballot box and poll books. Later, Wahl testified in federal court that one of the men said, "God damn you, turn it [the ballot box] loose or I will blow your brains out. We will show you how Conway County goes."[6]

By Any Means Necessary: The Murder of John Clayton

John Clayton lost the election by 846 votes. Federal indictments for fraud were issued, and Clayton personally investigated the election results, taking depositions in Plumerville. That night on January 29, 1889, someone, possibly Bob Pate, who had long been part of the efforts to fix election results, murdered Clayton by shooting him through a window while he sat down in a rooming house in Plumerville to write a letter to his children. Murdering an important white candidate in a federal election resulted in a great deal more interest than if the dead man had been black. Investigations occurred, and according to Barnes hundreds from Conway County testified at the federal courthouse in Little Rock. After Clayton's opponent Clayton Breckinridge had served almost his entire term, the Republican-controlled house of representatives declared the seat vacant.

The 1890 elections in Conway County were again violent with both sides claiming to match force with force. According to Barnes, "It was, however, Democratic violence that won out in the elections in September 1890." Again, ballots were stolen, but as Barnes notes, "Democrats counted the ballots, and Democrats won the election."[7] The November election was equally chaotic, but in this scenario a Republican "mob" from Center Ridge that included about a hundred blacks marched to the polling place in Plumerville and stayed with their weapons drawn until the results of the election were announced. Though Breckinridge won Conway County again, he lost to the Republican candidate by a hundred votes in Plumerville. Barnes argues convincingly that one can look at what occurred in Conway County in 1888 and 1890 and predict what was coming in the Arkansas legislature, for it was Morrilton lawyer W. S. Hanna from Conway County, elected to the state senate courtesy of the stolen election in 1888, who presided over the senate in 1891 as it wrote the law that had the effect of disfranchising blacks.

Conway County to Africa

Blacks in Conway County soon had little doubt about their futures in Arkansas. Barnes has pointed out "by the early 1890s, the dire situation for African Americans in Conway County fueled the back-to-Africa emigration movement."[8] Hundreds of blacks from Conway County applied. Morrilton resident N. M. Rogers, one of the few who was accepted and actually made it to Liberia, wrote his family that he would not return to Arkansas even if "some one would give me a place there and stock to work it." One of the things he liked best about Liberia was that it was not Conway County: "There are no white men to give orders; and when you go in your house, there is no one to stand out, and call you to the door and shoot you when you come out."[9] Barnes has documented that "despite the fact that Arkansas's black population was smaller than that of its southern neighbors" between the years of 1879 to 1899 "more Liberia-bound emigrants left from Arkansas than from any other state."[10] Approximately six hundred made the journey, and for each one who made the trip, "hundreds more applied unsuccessfully to go." Barnes argues that "the rapidity of this shift from relative well-being to subjugation, rather than the magnitude of the oppression, convinced many African Americans to leave not just Arkansas or the South but the entire United States."[11]

Similar Lessons in St. Francis County

But it was not only in Conway County that blacks learned the hard way that their days as active citizens were over. Writing in the winter 2001 *Arkansas Historical Quarterly*, Melanie K. Welch has shown that as in Conway County after Reconstruction ended blacks at first had no problems voting in the eastern Arkansas county of St. Francis, though whites were by far in the majority at that time. She acknowledges that while white Democrats had reacted to the strength of the coalition of the Wheelers and Republican Party in 1888 by "launching an effort to remove black Arkansans from politics," the behavior of the Democrats in St. Francis County "may have been particularly sharp there because of a distinct set of circumstances—St. Francis was becoming a black-majority county."[12] Welch documents that the same hardships suffered by farmers all over Arkansas—farmers losing their farms and becoming tenants—was occurring in St. Francis County. By 1900 70.7 percent of all farmers did not own their land, where in 1880 only 43.2 percent had been tenants. But what was different was that blacks in St. Francis County in a single decade went from 41 percent of the population in 1880 to 59 percent of the population in 1890. Instead of fusing with Democrats as occurred in places like Jefferson County, in 1888 black Republicans in St. Francis called on blacks to fuse with the Wheelers. Americus M. Neely, the editor of the *Advocate*, Forrest City's Republican newspaper, urged his readers in June 1888:

> Republican Clubs are being organized all over St. Francis Co. all the colored people should join. And stick together so that we can gain representation and recognition for the race. The wheelers are in favor of the above, and will

> give us a chance to have a free ballot and a fair count. And we should be men and act like men.[13]

Neely, also a Wheeler, was a grocer and generally a leader in the black community. The Democrats did not like this proposal one bit. Quoting the above comment by Neely, the *Forrest City Times* responded by saying this was a ploy to "break up the democratic party." As it turned out, the black Republicans got three candidates of their own on the ballot for coroner, treasurer, and assessor. Though the whites reserved for themselves the more important offices of county judge, sheriff, county clerk, and surveyor, blacks saw their chance for representation where they had none before, and it paid off. Their fusion ticket was elected on September 3 by a majority of 372 votes, and Norwood's majority for governor was 440. The *Forrest City Times* reacted angrily. "To elect the negro, is an insult to the intelligence of the county. . . . Proud St. Francis now has three negro county officials."[14] In May 1899 a test of the new politics presented itself with a school board election. All parties initially agreed to a fusion ticket of the entire political spectrum, including Democrats, but the agreement fell apart and added to the tensions before the school board election. Welch writes that

> growing anxiety about a black electoral majority had reached the point that some Democrats were prepared to use violence to install their candidates in office. A few days before the election . . . supporters were quoted as saying "that if necessary to carry that election against the negroes and their white leaders, shotguns and pistols would be used."[15]

Matters came to a quick boil on May 18 in what has become known as the Forrest City riot. Though accounts differed depending on one's political perspective, by the morning of the nineteenth Americus Neely, along with the Republican and Union Labor sheriff D. M. Wilson, Tom Parham (whose father had joined the Agricultural Wheel) and city marshal Frank Folbre (a Democrat) were dead. Black leaders quickly made themselves scarce for good reason, and the Democrats easily elected the school board. Welch writes, "Following Neely's murder, several black elected officials fled town. . . . Local Wheel members also found themselves under attack for their association with Republicans and blacks."[16] Wheelers were also advised to leave town.

As so often had happened and would again in the future, whites feared that blacks would extract their revenge, and it was rumored that "large number of negroes were congregated north of town, and prepared to attack and burn it."[17] Armed militia sent by Governor Eagle guarded the town with two hundred armed men. When no attack came, twelve men were detailed to investigate. The *Arkansas Gazette* reported they found no armed blacks, "but many cabins were deserted and the women and children of several families crowded into one house. No negro men were seen anywhere."[18]

When an election to select a new sheriff was held on July 15 in the large black township of Franks, it was reported that "the [neg]roes . . . did not go [to] the polls at all, and only Democratic [tic]kets were cast." Welch concludes that "it is evident from these reports that in the wake of the Forrest City Riot many blacks feared going to the polls."[19] The Democrats thus were able to elect a Democrat sheriff and assessor.

Two years later in St. Francis County the situation had calmed down enough that blacks returned to the polls and helped elect Union Laborites who took every office from county judge to representative. Interestingly, the Democrats in St. Francis County fused with Republicans, but blacks, despite their affiliation with the Republicans, obviously saw their interests differently. Though Governor Eagle won again, he did not carry St. Francis County, losing to the Union Laborite candidate.

As occurred in Conway County, in Welch's view, the Democrats "had had enough of the political uncertainty that events in St. Francis County over the previous two years had exemplified" and passed the 1891 election law whose "real purpose was to undermine the black vote."[20]

More Lessons in Crittenden County

In Crittenden County, where fusion had been the order of the day though blacks outnumbered whites by five to one, the summer of 1888 proved to be a sign of things to come. After tensions rose, two black officials were charged with drunkenness by the white sheriff. On the day of their trial, John Graves writes,

> A group of armed whites, including the sheriff, rounded up not only the accused but all other black officeholders and several black citizens, including a teacher, an editor, and a minister. The group of about twenty was then marched at gunpoint to the Marion railway station, placed on board a train for Memphis, and warned not to return.[21]

Eventually heading to Little Rock, the group petitioned Governor Eagle to intervene. He said he could do nothing without the support of the sheriff. Jeannie Whayne notes that

> when elections were held a few months later, county government was returned to white control. Not a single black candidate was elected, despite the fact that the county was overwhelmingly black. This not only ended black officeholding in Crittenden County but also signaled the end of "fusion."[22]

To the Back of the Elephant: The First Steps

Finally, nothing could have been more ominous to blacks in 1888 than the speech of former Arkansas Supreme Court justice and stalwart Republican leader John McClure who told the state convention that the Republican Party "has got him [the Negro] . . . and we can't get rid of him."[23] If it ever wanted to win again, the Republican Party would have to be all white or all black. As a biracial organization McClure said that it was doomed. It was not three months later that McClure and fifty other prominent Republicans began in Arkansas the long and tortured process of rendering black Republicans invisible and unwanted by organizing in Little Rock the Harrison and Morton Club, an all-white group that announced that the colored man need not apply for membership. Blacks were initially, at least, incredulous. A group attended the next meeting but sat near the door while the white group changed its name to the Lincoln Club. Then, within a week, five hundred black Republicans set up an all-black Harrison and Morton Campaign Club and passed a resolution that their club would deny political support to anyone that belonged to the Lincoln Club.

As recently as 1880 when Republican President Ulysses Grant had visited Little Rock and had been given a banquet in his honor, Mifflin W. Gibbs not only had attended but had been permitted to give one of the fourteen toasts; now, blacks were a millstone around the party's neck, and white Republicans didn't care who knew it. Historian Fon Gordon writes, "The lily-whites sought to attract white voters by rejecting black candidates and publicly expressing racist attitudes that had been barely concealed during Reconstruction and Redemption." As an example, she quotes the comments of a white Republican in the *Arkansas Gazette* in August 1890:

> So far as [the blacks] are concerned we don't care a damn for them. They are getting a little too smart. They have found out they can control any Republican convention that meets here and we want to show them their mistake. . . . I have voted at every election, national, state, county and city, and I have my first vote to cast for a negro.[24]

As will be seen, the fight to purge blacks would last for decades. Politicians of all stripes were quick to sense the change in attitudes that was sweeping Arkansas. At least one politician would apparently regard the dawn of this era as an opportunity to begin his career as Arkansas's premier racist demagogue. Future three-time governor and U.S. senator Jeff

Davis, in his campaign for prosecuting attorney in Pope County in 1890, promised to "fill the penitentiary so full of negroes that their feet would be sticking out the windows."[25] He would say far worse things about blacks before he was done.

The Separate Coach Act of 1891 and Black Protests

In Arkansas nothing would foreshadow the future of race relations more clearly in early 1891 than the decision of the house of representatives to remove the portrait of George Washington from behind the speaker's rostrum and substitute in its place a likeness of the president of the Confederacy Jefferson Davis. Soon Senator J. N. Tillman of Washington County introduced legislation to require passenger coaches and railroad cars to have "equal but separate and sufficient" compartments and facilities. John Graves has found that in Arkansas there was a copycat effect as to the timing of this bill. Tillman acknowledged that his bill, which easily became law, had been "modeled after the Mississippi [separate coach] statute," which had "been tested in the courts and pronounced constitutional."[26] In fact it was not until 1896 in *Plessy v. Ferguson* that the U.S. Supreme Court definitively upheld such legislation.

John Graves writes that some of the reaction by Arkansas newspapers to the proposed bill was "moderate and restrained," but other responses were from "out-and-out Negrophobes who made little attempt to disguise their hated for the blacks." The *Pine Bluff Commercial* warned that if the act did not pass there could be a "summary depopulation of some of the more impudent and venturesome negro districts."[27] Riding the trains forced whites to deal with "drunken, insolent blacks in the black districts of the State. A Saturday night train from Little Rock to Pine Bluff is hardly safe."

In *Caste & Class: The Black Experience in Arkansas, 1880–1920,* Fon Gordon writes that instead of presenting a united front on behalf of all African Americans and opposing the legislation in toto, the black middle class "responded immediately but conservatively to modify the provision for separation of the races by class."[28] As evidence of class bias, Gordon points to the statement made by Joseph A. Booker, president of Arkansas Baptist College, who argued that the proposed law be modified to give protection "especially for that part of the negro race that buys soap, goes to school and are progressive," in other words, those African Americans who were like himself and his friends and associates. Gordon further quotes from the statement made by Dr. J. H. Smith, a coauthor of the resolutions presented at the meeting:

> To force the better negroes into contact with the more degraded would be to force the race backward. . . . The negroes didn't want to ride in the cars with whites because they were ashamed of their own race, but they had educated men and women among them whose deportment entitled them to recognition in the way of first-class accommodations.[29]

Gordon argues that

> Jim Crow heightened color consciousness among African Americans and worsened the mutual antagonism between classes. . . . The middle class, often the descendents of interracial unions, resented the [one-drop of African blood] rule because it lumped them indiscriminately with the masses with whom they had nothing in common and to whom they felt superior.

She quotes a black editor of an Arkansas newspaper who addressed the issue of color within the black community:

> There is no use talking about the color prejudice of the white folks; it cannot equal the color prejudice among the colored folks. No one will call a black freeman a "nigger" so quickly as a light colored dude.[30]

Beginning Steps in the Disfranchisement of Blacks

At this same time the Arkansas legislature began to consider proposals to amend Arkansas's elections laws for the avowed purpose to cut down on the rampant fraud committed by voters. John Graves has summarized the proposed major changes, which, as he notes,

> would radically alter the future politics of Arkansas. One section established an elaborate centralization of the election machinery which effectively put control of local election procedure in the hands of Democratic officials; another section no longer allowed illiterate voters to have their friends help fill out their ballots but required them to apply to two of the precinct judges, who then would order all other electors to vacate the polling places. Afterward, the judges were instructed to prepare the illiterate's ballot as he desired.[31]

One could argue, and its proponents did, that the sole purpose of the proposal was to make the voting process less fraudulent, not more so, but its opponents were not about to concede that the supposed reforms were anything but a thinly veiled attempt to "oust Negro Republicans from control of the voting machinery in black districts."[32]

The no-holds-barred actions of Democrats in Conway, St. Francis, and Crittenden counties in 1888 and 1890 dramatically indicate that whites were already determined to come up with ways to limit or deny blacks' voting. But certainly it was easy enough for the Democrats to make the case for reform because, as Graves notes, in the black-majority counties,

> a number of recognized black leaders customarily selected their party's candidates for office, printed and distributed ballots, and then carted the faithful to the polls on election day. . . . The system was strikingly analogous to that found among the urban immigrant groups. . . . It gave black community spokesmen real power, which perhaps best explains why whites found it so loathsome.[33]

Encouraging Their Men: Black Women and the Ballot

It was "probably true," according to John Graves, that as whites "constantly charged, that individual black voters who refused to follow their leaders might be subjected to extreme social ostracism or even occasional physical violence."[34] Documenting this charge in the *Arkansas Historical Quarterly*, John Giggie shows that black women particularly took the lead in ostracizing individuals, including their own preachers who voted Democratic. A court trial in July 1889 in Little Rock demonstrated that white Democrats were correct. According to Reverend James Fleshman, pastor at the Missionary Baptist Corner Stone Church, he had been fired for exercising his right to vote in a way his parishioners did not like. "They told me . . . that if I voted the Democratic ticket that I could not preach."[35]

Apparently, intimidation was the rule in this election. Giggie summarizes the testimony in part.

> Black Republican men, women, and ministers surrounded voting stations, bellowed encouragement to colleagues, and scanned the queues for would-be Democratic voters. It was not hard to identify them, according to testimony offered in the Little Rock trial. By prior arrangement, black Republican voters revealed themselves through a secret code: they held the party ticket open in the palm of one of their hands while standing in line waiting to vote. Men that did not hold up the ticket were quickly yanked from the line and interrogated by black Republican strongmen. If those rousted men convinced their questioners that they were really dyed-in-the-wool Republicans and had simply forgotten their tickets, they got back in line unharmed. If not, Republicans cursed them, chased them home, and promised to beat, drown, or hang them.[36]

While the testimony amply demonstrated the need for a process by which all voters could cast a secret ballot and vote their consciences, it also shows unmistakably how totally committed African Americans were about trying to insure that they were represented in the Arkansas legislature and in county government. Too, it gives a rare picture of the political involvement of Arkansas African American women. An individual by the name of Sandy Barron testified, "Black women unsuccessfully tried to force him to switch his vote by physically threatening his wife, who subsequently 'beg[ged] him to leave the township." Others simply suffered ostracism when they voted Democratic. Black women "threatened to quit or to not associate with Democratic husbands, fathers, or brothers—an act of defiance that received a public blessing of sympathetic Republican clerics."[37]

The Poll Tax and Its Impact

With the passage of the "reforms" in the election law bill, a proposed constitutional amendment was introduced requiring that in order to vote an otherwise qualified voter would have to produce evidence that he had paid a one-dollar poll tax. The black members of the legislature were not united in opposition to this amendment. John Graves shows that five of the nine black Republicans in the house and the single black Union Laborite in the house voted to table it. Despite other opposition in the house, though with little discussion, the proposed amendment made it out of the legislature to the electorate where, according to Graves, some of its proponents openly campaigned for it as a way to stop blacks from voting. For example the Arkadelphia *Southern Standard* urged its readers to "vote for Amendment No. 2. It requires a poll tax receipt to entitle a man to vote, and compels thousands of worthless negroes to show a 'poll tax receipt' or be denied the sweet privilege of voting."[38]

Graves notes that the amendment was primarily touted as a reform measure that would make it harder for fraud to be committed, while its opponents argued that it would encourage vote buying. At the same time, one dollar was not a small amount of money given that laborers in that period made no more than a dollar for working all day. As Graves has pointed out, thousands of blacks did not vote in September 1892 on the poll tax amendment because the 1891 election reforms were now in effect, and many illiterates, but mostly blacks, did not vote. The poll tax amendment passed but had to be revoted two years later because of a technicality when it passed again. Monitoring the September 1892 election, an *Arkansas Gazette* correspondent wired from Hempstead County that "many negroes from pride failed to vote at all, and others scratched their ticket so badly the Judges had great trouble in deciding for whom they intended to vote."[39]

The election in 1892 with its new requirements proved a disaster for blacks and was a harbinger of things to come. By 1894 after the fall elections, the *Arkansas Gazette* editor wrote that "for the first time since the negroes have been allowed to vote there will be no representative of their race in either branch of the Legislature." Graves points out that in 1894 sixty-five thousand fewer people voted than in 1890. He concludes, "More than any other single measure, the 1891 election law established one-party rule and white supremacy as the central motif of Arkansas politics for well over a century."[40]

It was not merely that blacks disappeared from the Arkansas legislature; they disappeared from city and county government and jobs, as well. For example in 1895, now freed from any need to appease blacks politically, Helena authorities terminated the job of the last African American on the police force. He had served for twenty years but now was alleged to have used force against a white man. Commented the *Helena World*, "There was strong pressure, however, brought to bear to relieve the police force of all negroes, and Chief Clancy yielded to it inasmuch he considers it his duty to serve the people acceptably."[41] Suffice it to say that "the people" no longer included African Americans.

Lynching and Its Consequences

It is impossible to ignore the dramatic increase in the number of lynchings that occurred in Arkansas in 1891 and 1892 after blacks had taken such a beating in the legislature and also had begun to see their alliance with white Republicans start to unravel. But as suggested, the level of violence had already begun to escalate in 1888 and 1889 and, along with it, white Arkansans' speech began to reflect the contemptuous attitudes in dealing with blacks. Kenneth Barnes notes that the language grew more shrill, hostile, and snide. Previously, Barnes points out, the *Arkansas Gazette* called blacks, "Negroes, colored, or darkies. But by 1889 terms such as *nigger* and *coon* began to appear with frequency."[42]

In September 1891 in black-majority Lee County fifteen blacks were killed. Nine of the fifteen were hanged after an apparent attempt to organize a strike by a black man named Ben Patterson, possibly an organizer of the Cotton Picking League. His efforts had ended in the deaths of two cotton pickers who were possibly resisting efforts to convince them to join the strike. Patterson may well have been affiliated with a white Southerner named R. M. Humphrey, who became superintendent of the Colored Alliance, an organization of black farmers that like the Wheelers worked to secure economic justice for their lot. When planters in the region agreed with each other to not pay more than fifty cents per hundred pounds, Humphrey thought the area was ripe for a labor organization. The difficulty was that some of the Colored Alliance farmers were Lee County landowners whose interests were diametrically opposed to landless cotton pickers. Nevertheless, Humphrey organized the Cotton Pickers League, which apparently attracted no interest except in Lee County. After the deaths of the two pickers, whites under the leadership of the Lee County sheriff formed a posse to track down Patterson's strikers, two of whom had killed a plantation manager with whom they had a disagreement. Blacks from Lee County joined the white posse to search for the strikers and eventually tracked them down, killing two in the process and capturing nine.[43] What happened next was one of the worst lynchings in Arkansas history. According to a report from Memphis that appeared in the *Chicago Daily Tribune* on October 1, 1889,

> Sheriff Riddick and posse left Cat Island last evening with nine of the thirteen rioters conveying them to Marianna to jail. They were overtaken by an armed band of white regulators and after a desperate struggle the nine black prisoners were taken from the Sheriff and his men and hanged to a sycamore tree. . . . Without any ceremony the negroes were dragged to the nearest tree and inside of fifteen minutes nine bodies were swaying with the breezes. The mob poured a parting volley of bullets into the remains and dispersed as mysteriously and quietly as it came. The Sheriff was told to go home with his men, he proceeded to do so without delay.[44]

One has to take one aspect of the account given in the *Tribune* with a grain of salt. Vincent Vinikas observes that "in most cases the sheriff and his deputies merely stood by while the mob did its work, and later reported that the mob had taken them by surprise."[45] Though this collective act of mob violence has attracted little attention from historians of Arkansas race relations, in fact it was a watershed event because of its proportions and because, as Vincent Vinikas, writes, "With each unpunished killing, with every unprosecuted outrage, whites learned that, as citizens, blacks could be treated with complete contempt."[46] Suddenly, it was open season on Arkansas blacks. On March 24, 1892, Malcolm Argyle, an Arkansas black preacher, wrote to an individual in Philadelphia that

> all over the state, blacks were being murdered by whites:[s]ome being strung up to telephone poles, others burnt at the stake; and still others being shot like dogs. In the last 30 days there have been not less than eight colored persons lynched in this state.

And like the inattention paid to what had occurred in Lee County seven months earlier, "the white press of the South seems to be subsidized by this lawless element, the white pulpits seem to condone lynching."[47]

Nothing resulted in the departure of blacks like a spectacular lynching. Between 1870 and 1890 the black population in Arkansas had almost tripled: from 122,169 to 309,117, now 27 percent of the total. Now with increased violence and a deteriorating racial climate, blacks had begun to flee the state. "Ever since the burning of Coy . . . the Negroes have been leaving the state and the planters have been greatly alarmed over the exodus," wrote a journalist in the *Indianapolis Freeman* in May 1892. Barnes documents that hundreds left the state in 1892. "By the end of April 500 Oklahoma-bound settlers left Argenta [now North Little Rock]." Blacks were seen leaving Cleveland County in January 1893. Asked why they were leaving, Barnes notes that they answered, "We is tired of having the white folks rule us and we are gwine where the nigger has some say."[48]

Other Expressions of White Rage

Along with the violence the contempt expressed by whites was so blatant that suddenly nothing seemed out of bounds. In 1893 Robert Leigh, the editor of the *Morrilton Pilot,* disparaged the admission to a white college in Illinois of May Turner, a local black girl. "It's dollars to doughnuts that with all her musk and other refinements, she smells to heaven on a warm day just the same as any other nigger."[49] In Helena, the June 12, 1895, *Helena Weekly World* described two local black preachers.

> Jim Harvey and Sim Gibson are just a couple of common negro broilers, neither of them know anything about Christianity, nor are they governed by any consideration except the desire to work the gullible fools in the congregation for all the money they can get.

Writing about this period in Helena, Susan Huntsman notes that whites sneered openly at the practice of blacks in their churches "as a joke, a cheap and flawed imitation of white worship."[50] It did not matter how blacks, in fact, behaved because whites were going to interpret their actions in a negative light. Citing instances from the white owned *Helena World* in Phillips County, Susan Huntsman demonstrates "that blacks were often represented as having a 'scheming nature.'" When their plans failed, it was due to their stupidity. Paradoxically, "although blacks were often depicted as ruled by their emotions and lack of self-control, they also rarely committed a crime without it being premeditated or in cold blood."[51]

By 1900 Arkansas blacks were in a free-fall with no end in sight. The banishment of blacks from Arkansas politics would have far-reaching consequences for blacks because whites who formerly would have restrained themselves would now feel they had little to fear by giving vent to their worst instincts. None of the above was, of course, unique to Arkansas. All over the South blacks were being lynched, segregated, and disfranchised. Joel Williamson notes, "Beginning in the year 1889, in the South and in the nation at large, the lynching of Negroes increased markedly and within a few years reached its height. In 1892 the number peaked at 156."[52] It is impossible to convey adequately the terror and despair felt by blacks during this period as the South plunged toward the bottom, but Arkansas was just getting started good (though the numbers went up and down over the years) with lynching as its primary form of control of blacks.

The Meaning of Lynching

Vincent Vinikas postulates in the *Journal of Southern History* that "coming to terms with this variety of murder is central to understanding the history of race relations in the United States."[53] Building on the work of historians

Jacqueline Dowd Hall and George M. Fredrickson, Vinikas makes a number of points that support this thesis. Not only did lynching reduce the desire of blacks to participate as equals in society, it served, as well, to indoctrinate whites. "With each unpunished killing, with every unprosecuted outrage, whites learned that, as citizens, blacks could be treated with complete contempt."[54] The indelible message to both races signaled by this repeated and random horror was to reinforce the notion that "blacks were inherently inferior."[55] Lynching of blacks was increasingly part of one's education in the practical lessons of life after the end of Reconstruction. Once protected as property, now blacks had nothing. Vinikas writes,

> To rationalize and to justify the perpetuation of '[t]he incredible cruelty and barbarity of lynching . . . whites had to develop a perception of blacks that made this treatment seem reasonable. . . . To be able to accept the routinization of mob rule and mass murder in their society, whites had to come to view blacks as the vicious and beast-like predators that they were portrayed to be in the racist literature of the day. As a result, even the most oppressed and rigidly subordinated black sharecropper could serve as a symbol of terror for the white-supremacist imagination.

In psychological terms whites were projecting their feelings of rage onto blacks. By and large, it was not blacks in Arkansas who were perpetrating acts of violence against whites; rather, it was whites who again and again committed acts of violence against the black population.

Racial Expulsion: The Beginning

Given the violence against blacks that was occurring throughout Arkansas in the1890s it seemed only a matter of time before white Arkansans would begin in earnest the process of racial expulsion in urbanized areas of Arkansas, and in January 1898 the *Arkansas Gazette* reported that in the town of Lonoke there were "posted warning notes on the front gates of negro citizens, threatening them with dire vengeance unless they emigrate within thirty days." Thus Lonoke, according to the paper, was the scene of an "exodus of frightened negroes from the town."[56]

Jeannie Whayne also documents that in rural areas in 1898 racial expulsion, again motivated by economic considerations, occurred in Phillips County. The *Helena World* reported on February 23, 1898, that at Connells Point, just ten miles north of Elaine in Phillips County, a gang of whites began to ride against "the defenseless negroes of that vicinity until they have actually succeeded in driving the majority of them out of the neighborhood."[57] Planters banded together to protect the cheap labor supply and sought prosecutions against the gangs of white nightriders but were generally unsuccessful because of the difficulty of proving who the attackers were. The reference to "defenseless negroes" in the *Arkansas Gazette* article must be understood in the context of class antagonism between planters and landless whites who saw themselves in competition with blacks.

When blacks were "very troublesome" as they were said to be in Little River County in March 1899, whites forgot their own class differences in short order. On March 18 a black man by the name of General Duckett, possibly a tenant, killed a "wealthy planter," James Stockton, at Rocky Comfort. Typically, the *Arkansas Gazette* initially claimed it was "believed that the negroes had banded together for a race war." And just as typically, the paper made it clear that whites would rise to the occasion. The article continued "[but] when they [the blacks] saw how angry the citizens became over Stockton's murder, they gave up the idea." Not only was Duckett lynched by a mob four days later, the *Gazette* confirmed that including him "seven negro men have been lynched by the citizens of that section." The *Gazette* identified six by name including three brothers who were said to be "intimate with the assassination of Stockton and it was discovered that they were leading a scheme to avenge their comrade's death." The March 24 issue of the *Gazette* mentioned that there were twenty-three blacks who likely . . . have been strung up in the thickets," but provides no confirmation or follow-up the next day that additional persons had been lynched. It does mention that "negroes are fleeing from the district. Today three wagons full arrived at Texarkana, having crossed the Red River at Index."

The *Gazette* on the twenty-fifth provided reasons for some of the lynchings. Joe King had failed to give up his gun, "saying he wanted it for his own protection." He and one of the Jones brothers "had made ugly remarks concerning the murder of Stockton." Forgetting the "race war" explanation for the moment, the *Gazette* states, "The reason why Goodwin, King and Moses Jones were killed was that Jones' wife cooked for Duckett and Goodwin took it to him while he was hiding in the bottoms."[58]

As the decade ended and a new century began, the simple truth about lynching and racial expulsion was that Arkansas whites did not need an "imagined" race war to murder and banish their fellow citizens. All they needed was the most ephemeral of pretexts to unleash a rage that in the early part of the next century seemed to know no limits.

CHAPTER 7

Jeff Davis and His Legacy

Jeff Davis's long reign in state government began in 1899 as attorney general, followed by three terms as governor and then U.S. senator until interrupted by death in 1913. Lynching was apparently one of Davis's favorite topics, and as governor he did not care who knew it. When President Theodore Roosevelt visited Little Rock on October 25, 1905, Davis felt comfortable enough politically to give in his presence the white Southerner's justification for lynching.

> Charitable and indulgent as we have ever been to an inferior race, cheerfully contributing bountifully of our time and means toward their material and moral betterment, still, if the brutal criminals of that race . . . lay unholy hands upon our fair daughters, nature is so riven and shocked that the dire compact produces a social cataclysm, often, in its terrible sweep far beyond the utmost counter efforts of all civil power.[1]

One of the flaws in Davis's rhetoric was that "as early as 1905 it was documented," Tom Dillard writes, "that only one-third of lynched blacks were even accused of rape."[2]

President Roosevelt was at least aware of this statistic for he replied,

> To avenge one hideous crime by another hideous crime is to reduce the man doing so to the bestial level of the bestial scoundrel; and the hideous effects of lynch law are shown by the fact that three-fourths of the lynchings are not for that crime at all, but for other crimes.[3]

Piling on the Black Poor

The plain fact was that white Arkansans did not want to be bothered with the facts about lynching, and as Fon Gordon demonstrates, the leaders of the black middle class seemed to point their fingers at poorer blacks rather than challenge whites on the subject. When E. C. Morris spoke at the eighth meeting of the National Baptist Convention, he told the delegates that whites seldom noticed that rape charges involving blacks were brought against "the lowest element of the race."[4] Good Baptists would take the responsibility of "lifting up our people to a standard of Christianity which when attained will make impossible the heinous crimes with which so many hitherto have been charged."[5] Piling on the poor was not limited to Morris. Reverend William A. Holmes, who edited a black newspaper in Helena, wrote,

> The time is coming when nobody will care for that class of persons who are content to live in poverty. Such have neglected opportunities, misused means, and wasted time. They are content to know little and possess less. This class must go.[6]

With friends like Holmes, blacks struggling all over the state did not need enemies.

Vincent Vinikas, writing in the *Journal of Southern History*, observes that in Arkansas,

> by 1904 lynchings were essentially state-sponsored events. Campaigning as Governor for re-election during the new political primary which brought him into contact with thousands of Arkansans, Davis promised that "nigger" dominion will never prevail in this beautiful Southland of ours, as long as shotguns and rifles lie around loose, and we are able to pull the trigger.[7]

Davis was merely the messenger of a racism and white supremacist doctrine that already had become deeply ingrained in the psyche of white Arkansans. In any event, in an age that wanted red meat Davis was an absolute master at demagoguery. Giving blacks the vote during the Reconstruction era had been "the most cruel blow that was ever struck a helpless and defenceless [*sic*] people." Every successful demagogue carefully nurtures feelings of victimization in his audience, and Davis was a virtuoso when it came to wringing the very last drop of self-pity out of white Arkansans and converting it into righteous anger. A black voter was an "ever present eating, cankerous sore" on democracy.[8]

Nothing was too outrageous for Davis. He promised,

> We may have a lot of dead niggers in Arkansas, but we shall never have negro equality, and I want to say that I would rather tear, screaming from her mother's arms, my little daughter and bury her alive than to see her arm in arm with the best nigger on earth.[9]

The March of Jim Crow

In 1903 the Arkansas legislature passed a law requiring blacks to be seated at the back of streetcars and whites to be seated at the front, legislation that in its application caused confusion for over fifty years whenever the buses became crowded and the conductor had to exercise his discretion concerning the line of separation. Black Arkansans could not ignore the humiliation of such face-to-face discrimination. When the law took effect on May 27, 1903, they rebelled, even to the point of staging boycotts of the streetcars in Hot Springs, Pine Bluff, and Little Rock. This protest action went far beyond anything previously staged by blacks. Students at Shorter College edited a publication called *The Voice of the Twentieth Century* that said bluntly,

> The law was intended to humiliate negroes and every time a negro man, woman, or child goes to the back seat or sits on the cars while this iniquitous law is in force, the negro is humiliated. . . . Simply stay off the cars. Stay off the cars.[10]

This militant student involvement from a black school proved how important it was for blacks to build their own institutions without white involvement. Funds from the African Methodist Episcopal (AME) church financed the school originally begun in 1886 as Bethel University. Renamed Shorter University in 1892 in honor of AME bishop James A. Shorter, it was moved to Arkadelphia in 1891 but came back to North Little Rock in 1897.

Whites assumed that they could safely ignore protests by blacks, especially in light of the debates and outcome of the separate coach act in 1891, but at least briefly this short-lived movement transcended class lines. Writing that "the [1903] boycott obtained support from blacks of all social classes," John Graves shows that besides student involvement. In fact it was a streetcar porter who was president of the "We Walk League" that spearheaded the boycott, though "it had been launched by middle-class leaders."[11] This alliance across class lines, in fact, was a truly unique achievement and anticipated by half a century the Montgomery boycott in Alabama that launched the modern civil rights movement in 1956. Initially, ridership was down over 90 percent in Little Rock. Graves writes, "it appears to have fallen precipitously in Pine Bluff and Hot Springs as well; in all three cities the boycott continued for weeks."[12] What caused the boycott to falter is not known.

Black middle-class leaders in Arkansas were not oblivious to the irony that they were benefiting from segregation and oppression. In a speech to black churchmen in Pine Bluff in 1902, E. C. Morris pointed out that it was racial prejudice that

> gives employment to every Negro preacher, every Negro teacher, doctor, lawyer, that built all the Negro churches and school [*sic*], started every Negro store, hotel and restaurant, every bank, every insurance company, and in fact every enterprise owned and operated by the race.[13]

Following Booker T. Washington, Morris advised his flock at Centennial Church in Helena not to concern itself with politics, though Morris himself was active in the Republican Party. When blacks had raised themselves to the economic level of whites there would be time for political involvement.

Emboldened by their success with the streetcar legislation, the solons soon passed a law requiring segregation of prisoners in state custody: "separate bunks, beds, bedding, dining tables and all other furnishings."[14] This was followed in 1905 by a law mandating segregation by race in boys' and girls' industrial schools. In 1911 the legislature defined a black person as one having "any negro blood whatever," making it a crime punishable by one year in the penitentiary for whites and blacks to cohabit. Two more laws, passed in 1913 and 1919, dealt respectively with segregation by race in county jails—blacks and whites were forbidden to eat with one another or sleeping in the same bed—and coalmines were required to maintain separate washhouses for whites and blacks.[15]

The Second Worst Race Massacre

In 1904 the second worst race massacre in Arkansas's history occurred in St. Charles in Arkansas County. Though the murder of thirteen black Arkansans took place during the last week of the primary election season, Vincent Vinikas has found no connection with the campaign rhetoric of Jeff Davis.[16] Piecing together the news reports and recorded memories of the shooting deaths of thirteen men in a town of only five hundred people, one discovers that what originally started as a fight between a white and black gambling on a riverboat escalated into an assault on a police officer and the escape of the black assailant. Typically, the *Arkansas Gazette* cited reports that "negroes were organizing to defy law and order."[17] In fact, five blacks were already in jail in St. Charles on unspecified charges, but that did not stop men from a "number of towns" including De Witt, whose men arrived first, from going to the "scene of the trouble." From one incident that spiraled into rumor after rumor, as Vinikas shows, the *Arkansas Gazette* characterized the events as a race war: "Reinforcements to the Front." The five blacks were taken out of the jail by "indignant citizens" and murdered. In all thirteen blacks lost their lives. There was never any evidence whatsoever offered to show there that blacks were planning a race war. No whites were called to account.

Continuation of the Assault on All Blacks

The assault on black voting reached its apex in 1906 when the Arkansas Democratic Party passed a rule prohibiting blacks from voting in its primary elections. While the "White Primary" became a fixture all over the South, in Arkansas, not surprisingly, it was Jeff Davis who, according to his biographer, "probably did more to complete the process of black disfranchisement in Arkansas than any other politician."[18]

The phenomenon of racial expulsion continued in towns that had few blacks. In 1906 whites demanded that all blacks leave the town of Cotter in Baxter County.[19] Forty black families in Greene County were ordered to leave Paragould in 1908.[20] In 1905 and again in 1909 two campaigns of racial cleansing left the black population in Harrison in Boone County at one. It had been 115.[21]

Arkansas would never have another governor quite like Jeff Davis, but it hardly mattered because the doctrine of white supremacy was so thoroughly imbedded in every inch of Arkansas soil from the swampiest part of the Delta in Phillips County to the hardest rock in the Ozark Mountains on the Missouri border. It would have been easy to throw up one's hands at this point and simply submit, but, in fact, African Americans never quit trying to make a place for themselves at the table. The lives of two black male Arkansans during this era illustrate the very different choices available to African Americans.

Scipio Africanus Jones

There would be no one in Arkansas history who would wage this battle as carefully, as tirelessly, or as long as Scipio

Africanus Jones, whose complexity as a successful black lawyer and advocate for not only his race but for human dignity itself defies easy categorization. Too, Jones's commitment to the poorest and most downtrodden members of his race seriously weakens the argument that the black middle class abandoned the black lower classes. At first blush, Jones, born into slavery sometime in the 1860s and the son of a house slave and south Arkansas physician and planter, seems like a caricature of the Arkansas black middle-class personage, who as a lawyer reaped huge rewards from a segregated system. From a certain distance his life seems like a Jim Crow middle-class fairy tale. Like so many products of sex between master and slave, Jones, too, got a leg up when it most counted. The 1870 census reveals that, alone of his family, little Scipio learned how to read. A white father, once again, was clearly determined to see that his son was not going to go the way of the typical black man destined to break his back all his life in a cotton patch. Typically, the historical record is silent about the interaction between father and son, and it is also typically silent about Scipio Jones's innermost thoughts and feelings about his life. But it is known that the father helped the son, who had worked as a field hand and as a teacher, with the cost of an education at Philander Smith and across the Arkansas River at Shorter College. And then came the biggest break of his life, which could not have occurred without his father's help: Scipio Jones was allowed to "read law" in the offices of white attorneys. As a Little Rock attorney Scipio Jones appeared in federal district court and before the Arkansas Supreme Court "in 45 cases between 1891 and 1943," far more than most attorneys who practice law in Arkansas today.[22] As counsel for the Mosaic Templars, he would win most of them. In some ways Jones epitomized the aspirations of the black middle class. His spacious home at 1911 Pulaski was a prestige address in a community where numerous African Americans in Little Rock owned expensive and well-appointed Craftsman homes. At one point in his career Jones and his second wife, Lillie, hired a maid, and he employed a chauffeur to drive his Cadillac. Always immaculately dressed, he sometimes carried a walking stick. He was something of a dignified dandy, but why not? White folks behaved the same way if they had the money. Jones operated strictly within the confines of Jim Crow. Always mindful of the expectations of the whites who sat in judgment of his clients, he was not too proud to appear before white juries in criminal cases and beg for his clients, telling them that the man in front of him was just an ignorant colored boy: he hadn't meant any harm. Yet he was the same lawyer who in the memory of J. H. Carmichael, the dean of the law school in Little Rock, cross-examined black witnesses better than anyone he had ever seen. His behavior was so impeccable and correct within the Jim Crow tradition that his white colleagues in the Little Rock bar elected him to sit as a municipal judge and hear the case of two black litigants.

If Scipio Jones had done nothing else in his career than serve as counsel for the Mosaic Templars and numerous black fraternal organizations, he would have had a remarkable career, but he was so much more than an effective lawyer. Behind the affable mask of the black lawyer who "knew his place" was the mind and soul of a man who cared fiercely and deeply about social justice and was, on occasion, given the results, unbelievably successful in obtaining it. What put Jones in a class all his own was his uncanny ability and cheerful willingness to work with the most distasteful whites imaginable to help people who were not going to be helped any other way. Nothing illustrates this point more than his collaboration with Jeff Davis, who was then serving as attorney general. Jones approached Davis to ask him to help persuade the legislature to lower fines for blacks in jail. It was desperately needed legislation because of the terrible conditions, and poor blacks had to remain confined until their fines had been worked off. One can only imagine what it cost him emotionally to be in the same room with such an insufferable Negrophobe, but he did.

And amazingly Davis agreed to help and was successful in lowering fines for blacks.[23]

Jones studied whites closely for clues about their behavior and how to approach them, and then took whatever steps he needed to get in their good graces. An inveterate letter writer, he often sent polite messages of appreciation to governors and politicians sometimes over trivial things, flattering them but knowing how much each paid attention to their correspondents. He wanted them to know who he was and that he acknowledged their power. Sometimes, he left a bottle of whiskey in a drawer where he knew a judge would find it and would know who had left it. Jones possessed an inner confidence that few blacks in his era could understandably manage in such an inhospitable environment, for he never hesitated to go to the top and ingratiate himself with whites who had power. Governors have always had the authority to commute sentences, and nothing was more important to a criminal defense attorney, white or black, than to be friends with the governor. Scipio Jones claimed friendship with Governor George Donaghey who, though no supporter of blacks, was in no sense a Jeff Davis. Jones organized the "State Suffrage League" and campaigned hard to have blacks pay their poll taxes and get out and vote to defeat a constitutional amendment that would have allowed white illiterates to vote but at the same time would have required blacks to read and interpret the state constitution. His friend George Donaghey, on this issue, opined, "From every point of view it is better to eliminate the negro from politics. Until this is done, honest elections cannot be secured in Arkansas."[24] Democratic commentators after the election in 1912 at the time agreed that "amendment eleven brought out an unusually large number of black voters," and the amendment was defeated. Though as Fon Gordon has noted, it was a "pyrrhic victory." Since blacks already could not vote in Democratic party primary elections, blacks like Scipio Jones demonstrated that they never quit seeking racial justice no matter what the odds against them. It also demonstrated that middle-class blacks would pay their own poll taxes and go to bat for themselves but also for poorer members of their race.[25]

Scipio Jones was also active in Republican politics, and fought long and hard, though mostly unsuccessfully, to keep blacks from being driven from the party in Arkansas. His epic five-year and ultimately successful defense of the black sharecroppers in cooperation with the National Association for the Advancement of Colored People (NAACP) would not come for another six years in 1919.

James G. B. Polk

The short, tragic life of James G. B. Polk is mostly a mystery and is only known through Ruth Polk Patterson's previously mentioned chronicle of her family. Patterson describes James G. B. Polk, born in 1889, as the "darling of [grandfather] Spencer's family."[26] As a young man, according to the family, he was "handsome," "dashing," "brilliant," and, being Spencer's son, "very proud of his white ancestry," but in Arkansas in 1910 that all added up to trouble. One only has to read excerpts from letters to and from him to get a sense of his love for life but also of his potential. A young man like Jimmy Polk was intolerable to whites for the simple reason that he would not accept the place that whites dictated he must occupy. Unlike his father who had lived his life with his nose to the grindstone and playing by the rules of white men, Jimmy had his own ideas about what to do with his life. Admittedly spoiled at home by the family, as a young man "Jimmy liked fiddling and girls and parties and dancing. He also liked adventure and traveling and hunting and guns."[27] So many years after the fact, Patterson never found out precisely what was the racial incident that caused Jimmy to leave the successful family farm in Howard County. In a letter to his brother, Arthur Polk, Ruth Polk Patterson's father, Jimmy, who was living in Little Rock cleaning railroad cars, referred to his trouble in the following way: "Well, how's the race riot progressing? If you all think there's any danger, don't write."[28] As Patterson suggests, whatever Jimmy Polk had done that caused his departure from a law enforcement perspective could not have been too serious, or the story would have made the newspapers. James Polk never made it back home. On July 2, 1910, the *Nashville News* carried the following brief story:

> News reached this city last Wednesday of the killing of Jim Polk, colored, at Caddo Gap by officers, while Polk was resisting arrest. The negro had trouble with an engineer on the Gurdon and Fort Smith road, and when officers went to arrest him he showed fight, with the result that he was shot to death.[29]

Exactly why James Polk was put off the train and soon taken into woods by whites and killed was never discovered by the Polk family, but according to family members, Spencer Polk, still the reigning patriarch, never made an effort to get to the bottom of his son's probable murder. Told where his son's body was, Spencer Polk loaded up the wagon and with his daughter Frances went to claim his remains; however, young Polk's body was so decomposed by the time they reached it because of the extreme heat and mosquitoes that Spencer Polk buried his body on the spot. Patterson explains that her grandfather made no effort to confront the whites in power about his son's probable murder because he had spent a lifetime accommodating himself to Jim Crow. By Polk's death in 1910 in Arkansas whites had constructed a superstructure of racial dominance so strong that from the inside it all but seemed unchallengeable. According to newspaper reports that year lynch mobs took the lives of at least nine Arkansans.[30] One of these murders had occurred as recently as July 6 in nearby Union County when a mob hung a black man in the mill town of Huttig for allegedly burning down the house of a white man who was in church.[31] In actuality, as Vincent Vinikas has pointed out, what constituted a lynching was never clear to anyone, especially those in the newspaper business whose business was to report it. As he explains, the killings in St. Charles were mentioned in some papers as a lynching but not in others.

Though convenient and used here, lynching statistics as an indicator of acts by whites that resulted in the violent deaths of blacks in Arkansas must always be accompanied by the understanding that it is only one measure of this phenomenon and perhaps the least significant. James Polk's death was not in the classic sense strictly a lynching, but at some point the matter of definitions becomes purely academic. Any one who read the papers in this era learned of black Arkansans like Jimmy Polk who somehow died either "resisting arrest" or in "police custody." Jimmy Polk's death in 1910 did not count as an official lynching. The hundreds of blacks who were killed in the Arkansas race massacres of 1919 by white mobs and U.S. troops from Camp Pike do not count as part of lynching statistics kept, for example, by the NAACP. Killings of black Arkansans, whether by white mobs or by law enforcement personnel, and the never-ending brutality by town and county law enforcement have had a long and bloody history in Arkansas and did not end with the last official lynching in Arkansas in the 1930s.

Spencer Polk did not turn away from the white world as it became increasingly hostile and violent in relation to black Arkansans, however understandable it would have been had he and his family done so. Instead, he continued the tradition of having whites to his home. Ruth Polk Patterson has written,

> The respect and good will that the family enjoyed was more in proportion to how they behaved than to who they were or what they owned. Spencer's good character was measured in terms of his humility toward the mores established by the white community. . . . Thus, the Polks were tolerated, respected, and admired—as long as they stayed in their place. "Their place" was to exhibit an attitude of humbleness at all times and to cater to the needs and desires of the white community.[32]

The Coming of War and Black Migration

As the nation crept toward participation in a world war in 1917 that would change the way many African Americans in Arkansas thought of themselves, politically blacks in the state continued to be confronted with a one-way ticket out of a Republican Party that chronically found their presence a liability of the first magnitude. By June 1914 white members of the Pulaski County Republican Party were voting to hold their county conventions at the Hotel Marion, which excluded blacks. County chairman A. C. Remmel minced no words when he said, "If the Republican party in Pulaski county expects to grow and become a political force it must be controlled by white men, and the organization must be exclusively white."[33] For Remmel it was a question of doing the math. For example, whites in Pulaski County had given in 1908 William Howard Taft 3,500 votes, but the Republican candidate for governor received only 2,118. Arkansas whites would vote for a Republican but not if it meant joining with blacks at a state and local level.

In the second decade of the twentieth century thousands of black Arkansans poured out of the state to seek a better life in the north, but the exodus had started long before, and soon it changed the racial balance in the Delta. In 1890 there had been fifteen counties in the state, all in the Delta, with a majority-black population; by 1920 there were only eleven. The First World War with its sudden availability of jobs for blacks in the north had a major impact on outward migration. Between October 1916 and May 1917 over twenty-three thousand black Arkansans left for the north.[34] Some black Arkansans were eager to prove their loyalty and patriotism as the United States entered the First World War. As Fon Gordon demonstrates, they were "led by the middle class, [and] responded enthusiastically when the United States declared war in April of 1917."[35] All over the state, including Pine Bluff, Lewisville, Plumerville, Okolona, McNeil, and Magnolia, black communities held patriotic rallies to show support for the war. Black middle-class leaders, particularly ministers, met with local and state officials to receive instructions on draft and registration procedures after Congress enacted a draft in 1917. Not every black was eager to go. In fact, according to Kieran Taylor, only one in three blacks "in Arkansas responded to their draft notices."[36] Why would a race so callously abused respond cheerfully to the call for the chance to die or be maimed in a war ghastly with its gas and trench warfare and hideous suffering on every side? Whites wondered, too. In April the *Arkansas Gazette* reported that rumors were circulating that "German agents [were attempting] to induce negroes to turn in treason against the United States."[37] As always happened in moments of tension, whites, who expected revolt from blacks from day one of slavery, were easily panicked. In Hampton in Calhoun County, there were rumors that German sympathizers were agitating black labor, and the old insurrection fear blossomed overnight. "Blacks were arrested in wholesale quantity and ordered to cease holding meetings, whites fearing that Mexican agents had been contacted by Germans and were infiltrating black organizations with seditious thought." Before it was over, a black woman, Ollie Lumsey, made the mistake on April 5 of telling a white woman in Hampton in an incident at a store not to call her by her first name and was taken out that night and whipped for her insolence and told to leave town. Signs of anger from the black community were interpreted by whites as a possible insurrection and somehow connected to rumors by German sympathizers. A black was shot to death before it was over. As Todd Lewis documents, "To thwart any black resistance, an anonymous group of whites fired shots at two black men in another part of town, killing one of the men."[38]

Murderous incidents like this were the product of white paranoia generated, in part, by war hysteria as well as by the dreaded fear that blacks would someday rise up against their treatment, but they always had the same ending: whites blamed blacks for the murder they committed. The *Arkansas Gazette* wrote, "the ignorant negro, not possessed of enough intelligence to protect himself, must suffer because he had listened to the glowing promises [of German agents]."[39] White supremacy was going to be maintained at any cost, and black people were always going to be blamed when whites overreacted. This familiar rationalization of white behavior was as old as slavery itself. No German provocateurs were ever found. All it took was a rumor, and shortly blacks were slammed into their place.

Black Support for the War and Discrimination

Blacks, always afraid white violence would spiral out of control, attempted to pacify local whites. According to the *Arkansas Gazette*, the paper "was swamped with letters from individual negroes and copies of resolutions adopted by negro organizations" proclaiming loyalty to the U.S. government.[40] But it did not require murder for blacks to take a stand on the war. From top to bottom, black leaders, including W. E. B. Du Bois, editor of the *Crisis* in New York, to the AME bishop Conner in Little Rock seized on the war as a way to prove the worth of their fellow countrymen and hopefully to create a sense of obligation that would result in change when the war was over. Bishop Conner promised, "In the war we are going to do our part. . . . We are loyal to this country. . . . In this crisis . . . we should forget our creeds, classes, and conditions, and stand out for Americanism—unsullied, untrammeled, and undismayed."[41] Randy Finley summarizes the attitude and participation of the black community:

> By the end of the war, 104,835 Arkansas black males, aged twenty-one to thirty, had registered, and 17,544 were eventually inducted. . . . Black Arkansans made up 30.4 percent of those registered in Arkansas and composed 35.6 percent of those registered in Arkansas for World War I.[42]

Blacks not only signed up for the draft but also showed their loyalty by raising money. In particular, it was Scipio Africanus Jones who spearheaded a campaign by members of the Mosaic Templars to purchase war bonds during the First World War. On October 22, 1917, he stood on the stage of the Kempner Theater in Little Rock and, with Governor Charles Hillman Brough looking on, presented to secretary of the treasury William Gibbs McAdoo a check from the black community in the amount of fifty thousand dollars, telling the surely astonished official, "If you need $50,000 more you'll get it, Mr. Secretary."[43] By April of 1919, the Templars had done just that.

Randy Finley documents that racial segregation within companies, battalions, and regiments was not only expected at Camp Pike located outside of Little Rock but "was applauded by the Arkansas black elite, Scipio Jones. . . . Chester Bush [son of John E. Bush who had died in 1908] and J. M. Conner [who met] with Little Rock Mayor Charles Taylor to plan the perimeters of segregation," according to the *Helena World* on December 1, 1917.[44] Always alert to the possibility of white violence, Scipio Jones never hesitated to make sure blacks stayed out of the way of whites, for he knew only too well who would prevail if there was trouble. Finley writes that twelve Arkansas blacks were commissioned at a ninety-day officers school in Des Moines, Iowa, including four who came out of the intensive training as first lieutenants. One out of every five blacks who made it into the service from Arkansas served overseas.

For the most part Arkansas blacks did not find the respect they wanted. Todd Lewis documents numerous incidents at Camp Pike in which whites ridiculed blacks, mocking how they spoke and making fun of them. If black soldiers expected white officers to instill a different feeling in their men because they were soldiers on the same side, they were sorely disappointed, but more than this, they suffered blatantly unfair treatment. With the war over, whites were released from the military, but members of the 409th Reserve Labor Battalion (all black) were kept on for "ditching cutting down trees, hauling slop, and all sorts of hard chores."[45] This blatant discrimination provoked great resentment. Many black soldiers from the South did not return from Europe with an attitude of subservience. Besides having served their country, they often experienced a reception from white Europeans unlike anything they had known, and these positive encounters with foreigners engendered an unwillingness to accept the status quo when they returned to the United States after the war.

The Bloody Summer of 1919

In fact, the summer of 1919 was a disaster for race relations all over the country. Depending on one's definition, as many as twenty-five major race riots broke out during the summer as black troops came home to encounter the same racism that was now coupled with inflation and unemployment. There seemed to be no pattern as cities as disparate as Indianapolis and Knoxville erupted in racial conflict. Particularly violent clashes in Chicago and Washington brought death and destruction as local law enforcement proved inadequate to bring fighting under control. In Washington DC federal troops had to be brought in to deal with the carnage and property destruction. Nobody was safe. The mayor of Omaha came literally within a whisker of being lynched by a mob that placed a rope around his neck and burned the courthouse. The mayor would consider himself lucky to have survived with a gunshot wound.

In Arkansas the year of 1919 was a particularly tense time for race relations. As far as whites were concerned, blacks were coming back from overseas and getting completely out of hand. Lincoln Briggs, a black veteran of the war, was murdered in Star City in Lincoln County after it was claimed he made "insulting proposals to an eighteen year old white." A black veteran in Pine Bluff who refused to get off a sidewalk for a white woman was locked up to a tree with tire chains and shot "forty or fifty times" by a white mob. Whites in El Dorado burned to death Frank Livingstone after he was accused of killing two people in Union County. Will Ramsey was taken out of a jail in Blytheville by a mob of about a hundred whites and brutally whipped because he had written a letter to a young white girl.[46] The latter two incidents did not involve black men who had been in the service, but it seemed to whites in the Delta that there was a qualitative difference in race relations than had existed in the past. In Phillips County Gerard Lambert, a northerner who owned thousands of acres in the county, explained the phenomenon in his autobiography. Alluding to the common notion that whites once had a civilizing influencing on blacks, he recalled there had been much warmer relationships between the races, but Phillips County was a different time and place.

> Ours was a primitive and pioneer country where racial hatred was close to the surface. Here we had a tinderbox to be set out by the slightest spark. For this was the numerical imbalance. The colored men outnumbered whites by at least ten to one. White men, with their families on their minds, were constantly alert for the first signs of what they considered danger to their women and families. And the Negroes knew this. If they got out of line, they realized that there would be no compromise with sudden death.[47]

Given the attitudes of whites, one wonders why more blacks did not leave the state. Fon Gordon notes that some black middle-class leaders encouraged blacks to stay in Arkansas despite their own recognition that blacks had more than ample reason to leave the state. She cites as examples both Bishop J. M. Conner of the AME church and Rev. Joseph A. Booker, president of Arkansas Baptist College. Booker publicly attributed the northern exodus to poor schools for blacks and insufficient legal protections for them, but at the same time announced, "We have the best white people in the country." Gordon writes,

> How he reconciled his assessment of white Arkansans with their treatment of blacks is unclear. His moderate criticism and conciliatory, at times, almost groveling tone were all too familiar to black Arkansans. He sought

> to advance the prospects of African Americans by assuring whites that they had nothing to fear.[48]

Booker and men like him were, of course, were attempting to appeal to the best side of whites while at the same time suggesting needed changes that would improve the lot of black people. He and his conservative cohorts had to cope with white violence in an era unaccompanied by television cameras or a sympathetic federal government in any branch, whether judicial, executive, or legislative.

In the view of the newly formed NAACP in New York in 1909, the problem with the Booker T. Washington approach to race relations in the South is that it did little to stop racial violence or discrimination. The consequences for blacks in education alone were disastrous. An Arkansas survey in 1921 showed that the state was spending $17.06 for each white child compared to $5.61 for each black child. And what education there was for blacks was minimal. Almost three out of every four blacks were enrolled in the first four grades. According to Jay Barth, a 1930 study showed the reality of black education was even worse than it was reported. Three out of every ten blacks who were officially enrolled were not attending school, and of those that did, 61 percent were in the first three grades. Only 1.8 percent of the blacks receiving an education were in high school. Perhaps the most dismal statistic was that "77 percent of all black teachers had no college training whatsoever." Despite the grim statistics whites manifested an uncanny ability to deny its own evidence of discrimination. Indeed, the authors of the 1930 study concluded, "public education for the Negro is receiving fairly liberal support and cooperation."[49]

As spring turned to summer in the Arkansas Delta in 1919, black middle-class Southerners continued to argue that aggressive behavior in response to violence or discrimination by whites would only result in more violence by whites. Not all African Americans in Arkansas were content to follow their lead. The race massacres of 1919 in Phillips County would soon test that thesis.

CHAPTER 8

The Elaine Race Massacres

In his first successful race for governor in 1916, Charles Hillman Brough was ambushed by an opponent, secretary of state Earl Hodges, for being too soft on the race question. As a professor at the University of Arkansas, Brough had become chairman in 1912 of a commission that brought together eleven Southern universities to devise a scientific approach to the study of the race question in the South. Hodges thought he had found Brough's weak spot, for a 1915 article in the *Arkansas Gazette* had retrieved Brough's work and could be twisted to make it appear that as chairman he was supporting racial equality. In fact what Brough had preached back then was no more than what a number of racial conservatives had been saying for an entire generation: the present problem with race relations in the South was that there was no longer a healthy interaction between the races as there had been during slavery. Then, whites had taught blacks, had civilized them in effect, and blacks being the highly imitative creature-like persons they were had made real progress. According to Brough the work of the university race commission performed the role of an "intellectual aristocracy" that blacks in the South so badly needed to make their way from "the immediate, passionate, and unreflective life of the African savage toward a social order the nexus of which is rational rather than emotional or instinctive."[1] Brough had written in 1914,

> This close social contact of the races has now almost entirely disappeared. In the Southern states generally there are today no points of social contact whatever where the two races meet and exchange ideas. Separate schools, separate churches, separate telephones, the "Jim Crow" car, restrictions of the ballot, not to mention violent anti-negro political agitation in at least two of the states, have produced an alienation of the two races without parallel.[2]

Eureka! Brough had advocated "close social contact." Brough was for race mixing; the egg-headed professor with all the fancy degrees including a doctorate from Johns Hopkins was for social equality; there was no telling what mileage Hodges could get out of it.

The Education of Charles Hillman Brough

Brough was unlike most, if not all, gubernatorial candidates in the South in this era due to his educational background and the amount of time he had devoted to the issue of race and race relations. Of all Arkansas's governors, whatever the subject, he was the most intellectually prepared: not only did he have a doctorate in "economics, history and jurisprudence" from leading national university Johns Hopkins, where one of his professors was none other than future president Woodrow Wilson, but he had also picked up a master of arts degree in psychology at Mississippi College and a law degree from the University of Mississippi. By 1903, moving from Mississippi, he had become a professor at the University of Arkansas.

In his dissertation on Brough, Charles Orson Cook points out his appeal to Arkansans, which was no more in evidence than at his death in 1935 when there was an outpouring of emotion and affection for the former governor. Arkansans, defensive as ever about their state's image, were proud to have a well-spoken, erudite, and gentlemanly orator for their chief executive, someone who valiantly defended the state against the writer H. L. Mencken who delighted in exposing the state's political, economic, and cultural shortcomings to America. Mencken once wrote, "Not even the Red Cross, with all its munificence, could prevent the inhabitants [of Arkansas] from starving to death from congenital ignorance."[3] At all times, Brough above all was a booster of his adopted state, a proponent of the "New South," which had been in vogue for over a generation with its emphasis on attracting hands-on venture capitalists in order to remake the South into a paradise ripe for exploitation of its abundant natural resources and labor force.

The issue, as Brough saw it, was that "large numbers of semi-literate, sub-moral, and barbaric Negroes without the benefit of education and guidance from more advanced whites, threatened to debase southern society, or worse, jeopardize its physical security."[4] As a solution, Brough, following Booker T. Washington, prescribed a heavy dose of industrial education.

No demagogue, Brough did not want to campaign on race, but Hodges's attacks left him no choice but to respond. In Stuttgart, Brough told a crowd that the job of whites was "to make a better citizen of the negro and to cause him to render more efficient service to the white man."[5] To get his views made known in the state, he took out advertisements in a number of papers, leaving no doubt where he stood. "I am not . . . in favor of social equality. . . . I am not in favor of negroes serving on juries, I am not in favor of negroes holding political offices in the South."[6]

For somebody wishing to get elected to office in Arkansas, his views were hardly surprising, but at the same time if one did not know anymore about the man, one would find him, on balance, more favorably disposed toward blacks than most other Southerners of his time. But beneath his genial manner, Brough was as receptive as any racial Radical to the notion that blacks might some day rise up, and if that day came, he would know how to deal with it. In 1902 he wrote an article for the *Mississippi Historical Quarterly* about a race riot that had taken place in his hometown of Clinton. Three whites lost their lives at a political rally in 1875 just as Reconstruction was ending in Mississippi. The word went out for volunteers to end the violence, and former white Civil War veterans came from Vicksburg on a train and committed mayhem in the black community. There was no stopping them. The death toll was estimated at perhaps fifty, but no one really knew. Brough wrote, "An arrangement was made with the citizen soldiery, now fully 200 strong, that if they would end the killing of the negroes, the United States officers would not assume command but leave matters in charge of the civil authorities."

Most interestingly, Brough did not condemn or lament in any way the indiscriminate killing of blacks; instead he characterized the request for federal intervention by the Republican governor Adelbert Ames as a last-gasp plea from "the Carpet-bag Charlatan of a mongrel governmental mixture."[7] In Brough's mind what had occurred was simply history taught the hard way.

> The return of the terrorized negroes to their homes after the riot was gradual, and their return to municipal, county and State politics was like that of the ship homeward bound, but which never reached its long looked for destination. This lesson of Anglo-Saxon supremacy, written in letters of blood, will ever remain the most important of the many lessons taught in the modest college town of Clinton to the rising young manhood of a proud and untrammeled Commonwealth.[8]

Brough, Bolshevism, and Labor Problems in Phillips County

Though a progressive on domestic issues, embracing women's suffrage, education and tax reform, Brough had no qualms about using whatever means necessary as a panacea for every ill from the war in Europe to any perceived threat on the home front. And in his view, there were many threats, including "bolshevism," "IWWism," "anarchism, the Farmer-

Labor Party, [and] striking labor unions."[9] What was going on in Russia, suddenly steeped in revolutionary fervor, and what was going on in the cities in the north, with the labor clash between corporate America and the IWW (the Industrial Workers of the World, whose name said it all), all was of a single piece, and it seemed to be happening in Phillips County. In 1917 two white labor organizers attempted to induce some black railway workers to participate in a union. The two men, Red Wiggins and Roy Dramer, were promptly escorted to the Helena jail and charged with "threatening and intimidating" blacks workers. At their trial the municipal judge knew what was going on in the world and justified his decision to give them a year in jail and a five-hundred-dollar fine by announcing that "in the present crisis of the country it was a most unpropitious time for creating dissension in the ranks of labor."[10]

Indeed, it was, because, as noted, black workers were headed north in droves. Planters and their allies were doing what they could to keep them at home. Three weeks earlier, the Phillips County Business Men's League, the brainchild of E. M. Allen, a Yankee turned dyed-in-the-wool Southerner, had used its influence to overturn the decision of the U.S. Department of Labor that had begun recruiting blacks to build the military base of Camp Pike outside of Little Rock. Blacks were fired and "encouraged" to return to Phillips County. The headline in the August 10, 1917, *Helena World* read smugly, "Army Posts Will Use No More Black Labor."

An intellectual who was probably happiest when he was upstairs in front of the fireplace with its bird's-eye maple-finished mantle in his library on Scott Street in Little Rock after dinner and surrounded by his six thousand books, Brough was about as far from being a businessman as one could possibly be in temperament. But the "New South" philosophy was all about supporting business, which for Phillips County was primarily about planting and harvesting cotton, and it had turned Helena with its perfect location on the Mississippi River into a boomtown. The engine that made it run was docile black labor. No interference could be tolerated.

Apparently unaware of Brough's 1902 article on the slaughter in Canton, Mississippi, Orson Cook writes that "Governor Brough was certain that behind the Negro unrest in eastern Arkansas [the Elaine massacres] there lurked the agents of a Bolshevik conspiracy."[11] Brough may have allowed himself to believe that, but the difficulty with this explanation was that there was not one iota of evidence that "Bolsheviks" had anything to do with the creation of the black sharecropper union that began to appear in the summer of 1919.

Conditions that were to produce the Elaine Race Massacres in Arkansas were ripening to create a "perfect storm" of carnage in which Brough may have been more than an innocent bystander. One would be remiss in not mentioning that Brough had never had "his" war. He had never served, and perhaps because of this fact the military meant a great deal to him. His father, Charles Milton Brough, had served as a brevet captain of the 15th Pennsylvania Volunteer Calvary in the Civil War before meeting Brough's mother in Mississippi. In his writing and speeches Brough the teacher and politician gushed at length about Confederate war heroes including "the matchless life and character" of Admiral Ralph Semmes, the "brilliant dashes" of Stonewall Jackson, and Robert E. Lee, "the only person in human history without perceptible flaw."[12] More than just a scholarly interest, Brough's fascination with the First World War during his terms as governor was intensely personal. In addition to Brough's "frenzied support of the effort in World War I which he saw as a moral crusade," Orson Cook has observed that the Governor "seemed to experience the front lines vicariously."[13]

Thus, we have a picture of Governor Brough in September 1919 as the most progressive Arkansas governor ever on the issue of race. But he was also a man fully invested in the doctrine of Anglo-Saxon supremacy. Brough was psychologically primed to meet any perceived challenge to it with whatever force necessary and also a good bit more to teach a lesson that it was folly to do so.

A Black Sharecroppers Union in Phillips County

The specific impetus and details of the founding of the organization called the Progressive Farmers and Household Union of Arkansas by Robert Hill are unknown beyond the fact that the organization was incorporated in Monticello in Drew County. By the time Hill, a farmer with two children, moved the organization into Phillips County, the moment had long been right for labor agitation. Since the end of slavery sharecroppers in Phillips County had complained that they were cheated by the planters in a variety of ways, which came as no news to the white community. Ministers of the gospel who wanted to stay employed did not interfere in plantation economics, but things had reached the point where in 1916 Reverend Burke Culpepper had had enough. The *Helena World* reported the following:

> The evangelist took up another line of spiritual wickedness in high places in this community, in the unfair treatment of labor especially colored farm labor, on the part of those whose positions as financial and social leaders should make them above such practices. The evangelist evidently knows that some large fortunes in Helena have been founded on unfair and unrighteous treatment of negro farmers, and held all men guilty of such action up for the severest condemnation. . . . At the conclusion of the speaking, another large number of persons, most of them men of real worth in the community, went forward and professed conversion.[14]

This unique admission of wrongdoing was done and over in the blink of an eye, and it was back to business as usual. Alvin Solomon in October 19, 1919, a young Jewish man who was living in Helena, remembered,

> Most of these tenant farmers didn't get a break. They [planters] kept the books on them, and they were

> always in debt. They'd give them what they wanted to give them. There were exceptions to that but the exception was just against the rule.[15]

Over the years there had been and would be again federal investigations and occasional prosecution for the crime of peonage, also known as debt slavery, but the tradition of exploitation was too strong to break, and there were too many ways to do it. For example, as mentioned, planters charged outrageous prices for goods sold to their tenants; planters made agreements with other planters not to hire tenants who left owing money unless they paid their bills; and whites rationalized their behavior by telling themselves that blacks spent their money foolishly anyway and why keep detailed accounts when blacks did not bother themselves?

However, as mentioned, blacks were coming back from the war with a different attitude. African Americans, including those from Phillips County, felt if they had defended the country the least the country could do was reevaluate its attitude toward blacks. "We helped you fight the Germans, and are ready to help you fight the next fellows that get after you, but we want to be treated fairly," wrote Robert Hill, who by this time had become a fugitive after the race massacres in Elaine. Though Hill, had not apparently been drafted, he like many blacks was influenced by the militant positions taken in publications like the *Chicago Defender* and the *Crisis,* which made their way South and were passed from reader to reader. In these publications were article after article denouncing Jim Crow and the ceaseless violence against blacks in the South. Just how influential these publications were to blacks of all classes was indicated by Brough's futile effort to prevent them from entering Arkansas after the massacres in October 1919.

One individual could not keep himself from being cheated, but a cohesive group might, and in the summer of 1919 Robert Hill and his followers organized a number of "lodges" around the town of Elaine in Phillips County where blacks outnumbered whites by as much as ten to one. Tiny communities with names such as Mellwood, Ratio, and Hoop

Spur in addition to Elaine now hosted meetings in churches where blacks gathered far into the night to rally themselves and formulate strategies for dealing with the planters. They had begun to post armed guards outside to keep snooping whites away. Invariably, the word was getting out to whites as the summer wore on, but they were not taking these meetings seriously. It would be claimed much later that locals had known what was going on by having hiring a black detective to infiltrate the meetings and that this individual had told of a list that had been drawn up to kill planters. If that report had been true, doubtless the planters would have taken immediate action, but in fact they did nothing. The organization of the union had reached the point where in September members had talked with the Little Rock law firm of Ulysses S. Bratton to represent them in their dealings with the planters. Bratton, a fierce Republican and devout Methodist who was originally from rugged Searcy County in northwest Arkansas, had a reputation for representing the side of black sharecroppers against planters. He had at one time been an U.S. attorney and had prosecuted peonage cases for the government. By 1919 he was in private practice with his son Guy and maintained an office in Helena and had put his son Oscier, who was not a lawyer, on the train to travel to the Elaine area to meet with union members on October 1 and have them sign retainer agreements and collect money in order to represent them.[16]

The Slaughter by the White Mob

On the night of September 30, 1919, approximately a hundred black men, women, and children had gathered in a church for a meeting of the Hoop Spur Lodge three miles north of Elaine when at about midnight shooting commenced outside the church between the guards and three men who had pulled up in a car outside the church. Who fired the first shots will never be known, but given the contradictions in their accounts of the incident later, at a bare minimum the evidence shows the three had come to spy on the group or to harass it or both. Though it is not known how many blacks were killed in the shootout at the Hoop Spur church, W. A. Adkins, a security employee of the Missouri Pacific Railroad, was mortally wounded and a second, deputy sheriff Charlie Pratt, received injuries from which he would recover. The driver of the car, "Kid" Collins, a black trusty from the Helena jail, escaped unharmed.

What followed next was brutally familiar to Arkansas blacks. Whites immediately began to panic: rumors swept up and down the Mississippi on both sides of the river that blacks, who so outnumbered whites in this part of Phillip County, were said to be revolting. It is important here to understand the white mentality of this era. In her memoir entitled *Born in the Delta: Reflections on the Making of a Southern White Sensibility,* Arkansan Margaret Jones Bolsterli captures the fear and the response to fear felt by whites who lived in the Delta since the slave era. Overhearing but totally misunderstanding a conversation between a black child and her father at two in the morning, Bolsterli writes,

> I lay there in a cold sweat for hours waiting to be shot [by the child's father]. . . . In retrospect, and this is evidence of my acculturation to violence, the most frightening thing to me was not hearing the right noises of reassurance. I would have been comforted by hearing the action of my father's pump gun or the click of shells sliding into the chamber of his double-barrel twelve-gauge shotgun. . . . If I could expect the threat of violence, I expected to be protected from it by violent means. . . . All I'm trying to do is trace *my* pattern in the tapestry that depicts the Southern experience; my fear and expectation of violence are part of it.[17]

Earlier, she writes,

> I wonder if the traditional southern white fear of violence at the hands of blacks is at bottom really a belief that the whites deserve it, that one night the blacks will have taken all the abuse they can stand and will simply

> rise as one and murder the whites in their beds. On the face of it, this a fairly logical explanation, since the whites routinely have committed more violence on blacks than the reverse. The entire social structure from the time of slavery on has been organized for an easy assault on black people. Mary Boykin Chesnut describes such fear in her *Civil War Diary*, and it was prevalent in the Delta when I was growing up.[18]

There was, of course, only one solution for it: within hours of the initial incident that had taken the life of one white person, a mob estimated to be between six hundred and a thousand whites armed with shotguns and rifles poured into the Elaine area the next day on October 1 from Helena and Delta towns, such as Marianna in neighboring Lee County, but also from across the river in Mississippi and from Memphis, as well. Though whites in the area claimed that there had been no indiscriminate shooting of blacks, the evidence proves overwhelmingly that whites slaughtered blacks, including men, women, and children, the only unanswered question being how many. A sworn affidavit from H. F. Smiddy, a white posse member from Helena who was present, states, in part,

> Between nine and ten o'clock on the morning of October 1 a great many people from Helena and other portions of Phillips County, and from other surrounding counties began coming in, quite a large number of them, several hundred of them, and began to shoot negroes, and shotting [*sic*] them as they came to them.

In the affidavit which was prepared as part of court papers during the defense of blacks accused of killing five whites, Smiddy also swore under oath that a group of white Mississippians did their share.

> They shot and killed men, women, and children without regard to whether they were guilty or not. Negroes were killed time after time again out in the fields picking cotton, harming nobody.[19]

Smiddy's affidavit concerning the slaughter of the band from Mississippi is also confirmed by blacks in Elaine who were interviewed by Bessie Ferguson, a graduate of Hendrix College, who in 1927 wrote about the events in Elaine for her master's thesis.

> A party of twelve men from Mississippi equipped with eleven guns and an axe created havoc wherever they went. . . . Barberism [*sic*] such as cutting off the ears or toes of dead negroes for souvenirs and the dragging of their bodies through the streets of Elaine are told by witnesses.[20]

More confirmation of a racial massacre came from federal judge John Miller, prosecuting attorney for Phillips County in 1919. In a 1976 oral history interview he told historian Walter Brown that it was the group from Mississippi that "started the marauding. We wouldn't have any of that until—now I understand they had plenty of help over there in Arkansas. All they needed was some agitator and leader."[21]

Members of the lodges got word they were being attacked and tried to flee into the dense canebrakes that were such a part of the terrain in that part of Phillips County. Though they were running for their lives, at the same time they were eyewitnesses to some portion of the slaughter, and some of them gave their statements to Ida B. Wells-Barnett, the famous anti-lynching advocate, who published their statements in a pamphlet. Passing herself off as a family member, she was able to interview the twelve men who had been found guilty of murder by the state of Arkansas.

The statement given by seventy-nine-year-old Ed Coleman was, in part, as follows:

> And at 11:30 that day [October 1]. we saw near 300 white armed men coming and we all ran back of the field and when we go back of the field there was a big crowd of white men shooting and killing Jim Miller's family. . . . We were running and made it to the woods,

> where we were hid all night and all the next day. Then I came home to get my wife. She was about dead herself. When I got there, the white men had went and shot and killed some of the women and children.[22]

Ed Ware, one of the leaders of the union, told Well-Barnett,

> All of the while men were armed with guns and they had almost surrounded my house when the old man Charley Robinson and Isaac Bird and myself began to run. The old man was crippled and could not run and they shot him down and took him up from there and carried him and put him in my wife's bed and let him stay there for four days. They took the county broadcast and began to shoot down everything they saw like a Negro.[23]

Whites seemed to think they were entitled to take the possessions of union leaders according to the statements given by the men in prison and their wives. As examples of what occurred, Ed Ware's affidavit read, "I lost all of my household goods and 121 acres of cotton and corn, two mules, one horse, one Jersey cow, and one farm wagon and all farming tools and harness and eight head of hogs, 135 chickens and one Ford car."[24]

The wife of Frank Moore told Wells-Barnett when she returned to her house that

> everything was gone. She went to the landlord's wife and told his wife she had come to gather her crops and pay what was owed. She also asked Mrs. Archdale what had become of her furniture and clothes and where her husband was. Mrs. Archdale told her she would get nothing even though Mrs. Moore saw some of her furniture and clothes in Mrs. Archdale's house.[25]

Barnett put the value of items stolen by whites, including their cotton, at a million dollars.

The Boys from Camp Pike: Heroes or Part of the Slaughter?

On October 1 while all of this was occurring, Governor Brough received three telegrams from Phillips County whites, each more frantic than the last, advising of a race riot and requesting troops to quell it. The second telegraph requested "immediate dispatch of 500 troops with machine guns" to Elaine.[26] Finally, Brough, after bureaucratic delays in Washington, received permission from the war department to send troops to Elaine. Shortly after midnight Brough boarded a train out of Union Station in Little Rock with 583 U.S. troops from Camp Pike. Many of these troops were seasoned veterans, some of whom had fought at the Second Battle of the Marne. With units from the third and fifth infantry divisions, the hastily pieced together unit included twelve machine guns. The head of the unit was Colonel Isaac C. Jencks, a West Pointer whose field experience included the First World War and even went far back enough to include fighting Indians. To understand what occurred next, it is important to realize that by the time the troop train reached Elaine the following morning at eight o'clock and met with the townspeople of Elaine not a single plantation owner, farmer, woman, or child had been killed or wounded or would be. Instead of a black uprising that had resulted in the slaughter of whites, the actual number of white deaths, including W. A. Adkins, then numbered only four, and these included two Helena men who had come out with the posse to engage in what Phillips County sheriff Frank Kitchens called a "nigger hunt." With his intimate knowledge of Southern history, Brough would have suspected immediately that what was occurring was the mass slaughter of blacks, not whites. Clearly, whites in the area were in panic mode, fearing once again that blacks, with their vastly superior numbers, would overwhelm them. Fearful of an attack, some whites in the surrounding area of Elaine left their plantations and barricaded themselves in a store in Elaine. Sharing these quarters with them was Oscier Bratton who, unaware of the shootout at the Hoop Spur church the previous night, had gotten off the train before it arrived in Elaine and was meeting with blacks on behalf of his father's firm. Oscier Bratton had been taken into custody that morning by a group of whites who assumed that he was the leader of insurgent blacks. Later that day he would be taken to jail in Helena, and his observations in a letter to his father shed light on the conditions in Elaine on October 1. Not only there was no attack on Elaine, Oscier Bratton reported that the over-twenty-mile train trip into Helena was "uneventful," casting doubt on one report that blacks had fired on a train on October 1.[27] Though trial testimony demonstrated that a handful of black men from the union tried to resist as the mobs and posse hunted them down, their posture was almost invariably one of self-defense, as the mobs, posses, and then military rooted them out.

The arrival of the military at Elaine had the effect of ending the slaughter by the white mobs, but there was secondhand evidence that troops from Camp Pike conducted a slaughter of their own. One of the enduring questions of the Elaine massacres is what responsibility, if any, Governor Brough should bear for ensuring that the troops he had requested acted with self-restraint. The U.S. military has never officially admitted that even one soldier from Camp Pike was guilty of indiscriminate violence against blacks in Elaine. Governor Brough, who accompanied the troops on the train from Little Rock to Elaine and then was allowed to march with them to Hoop Spur as soon as they arrived in Elaine, proclaimed them military heroes. Commanding officer Jencks correctly and immediately ordered that both blacks and whites be disarmed, thus hastening the departure of the white mobs, who began leaving the area, taking their weapons with them.

The evidence that the U.S. military engaged in acts of indiscriminate killing of blacks in Elaine comes from numerous sources. Though official reports of the army put the number of blacks killed at twenty, unofficial sources have placed the number far higher. In his oral history interview federal judge Miller claimed that the troops misunderstood the intentions of blacks and

> must have killed 100 niggers right there. . . . You see that is what caused, really, the firing, that real slaughter down there. There was some shot fired . . . but they were fired in celebration of the army being there. That is what happened. There wasn't a soldier hit or anything.[28]

Louis Sharpe Dunaway, a salesman and reporter for the *Arkansas Gazette,* was not so charitable in his characterization of the soldiers' intentions at Elaine. In a chapter of his 1925 book *What a Preacher Saw Through a Keyhole in Arkansas,* Dunaway, who was from Arkansas and who had attended highly regarded Hendrix College for three years, wrote that the soldiers from Camp Pike "committed one murder after another with all the calm deliberation in the world, either too heartless to realize the enormity of their crimes or too drunk on moonshine to give a continental darn."[29]

Dunaway made the totally unsupported claim that "856 negroes were killed during the first days immediately following the first trouble at Elaine, most of whom were killed by soldiers."[30] This particular work by Dunaway has been called a "ridiculous little book" by Jeannie Whayne, who has argued the existing evidence is insufficient to support the view the troops commanded by Jencks murdered blacks at Elaine. Yet Dunaway's claims of murder cannot be so easily dismissed, for his lucid summary of the complex legal proceedings that followed the massacres in Elaine establishes him as a serious reporter of the events there.[31] What is almost entirely lacking in Dunaway's chapter about the events in Elaine is documentation of his claims. Had he done so, he would have had to verify also the murderous acts of civilian whites, as well, and he had no intention of exposing them.

> It was nothing more than expected, when a chivalrous white citizenship took up arms and immediately

> avenged the killing of seven or eight of [*sic*] their own color. While this summary action is not conducive to good government, yet it is not assailed for the reason we know of some of the leading characters in this tragedy, and we know them to be big and brave and true to the traditions of the "Old South."[32]

It is impossible after so much time to know the number of blacks murdered at Elaine. One can only piece together bits of information that suggest the dimensions of the slaughter. For example, the African American secretary of the Pine City Masonic Lodge George W. Davis reportedly paid insurance benefits for 103 members who died during the massacres. As an educated Arkansan, Dunaway plainly could not bear to go against the class of whites with whom he so clearly identified and thus adds almost off-handedly that the soldiers in their slaughter were "aided and abetted by a collection of low-lived creatures who call themselves WHITE MEN."[33]

Such was the stifling conformity and group-think of white Arkansans in this era that no one could go against the inviolate tradition of white supremacy, not even a man who was so clearly outraged by what he had discovered in writing about these events. In fact Dunaway felt it necessary to add that the "deepest regret" of the events in Elaine was the deaths of the whites and not the premeditated slaughter of hundreds of blacks. Finally, Dunaway would not have raised the following point had he not at some level wondered about it. He wrote, "We know that Gov. Brough did not sanction the soldiers' death-dance; we know that he was not aware of the butchery that was taking place in the guise of 'peace-making.'"[34] In the words of Shakespeare, Dunaway doth protest too much.

The Duty of a Governor

From the beginning, instead of distancing himself from the events in Elaine, Brough placed himself at the center. It was not necessary for Brough to ride over to Elaine with the troops, nor was there any military necessity for Brough, as he did, to march with a contingent of the troops to Hoop Spur immediately after arriving in Elaine, where it was reported that blacks were still in the area. It appears that Brough was living out his military fantasy throughout these events, capping it off by actually marching at the head of the troops when they entered Helena that afternoon. A day later, after returning to Little Rock, Brough wrote to a friend that he had "just had a very thrilling experience in Phillips County, in connection with the race riot out there."[35] As governor of Arkansas, at a minimum Brough had a duty to do whatever possible to prevent loss of life to both whites and blacks in Phillips County, but from the beginning he interpreted the unfolding events consistent with the unwritten rules of white supremacy in the South. To Brough it was appropriate and indeed necessary to counter any resistance by blacks with deadly and excessive force in order to accomplish two goals: to teach blacks a lesson of the consequences of resistance but also to teach, as he had written seventeen years previously, "the rising manhood of an untrammeled republic," what must be done to maintain that authority. Had Brough wished to even make an attempt to act evenhandedly in this situation, he would have made clear to the commanding officers by the afternoon of October 1 and to the public that he expected the soldiers to act with restraint because it was increasingly apparent that blacks, who had every opportunity to begin killing whites at midnight after the shootout at Hoop Spur, had not done so but in fact were fleeing for their lives into the canebrakes. There is no indication that he did so. By the afternoon of October 1 with no reports of the loss of life of white civilians, he would have understood that once again white mobs had gone beyond the pale with their acts of mutilation and wanton murder. Then or later, Brough never spoke publicly about the outrages committed against blacks in the Elaine massacres. In truth, the unwritten code of white supremacy among the white media was not to pursue these kinds of embarrassing questions, and this rule would be strictly honored. In his chapter discussing the events at Elaine, Dunaway takes his fellow journalists to task for ignoring what the military had done. He wrote,

> It is a strange coincidence that newspapermen, quick to get the news and usually accurate in their figures, were "unable to get the known Negro dead," or furnish a true description of the soldiers' march of death through the cotton fields of Phillips County. And it is a "strange come-off" that these same "news hounds" found time to write only "half the story" of all the Elaine troubles.[36]

The Committee of Seven Takes Charge

Ignoring all the evidence that hundreds of whites had come into the area and murdered innocent people, that afternoon after marching into Helena at the head of the troops Brough met with a self-appointed committee of the Helena power structure and made a deal with them. As a Southern progressive on race, Brough's mindset was such that he could interpret the evidence of barbaric behavior and mass murder that had occurred in Elaine as a wholly necessary adjunct of white supremacy, but at the same time he was appalled by the possibility of blacks being yanked out of jails by white mobs and murdered. In time it would be clear that he was not interested in seeing that blacks receive justice but only that they appear to receive justice. Though there is no written record of the meeting, from his press conference it is clear he extracted a promise from the so-called "Committee of Seven," which included three planters, the county judge and sheriff for Phillips County, a "furnish" merchant, and the mayor of Helena. The promise was that the committee would guarantee that there would be no lynchings but that Brough would accept the committee's version of events as well as its de facto control, as he surely was predisposed to do anyway.

On October 3, 1919, under inch-high headlines that

read "ELAINE INSURRECTION IS OVER: COMMITTEE OF SEVEN IN CHARGE," the front page of the *Helena World* contained a statement in the name of the committee written by its head, Mort Allen.

> The negroes at Hoop Spur have been under the influence of a few rascally white men and designing leaders of their own race. The people of Phillips County have never stood for mob violence and will permit none to occur under any circumstances.[37]

The Committee of Seven had much at stake: it was absolutely essential that blacks get back to work because the cotton would soon be rotting in the fields. To that end it would publish and distribute a circular on October 7 entitled "To the Negroes of Phillips County." It told blacks that the "trouble" was at an end and that

> soldiers now here to preserve order will return to Little Rock within a short time. . . . All you have to do is remain at work just as if nothing had happened. Phillips County has always been a peaceful, law-abiding community, and normal conditions must be restored right away. Stop talking! Stay at home—Go to work—don't worry![38]

The level of arrogance and contempt for blacks was such that the Committee of Seven's shifting version of events was so inconsistent as to be ridiculous. Anything it said was expected to be believed. Thus, blacks had planned to kill leading planters and had drawn up a list when the events at Hoop Spur had scuttled their plans prematurely. Somehow, blacks had been promised land; the leader of the union was in it for a "get rich scheme." Later, it would be revealed that blacks had been tortured by the military and local whites—and doubtless some blacks said under torture precisely what they were told to say—but there would be no credible evidence of any sort that blacks had planned an insurrection. What would finally become obvious to historians was that the shootout at Hoop Spur provided the perfect opportunity for whites to completely eradicate the labor union and its leaders, and that was accomplished within the first twenty-four hours.

Brough's story at his press conference in Little Rock on October 3 set out the general position that would be taken by whites for years to come. "The situation at Elaine has been well handled and is absolutely under control. There is no danger of any lynching." The five whites (including one soldier) who were killed became instant martyrs. Brough named them one by one and praised them profusely. "Phillips County [has] lost some of its most promising and most patriotic citizens."[39] The troops had acted in the finest tradition of the military, and a tragedy of epic proportions had been averted after the planned insurrection had been discovered. What Brough did not mention was more important than what he did. The actions of the mobs coming into Phillips County he totally ignored, nor was he apparently asked about them. Nor was he asked why no whites were arrested and hundreds of blacks were. He was not asked if blacks had been hunted and killed, nor how many blacks had died. He promised no investigation, no follow-up of any kind. Indeed, those functions were being handled with splendid thoroughness by the Committee of Seven. All was well or shortly would be. The governor looked tired, the reporter for the *Arkansas Gazette* noted. There was no mention that whites had cut off blacks' toes and ears.

Seeing No Evil: Group-Think in the Delta

The moment when the troops from Camp Pike began to use excessive force at Elaine is not clear. It may well have started in earnest on October 3, for the *Arkansas Gazette* reported that a railroad agent indicated that "several negroes had been surrounded near the village of Modoc, east of Elaine, and a detachment of soldiers had started for the scene to arrest them. He reported considerable shooting in the canebrakes about Elaine, where soldiers were engaged in a search for the hiding places of the negroes." As usual, there was no follow-up by the paper, and no paper nor the Associated Press ever did more than report hints of a slaughter. One can conclude there was an unconscious decision to ignore the dimensions of the massacres of blacks.[40]

Though University of Arkansas historian D. Y. Thomas concluded ten years later that the insurrection theory "was later shown to be incorrect," he neglected to explore the greater dimensions of the tragedy. The military reports submitted by Jencks and his officers are mysteriously vague and self-congratulatory. In the years following the massacres, there would be anecdotal information, for example, such as the error-ridden account by journalist and writer James Street who, in offering a one-page account, wrote, in part,

> Without comment and without haste the soldiers went about the tedious duty of ending the riot. They marched through the swamps shooting Negroes without question. Those who were not shot were herded into cattle cars for safety. For two days, the slaughter continued, but the riot was broken.[41]

The Elaine Race Massacres Legal Cases

The Elaine Race Massacres resulted in the arrest and detention of hundreds of blacks, ultimately to the consternation of planters in the area who demanded the release of their workers during the peak of the harvest. The overwhelming number of blacks in the Elaine area had nothing to do with the union and undoubtedly had never heard of Robert Hill, and the planters simply wanted them to get back in the fields at a critical time.

There is evidence that the soldiers worked together with the planters to get information from tortured blacks. In his autobiography Gerard Lambert recounts two incidents, one involving psychological torture and the other physical. In the latter incident, Lambert states he was told that troopers brought one of the leaders of the union at Lambrook to the

> company store and tied him with stout cord to one of the wooden columns on the other porch. He had been extremely insolent, and the troopers, enraged by the loss of two of their men that day in the woods [*sic*], had pressed him with questions. He continued his arrogance, and one white man, hoping to make him speak up, poured a can of kerosene over him. As he was clearly unwilling to talk, a man suddenly tossed a lighted match at him. The colored man went up like a torch and, in a moment of supreme agony, burst his bounds. Before he could get but a few feet he was riddled with bullets. The superintendent told me with some pleasure that they had to use our fire hose to put him out.[42]

The torture of blacks that occurred in the Helena jail was much more systematic. Both T. K. Jones and H. F. Smiddy gave affidavits in which they admitted that they had tortured blacks and watched others torture them to make them give evidence. T. K. Jones swore,

> I saw a great many negroes whipped on the third floor of the county jail to compel them to give evidence against themselves and others about the trouble. . . . I either whipped or helped to whip several of the petitioners. I don't know which, but I do remember that I helped to whip Frank Moore and J. E. Knox. Walter Ward, one of the witnesses against the petitioners was whipped two or three times and put in the electric chair to make him testify against the petitioners."[43]

Though no blacks would be removed from the jail and lynched, the white legal structure was determined to dispense its brand of justice in record time. Beginning on October 27, the Pulaski County grand jury began meeting, and by the thirty-first it had charged 122 blacks with crimes that ranged from nightriding to murder. Nightriding was generally reserved for whites who tried to run off black labor. Prosecutor John Miller released twenty-one blacks due to lack of evidence. Though today it would take years to try cases against a hundred defendants, by November 7 the Phillips County circuit court would have only a handful of these cases left on its docket.

The trials began on November 3 in front of Judge J. M. Jackson who appointed counsel from the local bar in Helena. These cases would be tried without any preparation by the defense attorneys whatsoever, including the failure to interview the client or any witnesses. There could be only one verdict, and that was guilty. The first case called set the stage for what was to follow. Jacob Fink, the attorney for Frank Hicks who was being tried for the murder of Phillips County posse man Clinton Lee, accepted the first twelve men called to sit on the jury and did not ask a single question. In his opening statement, he told the jury he had not "had time to talk to the witnesses in the case," asked for a fair trial, and sat down.[44] In fairness to Fink, the alternative he faced was to conduct an aggressive defense and run the risk of being lynched himself. This day had been promised to the mob. Outside the courthouse soldiers from Camp Pike stood guard. Had any of the defense attorneys done their job, they not only would have put themselves in danger but their families, as well.

Since there were no white eyewitnesses to the death of Clinton Lee, the prosecutor relied on the testimony of blacks, one of whom testified that he had seen Hicks fire his rifle in the direction of Lee who was over four hundred yards away from him. This "evidence" was enough for the jury who deliberated "8 minutes" before returning a verdict of guilty.[45] The entire capital murder trial had taken three-and-one-half hours.

The rest of the cases that day were handled in similar fashion. Judge Jackson called a new jury and tried the following individuals together: Frank Moore, Ed Hicks (the brother of Frank Hicks), Joe Knox, Ed Coleman, and Paul Hall. They were charged with "aiding and abetting Frank Hicks." The evidence in this trial was even less compelling than the first, but the race was on to get the trials finished as quickly as possible. All five of the men were found guilty before the day was out.

The next morning Alf Banks Jr. and John Martin were called to stand trial for the nighttime shooting of W. A. Atkins at the Hoop Spur church. Even without modern forensic evidence the case would have been difficult to prove. The prosecution's witness, deputy sheriff Charlie Pratt, could only testify that a dozen blacks had opened fire first. The jury was out only nine minutes.[46]

Albert Giles and Joe Fox then stood trial for the death of James Tappan, also a member of the Phillips County posse. Tappan had been killed while searching for blacks near Hoop Spur. The evidence against both men, in part, depended on the testimony of men who had been tortured, though this fact did not make it to the jury. Again, conviction of first-degree murder followed with a minimum amount of representation by defense counsel. William Wardlow was then tried for "aiding and abetting" in the killing of W. A. Adkins. Although there was evidence that Atkins was already dead when Wardlow, a guard outside the church that night, began shooting, the jury convicted and sentenced him to death.

With death sentences being handed out to the first twelve defendants, the effect on the remaining defendants to be tried was a foregone conclusion. Defendants, with the assistance of their appointed attorneys, rushed to enter plea bargains to avoid the very real possibility of electrocution. The *Helena World* reported on November 7 that a total of sixty-five men entered plea bargains and were convicted, including nine who were given sentences of twenty-one years for second-degree murder. It was not as smooth a process as it would have appeared. The *Helena World* also reported that the prosecutor John Miller, who would go on to careers as a congressmen, U.S. senator, and federal judge, succeeded in placing pressure on the court to increase the sentences of the men entering into plea bargains.[47]

One important trial remained. Ed Ware, thought to be a leader in the union, would be caught in New Orleans, brought back to Phillips County, and tried for W. A. Adkins's murder on November 16. The significance of this case arose from the importance of the prosecution witness, a black who had not testified previously. Suggs Bondsman had been arrested during the massacres but released without being charged, and now he testified that he had been present at a union meeting at the Elaine lodge in which he overheard Ed Ware "giving names of planters to be killed." Since the testimony of Ware's trial has never been found, the *Helena World's* account is the only instance where evidence of a conspiracy to kill planters was mentioned in any of the trials. As it developed, the credibility of his testimony would be impeached in a subsequent trial, but for the time being his testimony was understood to be proof positive of a conspiracy to kill planters.[48]

The Elaine Twelve, as they came to be known, seemed like so many other black men, destined to disappear into the brutally efficient jaws of Southern white supremacy. Judge Jackson set their executions for late December and early January.

The Governor's Biracial Commission

A footnote to the Elaine massacres was the November 24 meeting of the first biracial commission ever held in Arkansas, and at the state capitol at that. Given the tenor of the times, only a Charles Hillman Brough could have brought it off. Inviting the cream of the black male middle class, Joseph A. Booker, James Monroe Cox, Bishop J. M. Conner, E. C. Morris, and Scott Bond to name the leading lights, the governor was careful not to include men who would directly challenge him. Whites on the commission were men whose views were much like the governor's—sympathetic conservatives such as John Hugh Reynolds, president of Hendrix College. The reason for calling the meeting was to have "a heart-to-heart discussion of racial differences," the *Arkansas Gazette* reported Brough as saying. Yet Brough immediately took the issue of the mobs and military off the table by saying that the Phillips County affair was a "damnable insurrection." Further, he had been "on the ground the day after" and knew what happened there. "He said he did not need any assistance."[49]

This was quintessential Charles Hillman Brough on race: blacks could talk about racial problems but only if they accepted the premise that they were the cause of them. According to press reports, the blacks present did talk, but they did not confront Brough on the murders committed by the mobs or the military. James Monroe Cox later claimed that, "We have discussed the Elaine trouble again and again and the Negro members have expressed fearlessly their views concerning the whole affair." Well, not as fearlessly as Cox would have liked to have his readers believe, but there seemed extenuating circumstances. Here was a governor so unlike those who had become before him and would come after him that it would seem foolish to confront him on this issue when he was so adamant. Also, blacks were acutely aware that Brough had the power to commute the sentences of every black prisoner in the custody of the state, so nobody was going to contradict him directly on any subject.

Was anything accomplished by the biracial commission? So long as the white-supremacy lid was tightly bolted down, nothing substantive could be accomplished because Brough was incapable of admitting publicly any wrongdoing by whites on any subject that involved race. It is likely he did not even feel a twinge of hypocrisy when the objectives of the conference were announced: "Justice before the law, including the prevention of lynching and other denials of legal justice to the negro."[50] This was racial progress, 1920s style. But before then, there were no objectives, no biracial conference at all.

CHAPTER 9

The Aftermath of the Elaine Race Massacres and the Twenties

The most optimistic assessment of the successful fight to prevent the execution of the Elaine Twelve is that the highly complex legal proceedings that ensued proved that the Arkansas black middle class in Little Rock could rise to the occasion and successfully work, despite embarrassing setbacks, with a highly effective national organization to secure a degree of racial justice for the poorest blacks in the state. On a long-term national basis the success of the New York–based NAACP's collaboration with the black middle class in Little Rock became an important milestone and symbol within the institutional memory of the association. By no means, however, would this success mean the continued well-being of the recently formed Arkansas NAACP, which struggled from its birth in 1918 until it received a major boost in the 1940s from the activism of a dynamic lawyer by the name of Harold Flowers. The struggle would also demonstrate that there were a few white Arkansans who were capable of putting justice—at least criminal justice—ahead of white supremacy.

On a local level within the black community, this commitment to the struggle for freedom for his clients began with Scipio African Jones whose courage and persistence were the stuff of the rarest form of heroism. In again trying to understand what was at the core of this complex individual, one does well to remember that from the beginning Scipio Jones put black safety and survival far ahead of any kind of ideological commitment and would to his dying day.

The National NAACP and Southern Blacks

In early October even before the troops from Camp Pike had all returned to Little Rock, Jones had a visitor from the national office of the NAACP. He was an equally complex black individual by the name of Walter White who would one day be the NAACP's national executive director. No two African Americans could have been more different. The audacious White, whose skin was so fair that he had successfully pretended to be a newsman from the north and had gained an interview with Governor Brough to discuss the events in Elaine by using fake credentials, could not have been very impressed with Jones. He would have surely seen him as the typically cautious, conservative Southern black lawyer the NAACP wanted to avoid. When Jones learned that White planned to take the train to Helena to conduct an investigation, he warned the younger man not to try to talk to blacks there for fear of jeopardizing their safety. Whether White took his advice is not known, but he did go to Helena where he was lucky to escape being lynched. Probably the only advice White took from Jones was to seek the help of Ulysses S. Bratton, who was furiously trying to get his son Oscier released from the Phillips County jail.[1]

The simple truth was that the national NAACP staff in New York did not think much of middle-class Southern blacks nor of the black lawyers who practiced among them. Founded in 1909 in New York by a prestigious group of social activists and liberals that included both whites and blacks, the national board by 1919 was chaired by fifty-four-year-old Mary White Ovington, a white social worker and journalist whose private income allowed her to give generously of her time to the day-to-day operation of the organization. The executive staff in the national office was composed of three black field secretaries who, in addition to Walter White, were

James Weldon Johnson and the same William Pickens who had grown up in Arkansas. The executive director in 1919 was John Schillady, a white male whose almost-fatal beating by a mob in Texas caused him to resign in 1920. In the early years of the organization, the NAACP typically contracted with white lawyers in the South to represent black defendants and did so again in this instance, hiring upon the advice of Ulysses Bratton a Little Rock firm headed by George Murphy to seek a new trial and to try to save the Elaine Twelve from execution. Even at the advanced age of seventy-nine, Murphy, the former attorney general for the state of Arkansas and onetime candidate for governor on a reform ticket, was regarded as one of the best criminal defense attorneys in the state. A former Confederate colonel who had been severely wounded at the Battle of Shiloh, Murphy, along with Ulysses Bratton, was unique among white Arkansas lawyers for his willingness to champion unpopular causes.[2]

The Partnership of Colonel Murphy and Scipio Jones

Walter White had obviously not asked Scipio Jones if he was interested in helping to represent the Elaine Twelve, but it in no way stopped Jones from beginning to raise money and visiting the Elaine Twelve and their families. How Scipio Jones and Colonel Murphy, as he was called, formally got together to both represent the Elaine Twelve is not known. In the relationship as it began, Scipio Jones, as any black Arkansas attorney would have been given Murphy's criminal defense experience, reputation, and age, was clearly the junior partner. Their first mission was to travel to Helena to file motions for a new trial, a necessary requirement for appealing the cases to the Arkansas Supreme Court. As fully expected, Judge Jackson denied the motions on December 20, the same day they were filed. As he had promised, Governor Bough issued stays of execution to allow the appeals to go forward. Over the next five years the cases of the Elaine Twelve were litigated multiple times in both state and federal courts.

Arkansas always had its share of critics for its treatment of blacks from outside the state, but in 1920 pressure from an unlikely source caused major embarrassment in both white and black communities. Robert Hill, who had fled the state when he was about to be arrested on October 1, eventually made his way to Kansas. When Phillips County officials found out he was there, they began efforts immediately to extradite him. Ordinarily, the sole basis for one state's refusing to extradite a prisoner for trial to another state that has criminal jurisdiction over him is its belief that the individual will not receive a fair trial. The national office of the NAACP immediately saw the potential in this case and began a major effort to keep Hill from being returned to Arkansas. Hill was provided representation by three black attorneys of the local NAACP and would be defended at a hearing by Topeka prosecuting attorney Hugh Fisher, a white Republican who was about to make a run for the state senate and surely saw an opportunity to secure votes at no cost from the town's substantial black population. This was a standard NAACP tactic—put the influential white out front.[3]

An Outside View of Race Relations in Arkansas

While Governor Brough, without fear of public contradiction from either blacks or whites inside Arkansas, could proclaim to his heart's content that his adopted state provided justice for its black citizens, his words were greeted with the skepticism they deserved outside the state. Immediately pressure began to build on all sides. Black defenders of civil rights outside Arkansas were enraged by a letter signed by three influential black members of Brough's biracial commission who wrote the following,

> The citizens of Phillips County and the Governor have assured us that Hill will be guaranteed a fair trial and the right to change of venue. We believe the return of Hill is in the interest of justice to the negro and will materially strengthen this biracial commission in the work of promoting interracial justice.[4]

Nothing during the entire Elaine litigation highlighted the differences between the Arkansas black middle class and their counterparts in the north than the appearance of this letter. The black *Chicago Defender* denounced the three men in scathing, vitriolic language, calling them "rattlesnakes" and "animals." The *Defender* hissed,

> The names of Conner, [Cox] and Booker henceforth will be as a stench in the nostrils of self-respecting men and women and they should be shunned as a pestilence and hated as traitors of a type that would have made Benedict Arnold blush with shame.[5]

The dismay of the national office of the NAACP to the letter was palpable, but since it was working in tandem with the black middle class to raise money to defend the Elaine Twelve, the New York office could not afford to be so openly critical and judgmental of its brethren in Arkansas. The episode reveals the utter dependence of the Arkansas black middle class on the state's white leaders to do the right thing, despite every indication they would not. With Jim Crow in full flower for over a generation and their personal well-being invested in adherence to a system of second-class citizenship in which they personally benefited, middle-class blacks had extreme difficulty imagining any other strategy but to accept the promises of whites. Brough and his biracial commission were the only game in town. The sharecroppers' union had been wiped off the face of the earth along with hundreds of its members. In truth, it was a bit easy to call the black middle class names from the safety of the *Defender*'s office in Chicago.

James Monroe Cox provided a written response to the criticism. If Arkansas was such a "regular hell," why did blacks continue to choose to live there? The answer, of course, was that for the black elite it was no hell at all so long as it accepted white domination and shut its eyes to the horrors of Jim Crow. Cox wrote that after thirty-four years of living in Arkansas he knew it well. "In nearly all sections the most friendly feelings exist between the races."[6] If Arkansas whites were in denial about their treatment of blacks, it must be said that the capacity for denial by middle-class blacks exceeded that of whites. Thus, it was surely inevitable that Cox write William Pickens:

> Mr. Hill, if returned, will get a fair trial, he will not be molested. Governor Brough is one of the fairest executives in the country. The leading Negroes of Arkansas believe in him and he believes in the Negroes in Arkansas.[7]

Arkansas—a Regular Hell?

After the Elaine Race Massacres, there existed in the state an *Alice in Wonderland* quality on the subject among whites who agreed with their governor that the Elaine affair had been handled in superb fashion; the fact that whites had not stormed the county jail in Helena and roasted blacks was proof positive of Arkansas's eminently fair criminal justice system. For example, the *Arkansas Democrat* boasted, "The outside world ought to be informed, frequently and forcefully, that Arkansas stands with Phillips County" with regard to mob justice. Not only that, "Arkansas handled a negro insurrection . . . without the killing of a negro who was not actually menacing the lives of . . . white men."[8]

That blacks had been murdered in the cotton fields of Phillips County, that not a single white was ever arrested much less faced with prosecution, that blacks were tortured by the army and civilian jailers, that the property of the union leaders was stolen—these were all facts that could not and would not be discussed. This capacity to deny reality would continue to be a feature of Arkansas race relations through the advent of the modern civil rights movement. After the massacres in Elaine, it became a mantra that Phillips County had never had a lynching and never would.

That dubious claim went up in flames just two years later when in November a white mob of some "twenty-five to thirty men" took Will Turner from the sheriff and took him out of town and shot him. When his body was brought in by ambulance, a mob stopped the car and removed his corpse. "Burn the body!" the mob roared again and again. Turner's body was stripped naked and set on fire in front of the courthouse in Helena. Turner had been accused of assaulting a thirteen-year-old girl who had been on her way to work at a telephone exchange. As usual, lynching seemed to have a contagious quality to it. Just before Thanksgiving, to the south in Chicot County, Robert Hicks was found to have written an "insulting letter" to an eighteen-year-old white girl. A mob escorted Hicks four miles out of town and riddled his body with bullets. Then on November 25 a second lynching occurred in Phillips County. Dallas Knickerson, reported the *Arkansas Gazette,* "was shot by whites in Cypert for allegedly assaulting a white girl."[9] Needless to say, none of the murders warranted prosecution.

Lynching was not confined to Phillips County. Nothing would match the conduct of the Arkansas mob who lynched black tenant farmer Henry Lowery in 1921. After a dispute with his white landlord in Craighead County, Lowery killed him and his daughter and two sons on Christmas Day in 1920. Lowery was finally caught in Texas and brought back to the banks of the Mississippi River near the town of Wilson. There, he was chained to a log and literally cooked inch by inch in front of a mob of hundreds. "Every few minutes fresh leaves were tossed on the funeral pyre until the blaze had passed the negro's waist," read the story in the *Memphis Press.* "As the flames were eating away his abdomen, a member of the mob stepped forward and saturated the body with gasoline. It was then only a few minutes until the negro had been reduced to ashes." The *Memphis Press* reported on January 27, 1921, that "among those in the crowd were Lowery's tearful wife and children. . . . Lowery remained conscious for forty minutes. Not once did he whimper or beg for mercy." Lowery had tried to stuff ashes in his mouth in an effort to kill himself but they were kicked away by the mob.[10]

Two Separate Legal Tracks

For six of the Elaine Twelve, now miserably confined in the Marianna jail in Lee County in the Delta, the news of lynchings so nearby could not have been comforting. In fact it probably seemed something of a miracle to them that they were still alive. Certainly there had been prodigious legal efforts on their behalf to keep them that way. To summarize, the convictions of the six in the Marianna jail were overturned on a technicality. Now known collectively as the "Ware Defendants," they had been retried in May 1920 and convicted again. During the trial Colonel Murphy had become ill, and Scipio Jones had tried most of the cases. Legend would have it that during the trials in Helena he spent each night in a different house to avoid being attacked. Then in October Colonel Murphy died and was replaced by his partner Edgar McHaney who continued to collaborate on the cases with Scipio Jones. In December the convictions of the "Ware Defendants" were overturned again, this time because Murphy and Jones had preserved for appeal the legal argument there had been no blacks on the grand or petit jury. The major concern was now with the six men now known as the "Moore Defendants," whose convictions had been upheld by the Arkansas Supreme Court. Governor Brough had badly disappointed Scipio Jones by failing to commute a single one of the Moore defendants and left it to his successor, Thomas McRae, to set new execution dates on June 8, 1921. After a new flurry of legal petitions the cases of the Moore Defendants ended up before the U.S. Supreme Court in February 1923. In a groundbreaking decision that made constitutional history the Supreme Court ruled in favor of the Moore defendants, in effect suggesting that the original proceedings in Helena may have been a sham that had never been corrected by the Arkansas appellate courts. The Court said in part,

> If the case is that the whole proceeding is a mask—that counsel, jury, and judge were swept away to the fatal end

> by an irresistible wave of public passion—the right of the defendants to due process will have been violated.[11]

But instead of setting the Moore defendants free, the court sent the case back to the district court to allow the Moore defendants the opportunity to prove that the proceedings had denied them due process of law.[12]

Falling Out with the Republican Party

In the meantime the bottom continued to fall out for black Arkansans. For almost the last twenty years white Republicans in Pulaski County had made no secret of their desire to rid themselves of blacks, and 1920 was no exception. Not for the first time, whites announced that the convention for electing delegates would be in the Marion Hotel, which was segregated. After blacks led by E. C. Morris marched en masse from the Mosaic Templars to the hotel, someone turned off the electricity leaving them no option but to leave. But this time, the group returned to Mosaic Templars Building and selected for the first and only time their candidate for governor, Josiah H. Blount from Forrest City. Though, of course, having no expectations that Blount could win, blacks wanted to send the increasingly lily-white Arkansas Republican Party a message. Even a few whites voted for Blount, who received 15,627 votes to the Republican Party's candidate's 46,339. Democrat Thomas McRae received 123,604 votes. In fourteen counties, all in the Delta and including Pulaski, Blount outpolled the Republican candidate.

The Revival of the Ku Klux Klan

As blacks were wandering in the political wilderness, a disturbing new phenomenon was making its way to Arkansas. The Ku Klux Klan was back, albeit with a new style. Now reconstituted as a national organization steeped in hatred for all kinds of minorities in America, including Jews, Catholics, foreigners, and blacks, the new Klan cut across age and class divisions. According to the reporter for the *Arkansas Gazette* on February 10, 1922, the Klan attracted to a pasture four miles outside of Little Rock initiates that included "state, county, and city officials, preachers, lawyers, doctors, merchants [and] laborers." It would have been a chilling moment for a black to witness a gathering of 650 white men as they "knelt before the cross, kissed a Bible and an American flag . . . [and] swore absolute fealty to the tenets of the Klan."[13] The newest version of the Klan was begun in 1915, and though it was not nearly as violent as the old Klan, which terrorized blacks after the Civil War, it had more influence. Charles Alexander writes,

> Arkansas Klansmen only occasionally took action against "uppity" Negroes. . . . One of the surprising features of Klan history in Arkansas is not that men in white robes beat up a few Negroes, but that, considering the social acceptability of violence against Negroes, only a few were assaulted.[14]

Freedom: Scipio Jones Takes Charge

As the Klan was gaining political strength in Arkansas, it is somewhat ironic that at the same time the tide had begun to turn in favor of the Elaine Twelve and the other blacks who had entered plea bargains. What was becoming clear was now that H. F. Smiddy and T. K. Jones had signed affidavits detailing murder and torture of blacks white prosecutors suddenly were losing their appetite to go to court. In Lee County where the Ware Defendants were now being tried after a change of venue, prosecutors refused to bring the case to trial within the time allowed by law. On June 25, 1923, the Arkansas Supreme Court ordered that the six men be released from the Marianna jail. Fearful that they would be lynched, E. D. Robertson, the new presiding judge, put them on a train to Little Rock. Six of the men were free at last.

Rather than returning to federal court to attempt the risky

proposition of factually proving that the circumstances of the original proceedings had made a fair trial impossible, Scipio Jones, acting on his own, entered into an agreement to shorten the terms of the remaining Moore defendants. It required the cooperation of governor Thomas McRae, who finally honored the agreement on his last day in office on January 14, 1925, after a personal visit with Scipio Jones the day before. In the meantime the dogged persistence of Jones had also resulted in the early release of the other sixty-five men who had originally been pled guilty in the Elaine cases. The results of the work done by Jones, a man born into slavery, in ultimately achieving the release of all the Elaine defendants was nothing short of phenomenal and showed how one lawyer working within the system at the height of Jim Crow could obtain judicial relief for black men who were otherwise doomed. For those who would criticize Jones as a man who was too cozy with Jim Crow, it should be said that no other lawyer in the country at the time could have achieved his results. As the ultimate pragmatist, his goals for black people were freedom and physical safety in an era when they were neither free nor safe. Barely two years later, the most revolting lynching in the history of Little Rock would take place in the very center of the black community where Jones worshipped and worked.

The Last Lynching in Little Rock

It all began on April 12, 1927, when twelve-year-old Floella McDonald did not come home after last being seen in the Little Rock public library.[15] On April 30 the child's mutilated body was found a few blocks away stuffed in the bell tower of the First Presbyterian Church. Frank Dixon, the black church custodian, had discovered her body because of the odor coming from the tower. After a full day's interrogation, Frank Dixon's fifteen-year-old son, Lonnie, admitted to the crime. When the news of his confession was announced by Little Rock police chief Burl C. Rotenberry, thousands of whites raged in the streets at the police station, screaming for Lonnie Dixon to be turned over to them. The chief managed somehow to sneak father and son, hidden in the rumble seat of a new Studebaker, out of town. Thinking to calm the mob after it broke through police lines and beat at the front doors, Rotenberry permitted a delegation to conduct a futile search at the jail that only angered them more. Furious, the mob finally dispersed when a contingent of soldiers arrived at eleven in the evening. Instead of giving up and going home, a group stormed the state penitentiary known as "the Walls" where members of the Elaine Twelve had been forced to build their own coffins while they waited to be electrocuted. Breaking open the doors, 150 rushed onto the grounds where they were stared down by warden Todhunter who pointed a six-shooter at them. Even so, he also permitted a delegation of five to search the prison and satisfy themselves that Lonnie Dixon was not among the prisoners.

This successful effort to avert Dixon's lynching merely fed white rage. Seen as a traitor to the tenants of white supremacy, Chief Rotenberry received death threat upon death threat and went so far as to install a machine gun in his living room aimed at his front door. Soon, he took his family to Memphis to hide while mobs continued to roam the streets of Little Rock.

In truth, Lonnie Dixon might as well already have been dead, for the mayor of Little Rock Charles Moyer told the press, "Lonnie will not escape the electric chair. We [will] allow Lonnie's execution to be done according to law."[16] As at Elaine, white citizens were promised his trial would be a formality, and, in fact, this announcement seemed to cool down the hot-house atmosphere, so much so that the state's governor, John Martineau, felt it safe to leave Little Rock and travel to Van Buren to serve as guest of honor for the strawberry festival. His decision turned out to be a mistake, for Martineau was possibly the only publicly elected official in the state who had the strength of character and will to meet a howling, racist mob on its own terms. During the

Elaine affair, as a Pulaski county chancellor, he had issued a writ of habeas corpus to stop the execution of the Moore Defendants and had openly run as an anti-Klan candidate for governor when the Klan candidate, Tom Terral, had won going away.

Little Rock's blood lust would not be satisfied until it found a victim, and one presented himself the morning of May 4 at 10:30. John Carter, a thirty-eight-year-old black man who was later said to have mental problems, allegedly whacked Mrs. B. E. Stewart and her young daughter Glennie with an iron bar outside the city limits of Little Rock. A passing car scared Carter off. When this news got out, the mob again went wild and descended on the woods where Carter was said to be. Carter was quickly found and with policemen looking on was forced to jump off an automobile with a noose around his neck. Then his body was riddled with two hundred bullets. The horror had just begun.

The Shame of a City

Mrs. Stewart's husband recalled later that he then yelled, "Everybody that want to drag the nigger down Ninth Street and burn him, gimme your right hand." Every hand shot up, including those of the policemen present, Stewart added.

As had happened so often in the past, it was time once again to teach blacks a lesson, for the mob, of course, knew Ninth Street was the heart and soul of the black community. Carter's mangled body was first thrown across a Ford and driven into downtown Little Rock, where at Ringo and Fourteenth streets it was tied headfirst to another automobile. Then, with a motorcyclist leading the way, a twenty-six-block-long procession of vehicles full of snarling, hate-crazed whites drove through black neighborhoods in downtown Little Rock.

The response of the black community was dictated by absolute caution as whites went on their worst rampage in the capital city ever. Knowing whites as he did, Scipio Jones had always feared the worst, and the worst was coming to pass right in front of his eyes. Besides the deaths of possibly as many as three hundred blacks, the Tulsa Riot of 1921 had destroyed a thousand homes and burned thirty blocks of black-owned property. At noon Jones and nine black leaders called the sheriff to offer their assistance, a gesture that was refused. Their next move was to go from house to house and demand that no blacks respond in kind. No yelling, no guns, no going into the streets. No resistance of any kind so as not to give whites any excuse to go off on anyone.

Finally, to show their contempt for law and order and for the people who were responsible for it, the mob dragged Carter's body past city hall and then south on Broadway to Ninth Street where at seven in the evening between the two most significant landmarks in the black community—Bethel African American Episcopal Church, the largest black church at the time in Little Rock, and the Mosaic Templars Building—whites ignited a gigantic bonfire on the trolley tracks.

When a black man accidentally came toward the blaze, he was beaten unconscious but somehow survived. To feed the fire, the mob broke open the doors of the church and ripped out the pews. As had been their intention since shooting him, they threw Carter's body into the fire. For three hours the mob raged. The response of the city police was to remain inside. Finally, at nine o'clock the city council took action. It "deemed it best that our small force of men not be sent to the scene of the burning."[17]

Mayor Moyer went into hiding; no one could find him. The police chief was hiding with his family in Memphis. There was not a single city official who was going to risk his life regardless of what happened to the black community of Little Rock. Finally, Governor Martineau was reached by telephone and immediately ordered the National Guard to the scene to disperse the mob. As the guard approached from the east on Tenth Street from the Arsenal Building in McArthur Park, "the first thing they observed was a man directing traffic with a badly charred arm which had been broken from Carter's body."[18] Faced with armed troops, the mob melted away. Patrols throughout the night secured black neighborhoods. Martineau commanded a special train and was back in Little Rock by 4:30 in the morning. He had ordered troops to shoot if necessary.

The breakdown of law and order had been complete, and the *Arkansas Gazette* had the decency to admit it on May 5. Its headline read: "WITH OFFICERS MAKING NO ATTEMPT AT RESTRAINT MOB BURNS NEGRO'S BODY AND CREATES A REIGN OF TERROR."[19] At least some whites had felt shame at what had occurred, but not enough to take action. A grand jury was convened but returned no indictments. In defense of their cowardice, the mayor and sheriff said it was a good thing that no action to interfere with the mob had been taken; it would have simply resulted in people getting killed. Not needing to be said was that the "people" they were referring to were white.

There was still Lonnie Dixon to deal with, and given the actions thus far of Little Rock whites, giving him his day in court was not a pleasant prospect. In fact the legal community performed worse than it had in Helena. To decide who would represent him, attorneys drew names out of a hat on May 17, a mere two days before the trial. On May 19, 150 deputies surrounded the courthouse with guardsmen at the ready. The unlucky lawyers, Ector Johnson and J. E. Wills, did not bother to ask for a change of venue, nor did they appeal the verdict of the jury, which was out a total of only seven minutes, despite the fact that Dixon had retracted his confession and maintained his innocence despite rigorous cross-examination. Some two hours before he was executed on June 24, Lonnie Dixon said he was guilty.

The Reality of Jim Crow in an Urban Environment

In Little Rock, as in some other urban areas in the state with significant black populations, middle-class blacks continued to carve out a niche for themselves. In her history of

West Ninth Street in Little Rock, Berna J. Love documents the growth of West Ninth Street as an area for black businesses. In 1899 there were "twenty-two vacancies in the heart of the commercial district; by 1920 there were none. More substantial businesses like clothes cleaners had replaced bootblack street stalls. The commercial atmosphere and its atmosphere of economic success drew black professionals like Scipio Jones and physician G. W. Hayman among others. In 1920, eleven physicians had offices on West Ninth, the record for the street."[20] Yet in fact, the year 1920 seems to have been the high-water mark for black community business efforts in Little Rock. In an *Arkansas Historical Quarterly* article entitled "Mirage and Reality: Economic Conditions in Black Little Rock in the 1920s," Gene Vinzant documents that though there were continuing success stories among the black middle class during the 1920s there was no "substantial growth in the number of black-owned businesses over the course of the decade and that the economic condition of the typical black citizen remained bleak."[21] Vinzant shows that black business concerns in the 1920s were concentrated in personal services or small retail establishments. Blacks in Little Rock during this decade were completely absent from certain businesses including "bakeries, car dealerships, and clothing, department, furniture, hardware, and lumber stores." There were no accountants, architects, civil engineers, or insurance agents, nor were there any black-owned banks, hotels, or cotton brokerages in Little Rock. During the decade "despite the almost 13 percent increase in the black population, the number of lawyers dropped from ten to eight, while the number of physicians barely increased from nine to ten."[22] Vinzant's point is that though the black middle class had seemed poised for significant growth during the 1920s it did not occur. Racial segregation now affected blacks in the pocketbook. In an earlier era,

> Black businesses, such as black barbershops, dentists, blacksmiths, and retail stores were patronized by whites. Whites often relied on skilled blacks for carpentry, black-

> smithing, and bricklaying. Due to their strength in the Republican party, blacks had also benefited from government jobs, filling roles at the local, state, and federal level as railway postal clerks and policemen.[23]

Now, economic segregation held sway. Instead of working-and-middle-class blacks participating in an integrated economy, blacks bought from whites, but whites bought only from each other. As Vinzant point out, Jim Crow had as much to do about creating a servant class as it did about segregation.

Rural Blacks Go Their Own Way

Though middle-class blacks in the urban areas continued to align themselves with whites who held power after the Elaine Race Massacres, Mary Gambrell Rolinson has shown that many blacks in the Arkansas Delta, despite the destruction of the union, charted a much different course, emphasizing racial separateness, self-defense, race pride, and self-help as they embraced the philosophy of Marcus Garvey. Rolinson documents the widespread appeal the philosophy of Marcus Garvey had for Arkansas blacks of a certain class by showing the organizational breadth of the Universal Negro Improvement Association (UNIA), which, with forty-one of its forty-six "divisions" in the Delta, was an entirely different approach to race relations than taken by the black middle class. Thus, UNIA existed in towns up and down the Delta such as Blytheville, Wynne, Brickeys, and Cypert. Rolinson shows the membership base of UNIA to be overwhelmingly middle-aged married sharecroppers with families who identified themselves as black, rather than mulatto, and with strong church ties. In her dissertation entitled "The Garvey Movement in the Rural South, 1920–1927," Rolinson contends,

> The independence from whites espoused by the UNIA made more sense in the wake of the Phillips County slaughter than the cooperation or legal solutions which had failed before. The UNIA built its strength in the

> immediate vicinity of Elaine on both sides of the river less than two years later and amidst the rigorous appeal process underwritten by the national NAACP and pursued by a black lawyer named Scipio Africanus Jones. The theme which gained even more pertinence after the Delta incident, a desire for self-defense, lingered in the form of Garveyism.[24]

In short, the background of UNIA members was precisely that of the men and women who were meeting in the Hoop Spur church on the night of September 30, 1919. Rolinson establishes that the NAACP with its commitment to racial inclusiveness had little appeal in this period in the Arkansas Delta. Though the struggle for the Elaine Twelve begun in December 1919 with the motions for a new trial and climaxing in 1923 with the victory in *Moore v. Dempsey* gave maximum visibility and publicity to the NAACP, only "two branches" were organized in the Delta, "one of which was in an all-black town ten miles west of Memphis and the other formed in St. Francis County, which held at least four UNIA divisions."[25]

Given what had occurred at Elaine, it is not surprising that rural blacks would look to find their own strength in themselves. Middle-class blacks meeting with Governor Brough in Little Rock might be impressed by the governor's willingness to talk about racial problems, but Delta blacks now knew, as perhaps they had never allowed themselves to admit before, that they had only themselves to rely on. In a word, they did not trust whites nor had any reason to do so, whether they were in the governor's chair or the sheriff of Phillips County.

Rolinson notes that the Arkansas movement toward racial separation during this period had roots in the earlier back-to-Africa movement, previously discussed. The urge to escape the presence of whites and rely on self-help measures had long been part of black thinking in rural Arkansas. Membership in UNIA was not entirely a rural phenomenon. Pine Bluff and Fort Smith had middle-class members of UNIA, but it was blacks in the smallest hamlets who primarily joined UNIA. Perhaps as a result of the massacres of 1919, it was no accident that the

> UNIA enjoyed broad support among the blacks of Phillips County. . . . Numerous Arkansas UNIA divisions formed west of Helena in the interior of Phillips County and into Monroe County even further to the west. . . . Husbands and wives apparently attended meetings of the UNIA together at small places like Southland, Lexa, Oneida, Cypert, and Postelle.[26]

What is missing from the historical record are concrete examples of how membership in UNIA affected relationships with whites on a day-to-day basis and its general influence on race relations in the Delta. In John M. Barry's *Rising Tide,* the saga of the 1927 flood that devastated the Arkansas Delta as well as other states in its path, the author documents how powerful whites turned the Greenville, Mississippi, levee into a vast work camp where blacks received no pay and were not allowed to leave. It would be interesting to know how UNIA members reacted to such orders from whites. There is no equivalent study on the Arkansas side of the river though tantalizing details suggest similar situations occurred. Michael Dougan notes that Nathan Nunley, a black man,

> was shot dead by local road crew foreman Pearl Drowns, who was directing the crew filling sandbags. . . . Nunley protested when ordered to work by Drowns, saying he could not work because he had been sitting up all night with a critically ill wife and was on his way to get the doctor.[27]

Pete Daniel writes about the operation of the camps:

> Although no court case was brought to establish whether the relief camps served in effect as prisons where debt-ridden workers were held against their will, there is evidence that such was often the case.[28]

Even as planters were desperate to hold onto their black labor, there were individuals who shared what they had, regardless of color. Daniel quotes former Arkansan Albert

Tilbury, who fled the flood in Wilmot in 1927. Tilbury said that his father

> had eight or ten colored families on the place and two or three white families. Well, they all come up here with us, and we all stayed in the Deep Creek schoolhouse, and everybody cooked together and et together.[29]

Paternalism and Iron Rule in Mississippi County

Jeannie Whayne has shown that hundreds of African Americans seeking work and a safer environment in the Arkansas Delta found one in the gigantic Wilson operation in Mississippi County. In fact, as Whayne discusses, about the only decent opportunities for black newcomers to Mississippi County was to work for Robert E. Lee Wilson. "African Americans faced intense competition from whites for jobs in the lumber industry and for places on the growing number of plantations, competition that often erupted in violence."[30] Typically, the violence appeared to go only one way. Whayne writes,

> Whitecapping activities in Mississippi County resulted in no high-profile arrests or convictions, but references to violence against blacks and a "white only" mentality surfaced in south Mississippi County's major newspaper, the *Osceola Times*.[31]

At the time of his death in 1933 Robert E. Lee Wilson owned sixty-five thousand acres of land and a business operation that he ruled over like a feudal baron. Wilson's domain provides a window on the nature of paternalism and control exercised by plantation owners. Wilson, Whayne finds, "provided an attractive alternative to the uncertainty prevailing elsewhere in the violence-ridden Delta." For his African American tenants and sharecroppers he provided a black doctor, schools for their children, a black dance hall, and picnics. The housing for them "was far superior to that occupied by those on other plantations and many homesteaders." Perhaps even more important, if blacks were mistreated, Wilson took action on their behalf to see it did not happen again, firing white workers and reporting them to the sheriff. "I had Carpenter in my office this morning and I told him to get off the premises and stay off. . . . I am positive that no sons-of-bitches like this can stay on any of my property," Wilson wrote about one of his "unpaid deputy sheriffs" who had extorted money from one of his black sharecroppers.[32] Paternalism and self-interest went hand in hand. Money, paid in coupons issued by him and called "doodlum," rarely left his operation since it was redeemable only in his stores. It is not too much to say that Wilson, in terms of his tenants and sharecroppers, thought as himself as much like a king. He owned everything. As Whayne says, tenants and sharecroppers "had earned the right to possess the property while under his protection, but to leave the plantation with it was out of the question."[33] The plantation kept the accounts. One was always in debt for something. As the saga of William Pickens indicates, since the beginning of the sharecropper system after the Civil War, black families saw their only escape as coming in the middle of the night, and leaving Wilson's land was no different. A black organizer for the Southern Tenant Farmers' Union (STFU), George Smith, recalled that "his sister and family worked on the Wilson plantation in the 1920's, and when they decided to depart, they left all their possessions and slipped away late one evening."[34]

Wilson had no doubt about any outcome that involved his tenants. Hoping to get a settlement, Scipio Jones threatened to sue Wilson on behalf of two blacks and the estate of a third in "federal court for damages based upon alleged acts of peonage." Wilson told him to sue if he wanted. It made no difference to him that in one of the cases his labor agents were accused of beating to death a black who had tried to leave his plantation with a debt. "This is not true," Wilson replied. "You can take any steps that you see fit."[35] Apparently, Wilson had no doubt about the outcome of litigation in eastern Arkansas.

Black Politics, Urban and Rural

Nothing would illustrate the difference between the approach of the urban black middle class and Garveyites in the Delta during the 1920s than the appearance of the Arkansas Democratic Negro Association (ANDA) in 1928. Its founder, Dr. John Marshall Robinson, a native Mississippian, had passed the exam given by the Arkansas board of medical examiners and eventually set up a practice in Little Rock at Seventh and Main Street in 1905. Though one of the charter members of Little Rock branch of the NAACP in 1918, Robinson apparently was not active in the many black fraternal groups in Arkansas. While the Little Rock branch of the NAACP had supported the defense of the Elaine Twelve in 1919, it was not a militant organization at its conception, and as John Kirk has said, "initial interest in the NAACP soon faded away."[36] ANDA came into being at a meeting in England in Lonoke County attended by seventy-five blacks who organized the Smith-Robinson Club in support of the Democratic ticket of Alfred Smith and Joe T. Robinson. Elected president of the group, Robinson reflected the same accommodationist philosophy found in the rest of the black middle class. At the meeting, besides noting that blacks were "no longer slaves of the Republican Party," Robinson told the group,

> The Southern white man lends us money, feels our sorrows and helps bear our burden. He extends business courtesies and to a large degree makes possible our success. When we want a favor, we go to him and usually get it.[37]

While rural Delta blacks reacted to the Elaine Race Massacres by withdrawing from whites even further, the black middle class in Arkansas had watched the absolute unwillingness of the white authorities in Little Rock to protect them during the John Carter lynching and apparently concluded blacks had no choice but to try to involve themselves politically through participation in the only game in town—the

Arkansas Democratic Party. In his approach to politics in 1928, Robinson resembled no one so much as the deferential Scipio Africanus Jones, who had long fought for a place in the now mostly lily-white Republican Party. While Robinson's extreme politeness to whites may grate on the modern sensibility, as John Kirk points out,

> alienating the white power structure would have made any real chance of progress, certainly in making headway into the Democratic Party, impossible. . . . If offering an olive branch and genuine support for the cause could not bring the desired ends, other methods and devices of petition were to be available, too.[38]

Rebuffed by the Arkansas Democratic Party, which had no intention of allowing blacks to become Democrats, ANDA under Robinson's leadership filed suit and thought it had won a major victory when circuit judge Richard M. Mann, sitting for chancellor Frank H. Dodge, entered an order in November 1928 against the Arkansas Democratic Party prohibiting it from barring blacks from voting in the Democratic Party. This was overturned in August 1929 by Judge Dodge whose decision was upheld by the Arkansas Supreme Court. The U.S. Supreme Court refused to hear the case, and this issue would not be won for years. In retrospect, one may say that Robinson was ahead of his time. Yet as John Kirk notes, while Robinson and ANDA were pioneers in "the struggle for black participation in politics through the Arkansas courts," he and his followers

> stood for a participation in politics led mainly by the educated few. . . . There were no appeals for social equality or mass participation by blacks in politics . . . nor a strategic use of the black vote at elections. In this sense they reflected the more "accommodationist" and non-conflict seeking models associated with black leaders and organizations at the time.[39]

Robinson's leadership thus stands in sharp contrast to the approach of Arkansas followers of Marcus Garvey and lends support to Fon Gordon's criticism that the black elite of Arkansas attended to their own needs while essentially forsaking the concerns of poorer and less educated blacks. At the same time, ANDA's decision to challenge the "White Primary" rule through litigation was no small step in confronting white supremacy. As we shall see in chapter 11, ANDA endured and, as John Kirk has pointed out, paved the way for a successful challenge by others in the 1940s.

Interracial Sex and White Supremacy in the 1920s

As a final note to the end of the decade, despite lynching, fraud, and repression of Arkansas African Americans, there was one area of race relations that proved to be impervious to change, and that was interracial sex. In January 1929 the Arkansas Supreme Court handed down its decision in *Wilson v. State* in which the court reversed the trial court's conviction of Martha Wilson, a white woman, and Ulysses Mitchell, a black male. The court found that although the evidence was clear that these individuals had engaged in sexual intercourse on a number of occasions they had not broken the law. For them to be in violation of the anti-miscegenation law they had either to be married or to, in fact, actually live together. Since the evidence showed that Mitchell lived elsewhere, the court reversed. In his *Arkansas Historical Quarterly* article entitled "Most Shamefully Common: Arkansas and Miscegenation," Charles F. Robinson demonstrates that typically the Arkansas high court rarely found reason to sanction individuals who were alleged to have trespassed this provision of a law that had been on the books since 1837, a law that at most imposed a sentence of a year in jail. Robinson rightfully concludes that

> Arkansas's anti-miscegenation laws proved to be largely symbolic expressions of the desire of whites in the state to maintain a white over black social structure. . . . In Arkansas, interracial sex, even between black men and

> white women, did not automatically trigger the hangman's noose or the fervid, vicious anger of a white mob. Often, it produced nothing more than a relatively harmless vituperation.[40]

In their private relationships, white Arkansans were hardly consistent in their application of the color line, whether in the bedroom or in ordinary dealings with blacks. If anything, white supremacy meant the power to make exceptions for one's conduct. As long as disapproval was expressed, all was well in a state in which sexual hypocrisy was so much a part of the social fabric it was unremarkable.

CHAPTER 10

The Great Depression and the Southern Tenant Farmers' Union

The pain of the Great Depression in the 1930s was so deep and wide for some in the Arkansas Delta that for a brief time the misery it brought transcended race. On the surface at least, black and white came together in the movement known as the Southern Tenant Farmers' Union (STFU). Though the national financial markets had crashed in 1929, in Arkansas where so much of the economy and daily life revolved around agriculture it was not until the drought of 1930 that hunger and choking dust became an everyday companion. The pain was real not just on the plantations. While much attention has rightly been paid to the labor struggles on the plantations in the Delta during the Depression, historians have tended to overlook the final years of the former slaves whose lives were winding down in the towns during this era.

Tales from the Great Depression: The WPA Interviews

As suggested earlier, the interviews conducted by the employees of the Federal Writers Project provide glimpses of race relations in Arkansas through the depiction not just of slavery and succeeding eras but also of the times in which the interviews were conducted. Thus, a handy reference guide to the day-to-day economic horror in the relatively urbanized areas of Arkansas during the Great Depression for former slaves is George E. Lankford's *Bearing Witness*. While white Arkansans starved and suffered along with blacks during this era, the WPA interviews capture the results of a lifetime of exploitation of the former slaves. What is particularly poignant about the interviews is often the stoic recognition of their condition. Always the working poor, now they could no longer work and had next to nothing as they waited for death. The ravages of a lifetime of discrimination and contempt had left them aged, diseased, maimed, and starved. Augustus Robinson, seventy-eight, Little Rock:

> I worked for [Missouri Pacific] from 1891 to 1935. . . . although I worked for forty-four years and gave entire satisfaction, there has been a disposition to keep me from the pension. While in service [to the company] I had my jaw broken in two pieces and four front teeth knocked out by a piece of flying steel. . . . Also, I lost my right eye . . . when a hot cinder from the furnace flew in it while I was doing my regular work. Then I was ruptured because of the handling of heavy pieces of iron at my work. I still wear the truss. You can see the places where my jaw was broke and you can see where my teeth were knocked out. . . . I get a little assistance from the Welfare, and I get some commodities. If it wasn't for that, I would be broke up.[1]

Lucy White, seventy-four, Marianna, said, "I gets ten dollars and some little things to eat along. I say it do help out. I got rheumatism and big stiff j'ints (enlarged writs and knuckles)."[2] Frank Briles, eighty-two or eighty-three, Little Rock, said, "I am sick now. My head looks like it's goin' to bust open. . . . I ain't able to do no work now 'cept a little pittling here and there. I get a pension. It's been cut a whole lot."[3] George Benson, age eighty, Pine Bluff, said, "I been farmin' all my life and what I got? Nothin.' Old age pension? I may be in glory time I get it and then what would become of my wife?"[4]

Of course, whites suffered terribly in Arkansas during the Depression, as well, but not as much as blacks. In *Arkansas Odyssey,* Michael Dougan documents the statistics of discrimination during the Depression years. In Little Rock blacks totaled 20 percent of the city's population, but 54 percent of them could not find work. A white family on welfare received twelve dollars; a black family got only half of that. Few blacks were hired to work on WPA projects

> because the prevailing wage scale was so far above what blacks normally were paid that it was feared racial unrest would result. When WPA wages were reduced in the fall of 1935 from 35 cents to 20 cents an hour in response to the protests of planters, blacks protesting at the Little Rock WPA office were clubbed and arrested by the police.[5]

At least most black women were able to find something—over half were employed: 86 percent of them worked as maids earning two to five dollars weekly.[6] Their situation was not helped by their exclusion from the new Social Security Act.[7] Discrimination against blacks covered every facet of daily life but perhaps nothing quite so scandalous as in education. Whites simply stole funds intended for black schools. The town of Crawfordsville in Crittenden County spent one dollar on black education for every fifty-seven on whites. The disparity in Crittenden County would continue to be so great it would become a national scandal years later.

The position of whites that blacks were going to remain subservient was not limited to the Delta. Arkansas's only Pulitzer Prize–winning poet, John Gould Fletcher, took it upon himself to write the *Nation* in 1933: "We do no Negro to death because of his political affiliations. But we are determined, whether rightly or wrongly, to treat him as a race largely dependent upon us, and inferior to ours."[8]

Hunger Everywhere You Look

No matter how much whites discriminated against blacks, nothing could protect them against the Depression. Though it would be the town of England in Lonoke County that would get the national headlines, in *Arkansas and Modern America: 1930–1999* Ben Johnson III states that "dozens of people raided stores in Conway, Forth [*sic*] Smith and Pine Bluff to seize foodstuffs."[9] In England in January 1931 town authorities avoided a "food riot" by an angry crowd of five hundred by opening grocery stores to them. After the *New York Times* ran the story, the national Red Cross between January and March "provided over three million dollars to feed 180,000 families," but it would be the same old story: the white leaders in Arkansas had concerns that the nation's charity would harm blacks. As Ben Johnson writes,

> In eastern Arkansas, planter-dominated committees balanced charity with labor management. One committee report revealed the familiar assumptions. We do not believe we should give enough food to be comfortable for this would destroy the incentive of our negroes to work and might even ruin our labor force for years.[10]

The Arkansas Delta

The shortsightedness of the Arkansas planter class and its allies was hopelessly time worn but, indeed, legendary. To every problem there was the same solution: a docile black labor force was the cure-all. This time, however, keeping blacks hungry enough to stay in the fields and accept whatever whites wanted to give them was not enough. The reality was that conditions in the Delta resembled the economic, political, and judicial horrors usually associated with totalitarian countries. The American dream of pulling one's self up by the bootstraps into self-sufficiency and ownership of land had turned into a nightmare of poverty and exploitation not just for blacks but for whites, as well. In *Arkansas Odyssey,* Michael Dougan offers quotations from a number of individuals who had seen something of the world.

> "I have never seen worse living conditions or lower standards of living, even in backward sections of

> Europe," wrote free-lancer writer Fred Kelly. . . . "I have traveled over most of Europe and part of Africa, but I have never seen such terrible sights as I saw yesterday among the sharecroppers in Arkansas," wrote Naomi Mitchinson, an English novelist.[11]

What visitors uniformly saw were sickly, poorly fed men, women, and children who survived without basic medical or dental care and who often dressed in clothing that offered little protection against the cold, damp Delta winters.

> Sharecroppers lived in box houses, thrown together from rough lumber without studding. Screen wire and electricity were nonexistent. Houses were rarely painted and had newspapers or colorful pictures tacked to the walls to keep out the cold. The family lived around the cook stove, ate from an oil cloth covered table, and slept as many to an iron frame bed as family size dictated.[12]

The problem for the planter class and its allies was that squeezing its black labor was no longer enough. Whites were joining the sharecropper class at an alarming pace. Ben Johnson reminds the reader that in 1930 80 percent of Arkansans dwelled in villages on small farms. With the drought that year, Red Cross workers captured third-world images in eastern Arkansas: in the cabins of tenants children were "barefoot and without decent clothes, no meal, no flour in the bin, ragged children crying from hunger . . . nothing but hunger and misery . . . far worse than the [1927] Mississippi Flood." A visit to thirty-seven shacks in St. Francis County by the Arkansas Red Cross director revealed only two families with milk.

The Arkansas Red Cross reported that it did not have enough supplies to take care of the "estimated 100,000–200,000 families without subsistence."[13] The number of cotton bales harvested was down 40 percent from the previous year, and prices plummeted by 42 percent. Capitalism did not seem to be working, and as Johnson shows, in stressful times blacks were the usual targets. In August 1930, in an action reminiscent of the days of "whitecapping," whites who wanted public works jobs "fired at a group of black road construction workers near Lonoke."

At the same time, education was minimal or non-existent, and even where there were schools, it was often impossible to get to them because the roads were impassable. In addition entire families worked the fields to maximize what little income was available. As difficult as conditions were, African Americans suffered "disproportionately." Dougan notes that reported black infant mortality was at least twice as high as that of whites and probably much higher. He writes, without exaggeration that in the Arkansas Delta, "sharecropping stood on the brink of revolution there in 1932."[14]

The Federal Government and the Farm Crisis

A political revolution in America was about to take place: the notion that the federal government had to intervene in the lives of ordinary Americans to deal with a national catastrophe. Help was coming to the nation's agriculture in the form of a federal program created by the administration of Franklin Roosevelt. Unfortunately for black as well as white sharecroppers, those in power in the state were determined to control the aid coming into the state for agriculture with predictable results. However they tried to rationalize their actions, landowners in Arkansas simply stole federal money intended for destitute sharecroppers. In 1935 Mary Myers, a federal investigator for the Agricultural Adjustment Administration (AAA), came to Arkansas and "secured hundreds of scrawled statements from cheated sharecroppers and tenants."[15] "At cotton picking time he [landlord C. E. Hughes] brought some blank sheet of paper for us to sing [sign] ant told us we had to sing them or not sell cotton. . . . Our pardie [parity] money we have not got it."[16] In St. Francis County sharecropper Dorothy Real described what happened to her husband's check after the first one was taken by his landlord. "My husband couldn't read or write. I tried to teach him but he just couldn't learn." With the arrival of his next check at the county agent's office, in a room "crowded with white riding bosses from all of the plantations," his check was snatched out of his hands, and he was told to sign it over to his plantation owner.[17] Quoting directly from Myers's report, Michael Dougan writes that the interaction between planters and sharecroppers "was one long story of human greed."[18]

The Agricultural Adjustment Act resulted in fewer tenants but not in the way the federal government had intended it. Nan Woodruff observes, "In some ways planters in the 1930s used the AAA to legitimize actions they had always engaged in, such as driving sharecroppers from the land after they had planted the cotton, then hiring day labor to pick it."[19]

The Agricultural Adjustment Administration was supposed to help both planters and sharecroppers alike by taking land out of production, decreasing the amount of produce in order to raise prices farmers could get for their crops. Financial payments were supposed to be made to both planters and sharecroppers. Within the federal government itself a battle was waged by the legal department in the Department of Agriculture that advocated an interpretation of the AAA to reduce the arbitrary power of planters to evict their tenants. Politics won out. Agricultural secretary Henry Wallace, who had been a hero to many because of his support for the poor tenant farmer, bowed to pressure from Franklin Roosevelt and "purged the liberals after they attempted to prohibit tenant evictions." The secretary charged that the dissidents were motivated by "social preconceptions."[20]

The Southern Tenant Farmers' Union

In Arkansas the Southern Tenant Farmers' Union was started most improbably in 1934 in Tyronza in Poinsett County by two white socialists, H. L. Mitchell, the owner of a dry cleaners business, and Clay East, who owned a service station. The two men had originally worked together to help

Poinsett County tenants who had been excluded from the Civil Works Administration program. Famously, the first meeting in July 1934 included eleven whites and seven black tenants who came together at the Sunnyside schoolhouse on the Hiram Norcross plantation in Poinsett County. Much has been made of the interracial nature of this union, which has become a legend in working class circles, and certainly the willingness of members of both races to be identified in a common cause in an era in which white supremacy ruled with such fervor was unique. It is also noteworthy that one of the founders was Ike Shaw, who had been a member of the ill-fated union at Elaine. Shaw was remembered to have said, "As long as we stand together, black and white together in this organization, nothing can tear it down."[21]

A Garveyite's View of the STFU

Mary Gambrell Rolinson contrasts the interracial solidarity expressed by Ike Shaw with the growing disillusionment of Britt McKinney, an indispensable black organizer of the STFU. Despite Shaw's idealism, in order to maintain interest and keep both races satisfied with the union, STFU leaders felt they had no choice but to use black organizers to attract black members and white organizers to attract white members. Since blacks constituted one-half to two-thirds of the members of the thirty-thousand-person union, McKinney was a key but contentious figure who appears to have held a complex set of beliefs about the efficacy of working with whites, most of whom he distrusted with the exception of H. L. Mitchell. Rolinson shows that McKinney felt that too much money of the union was going into administrative expenses and travel for the leaders and not into helping the rank and file. At one point in 1937 McKinney was encouraged to attend an NAACP conference but had considered raising money to send himself to a UNIA conference in Toronto. This led to a call for his expulsion by J. R. Butler, who claimed he was attempting to divide the organization on racial lines. As a

Garveyite, McKinney may well have preferred an organization that was separate from whites. Correspondence to a friend reveals the depth of his distrust.

> I am aware that the forces are working to stop us from trying to help ourselves, showing all sorts of scar [*sic*] crows, waving at us the Elaine Riot and the KKK. I am sure they know lot about both. For they are the very element who made us both. We have always been tools in the hands of those who have kept us down.[22]

Whatever original hopes white and black union leaders had that interracial cooperation would be enough to deal with planters and their allies would soon be in doubt. Though obviously different in important ways, the Progressive Farmers and Household Union of America in Elaine in 1919 and the STFU of the 1930s elicited the same oppressive and violent response from the Delta white power structure.

Dealing with the Union: Intimidation and Violence and More Violence

In *Cry from the Cotton: The Southern Tenant Farmers' Union and the New Deal,* Donald Grubbs chronicles the intimidation and violence visited upon both races for their participation in the STFU.

> It began on a chilly weekday afternoon in the middle of January, [in 1935] with a number of landlords and lawmen sprinkled among the hundreds of farm tenants gathered in Marked Tree's town square to hear STFU spokesmen tell of [New Deal Agricultural Secretary] Henry Wallace's promise to begin an investigation of AAA operations in the Delta. [23]

In 1935, it made no difference to whites in authority in the Arkansas Delta what, if any, sympathy the plight of the sharecropper aroused in Washington. On the contrary, what lawmen and landlords heard and saw that afternoon in Marked Tree infuriated them. It was their worst nightmare coming true, for the crowd heard Britt McKinney introduced as "Mister McKinney" in total disregard for the customs of white supremacy. Worse, McKinney had the nerve to announce that the union had received "telegrams of support" from "European countries." A year later a planter remembered, "He [Ward Rodgers, a white organizer] stressed Russia . . . [and] talked along there about the people starving to death and of the awful conditions of the people that were there and just that general line of Communistic talk."[24]

The first casualty was the First Amendment. Ward Rodgers was soon arrested for "criminal anarchy." The prosecutor informed a hastily convened jury that Rodgers was "an organizer for the Communist Party and is advocating racial equality right here in Arkansas."[25] Reminiscent of the trials in Helena in 1919, the jury spent a total of ten minutes deliberating and returned with a verdict of guilty. Justice of the peace J. C. McCroy sentenced Rogers to six months in jail and gave him a fine of five hundred dollars and court costs. The white response did not end there. In short order, at a black church outside of Gilmore and then again later in the jail, sheriff's deputies beat Lucien Koch and Bob Reed for "addressing a mixed meeting. " In Marked Tree, Clay East was forced to leave his home; Mary Hillyer, a member of the League for Industrial Democracy, was forced to leave the same town. Britt McKinney's home was fired on, his two sons wounded. Grubbs notes that "several STFU meetings in Negro churches were disrupted and most of the members clubbed, without regard for sex or age."[26] After a failed attempt to murder John Allen, the black secretary of the STFU, law officers in Cross County "pistol-whipped" a woman who supposedly knew his whereabouts. In the process, her ear was severed.[27] In addition to Clay East, many of the STFU leaders fled for their lives across the state line to Memphis. Ignoring the violence of its town's citizens, the *Marked Tree Tribune* saw the situation differently. "Citizens Ask Reds to Leave" read a headline.[28]

"There ain't goin' to be no speakin' here"

When Socialist leader Norman Thomas[29] began his speech on behalf of the STFU in Mississippi County in March 1935 , he was dragged from the stage by men wearing deputy sheriff badges and told,

> There ain't goin' to be no speakin' here. We are citizens of this county and we run it to suit ourselves. We don't need no Gawd-damn Yankee Bastard to tell us what to do with our niggers and we want you to know that this is the best Gawd-damn county on earth.[30]

Though Thomas was not hurt, in Birdsong in Mississippi County lawmen beat up other members of his entourage.[31]

At Elaine, the sharecroppers union had been destroyed before it had ever made a single demand. However, the STFU had important and effective allies come to its aid from the beginning, including the American Civil Liberties Union (ACLU), which agreed to represent Ward Rogers and others. The STFU was not going down without putting up a fight. Despite arrests and repeated acts of violence against its members, in Crittenden, Cross, Mississippi, Poinsett, and St. Francis counties the first strike called by the STFU kept thousands of cotton pickers out of the fields for a time at the height of the harvest in 1935. It resulted for some in a temporary raise of wages from forty to sixty cents per hundred pounds picked to seventy-five cents.

More effective than beating union members was evicting them and daring them to do anything about it. With increased membership because of its successful strike in 1935, the STFU geared up for another one the next year, but the planters were ready for them. In response to union activity "planters blacklisted STFU members all over the Delta . . . evicting thousands of families."[32] Additionally, the white power structure in the affected counties escalated the violence and increasingly was more brazen about how it went about it.

Even if it did not seem to make a difference at first, the tactic of focusing the glare of publicity on the Arkansas Delta seemed the STFU's best hope. When plantation owner C. H. Dibble, who farmed near the town of Parkin, ordered approximately one hundred persons off his land by January 16, the union set up a "tent colony" on the side of the road. An observer driving through the Delta noted in January 1936, "The utter brutality and callousness with which the planters are throwing off families is beyond belief."[33] During the evening of January 16, 1936, two deputy sheriffs, Paul Peacher and Everett Hood, burst into St. Peter's Methodist Church near Earle in Crittenden County to break up a union meeting. When member James Ball grabbed for his gun, Peacher hurled him to the floor and arrested him and charged him with intent to commit murder. The two lawmen came back to the meeting and began shooting. Two men were wounded in the back as they ran for their lives. Law enforcement arrested three members.[34] The lawmen were not done because they soon found out that Willie Hurst, a black man, had not only witnessed what had taken place but had said he would testify as to what he had seen. According to Donald Grubbs, Peacher and Hood unsuccessfully tried to intimidate Hurst into giving a statement that cleared them.[35] Soon afterwards Willie Hurst was killed by two masked men who were said to resemble Hood and Peacher. No one was ever charged. With the witness no longer alive who would have been able to prove that he was innocent, James Ball was convicted and ordered to serve seven years in prison. The sentence was later reduced to a year by the Arkansas Supreme Court, which also "reprimanded Deputy Hood for violating the right of free assemblage."[36] According to Donald Grubbs, it was the only time that a conviction of an STFU member was not overturned on appeal.

The reign of terror against sharecroppers continued. Within twenty-four hours of the beating of James Ball, Deputy Hood led a gang composed of riding bosses as well as planters into a meeting of approximately 450 black sharecroppers outside of Earle at the Providence Methodist Church in Crittenden County. Grubbs writes,

> They immediately began slugging the sharecroppers with ax handles and pistol butts, guffawing loudly as they cracked the skulls of screaming women and children. Deputy Hood promised one of the leaders, Howard Kester, "There's going to be another Elaine Massacre, only the next time we'll kill whites as well as the niggers."[37]

National Politics and Friends in Arkansas

In fact, there would be no need for another Elaine massacre to destroy the union. Had there been a wholesale slaughter, it might have been the one event that could have kept it viable. The leaders of the STFU were much more effective in focusing outside attention on the union than conducting strikes or bargaining with planters, but the deck was heavily stacked against them. Political considerations carried the day. President Roosevelt had no intention of embarrassing his loyal majority leader in the U.S. Senate, Joe T. Robinson of Arkansas, himself a planter. For his part, Robinson wanted to avoid a congressional investigation of the violence in Arkansas and thus exerted so much pressure on his fellow planter, Governor J. M. Futrell, that Arkansas's chief executive conducted his own inquiry in 1936, with predictable results. After hearing complaints from sharecroppers, Futrell advised, "You had better listen to the white folks who have always been your friends. . . . There are people who will get you into trouble if you listen to them."[38]

Governor Futrell's remarks during his visit to Earle in Crittenden County illustrate the iron grip of white supremacy within the state and, not incidentally, how whites in power used their own interpretation of history to buttress their position. Futrell made reference to the "Elaine affair" and warned blacks away from the union. Ignoring the lack of credible evidence that whites had ever supervised blacks in a plot to kill planters at Elaine, he repeated the discredited version of the Committee of Seven that "negroes under the guidance of the white men had planned to dispatch several owners of land in that country. A fortunate circumstance prevented the killing of a half dozen landowners within the same few minutes."[39] The point of all this, he said, was that white planters rightly feared unions. After all, the "Negro is easily excited into the most unbridled violence. This has happened in eastern Arkansas."[40] Given the governor's private views of sharecroppers, his remarks came as no surprise. Michael Dougan writes, "In correspondence with Senator Robinson, Futrell enunciated his belief that tenant farmers were sub-human."[41]

It just so happened that the president of the United States was scheduled to make a visit to Little Rock in the summer of 1936 to praise his ally Senator Joe T. Robinson and the state of Arkansas. Union leaders made an effort to meet with the president but were not allowed to get within "100 ft." of President Roosevelt, who never mentioned the dire circumstances of the sharecroppers in the eastern part of the state.[42] Despite the idealism that provided the impetus for so much of the New Deal legislation, practical politics dictated the agenda of the president's visit. Though the investigative report made at the direction of Governor Futrell was labeled a "whitewash" by the STFU, it did acknowledge that "the legal system was being abused by planters."[43]

The Importance of National Publicity to the STFU

An incident occurred in June 1936 that brought nationwide attention to the STFU and the conditions in which its members lived. According to Donald Grubbs, a black member of the union, Frank Weems had been beaten into unconsciousness by a group of whites while one of them held a shotgun on him. When his friends came to collect his body, it was nowhere to be found. Law enforcement in the Delta claimed the STFU was pulling a trick when the union sought to capitalize on his disappearance because of the national publicity generated by the incident. Hoping to keep the interest in the story alive, the union persuaded Reverend Claude Williams, then one of the most famous preachers in the South, to give the funeral sermon for the missing man. Stopping at the STFU office, Williams met a young, white woman by the name of Willie Sue Blagden who asked him to allow her to go to the funeral. Blagden, it so happened, was from a prominent Memphis family. She and Williams stopped at a drugstore in Earle when they were ordered outside by five white men in "summer whites." All piled into Williams's car and headed out into the countryside. Williams was ordered to take off his shirt and was flogged with "harness straps," and then the five men made the fatal error of spanking Willie Sue Blagden. As Grubbs notes, for decades blacks had been murdered, raped, tortured, and terrorized, "but now the planters had made the mistake of beating a minister and smacking a white woman's posterior."[44]

The incident, involving the sacred honor of white Southern womanhood, provided the basis for the media to take another look at what was occurring in the Arkansas Delta. Their conclusions were not flattering. For example, the headline in *Time* ran, "Slavery in Arkansas."[45] Donald Grubbs writes that

> more than any other single event, the beating made the nation demand action on behalf of sharecroppers; little more than six weeks elapsed between the bruising of Miss Blagsden's bottom and the appointment by President Roosevelt of a special commission on farm tenancy, and the proximity in time was not incidental.[46]

The issue of whether slavery still existed in Arkansas had to do with the practice of Delta planters taking convicted prisoners and working them on their plantations until their fines were paid off. Actually, this practice was similar to the infamous convict lease system that had existed at the state level. The STFU and its civil rights allies argued repeatedly that this practice was nothing but a form of peonage, in other words, debt slavery. The white power structure in the Delta saw absolutely nothing wrong with this practice since it had existed in one form or another in Arkansas since the formal end of slavery. After all, planters desperately needed human labor to get their crops in the ground and then get them harvested. Why shouldn't prisoners work to pay off their fines? A Crittenden County grand jury was presented with this very issue in the fall of 1936 and refused to issue a single indictment, but quite sensationally a day later a federal grand jury filed an indictment against "Paul D. Peacher, Deputy Sheriff of Crittenden County, for 'aiding and abetting in holding in slavery.'"[47]

A Federal Indictment and a Strong-Willed Judge

Though the STFU and other organizations had been complaining for years against the practice of peonage in the Delta, it took a complete outsider whose personal investigation in the summer of 1936 finally resulted in an indictment in a case involving the operation of a private prison farm in Arkansas. Dr. Sherwood Eddy, an official of the national Young Men's Christian Association (YMCA), had decided he would come to Arkansas and personally investigate Peacher's operation and had gone out to his farm. While Peacher was not present, Eddy interviewed thirteen black prisoners who all told him they had been charged and convicted of "vagrancy," despite the fact they were all long-time residents of the area. Some were even property owners. Not a single one had an attorney appointed to represent him, nor could any of them tell Eddy exactly why he had been convicted. None of these facts impressed Fred Isgrig, the U.S. attorney for the eastern district of Arkansas, who himself was a "prominent member of Little Rock's conservative Planter's Club."[48] He did nothing with this information.

Despite the fact that President Roosevelt had been loathe in June to criticize men like Joe T. Robinson in their own backyard, the president now made sure that complaints about sharecropper treatment went to his Department of Justice in Washington and no longer to the Department of Agriculture, which had proved powerless to influence events. By August 1936 George P. Jones, an U.S. attorney from Minnesota, was suddenly in charge of the grand jury investigation, and the "good ole boy" system was, at least temporarily, no longer in operation in the eastern district of the federal courts in Arkansas.

Jones, working with the full cooperation of the U.S. attorney general's office in Washington, still had to convince a federal jury sitting in Jonesboro in Craighead County that Peacher's operation was illegal, and that was going to be no easy matter, given the racial attitudes in Arkansas. Few white Arkansans in 1936 would have disagreed with the statement that one way or another most black people had to be made to work, or in the words of Peacher's defense attorney N. S. Lamb, "You can't expect negroes in a short time among civilized people to rise to the level of good citizens."[49]

It was not enough to have an aggressive U.S. attorney on the case: if the presiding judicial officer was not sympathetic to the claim that a form of slavery still existed in Arkansas, a peonage case would have gone nowhere. But it so happened that the federal judge in the case was John Martineau. Now, still serving as the guardian of racial justice seldom seen in the Delta, Martineau acted again. According to Michael Dougan, he bluntly told the jury that "every circumstance in this case points to the guilt of this man."[50] As Donald Grubbs writes, "the jury of Jonesboro white men was so reluctant to convict Peacher that Judge John Martineau all but directed the inevitable guilty verdict."[51]

Though Peacher's fine of $3,500 was quickly paid off by his fellow planters, two historians who have written about this era contend that this verdict and the resulting publicity proved a turning point in the history of peonage. Grubbs states that "it so discredited the practice of peonage that private prison farms began to disappear everywhere. Before World War II began, Arkansas, for example, outlawed such farms altogether."[52] Similarly, Michael Dougan writes that the victory "led to the abandonment of some of the worst abuses of local law enforcement. A new state law in 1938 banned the hiring out of county prisoners, but the practice of loaning seems to have continued."[53]

Once again, outside pressure caused whites in power in Arkansas to ameliorate practices and conditions that had long harmed its reputation. In the fall of 1936 Governor Futrell appointed a group within the state to study tenancy and was cornered into publicly stating that two "STFU spokesmen [were] to consider themselves members of the commission."[54] The report that was eventually issued by the commission was a significant document that not only recognized that farm tenancy "has become a serious menace to American institutions" but also recommended far-reaching changes. Basic reforms in the relationship between planters and tenants were addressed. For example, "tenants should have standard written contracts with their landlords and the right to prompt, impartial arbitration of landlord-tenant disputes."[55]

Like so many things in America affected by technology and the bottom line, these matters, so urgent at the time, were soon to be ushered off the stage as farming was revolutionized, and tenancy in Arkansas and elsewhere in the country became a historical footnote. The reforms were, in the main, given lip service, but tenancy was soon to disappear anyway. Like farm tenancy, the STFU, never a dues-paying proposition because of the poverty of its members, would, too, in a short time become a memory and a field for scholars. Always carried by outside contributions, the STFU unsuccessfully sought survival through affiliation with the mainstream labor movement because it had no internal resources of its own to carry it forward. Though it struggled on, by 1938 it had begun to fade away in earnest.[56]

From the perspective of landowning farmers, there was nothing guaranteed about the sharecropping system. Their creditors, the banks, were always in line to be paid. Margaret Jones Bolsterli remembered her father simply refused

> to mortgage the land for furnish money and listed as collateral worn-out combines and cultivators and hay balers that had not worked for years. The responsibility my father had for lending his money carefully, because he would be called upon in turn to pay it back to the bank, led to extreme parsimony when it came to letting tenants have what they asked for. I remember particularly long discussions he had with a tenant named Arthur Thomas, who had a large family, always made money for us, and consequently had a lot of requests that he, quite reasonably, thought should be listened to, but that my father met with almost pathological skepticism.[57]

It is little wonder why there was such hatred of the system from both sides of the economic equation.

CHAPTER 11

The Beginning Challenge to Jim Crow

Given the grim statistics of most black life in Arkansas during the 1930s, it is frankly difficult to imagine that the next decade would see significant challenges to Jim Crow. In fact, had there not been two black communities, themselves unequal, challenges to Jim Crow would have been unthinkable. Though tiny in number and as a percentage of the black population, the so-called "black elites" in Arkansas persisted in their efforts to achieve their vision of the American dream.

The Views of Samuel S. Taylor

Writing in the 1930s in a draft of a publication of the Urban League of Little Rock, black researcher Samuel S. Taylor, who had done graduate work at Columbia University in New York, noted as had Charlotte Stephens in her WPA interview the vast class differences between blacks. "The Little Rock Negro has his social strata. At the top stand the old and established families, and at the bottom stand the denizens of the slums, and there is little in common between them."[1] The difficulty for African Americans was how few of them had a toehold on middle-class life. By 1940, John Kirk writes, no more than 3 percent of blacks in Little Rock belonged to this "top" social stratum made up of black physicians, pharmacists, dentists, lawyers, college professors, teachers, ministers, and businessmen. Just below this group were skilled blue-collar workers.[2]

Given his education, obvious intelligence, and his background as an observer of race relations in Arkansas (Taylor's interviews of former slaves as a WPA interviewer were considered the best in the state), Taylor's views and findings are noteworthy if for no other reason than he was the only black commentator in the 1930s on the subject of race in Arkansas. However, much more important than his uniqueness as an African American researcher and writer was his ability and candor on the subject of race. What united the two classes, in Taylor's opinion, was fear of whites.

> The Negro in Little Rock, like the Negro everywhere, lives with the ever present dread that some normal free action of a well meaning Negro may be given a racial interpretation or that the abnormal act of some Negro criminal or moron may be considered typical of the Negro race. There are Negroes in Little Rock who . . . believe that Negroes will not be given justice where serious white interests demand otherwise. There are some outstanding cases of Caucasian justice. But the feeling lingers. There is little bitterness and little hate, but th[ere is] a good deal of distrust and fear.[3]

As noted in the introduction, blacks in Pulaski County would confirm the same profound feelings of distrust seventy-eight years later. Even though they rarely spoke about it publicly or perhaps even to each other, blacks in central Arkansas no more forgot the last lynching in Little Rock than blacks in the Delta forgot the Elaine Race Massacres of 1919. But as Joel Williamson has emphasized, even more devastating to the black community than white violence was black-on-black crime during Jim Crow. Acutely aware of what black crime was still doing to his community, Taylor wrote,

> Acts of violence committed by Negroes against members of their race are frequent in the community. . . . Many Negroes carry knives and other dangerous weapons, and brawls resulting in serious and sometimes fatal injuries are common.[4]

In his report Taylor called "for a stricter law enforcement program among Negroes and vigilant patrolling of Negro night spots." He observed that for the first six months in 1938 slightly over 36 percent of those convicted of crimes in Little Rock were black, but only 24 percent of the population was black. Yet even as blacks were convicted at a disproportionate rate, there seemed to be a double standard at work.

> Ordinarily, Negro crimes against Negroes are not severely punished. There seems to be an attitude of indulgence on the part of the community toward Negro crimes not committed against whites, and this tolerance has resulted in increasing lawlessness and disorderliness at beer parlors and other places of recreation.

A Servant Class and the Cause of Black Poverty

Much of the problem in Little Rock and North Little Rock, as Taylor saw it, was that whites seemed determined, as much as possible, to maintain a servant class composed of African Americans. Almost half of all employed black men and women were employed in personal and domestic service jobs, making between two and five dollars a week.[5] Nearly 86 percent of employed black women were domestic or personal service workers. Over half of all adult black women were employed and represented almost 40 percent of all the women in the workforce. Taylor concluded that

> the problems of the Negro wage earners in Little Rock and North Little Rock lie at the root of virtually all other basic difficulties of the Negro's existence—illiteracy, lack of proper food, inadequate clothing, unsanitary homes. The most serious of these problems are . . . low wages, . . . narrow range of available jobs, lack of opportunity for advancement and limited facilities for training or apprenticeship.[6]

Taylor's report also documented the serious health problems resulting often from poverty in the black community.

The 1930 census revealed the disproportionately high black death rate in Little Rock and North Little Rock. For example, blacks, who constituted only one fourth of the population, were nearly 60 percent of the deaths from tuberculosis. "The low economic level of the Negro is a fundamental factor in the virulence and spread of tuberculosis. Low wages and unemployment force the Negro family into cheap, unsanitary living quarters."[7]

Taylor did not avoid controversy in presenting other statistics even if they gave ammunition to whites. "Of the 402 cases of syphilis in Pulaski County reported to the State Bureau of Vital Statistics in 1938, 322 were Negro." But Taylor knew this statistic was only the tip of the iceberg.

> Because not all cases of syphilis and gonorrhea are reported to health authorities, available statistics do not indicate the true extent of venereal disease either in Pulaski county or the two cities with which this survey is directly concerned.[8]

The epidemic in sexually-transmitted diseases among blacks most likely had been a public-health problem for decades but not one whites appeared to care about, just as they did not seem to be concerned about how many blacks lived in poverty and their part in causing such poverty. Slavery's abolishment had meant whites felt no responsibility for black welfare except in those cases where bonds of paternalism had created a sense of obligation. Of course, blacks lived in shacks and contracted preventable diseases. In the mind of whites, that's just how blacks lived.[9]

Turning to education, Taylor was quick to admit that black schools in Little Rock in the 1930s were the best in the state and paid better salaries, but blacks

> receive salaries averaging only slightly more than half those paid white teachers. The pupil-load is too heavy for efficient work; at Dunbar Junior and Senior High School teachers daily conduct as many as 7 classes of from 40 to 50 pupils each, as well as supervising a study hall which may contain as many as 300 pupils.[10]

How much of Taylor's work was read and absorbed by whites is not known, but it seems to have attracted little attention. Soon Taylor went on to employment with the *Arkansas State Press* in the 1940s and had an opportunity to repeat his criticisms of Jim Crow in collaboration with his employers L. C. and Daisy Bates. Confined to Little Rock and North Little Rock where blacks had always enjoyed more opportunities, Taylor's survey, of course, did not reflect the totality of the conditions of Jim Crow, which was often more brutal and humiliating in the small towns and rural areas in this era. Maya Angelou, the gifted black writer from Arkansas, who following tradition was invited to compose and read her poem at Bill Clinton's first inauguration, recalled in her famous memoir, *I Know Why the Caged Bird Sings,* what life had been like in the town of Stamps in southwest Arkansas in the 1930s. Angelou remembered that as a child she had suffered a terrible toothache, and her grandmother had taken her to the town dentist. Though Angelou's grandmother had loaned money to him, he told her, "Annie, my policy is I'd rather stick my hand in a dog's mouth than in a nigger's."[11]

Even in "decent" white families, white paternalism extended only so far. In her memoir about growing up in the Arkansas Delta on a four-hundred-acre farm during the 1930s and 1940s, Margaret Jones Bolsterli recalls that her father refused to be responsible for the hospital bill of one of his tenant's newborns when told the infant needed special care and would die. "'Why, honey, I never even heard of putting a nigra baby in an incubator,'" he told his enraged daughter. As Bolsterli explains, "There were things that white people did not think of in terms of black people, and expensive medical care was one of them."[12]

Harold Flowers and the First Black Mass Movement

In the teeth of such blatant and arrogant cruelty, perhaps it is poetic justice that the first effective black political leader devoted to civil rights came from Stamps. Born in 1911, Harold Flowers was the son of a schoolteacher and insurance salesman and thus a member of the tiny black elite. Given his relatively privileged background, Flowers could have embraced the attitudes of his middle-class peers and carved out for himself a relatively comfortable life as part of the black bourgeoisie wherever he chose. Instead, at the age of sixteen on a visit to Little Rock with his father, he personally witnessed the unforgettable behavior of whites during the lynching of John Carter in 1927. He would never be the same. That experience, he later recalled, "truly converted him to be a lawyer."[13]

Flowers's outlook was considerably broadened by the years he spent outside Arkansas with two years at Lincoln High School in East Saint Louis and a night school legal education in Washington DC at Robert H. Terrell School of Law. When he returned, his approach to Arkansas politics was radically different than anyone's before him. Though a Republican, Flowers had a different agenda than the traditional black political leader in Arkansas who typically had used politics as a way of benefiting himself or members of his class. Beginning with a meeting in his hometown of Stamps on March 10, 1940, Flowers set forth his vision of non-partisan statewide collective action by blacks in a "single organization sufficient to serve the social, civic, political and economic needs of the people."[14]

In fact, the Committee on Negro Organizations (CNO) was an umbrella organization that brought together blacks from a community's churches, lodges, and other groups under one non-partisan political banner. A gifted speaker, Flowers was an immediate success, attracting large, enthusiastic black audiences across the state that obviously had been waiting for a leader to appeal to them across class lines. At Hope, the later boyhood hometown of Bill Clinton in south Arkansas, he attracted three hundred; at Postelle in east Arkansas six hundred turned out to hear him. Using the strongest local organization in each community as a rallying point, Flowers turned out two hundred at the Negro Business Club of Morrilton. Flowers preached a unity of purpose that had been foreign to the ears of black Arkansans. It was not a call to black nationalism but rather a summons for blacks to use their numerical strength to force changes by whites. His message was simple. Blacks must organize into a single group whatever their other affiliations, they must pay their poll taxes and vote, and they must combat discrimination together. At a meeting in Lake View in Phillips County on September 27, 1940, Flowers ticked off his organization's achievements: thirty-five investigations of discrimination in public works employment that had resulted in employment opportunities under the National Youth Administration, four thousand people had attended sixteen mass meetings, twenty-one organizations had endorsed the CNO, and the state of Arkansas had agreed to hire its first black census taker. In fact, in terms of actual change, initial progress was small, but the potential was clearly there. And the national offices of the NAACP, which had originally done nothing to help Flowers other than encourage him, soon realized that for the first time in its history Arkansas had a natural leader who could make a difference. As a result of Flowers's efforts in coordinating voter registration campaigns, eligible black voters in the state increased from 1.5 percent in 1940 to 17.3 percent by 1947.[15] But it was not only the national office that recognized a star in the making.

L. C. and Daisy Bates and the *Arkansas State Press*

In 1941 Lucious Christopher (L. C.) Bates, a one-time owner of a newspaper in Pueblo, Colorado, together with Daisy Gatson, whom he married the next year, began publication of the *Arkansas State Press* and instantly became a fan of Harold Flowers. Unlike any newspaper in Arkansas, the *State Press* was, from its beginning until its demise in 1959, a hard-hitting, tabloid-style advocate for civil rights and the NAACP. Originally from Liberty, Mississippi, by 1941 L. C. Bates had only one year of college but several years of experience in the newspaper business including a stint on the black-owned *Kansas City Call* where he worked under future national NAACP head Roy Wilkins. Bates modeled the newspaper on the publication of black newspapers such as the *Chicago Defender* and the *Crisis,* a magazine published by the NAACP. Though the *State Press* gave particular attention to incidents of police brutality and discriminatory treatment of black citizens, it also provided coverage of black involvement in sports, social events, entertainment, and politics. The *State Press* was distributed weekly not just in Little Rock but towns in Arkansas where there was a substantial black population.

Because of her later prominence, a word needs to be said here about Daisy Bates and her involvement with the *State Press.* After she had become famous for her role in the 1957 school desegregation crisis in Little Rock, Daisy Bates would be celebrated as copublisher of the paper. In fact, it was L. C. Bates who put the paper out and made editorial decisions. Daisy Bates, who would be selected as woman of the year in education in 1957 by the Associated Press, worked at the *State Press* under her husband's direction, for she had no experience in journalism and even less formal education. As the wife of L. C. Bates, Daisy Bates had input into the paper and in 1945 became city editor, but it was always L. C. Bates who ultimately made decisions about content and the business of running the paper. Indeed, at the height of her fame in 1957 and 1958 Daisy Bates spent little time at the *State Press.* Initially, the friendship between L. C. and Daisy Bates and Harold Flowers was made to order for all concerned. *State Press* employee Preston Tombs remembered, "Every Monday he [Flowers] would come in. He'd be there all day on Mondays. That was his headquarters."[16] Nothing would be more important to L. C. Bates than blacks using the power of the ballot to force change, and voting was also Flowers's bread-and-butter issue. "Drive to Increase Race Votes Is Successful," the headline ran in the *State Press* after poll tax drives in September 1941. On March 6, 1942, L. C. Bates ran a photograph of Flowers under the headline, "He Founded a Movement. "

The *State Press* and Black Protest in Little Rock

As much as the *State Press* trumpeted the achievements of Flowers, the paper soon demonstrated it had muscle all its own. On March 22, 1942, two white military policemen arrested a black soldier named Albert Glover on Ninth Street in Little Rock for being drunk and disorderly. At that point Abner Hay and George Henson, two Little Rock policemen, decided to assist the two MPs by clubbing Glover repeatedly until he was bleeding. When a crowd of blacks appeared outside of a makeshift first aid station, a panic-stricken Henson trained his pistol on them. Thomas Foster, a black sergeant, appeared out of the crowd and insisted he had authority to investigate and take charge of incidents that concerned men from his unit. He refused to allow Glover to be taken back to his unit until he had been given a satisfactory explanation of what had taken place. Instead of taking the trouble to make him aware of the facts, the two MPs arrested him and began to drag him down the street. Foster broke free and ran into the alcove of a nearby church where he stood his ground. A bad situation was about to turn worse.[17] Here, Officer Hay offered to bring in Foster if the others would clear a path for him. When it became apparent that Foster was winning the fight, the policemen began clubbing Foster until he let go of Hay. Immediately, Hay pulled out his revolver and shot Foster in the stomach three times and once in the arm. As Foster lay dying in front of him, Hay took out his pipe, filled it, and began to smoke while an ambulance was called. All of this occurred in front of a large crowd of blacks, who having witnessed a cold-blooded murder, were understandably furious. Immediately, officials from Camp Robinson averted further trouble by sending a convoy of trucks to the area and returned all soldiers to the base. Predictably, an investigation by Little Rock police found that Foster's death was justifiable homicide.[18]

The reaction of the *State Press* was unprecedented for a black newspaper in Arkansas: "NEGRO SOLDIER, BODY

RIDDLED WHILE LYING ON GROUND, WHITE MILITARY POLICE LOOK ON" roared the front page headline. "One of the most bestial murders in the annals of Little Rock tragedies was witnessed Sunday afternoon at 5:45 o'clock at Ninth and Gaines streets, by hundreds of eyewitnesses."[19] The paper's tone throughout the article was a militant call to action with no pretense of objectivity. The refusal to hold a white man accountable for the murder of a black person had its roots firmly anchored in the history of Arkansas white supremacy, and for the first time a black Arkansas newspaper demanded, not pleaded, for justice. The article and subsequent ones like it galvanized blacks throughout the city. Instead of reacting by heeding calls for calm by whites, Little Rock blacks formed the Negro Citizens Committee and conducted their own investigation of the incident. Hundreds squeezed into the First Baptist Church on March 29 to hear the results of the committee's investigation. Its report contradicted every finding made by whites of the incident. It would be difficult to overestimate the significance of the sea change in the black response. Twenty-three years earlier blacks on the Governor's biracial commission had sat in silence as Governor Brough had whitewashed the slaughter of hundreds of their race. The *State Press* challenged the black community to confront one of white supremacy's oldest traditions: any effort to ameliorate an injustice should be made by a black supplicant who came around to the back door and pleaded respectfully and in hushed tones for an influential white to intercede. An editorial by Bates on April 3 in response to a letter to the editor urging blacks to move on flatly refused. "The bestial murder of Sgt. Foster shall never be forgotten."

Not able to reverse the city's decision, the Negro Citizens Committee called for federal intervention, and because of the propaganda value to the country's enemies during a war, the whites in power in Little Rock encountered scrutiny they routinely avoided.[20] With the *State Press* keeping the heat on in editorial after editorial, the city finally capitulated by agreeing to hire black policemen to patrol Ninth Street. It was a victory for the black community that came with a price for the *State Press*. The bombastic, tabloid style and content of the paper during this period was enough of a threat to the white political and business community that it instructed E. Hobson Lewis, the manager of the Little Rock Chamber of Commerce, to offer L. C. Bates a bribe. Years later, Bates recalled, "He told me that he had been authorized to keep my paper full of ads. I asked him by whom. He said by the merchants of the city."[21] As poor as the black community was, whites always had assumed any of its residents could be bought, but L. C. Bates had no intention of softening the "tone" of the paper he had created. What followed next was a boycott of the paper by white merchants who had advertised in it. Soon, the *State Press* was quickly being strangled to death. Daisy Bates recalled she told her husband, "We can't operate without advertisers. Let's quit now while we still have train fare."[22] But L. C. Bates was not about to quit. Energy that once had gone into selling ads now went into increasing circulation. The strategy worked. The paper more than doubled its circulation from ten to over twenty thousand and continued its scathing criticism of Jim Crow at every opportunity. As time passed, Daisy Bates herself became increasingly interested in the paper, for clearly the *State Press* was where the action was. Once content to stay in bed and wait for her husband to come home and serve him brunch and then go in for a few hours with him, Daisy Bates found she had a "nose for news," according to her husband. Located on Ninth Street, the *State Press* was a must stop for prominent blacks visiting the city. Athletes and entertainers, such as Lionel Hampton and his wife, stopped by the paper to get publicity for their appearance. With her warm personality and boundless energy Daisy Bates was a natural reporter of events and a supporter of causes in the community. L. C. Bates preferred to stay in the background; his wife liked to see and be seen. Throughout the life of the paper, they worked well as a team. Though neither had a college degree, thus foreclosing them from membership in the all-important black sororities and fraternities, they operated across class lines, and it was their willingness and ability to do so that perhaps distinguished them a bit from some of the rest of the black elite in Little Rock and made the *State Press* successful.

Their identity with the NAACP was front and center from the beginning. As an organization that pushed hard for the rights of all blacks, the NAACP demolished the fiction that the black elite in the South could remain content with the status quo. Still, the Bateses were not everybody's cup of tea in the black community. But L. C. Bates, in particular, had no interest or desire in placating his enemies or his friends for that matter. He was quoted more than once to the effect that he would sacrifice a friend but not a principle. In his role as community scold, he was harder on blacks than whites. For a while he ran a column entitled "Mornin' Jedge" that chronicled the arrests and convictions of blacks in municipal court. And until the *State Press* was forced out of business in 1959, he ran a cartoon that purported to educate blacks about their behavior in public. For example, "Don't Spit in Public," ran one cartoon. Though every educated black person was acutely aware of the sometimes loud, boorish offensive behavior of poorer blacks, only L. C. Bates would publicly instruct his fellow blacks in print on how to behave.

The Litigation to Equalize Teachers' Salaries in Little Rock

Despite Little Rock's reputation for "good" race relations, class action litigation sponsored by the national NAACP in 1942 to equalize Little Rock teacher salaries showed how determined whites were to not give an inch over an issue that mattered to them. Out came the legal bare-knuckles approach to signs of black activism. The district refused to renew the contract of Sue Cowan Morris, the teacher who brought the litigation. Dunbar principal John Lewis who courageously testified for Morris lost his job as did John H. Gibson, head of the black teachers association. Annie Griffey, a white supervisor of primary teachers with thirty-one years of experience, testified at the trial that "regardless of college degrees and teaching experience no white teacher is inferior to the best Negro teacher," thus it made sense to pay different salaries based on race. The relentless attack by the Little Rock School District on blacks during the litigation even impressed national NAACP counsel Thurgood Marshall who admitted the district had employed for the case "top flight lawyers."[23]

After a delay of a year, Arkansas federal district judge Trimble ruled against the plaintiffs who appealed the decision to the Eighth Circuit Court of Appeals. The appellate court promptly reversed the trial court's decision and held that black teachers were entitled to equal pay. Though an important victory for black school teachers, the bad faith of the Little Rock School District in some ways made the ruling more symbolic than real. John Kirk has noted that though some black teachers got raises, the school district implemented a merit increase that was used to prevent some black teachers from receiving raises.

In any event, the legal victory for the Dunbar teachers put the NAACP in Arkansas back on the map. The national NAACP in this era had determined that the most effective way to dismantle Jim Crow was to make it as expensive as possible to maintain. Every victory was deemed important, and institutions like the NAACP and the *State Press* were determined to keep the pressure on the white community. Discrimination was a part of everyday life in Arkansas, and one of the most important contributions the *State Press* made during the 1940s was to document the racism encountered by blacks in Little Rock and throughout the state. For example, L. C. Bates called attention to the blatant discrimination faced by black workers at Pekin Wood Products in Phillips County. White workers walked off the job taking forty black workers with them. Bates described what occurred:

"Through intimidation and brutal treatment they [the black workers] were pulled off their jobs and made to stay off their jobs until . . . the white workers could get something better."[24] In this era discrimination was so common and blatant that when the entire plant had been given a three-cent-an-hour raise, whites would not let anyone work until they got a raise over the blacks. L. C. Bates wrote that it did no good for the blacks to join a white-dominated union. "We would say, 'Hell, no!! Stay Out.'" After all, blacks were in the majority. "If you feel you should have an organization to bargain for you, why not choose your own?"

Internal Squabbles, External Victories

With strong personalities like the Bateses and Harold Flowers on the scene, it is easy to forget how thoroughly white supremacy dominated black life in Arkansas. One would have expected the state NAACP to begin to show even more strength, but the organization began to be torn apart in the 1940s by vicious infighting. The traditional conservative black leadership eventually ran off Harold Flowers who had been responsible for much of its recent growth. A member from Texas wrote, "No place in the country is there so much strife and division amongst Negroes as it is in Arkansas."[25]

Despite the internal squabbles, events were taking place outside Arkansas that would bring progress for blacks inside the state. Though "separate but equal" was still the law, in 1938 the U.S. Supreme Court ruled that the state of Missouri could not deny admission of an African American to its all-white law school where it had not established a separate law school within its own borders. The fact that Missouri was willing to pay tuition for blacks to go out of state to law school was not considered sufficient justification to rule in the state's favor. With its meager resources, in the next decade Arkansas made no move to create separate professional or graduate educational schools for blacks. With no legal or factual basis to refuse him, the highly respected dean of the law school, Robert A. Leflar, who was given responsibility for the decision, admitted Silas Hunt as the first black law student to the University of Arkansas in Fayetteville on February 2, 1948. The terms of his admission were humiliating and embarrassing to everyone concerned. Initially, Hunt, an army veteran who had been seriously wounded at the Battle of the Bulge, was required to attend classes by himself in the basement of the law school. Prohibited from dining with other students, he could only use the library through the help of another student. Through this shameful period, a few students rebelled and began to study with Hunt. Tragically, because of his war wounds, Hunt was not even able to complete a year, dying at a Veteran's Hospital in Springfield, Missouri, within months of his initial enrollment. But Hunt would always be remembered as the first to break the color bar. He was followed by Jackie Shropshire, who, though not required to attend law school in a basement, was separated from the rest of his classmates by a railing. Again, students rebelled and the railing mysteriously disappeared.[26]

It was never just a matter of being isolated. Besides receiving death threats, George Haley, who began at the law school in 1949, had a bag of urine thrown in his face and a noose hung in his room. He was taunted with such statements as, "Hey, missing link, why don't you walk on your hind legs."[27]

Other blacks would soon follow, including Wiley Branton, Christopher Mercer, and George Howard Jr. Each of the three would have important roles in the Arkansas civil rights movement.[28] Meanwhile in 1948, Edith Irby was admitted to medical school and graduated as the first black doctor from the University of Arkansas for Medical Sciences.

The Seeds of Little Rock Housing Policy: The Master Plan

Historians of race relations have shown that despite the imposition of Jim Crow laws and customs going back to the

1890s, even until the middle of the twentieth century housing in certain areas of Little Rock was racially mixed. For example, Cheryl Nichols has identified specific racially-mixed areas within the historically black Dunbar neighborhood. Discussing housing patterns in this area, Nichols writes that

> certain blocks—notably the 1000, 1100 and 1200 blocks of Ringo, Cross and Pulaski Streets—originally were populated by white residents and remained predominantly white until about 1950, probably because of the presence of a white church.[29]

But even as blacks in Little Rock and throughout the state began to push against the barriers of Jim Crow in the 1940s, historians have traced to this era the initial efforts by whites in power to structure segregation within the capital city. Indeed, John Kirk concludes, "Without doubt, city planning policy shaped race relations more fundamentally over the long term than the short-term effects of the school crisis."[30] Kirk documents that as far back as the 1930s Little Rock policy makers began to realize that segregation could be maintained through the implementation of city-planning policies. Faced with pressure from blacks and some white allies who pointed to the undeniable fact that Little Rock maintained six public parks for whites and none for blacks (there were three private parks for blacks), the city passed bond issues in 1937 that included a provision for a park for blacks. Instead of following through with the creation of a park, for years city authorities desultorily entertained various proposals from the black community that was divided on a number of issues, including whether blacks should accept a segregated park. A threat to litigate the issue of the lack of black recreational facilities by new black community leaders I. S. McClinton and Charles Bussey in 1948 finally put the city on the spot because of the increase of successful lawsuits around the country challenging Jim Crow policies. The city put before the voters a bond issue in the amount of $359,000 that included a proposal "for the development and improvement of Gillam

Park." With only a 19 percent turnout, the narrow passage of the bond issue in 1949 was significant because it ultimately highlighted a split in the black community's leadership. L. C. and Daisy Bates had no confidence the money would be spent on the black community. In 1947 L. C. Bates, writing about the proposal in the *State Press* under the pseudonym of A. M. Judge, had directly challenged the policy of segregation. Little Rock "has no business trying to support a dual system for segregational [*sic*] purposes."[31]

The skepticism of the *State Press* was completely warranted because, as John Kirk explains, with the passage of the federal Housing Act of 1949 it was now possible for the city "to use the black park bond issue not to improve the condition of black facilities but, instead, to embark upon an aggressive plan to create a more geographically segregated city."[32] Kirk shows that in the 1950s the city took this bond money and leveraged federal money for slum clearance that resulted in the eviction of black residents and the construction of "black public housing units on the edge of the city, as far away from white neighborhoods as possible."[33] In Kirk's words, "Slum clearance" quickly translated into "Negro clearance" just as its successor "urban renewal" later became known as "Negro removal."[34]

Little Rock blacks did get their own Gillam park, including a swimming pool in 1950, but as the *State Press* complained, most "blacks did not want a swimming pool built out of the city in an insect infested mountain."[35]

Kirk shows that beginning in the 1950s there was little need for Little Rock whites to write into law discriminatory legislation affecting blacks. Policies of the city accomplished the goal of racial segregation in ways that could be more easily defended. Kirk contends that "what prompted segregation laws from the 1890s onward was the amount of racial mixing that was actually taking place in rapidly expanding towns and cities."[36] Little Rock was the primary example of an urbanized area that attracted a broad spectrum of African Americans. So long as they accepted their status as servants, they were welcome into the homes of whites to clean, cook, and care for their children. But with nightfall, they had to leave. Discrimination was a given, but as Kirk writes, "Geographical segregation replaced segregation as an instrument of racial discrimination, by ensuring that many city facilities would remain race-specific by virtue of their location close to black or white areas of residence."[37]

In fact, the evidence brought forth in a federal court trial in the 1980s in Little Rock confirms that segregation in Pulaski County had long involved a multitude of white players, including state, city, and county officials as well as business interests. In a suit filed by the Little Rock School District against the Little Rock Special School District, the North Little Rock School District, and the state to consolidate the three school districts into one giant district for the purpose of integration, the devices used to perpetuate segregation within the county were offered into evidence by the attorneys for the Little Rock School District in an effort to convince judge Henry Woods that a countywide legal remedy was appropriate. In a decision in which Judge Woods's factual findings were accepted in toto by the court of appeals, the evidence showed that before the federal judiciary began requiring meaningful integration the Little Rock School District, the North Little Rock School District, and the Pulaski County School District often worked together with the help of the city of Little Rock to manage black education within the county in a way that accommodated the interests of each district. Judge Woods ruled:

> The development of the Granite Mountain [Housing] project together with the Federal Housing Administration's development of an all black subdivision adjacent to the project serves as a good example of the manner in which blacks have been located to the south and east in Little Rock.[38]

The court found that in North Little Rock the same policies existed as to low-income housing. As long as whites in the county could segregate blacks as they wished, an attitude of cooperation among the various authorities continued. For example,

> The only major clearance project in North Little Rock was a complete clearance of the Military Heights area lying south of Interstate 40 and west of Interstate 30. This project had become all black and when it was razed, blacks were moved to Little Rock as well as south and east in North Little Rock.[39]

The evidence submitted by the Little Rock School District was comprehensive in showing that whatever decisions were needed to be made to preserve housing segregation throughout Pulaski County were undertaken cooperatively by whites. As have historians of Arkansas race relations, Judge Woods found

> The existence and location of the housing projects, the location of other government-subsidized housing units, the failure to build projects within the geographic boundaries of the county district, and the private and public steering and redlining practices are major contributing factors to the residential segregation in Pulaski County which exists today.[40]

In chapter 19 we will return to Judge Woods's opinion in the case of the *Little Rock School District v. Pulaski County School District, et al.* It is enough now to note that there is sufficient evidence to state that segregation was accomplished in numerous ways by whites working together behind closed doors. Ironically, it would be the Little Rock School District that would break ranks.

Voting and the Democratic Party: A New Era begins

Now that the door was opening a bit in the area of graduate education thanks to outside pressure, the NAACP continued to press the fight for voting rights for blacks, and here again the NAACP in Arkansas also benefited by favorable decisions from other jurisdictions. As chair of the legal redress committee of the Little Rock NAACP, L. C. Bates advised the Arkansas Democratic Committee in May 1950 that litigation was about to follow if it did not change its rules and permit Rev. J. H. Gatlin to run in the Democratic primary for city alderman. When the Arkansas Democratic Party tried to stall, Little Rock attorney J. R. Booker and national NAACP staff attorney Ulysses Simpson Tate filed suit and immediately got a good decision from Judge Trimble who had little choice but to hold that the primary election was "an integral part of the state election system . . . tantamount to election at the general election." He further held that "it is not sufficient that a citizen have a token exercise of his right and privilege [to vote]."[41] Of course, the court's logic applied at the turn of the century, but clearly now there was change in the air. Instead of renouncing support from blacks as had Ben Laney, the state's former governor, in his closing speech to the Democratic state convention, Sidney McMath, the state's new chief executive, told the party faithful that he was "proud, and I know you are proud . . . [that the convention] . . . has said the Negro citizen is entitled to the rights and privileges of Party membership."[42] Though McMath's administration foundered as a result of charges of corruption in the administration of highway funds, his attitude toward blacks as new political partners was a defining moment with long-range consequences for the Arkansas Democratic Party. Jim Lester has traced Sidney McMath's efforts to create a more moderate climate of race relations in the state. Though McMath had no choice politically but to remain committed to a policy of segregation, he called attention to the fact that black educational institutions were not receiving equal funding. Early in his first administration department of education officials publicly charged that "state school funds were being diverted from black to white schools on the local level." In fact, according to Ed McCuiston, state director of negro education, "the diversion had amounted to $4,250,000 the previous year alone." In a public statement days later, McMath demanded that local school districts end the practice and threatened litigation if they did not. McMath was also able to increase funding for Arkansas AM&N, which had long been neglected by previous administrations. Perhaps, his most significant contribution was to use his influence to keep Arkansas from bolting the Democratic Party for the Dixiecrat Party in 1948.[43] A new world was opening to blacks, but as L. C. Bates would learn to his consternation, they did not always exercise their right to vote in the way the *State Press* urged.

Signs of Progress in the Capital City

If there was going to be racial progress anywhere in the state, it was going to be in the city of Little Rock where there was a continuum of interracial groups. At one end was, of course, the NAACP, in fact more specifically, the Little Rock branch's executive committee, made up of a number of dedicated and conscientious people. Besides Daisy and L. C. Bates, they ranged from Rev. J. C. Crenchaw, a forty-year member of the NAACP and pastor of Mount Pleasant Baptist Church who earned his living as a tailor, to J. R. Booker, a stalwart Republican lawyer who had helped litigate the Little Rock school-teacher-salary case. Two others who would later achieve prominence in the 1960s in the black community were optometrist William H. Townsend, who would take his place as the first black legislator, and Ozell Sutton, a journalist who would be one of the leaders to negotiate an end to segregation in downtown Little Rock. Two white members of the executive committee were highly qualified professors at Philander Smith College, Georg Iggers and Lee Lorch, who, with their wives Wilma and Grace, were that rarest of species in the South—white idealists who were deeply committed to racial integration and social justice for African Americans. It was the Little Rock branch of the NAACP that was the most fervent in its demand for racial integration, but it must be kept in mind that white supremacy and segregation were so total that initially any small steps that could be taken to roll it back were seen as important progress. As radical and militant as the organization appeared to the typical white or black in Arkansas, in no sense was theirs a group that expected an immediate end to Jim Crow. For example, hoping to expand the availability of reference works for his students at Philander Smith, Georg Iggers negotiated an initial arrangement with the Little Rock library to permit blacks on a quite limited basis to use it. So impressed with what Iggers had accomplished, the Little Rock branch's executive committee invited him to be a member.[44] In 1952 Daisy Bates was chosen for the top spot in the state NAACP. In fact, her responsibilities were generally limited to presiding over the annual meeting and collecting dues. And though in 1957 she would become the spokesperson for blacks in Little Rock involved in the school litigation and thus become the focus of much attention during Little Rock's school desegregation crisis, until 1956 she functioned primarily as a committed team member of the Little Rock branch's executive committee. Next along the continuum of interracial support groups was the Little Rock branch of the Southern Regional Council, which operated under the name of the Arkansas Council on Human Relations (ACHR). Most members of this small group favored gradual integration, but in the increasingly shrill atmosphere that would come to be the norm in 1957, many were timid and circumspect in their support. It took courage for whites to join even this group that primarily favored dialogue and had no litigation capacity of its own. Finally, there was the Urban League, which supported "racial uplift" but not much else, or, as John Kirk has written, for improvement of "black life and opportunities strictly within the bounds of Jim Crow."[45] Though blacks and whites could and did join all three organizations, Daisy Bates initially turned down an opportunity to join the board of the Urban League by telling her white friend Edwin Dunaway that the executive board was "just a bunch of niggers who want to sit next to white folks once every two weeks."[46] Still, it had been the Urban League that had pointed out the disparities between blacks and whites in the

1930s. A coalition involving these three groups appeared to have nearly achieved a modest breakthrough in school desegregation in 1952. The coalition, whose spokesman was Lewis Deer, a white minister of the Pulaski Heights Christian Church, apparently very nearly persuaded the Little Rock School Board in 1952 to allow black students from Dunbar to come to Little Rock Central High School and take courses that were not offered at the black high school.[47] One, however, must keep in mind that white supremacy was not at issue in these modest proposals. So long as whites in authority in Little Rock were approached by blacks respectfully and led by white allies, token adjustments were made in the color line such as allowing blacks certain times to visit the zoo and parks.[48] Though signs designating which race was to use which drinking fountain—"white" or "colored"—began to disappear in downtown Little Rock stores in this period, blacks who needed to use the bathroom were still out of luck.

Militants on the Verge

Of these three groups, the Little Rock NAACP was the most aggressive at every turn. As far back as 1952, some members of the executive committee, including Daisy and L. C. Bates, were advocating that a suit be brought to force the Little Rock School Board to integrate the school system; however, they were dissuaded by the national office of the NAACP, which already had lined up the cases which would challenge the "separate but equal" doctrine that had been the law since *Plessy v. Ferguson* in 1896. As these five cases made their way up to the Supreme Court for its momentous decision in 1954, it is imperative to remember that while *Brown v. Board of Education* would begin a revolution in race relations, white supremacy dominated the psychological climate then and for years afterwards. As Taylor Branch explains in his history of the civil rights movement, the original goal of the leaders of the Montgomery, Alabama, bus boycott, which catapulted Martin Luther King Jr. to the leadership of the civil rights movement in 1956, was not to end segregation on buses but to stop the practice of blacks having to give their seats up to whites. It would take a lawsuit to end segregation on buses. The point is that white supremacy had become such a part of the American psyche, whether that American was white or black, rich or poor, liberal or conservative, that its overthrow was not going to be suddenly accomplished by judicial fiat or by legislation. Examples nationally and locally abound in the early 1950s within the white and black community during this era, but three will suffice. Walter White, executive director of the NAACP in New York, wrote an article for *Look* magazine praising the virtues of a skin whitener. He divorced his wife of twenty-seven years and rather improbably married a white socialite from South Africa. Embarrassed by his actions, the board stripped him of his power but still retained him as a figurehead. Meanwhile, Dwight Eisenhower, the president of the United States, "passed along the latest 'nigger' jokes from his friends at the Bobby Jones golf course in Augusta." Taylor Branch writes that Eisenhower "bridled at the company of Negroes."[49] It would be in this social and psychological context that the U.S. Supreme Court in May 1954 would decide a direct challenge to segregated education in public schools. Meanwhile in the Arkansas Delta segregation and inequality ruled supreme. In 1949 *Life* magazine in its March 21 issue ran a story about schools in West Memphis in Crittenden County. In 1948 West Memphis spent an average of $144.51 for each white child's education and $19.51 for each black child's education, according to the *Life* article. The occasion for the article was the hideously crowded conditions in the black school that had been partially destroyed by fire. A new $300,000 facility for nine hundred white children had just opened, giving the whites two schools, while 310 black students and their five teachers squeezed into five rooms of the gutted school, and 370 students were jammed into a black one room church. The statistics seem unbelievable until one sees the pictures that accompany the story. On September 27, 1949, a proposed bond issue for a black school was defeated by the people of West Memphis.[50] Such was the tenor of the times before the *Brown* decision.

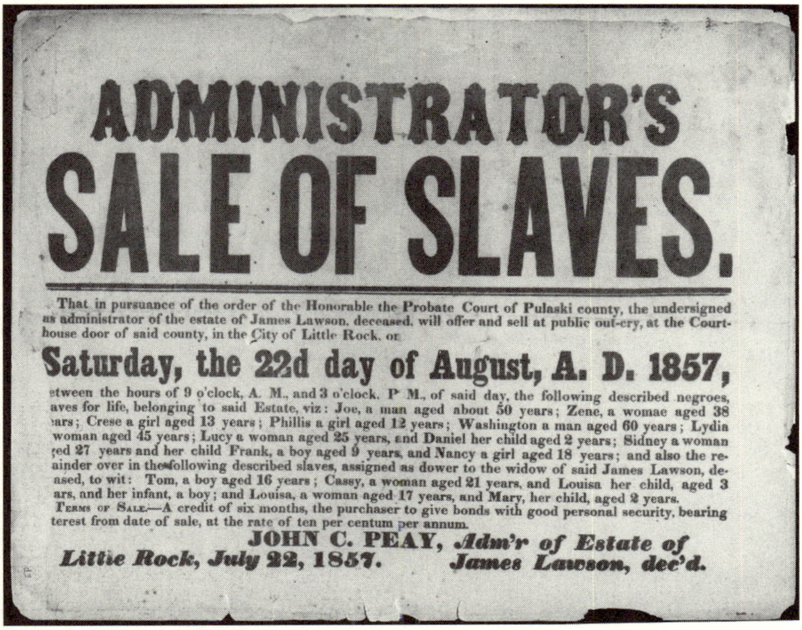

ADMINISTRATOR'S SALE OF SLAVES.

That in pursuance of the order of the Honorable the Probate Court of Pulaski county, the undersigned as administrator of the estate of James Lawson, deceased, will offer and sell at public out-cry, at the Court-house door of said county, in the City of Little Rock, on

Saturday, the 22d day of August, A. D. 1857,

etween the hours of 9 o'clock, A. M., and 3 o'clock, P. M., of said day, the following described negroes, aves for life, belonging to said Estate, viz: Joe, a man aged about 50 years; Zene, a womae aged 38 ars; Crese a girl aged 13 years; Phillis a girl aged 12 years; Washington a man aged 60 years; Lydia woman aged 45 years; Lucy a woman aged 25 years, and Daniel her child aged 2 years; Sidney a woman ged 27 years and her child Frank, a boy aged 9 years, and Nancy a girl aged 18 years; and also the re-ainder over in the following described slaves, assigned as dower to the widow of said James Lawson, de-ased, to wit: Tom, a boy aged 16 years; Cassy, a woman aged 21 years, and Louisa her child, aged 3 ars, and her infant, a boy; and Louisa, a woman aged 17 years, and Mary, her child, aged 2 years.

TERMS OF SALE.—A credit of six months, the purchaser to give bonds with good personal security, bearing terest from date of sale, at the rate of ten per centum per annum.

JOHN C. PEAY, *Adm'r of Estate of*
Little Rock, July 22, 1857. *James Lawson, dec'd.*

Advertisement for the sale of slaves in Pulaski County, Arkansas, 1857. *Digital collection, Special Collections, University of Arkansas Libraries, Fayetteville*

Arkansas General William L. Cabell, the commanding officer of Confederate troops who refused to allow unarmed African American soldiers to surrender at the Battle of Poison Spring, 1864. *Courtesy of the Butler Center for Arkansas Studies, Central Arkansas Library System*

The Ku Klux Klan, a terrorist organization composed of Southerners who resisted Reconstruction and sought to maintain white supremacy after the Civil War. *Courtesy of the Arkansas History Commission*

In 1874 Augustus H. Garland, the first Democrat to serve as governor after Reconstruction and, though one of the "Redeemers," implementer of racially moderate policies. *Courtesy of the Butler Center for Arkansas Studies, Central Arkansas Library System*

Jeff Davis, a three-term governor and U.S. senator, who was the most racially demagogic leader in the history of the state. *Courtesy of the Butler Center for Arkansas Studies, Central Arkansas Library System*

John Carter, who became in May 1927 the last African American lynched in Little Rock. *Courtesy of the Butler Center for Arkansas Studies, Central Arkansas Library System*

Governor Charles Hillman Brough, who allowed the Phillips County "Committee of Seven" to have a free hand during the Elaine Race Massacres of 1919. *Courtesy of the Butler Center for Arkansas Studies, Central Arkansas Library System*

Attorney Scipio Africanus Jones with six of the Elaine defendants whom he helped save from the electric chair. *Courtesy of the Butler Center for Arkansas Studies, Central Arkansas Library System*

Arkansas farm workers listening to the speaker at a meeting of the Southern Tenant Farmers' Union, circa 1934. *Louise Boyle, photographer. Photograph number 3472, Southern Tenant Farmers' Union Records, Southern Historical Collection, Wilson Library, University of North Carolina at Chapel Hill*

Dispossessed Arkansas farmers in Bakersfield, California, in 1935. *Library of Congress, Prints & Photographs Division, FSA-OWI Collection (reproduction number LC-USF34–002327-C DLC)*

Legal pioneers Wiley Branton and Harold Flowers with Silas Hunt as he seeks to become the first black student admitted to the University of Arkansas School of Law. *Geleve Grice, photographer, Geleve Grice Collection (MC 1463), Special Collections, University of Arkansas Libraries, Fayetteville*

Sue Cowan Williams, a noted black educator, who in 1942 served as the lead plaintiff in successful litigation to equalize public school teacher salaries in Little Rock. *Courtesy of the Butler Center for Arkansas Studies, Central Arkansas Library System, Tom W. Dillard Black Arkansiana Collection*

Adolphine Fletcher Terry, a member of one of Little Rock's leading families, who helped organize the Women's Emergency Committee to reopen the city's high schools. *Courtesy of the Butler Center for Arkansas Studies, Central Arkansas Library System*

Governor Orval E. Faubus, who provoked a major constitutional crisis by ordering the Arkansas National Guard to prohibit the desegregation of Central High School. *Courtesy of the Butler Center for Arkansas Studies, Central Arkansas Library System*

The Little Rock Nine with Daisy Bates, president of the Arkansas Conference of Branches of the NAACP, at the forty-ninth NAACP convention. *Daisy Bates Papers (MC 582), box 11, photograph number 24, Special Collections, University of Arkansas Libraries, Fayetteville*

Daisy Bates with L. C. Bates, whose weekly *State Press* was a staunch advocate for civil rights from 1941 to 1959. *Daisy Bates Papers (MC 582), box 11, photograph number 443. Special Collections, University of Arkansas Libraries, Fayetteville*

Republican Winthrop Rockefeller, who changed the tone of race relations in the state during his two terms as governor. *Courtesy of the Arkansas History Commission*

SNCC worker William Hansen marching in Pine Bluff in 1963. *Arkansas State Police surveillance photograph, courtesy of the Special Collections Division, University of Arkansas Libraries, Fayetteville*

Olly Neal Jr., a militant civil rights advocate in the 1970s in Lee County, who later became a prosecuting attorney, a trial judge, and a member of the Arkansas court of appeals. *Courtesy of the University of Central Arkansas Archives*

Governor Bill Clinton surrounded by African American staff and appointees in 1984. *Courtesy of the Arkansas History Commission*

CHAPTER 12

Brown v. Board of Education and the Central High Crisis

The real and symbolic importance of the Supreme Court decision of *Brown v. Board of Education* in May 1954 to black Americans in the United States can hardly be overstated. Written in plain English, the court's decision is as much about morality as it is about legal rights. The unanimous court's ruling struck down segregation in public education in those states where it had been law. The decision, written by Chief Justice Earl Warren, found that "segregation on the basis of race had caused Negro children to carry within themselves a sense of inferiority that was harmful to their ability to learn." This factual determination by the Court of the effect of racial segregation on black children's ability to learn was the underlying premise for the Court's conclusion that "separate educational facilities are inherently unequal." Largely on the basis of testimony by black psychologist Kenneth Clark, the court implicitly assumed that if blacks and whites went to school together and received the same education then blacks' sense of inferiority would be overcome and, as a result, blacks would eventually achieve educational parity.

From a purely legal perspective the Court's decision was grounded in the Fourteenth Amendment's guarantee of equal protection. Educational "opportunity where the state has undertaken to provide it, is a right that must be made available to all on equal terms."[1] And equal terms no longer meant separate but equal. Simply put, in order to comply with *Brown,* blacks must attend public schools with white children. Significantly, the opinion in *Brown* left the issue of how fast school integration must take place for another day. The lawyers were told to submit additional arguments.

The Calm before the Storm

In Arkansas, unlike Mississippi and Georgia, for example, the immediate official reaction to *Brown* was one of a deceptive calm. Governor Francis Cherry solemnly intoned, "Arkansas will obey the law. It always has."[2] Of course, white Arkansans had not obeyed the federal requirement of providing separate but equal education or separate but equal public facilities in other public institutions such as hospitals and mental institutions. Yet the white supremacist mindset was so ingrained that white Arkansans could make such a statement without any conscious sense of hypocrisy.

After the first decision in *Brown* there were a handful of school boards in Arkansas that voted to end their dual system of education primarily for reasons of economy. In Fayetteville, the home of the University of Arkansas, nine black students had been bused across the mountain to Fort Smith at a cost of five thousand dollars. Its superintendent, Wayne White, issued a statement that "segregation was a luxury we could not longer afford."[3] His announcement was met with no focused opposition and not a single patron of the district visited with school board members to protest the decision.[4] In Charleston and Bentonville, virtually all-white towns far outside the Delta, school boards voted likewise. In Sheridan located in Grant County in south Arkansas, the school board had reacted to *Brown* by first voting to desegregate its schools but reversed itself the next night after their white neighbors had erupted in a "firestorm of protest."

By 1955 Arkansas had a new governor, Orval E. Faubus, who first tried to avoid the issue of school desegregation. Though saying initially that he would make race an issue in his campaign against incumbent Francis Cherry, Faubus did not. In fact, he tried to defuse the issue by saying desegregation was a matter for local school boards. His strategy worked well enough until the Supreme Court issued its second ruling in *Brown* on May 31, 1955.[5] Also unanimous, its declared intention was to allow school districts good faith flexibility in determining whether there were administrative obstacles that would impede immediate conversion to a unitary school system and to allow time for these problems to be overcome. The debate has never ended whether the U.S. Supreme Court, in reacting to the furor caused by its initial ruling, deliberately sabotaged its decision in *Brown I* by its language in *Brown II*. Instead of insisting upon good faith compliance, the court seemed determined to give school districts an excuse to delay integration of their schools. Catch phrases in the opinion such as "varied local problems," "practical flexibility," "adjusting and reconciling public and private needs," and "all deliberate speed" were seized upon by school boards all over the South to avoid compliance with the original intent of the first *Brown* decision.

Hoxie: The First Battleground

Unique among school districts in Arkansas after *Brown II* was the reaction of the Hoxie School District in the summer of 1955 in northeast Arkansas near Jonesboro, which through its superintendent, Howard Kunkel, announced that it would integrate its system because it was "right in the sight of God," because it was the "law," and lastly because it was "cheaper."[6] The introduction of morality as a stated reason for the decision of a school board to desegregate was unprecedented in the history of Arkansas. Though involving only a handful of black students, the decision of the Hoxie School Board and its desegregation of its school system brought with it the opportunity one Arkansan in particular had been waiting for. Jim Johnson, director of the state White Citizens Council, a more respectable substitute for the Ku Klux Klan though the Klan was active in Arkansas, was from Crossett in Ashley

County near the Louisiana border. As a self-appointed defender of the message of white supremacy, Johnson, a lean and handsome lawyer, mesmerized audiences who responded to his often crude racist message. *Arkansas Faith,* the magazine that he founded in 1956 and put out by his sidekick Curt Copeland, pushed every button available to the demagogue. A typical editorial started off,

> The National Association for the Agitation of Colored People (NAACP), also referred to as the National Association for the Advancement of the Communist Party, has been screaming 40 years for race-mixing in the schools, mixed churches, mixed marriages, mixed children, etc.[7]

As propaganda *Arkansas Faith* proved superb at arousing the instincts of its readers to engage in age-old self-pity at what had been done to them over time by the federal government but most recently by the Supreme Court. For Johnson, it was a perfect opportunity to fan the flames of Southern racism, and he and others, Amis Guthridge, in particular, a lawyer from Little Rock who was executive secretary of White America, Inc., excelled at this task. Soon, black parents and school board members were receiving visitors who thought they had ways of changing their minds about the decision to desegregate the Hoxie schools.

Instead of caving into pressure and intimidation, the Hoxie School Board hired a lawyer to defend it. From the nearby town of Jonesboro, Bill Penix was white, smart, and aggressive. With the help of the Justice Department, which filed a friend of the court brief, he obtained for his clients an order in federal court prohibiting interference and harassment by the White Citizens Council. Flabbergasted that an Arkansas judge would rule against it, the council filed numerous appeals, which were all denied.

Aaron v. Cooper: The Little Rock NAACP Files Suit

The success at Hoxie surely helped convince the Little Rock NAACP to sue the Little Rock School District in federal court, but bearing more on its decision was the continued shifting of the district's plans as pressure came from the white community to do as little as possible. As early as August 1955 the Little Rock NAACP had lost whatever confidence it had in Superintendent Blossom and the Little Rock School Board to implement in good faith a plan to desegregate its schools and began planning litigation.[8] The plans of the Little Rock School District seemed to shift every week, but the final version turned out to be that Central High School was the only school where even token integration would take place. In the litigation that followed, the case of *Aaron v. Cooper* filed in February 1956 would for the next three years make the Little Rock NAACP and particularly Daisy Bates the focal point for civil rights activity in Arkansas.

While positions were radically beginning to harden within the state and the South on the issue of school desegregation, whites in Arkansas were discovering that black leadership was beginning to assert itself during the pretrial phase of *Aaron v. Cooper* in a way it had never done in the past. During a deposition taken of Daisy Bates, who was still serving as president of the Arkansas Conference of Branches since her election in 1952, Leon Catlett, an attorney specially hired for this case at the recommendation of the regular board attorney Archie House, continually referred to Daisy Bates by her first name. There was nothing unusual about this "time-honored control technique of white supremacy which was to strip blacks of their dignity by calling them by their first names as though they were children."[9] Not only did Bates correct Catlett on the pronunciation of the word "Negro," she told him, "You addressed me several times this morning by my first name. This is something that is reserved for my intimate friends and my husband. You will refrain from calling me Daisy." Without hesitating, Catlett shot back, "I won't call you anything then."[10] Reported in the *Arkansas Gazette* the next day, this sharp exchange was in fact a signal to both whites and blacks that there was a sea change taking place in the black leadership in Little Rock. Daisy Bates was supposed to act deferentially, but there was none of that in her responses or demeanor. For blacks, they had found a leader, but it must be said that many African Americans were rightly concerned that Daisy and L. C. Bates would bring the wrath of powerful whites down on them.

Though the NAACP did not win the lawsuit because both the federal district judge and the Eighth Circuit Court of Appeals accepted the claim of the Little Rock School District that it intended in good faith to start integration in the fall of 1957, the case remained in court because the decision of the eighth circuit made clear the federal district court judge had the responsibility to see that integration occurred.

Especially after the 1955 ruling by the Supreme Court, many whites in the South and in Arkansas began increasing the pressure on school board members and politicians to demand that the *Brown* decisions be resisted. In March 1956 Southern politicians in Congress, including the entire Arkansas delegation, weighed in as signatories to a document called the "Southern Manifesto." Signed by all but three U.S. senators, one of whom was future president Lyndon Johnson, the manifesto read in pertinent part, "We pledge ourselves to use all lawful means to bring about a reversal of this decision [*Brown I*] which is contrary to the Constitution and to prevent the use of force in its implementation."

As the pressure increased, Governor Faubus tried to appease white voters by supporting in 1956 an unlawful constitutional amendment and legislation in 1957 that sought to preserve segregated schools. Federal law, of course, is supreme over state law, a fact the governor well knew and had, on one occasion, admitted. One of the laws passed in 1957 was particularly abusive of democratic government. The NAACP was now required to report its membership and finances. The right to privacy and free association were put at risk. This law was used to crush the Arkansas NAACP before it was declared unconstitutional.[11] Supporters of these measures claimed that the forces of international communism were responsible for black citizens seeking their constitutional rights. In fact the number of Communists in the entire state during this era probably could have been counted on one hand.

Within the city of Little Rock, as ordinary white citizens began to realize that Central High School would be the only school to experience integration in 1957, they felt themselves the victims of class warfare since many wealthier and socially prominent whites lived outside Central's attendance zone.[12] Organizing themselves as the Capital Citizens Council (CCC), they began to insist that Governor Faubus and the Little Rock School Board devise a way to avoid integration. Advertisements in the *Arkansas Democrat* taken out by the CCC raised the age-old fear of "race-mixing." During slavery and continuing into the present, whites had engaged in sexual relations with African Americans, but the possibility that one's children could be involved in such a scenario was a scare tactic that was ready-made for the era. "Will [blacks and whites] be permitted to stay in the same motels" on school-sponsored trips? "Would the negro boys be permitted to solicit the white girls for dances" at school functions? The hypocrisy of such advertisements went unnoticed. They touched the rawest nerve in the white Southerner's body. The advertisement was a public-relations masterpiece because of the fears it raised.[13] According to Elizabeth Jacoway, white Southerners were terrified of "miscegenation, or more specifically allowing black men to have access to white women."[14]

By the time school opened in September, most whites in Little Rock wanted something to be done to stop any black students from entering Central High School. Under pressure from white parents, the members of the Little Rock School Board began to say publicly they were segregationists. Virgil Blossom now said the plan was designed to permit as little integration as legally possible.

From every corner white Arkansans were applying pressure to stop the district from desegregating the school district in September. On August 22 Georgia governor Marvin Griffin and Roy V. Harris appeared at a Capital Citizens Council banquet to remind the group that in Georgia his administration had passed legislation to stop integration. Harris pointed the finger at Communists who he said "for twenty years . . . have conducted a brainwashing campaign through the churches, the two political parties and national organizations, and have been so successful." In his biography of Orval Faubus, Roy Reed writes, "Griffin's appearance quite suddenly convinced large numbers of people that the entire integration problem could be solved quickly and simply."[15]

Afterwards, the governor and some members of the Little Rock School Board arranged to have a lawsuit filed in an Arkansas state court to delay integration because of alleged possible violence, but a new federal judge hearing the case, Ronald Davies from North Dakota, ruled that the school board's plan must go forward. Much has been written about Governor Orval Faubus's decision on Labor Day to order members of the National Guard to surround Central and prevent the nine African American students from entering the next day. Fifty years later Faubus's ten-page speech on statewide television that night reads as if it could have been written for him by members of the Little Rock white elite who, in the aftermath of what occurred, so bitterly opposed him. He began by listing all the progress the state had been making in integration. Indeed, three of the ten pages were devoted to the gains blacks had made in recent years. As he pointed out, blacks were in law school, medical school, graduate programs, and the Democratic Central Committee and had "been integrated into the public school systems of the state where it was acceptable to the majority and could be peaceably accomplished." The difficulty was that

> now that a Federal Court has ruled that no further litigation is possible before the forcible integration of Negroes and whites in Central High School tomorrow,

> the evidence of discord, anger and resentment has come to me from so many sources as to be a deluge. There is evidence of disorder and threats which could have but one inevitable result—that is violence which can lead to injury and the harm to persons and property.[16]

Historians of the crisis now generally agree that at a minimum there was the potential for violence. Faubus's biographer Roy Reed has shown that Faubus "had a credible reason to expect violence," having earlier received a telephone call from Joe Foster, the town marshal of England, who had "just intercepted two carloads of angry men from Phillips County who were headed for Little Rock with lots of guns." According to Foster, "Their intention was to go to Central High and keep the Negro students from entering." He had told them to wait until they saw what the National Guard was going to do and then had called the governor.[17]

Assuming violence was about to occur, the governor had at least two choices. Since Faubus himself knew and had stated publicly that federal law was supreme over state law, he could have ordered the National Guard to protect the nine children who were to enter Central the next day. However, instead of assuming the responsibility for enforcing the constitutional rights of the black students, he ordered the National Guard to keep the black students from entering Central. The question of his motives has been debated ever since. Even if one accepts the view that he was trying to keep the peace, it seems clear that at the same time he was trying to provide himself with as much political cover as possible because he knew the federal government would be forced to act. Harry Ashmore, editor of the *Arkansas Gazette,* insisted repeatedly in editorials in the paper that the governor created a constitutional crisis by disobeying the federal court's order to proceed with integration. The paper lost large amounts of money as local businesses in Little Rock withdrew their advertising accounts. Ashmore and the *Arkansas Gazette* each won a Pulitzer Prize for advocating what became known as the "Southern Moderate" position. Those who held this view urged their fellow Southerners to accept the decision of the Supreme Court as the law of the land. According to the selection committee, in so doing the *Gazette* had "demonstrate[d] the highest qualities of civic leadership, journalistic responsibility and moral courage in the face of mounting public tension during the school integration crisis of 1957."[18] It must be pointed out that Southern Moderates were committed to tokenism and would use every device possible to delay school integration while at the same time giving lip service to compliance with federal law. The tenor of the times was such that Southerners could win accolades from the rest of the country by merely agreeing that federal law was supreme.

Surrounded by National Guard troops, Central High opened as scheduled the day after the Labor Day holiday, but no black students made an effort to attend in order for the Little Rock School District to work out a plan that would allow them to try to enter the school as directed by Judge Davies. Daisy Bates initiated the idea of having a group of ministers to accompany the students the next morning but forgot to tell fourteen-year-old Elizabeth Eckford where to meet them at the school.[19] A photograph of Eckford being harassed by a mob of angry whites on the grounds of Central High after she was turned away by the National Guard has become has become an enduring symbol of the hatred and violence displayed by white Arkansans during this era but also of the courage of the nine black students who would finally be admitted to classes. Though there was a meeting between President Dwight D. Eisenhower and Governor Faubus to discuss the situation, the governor refused to back down until after another federal court hearing after which he ordered the removal of the National Guard. During this time, Governor Faubus received positive responses from many Southerners inside of Arkansas as well as throughout the South for his attempted defiance of the federal government. Though he had claimed that he had acted to preserve the peace, the governor left the state to attend a Southern Governors Conference, aware of the turmoil that would occur when the Little Rock Nine, as they would be known, once again attempted to enter Central High School on September 23. Though the Nine did enter Central that morning with police protection, by the afternoon they were forced to evacuate the building because of fears for their safety from the mob of a thousand whites outside the school. Newsmen covering their entrance that morning were beaten and injured by the white mob. No whites would be charged for their unlawful behavior either by the state of Arkansas or federal government.

The news and pictures of the beatings again went round the world, and the enemies of the United States, particularly Communist governments with whom the U.S. was engaged in a "Cold War," seized on the hypocrisy of the "world's greatest democracy" that had one law for whites and another for blacks. Little Rock had become a symbol of white hatred but was increasingly a foreign policy issue. President Eisenhower, in a controversial but decisive move, ordered the next morning a thousand troops from the elite 101st Airborne Division to Little Rock to accompany the Little Rock Nine to Central. At the same time he issued an order federalizing the Arkansas National Guard troops. Upon the arrival on the twenty-fifth of the soldiers at the house of Daisy and L. C. Bates to escort the students, Minnijean Brown said, "For the first time in my life, I feel like an American citizen."[20]

In many ways the school year would be extremely difficult for the Little Rock Nine at Central because a small group of students within the school tormented them for the entire year and were only rarely disciplined. The Nine were cursed, spit on, hit, and isolated. As Thelma Mothershed remembers, "There were some mornings I got up and my throat was tight. I didn't want to go because I knew I would be ignored all day for the most part."

A diary kept by Melba Pattillo between 1957 and 1958 that became a published memoir of that school year deals with middle-class, Southern, female teenaged life in the Bible belt during the 1950s, whether black or white: friends, family life, church, boys, and school. As Pattillo wrote in her diary about the reception she received from whites at school, "I longed to tell them, 'I won't hurt you, honest, give me a chance, come on I'm an average teenager, just like yourself . . . with the same aspirations and heartaches.'"[21]

But it was not to be. Because no white students were willing to corroborate the incidents, it did no good for the Nine to report them to the principal's office since the administration took the position that unless a teacher saw what had occurred it could not punish the behavior. In April 1958 the *New York Post* ran an article in which it listed forty-two separate incidents ranging from outright attacks to harassment of the Nine. As justification for doing nothing, Virgil Blossom responded,

> The segregationists are now only a hard core, and we don't intend to give them some martyrs which will enable them to spread their influence. . . . The temper of the community is such that we must be prepared to see each case through court.[22]

By its failure to remove permanently even a single white student during the entire school year despite acts of violence that rose to the level of criminal behavior, the Little Rock School District signaled it ultimately had no intention of standing up for its defenseless black students. Rather, by its decision to dismiss Minnijean Brown for the rest of the school year after two incidents in which white students successfully goaded her into retaliatory responses, the district gave hope to the group of parents and students who had been trying all year to force the Little Rock Nine to quit. Brown's expulsion came after she had dropped the contents of a bowl of chili on a boy's head and then called a girl "white trash." White students wore buttons that read "one down; eight to go." Countering this group was a handful of white individuals, including teachers, administrators, assistant principals Elizabeth Huckaby and J. O. Powell, and students who were genuinely sympathetic to the plight of the Nine. Of these individuals, the experience of watching their abuse and the stoicism with which they endured it effected a moral transformation in J. O. Powell. In a part of the manuscript *The Long*

Shadow of Little Rock that did not appear in the book, Daisy Bates wrote that Powell, "who had been completely indifferent" to the Nine, became in the course of the year "obsessed" with their fair treatment. "We could never have kept the children in school without his help." As Bates explained, Powell's assistance had to be rendered quietly. "He used to sneak over to see us in the middle of the night to bring information dressed in old fishing clothes."[23]

The War on the NAACP

Whites, including local and state authorities, repeatedly attacked the Bateses and the NAACP on many fronts. Nothing was more intimidating than the well-publicized effort to force the NAACP to turn over its membership lists and contributors. With most black adults in Arkansas vulnerable to economic pressure, the possible disclosure that one was either a member or had contributed to the NAACP was itself enough to destroy the organization in the state. Yet it was not only blacks who were intimidated; whites were, as well, as the pressure intensified. Pine Bluff attorney George Howard Jr., then a member of the NAACP legal redress committee in 1957 and who much later became the first black federal judge in Arkansas, remembered that there "were whites who were encouraging her [Daisy Bates], . . . whites who brought in contributions to assist her. . . . If [her opponents] got these records, it would bring a halt."[24]

In fact, the fear by itself was enough. As Daisy Bates later noted bitterly in an interview with historian Elizabeth Jacoway, "Of course, all my friends stopped coming, because they were afraid."[25] Contributions to the NAACP from Arkansans dwindled to almost nothing.

A Police State in Little Rock

In the two years following his decision to confront the federal government, Faubus became a different man. From a relatively liberal politician who had been "cautiously supportive of the aspirations of blacks," in the words of his biographer, Roy Reed, he now was a man

> who could allow himself to believe that their efforts to vindicate their constitutional and human rights were part of a vast Communist conspiracy when there was no meaningful evidence to support that view.[26]

As a zealot he lost any sense of restraint, and winning election after election, he controlled all levers of power in state government. Thus, it was a small step to using the Criminal Investigation Division (CID) of the state police to spy on his enemies. Who were his enemies?—anyone thought remotely to be sympathetic to integration. Roy Reed provides indelible snapshots of a spy operation worthy of totalitarian countries that operated in Little Rock "from 1957 until the end of Faubus's tenure in 1967." The CID

> infiltrated organizations, tapped telephones, secretly tape-recorded meetings, compiled lists of group members and suspected sympathizers, traced car ownership through license numbers, fingered state employees suspected of integrationist or anti-Faubus sympathies, and collected damaging personal information on political opponents and seemingly ordinary citizens.[27]

At the end of the year in 1957 Daisy Bates was named by the Associated Press "Woman of the Year in Education." Carrying with it international recognition, this honor infuriated many whites and institutions in Little Rock, including the *Arkansas Democrat,* which mounted a personal attack on her. Nothing would have made the enemies of Daisy Bates happier than to show she was a Communist or even a Communist sympathizer, but despite years of surveillance by law enforcement, her FBI file revealed in numbing detail that she and L. C. Bates were simply loyal Americans who fought for civil rights. The only real connection Daisy Bates ever had with Communism was her friendship with Lee and Grace

Lorch. A tireless worker in the Little Rock branch of the NAACP, Lee Lorch had admitted to once having been a Communist but successfully fought attempts by the Congress's House Un-American Activities Committee to answer questions about whether he was presently a Communist Party member. Grace Lorch did likewise. The real sin of the Lorches was their idealism and commitment to racial equality, and Daisy Bates never turned her back on them.[28]

Despite a campaign of harassment that never ended the entire year, Ernest Green, the lone senior, graduated from Central on May 27, 1958, in an event invested with such symbolic importance that the ceremony was attended by Martin Luther King Jr. Among many other awards from civil rights organizations the Nine and Daisy Bates received that summer was the Spingarn Medal, the highest honor given by the NAACP.

The Case for a Delay

On June 20, 1958, Harry Lemley, a Southerner who had replaced Ronald Davies as federal district judge in the litigation of *Aaron v. Cooper*, granted the Little Rock School District's motion for a two-and-a-half-year delay in proceeding with school desegregation. The NAACP interpreted Lemley's decision as a color-coded victory for continued white supremacy and discrimination at the expense of the students' constitutional rights and appealed it to the eighth circuit. On August 18, the Eighth Circuit Court of Appeals voted six-to-one to overturn Judge Lemley's decision; however, since the rules permitted a single dissenting judge (Chief Justice Gardner) to delay the implementation of the decision while the case was being appealed to the U.S. Supreme Court, the NAACP requested an expedited appeal. The U.S. Supreme Court signaled the importance of the case by agreeing to hear the case almost immediately. Normally, an appeal to the Court takes months or even years.

Orval Faubus's Solution

Governor Faubus, then in complete control of the legislature, expected, as it quickly did, that the U.S. Supreme Court would rule that the Little Rock School District would have to go forward with its plan of desegregation. If necessary, the governor was prepared to try to engineer, through the legislative process, a transfer of the Little Rock high schools into private hands. Thus, as soon as the Supreme Court ruled against the Little Rock School District, Faubus signed the "School Closing Act" and arranged to set an election to be held on September 27 for Little Rock voters. The election purported to give Little Rock voters the choice of closing the city's high schools or total integration. In fact, as the governor and his supporters well knew, compliance with federal law would mean token desegregation, but with a well-organized and financed group behind it, the Save Our Schools Committee (SOS), the measure passed overwhelmingly, 19,470 to 7,561. Astonishingly, in the name of segregation and states' rights, the governor of Arkansas and a group of determined supporters had convinced the residents of its capital city to do away with its most important resource, the public education of many of its citizens. It was an extraordinary moment in the history of Little Rock and had disastrous consequences for the city's economic growth, not to mention the individual hardships on children and their families. Blacks found it incomprehensible that whites chose such a self-destructive path. An editorial in the *State Press* expressed amazement over the vote: "We never anticipated their speaking out in defense of Negro children, but we did think they would come to the defense of their own children."[29]

The Lost School Year of 1958–1959

For many black students, the "lost year" was a disaster. J. Harvey Walthall documents that 376 black students or 50.1 percent of black students "attended no schools at all" between 1958 and 1959. Two hundred seventy-seven went to black public schools in Arkansas, and ninety-one went out of state. Six entered college early, making a total of 750 who were "displaced" by the school closings. A total of 208 white students or 7.1 percent did not attend school that year. Sondra Gordy writes about the consequences to both black and white students.

> One can measure it with statistics but nothing clarifies it more than the words of one displaced black student. "I remember running the streets, taking odd jobs when men came into the 9th Street pool halls looking for laborers. . . . I became cynical, lost any respect for authority I had, and blamed adults for not doing the right thing by young people. You take on certain characteristics when you do not have structure in your life. You couldn't tell me anything. . . . The only school I ever graduated from was the school of hard knocks."[30]

Though doomed to failure, Faubus's scheme was to try to reopen the high schools in Little Rock as a private corporation that could admit whomever it pleased. Though the Little Rock School Board signed a lease with the newly formed private school corporation, this subterfuge to try to avoid integration was declared void by the federal judiciary through a challenge brought by the NAACP, but it took months of litigation, and the high schools in Little Rock stayed shut the entire academic year.

Women to the Rescue

Even though Faubus had achieved his goal of stopping integration in Little Rock through the September 27 election, a new organization in Little Rock had just formed, though not in time to be successful. Called the Women's Emergency Committee (WEC), this group of women, for the most part composed of upper-class whites whose husbands were part of the business and professional community that ran Little Rock, had much more success in the coming year. Where their husbands had been outmaneuvered at every turn by Orval Faubus, these women were determined to organize themselves into an effective political force to get the schools open. To do so, they immediately were faced with a tactical decision. At their initial meeting at the home of Adolphine Terry, "several women in the audience quietly left" after plans were announced to recruit blacks to the organization. After learning the organization had decided not to allow blacks to join, black contributions dropped off sharply but its decision may have insured the ultimate success of the Women's Emergency Committee.[31]

The Arrogance of Power

On May 5, 1959, three members of the school board voted to fire forty-five teachers and administrators whom they identified as having sympathy for integration. This attempted purge would not have stood up in court since three others had walked out to prevent a quorum from being present. It was this arrogant, brazen act of creating a litmus test for cherished teachers and administrators that prompted a group of 179 Little Rock civic and business leaders to meet and form an organization they called STOP (Stop This Outrageous Purge) for the purpose of trying to recall the three members who had voted to fire the teachers. In fact, in order to ferret out integration sympathizers the 1958 Arkansas legislature had passed "Act 10," which required teachers and other state employees to list their membership in organizations and even those groups to whom they contributed money. It was not until 1960 that this legislation was declared unconstitutional. Despite her understandable resentment of WEC policy, Daisy Bates was enough of a pragmatist to help turn out black voters on May 25 to participate in a special recall election of school board members. Even as the white power structure joined with blacks to vote for recall of the three radical segregationists, the segregated nature of their alliance was real.

For example, blacks attended a rally a few days before the election at the Dunbar Community Center; white STOP supporters packed into Robinson Auditorium. WEC members conducted a highly efficient grass-roots campaign, using sophisticated techniques aimed at likely white voters; Philander Smith students organized rides to the polls for blacks. In the end, as historian Ben Johnson notes, almost three out of every four votes in "both the upper-income white ward and predominantly African-American precincts" went for the so-called "moderate" position.[32]

And to put the icing on the cake for the victors, on June 18 a federal court overruled the Arkansas Supreme Court and held unconstitutional the school closing law. The power over the Little Rock School Board was now broken, and Faubus, the consummate political realist, soon began to tack toward the center to feed his now ravenous appetite to maintain himself in power.

The Reopening of the Little Rock High Schools

The recent victories did not mean that all went smoothly. On the contrary, police chief Gene Smith ordered fire hoses turned on a howling, Confederate flag–waving mob of a thousand at Central as school opened on August 11. Using the "Pupil Placement Law," the Little Rock School Board permitted only six blacks to attend schools with whites, three at Central and three at Hall.

During this crucial time, the level of violence skyrocketed. Besides continued harassment and attacks on the home of Daisy and L. C. Bates, which had been going on since 1957, on Labor Day bombs exploded at the Little Rock School District office and at the place of business of the new mayor of Little Rock. Though only doing minimal damage to these targets, the bombers managed to damage the vehicle of Little Rock's fire chief, presumably because he had betrayed his Southern heritage and had followed orders to turn the fire hose on white demonstrators at the Central campus. Of the bombers, E. A. Lauderdale, a member of the Capital Citizens Council, was given a three-year sentence, but the governor saw to it that he was released after only six months and returned his fine of five hundred dollars.

Within this police-state culture it was notable that during the school year of 1959–1960, Ted Lamb, a member of the Little Rock School Board, began publicly calling integration a "moral" issue, a position never before taken by any board member. Daisy Bates credited him for having "led the fight to get the three additional children admitted to Central."[33] Soon Lamb, who owned a successful advertising business, began insisting on genuine integration of the Little Rock School District. Within months he lost his advertising business and was defeated when he ran for a new term.

On October 30, 1959, the last issue of the *State Press* appeared in Arkansas. For eighteen years the paper had been a weekly reminder to Arkansas citizens of the injustices black people faced. Daisy Bates wrote the NAACP in New York,

> There comes a time in everyone's life when one must realize that there are forces too powerful to withstand. For more than a year, L.C. and I have watched our white friends and supporters being picked off one by one for daring to stand up for what is right. Each month agents [who sold the *State Press*] grew fewer and fewer. Our friends, teachers and principals from whom we get most of our state support, reported in September that they could not support the paper any longer because of local pressures.[34]

As the 1950s ended in Arkansas, for those who believed in the cause of civil rights for blacks there seemed very little to cheer about. Though on paper local chapters of the NAACP continued to exist in the state, there had become empty shells stripped of active members and financial support. Despite major legal victories upholding First Amendment rights to privacy and freedom of speech, the NAACP in Arkansas now existed in name only. During the last of the decade Arkansas was governed by a man who found great political success in pandering to the worst instincts of the electorate. As Roy Reed has said about Faubus after 1957, "Much of his political behavior during the next several years was a blend of coded white supremacy and McCarthyism."[35] It must be said that Faubus's worst sin was not that he initiated the 1957 Little Rock school desegregation crisis. Enough questions have been raised about his motives to delay, perhaps forever, a final judgment about that issue. What Faubus did was infinitely worse: with no justification whatever, he turned the city of Little Rock for a time into a police state and attacked civil liberties of African Americans as well as whites throughout Arkansas through his willingness to go along with the persecution of the NAACP.

CHAPTER 13

Wandering in the Wilderness of Race: 1957–1960

The 1957 Central High crisis and its aftermath proved historic for both the state and the nation. The story requires a closer analysis of some of the actions of a number of the primary participants in this period.

The Southern Moderate

In 1957 J. N. Heiskell, publisher of the *Arkansas Gazette,* was an astonishing eighty-five years old. His family had controlled the paper since 1902 and had long ago bought out his partner. Going so far back, Heiskell had a long track record in his thinking about blacks. Once he had "justified lynching of blacks on the theory that some plantations were so remote that nothing else would deter their savage behavior," but ultimately had come to the conclusion that lynching was "uncivilized" and had opposed it.[1] Blacks could not be trusted to vote responsibly, and at one time he had supported, as many other Arkansans had, the repeal of the Fifteenth Amendment. Favoring the swift execution of the twelve blacks convicted in Helena in 1919, he never changed his mind about that and regarded the lengthy litigation efforts on their behalf as a travesty of justice when the system capitulated to outside pressure, resulting in their freedom. However, he was plainly shocked by the shameful behavior of his fellow white citizens during the John Carter lynching in 1927 and took them to task repeatedly. Now, thirty years later the rumors were rife that Orval Faubus was going to throw his lot in on this issue with a segment of the population that was not embarrassed cut to the quick.

In a now-much-celebrated meeting on the Sunday before Labor Day with editor Harry Ashmore and his son-in-law, *Gazette* publisher Hugh Patterson, owner Heiskell is portrayed as having to make a decision then and there about the paper's direction. Harry Ashmore told Heiskell, "The position you have to take is to support the school board but I can't make that decision. It's your newspaper and it's costing you money." According to Roy Reed, Heiskell ultimately responded, "I won't let people like that take over my town."[2]

"People like that" were, of course, those men and women who were going to cause major embarrassment to the city of Little Rock and damage its reputation and business climate. But not only that, they would possibly behave in a way that recalled the indelible nightmare of thousands of Little Rock whites participating in the blood ritual lynching of John Carter. Heiskell, it needs to be said, was not objecting to the continuation of white supremacy but the manner in which it was carried out.

On September 4, 1957, the *Arkansas Gazette* went toe-to-toe with Orval Faubus with its editorial entitled, "The Crisis Mr. Faubus Made." After setting out the scenario of the National Guard surrounding Central, Harry Ashmore wrote, "The issue is no longer segregation vs. integration. The question has now become the supremacy of the government of the United States in all matters of law. And clearly the federal government cannot let this issue remain unsolved, no matter what the cost to this community."[3] With this editorial, the "Southern Moderate" position was born. In editorial after editorial, Harry Ashmore confronted Faubus repeatedly with the consequences of his defiance. Once a Faubus supporter (he wrote a key speech for Faubus explaining his sojourn at socialist Commonwealth College during his runoff election with Francis Cherry), Ashmore wrote on September 20, three days before real violence erupted at Central, "Mr. Faubus has made it quite clear that he will not contribute to an orderly solution. He will, he has said, withdraw his forces from Central High School if he is ordered to do so. But he will do nothing to uphold the law and prevent the violence his flagrant actions have invited."[4]

Ashmore's approach, approved by his employer, J. N. Heiskell, had nothing to do with the morality of the issue of segregation. According to Nathania Sawyer, editor of the *Encyclopedia of Arkansas* and the author of a master's thesis on Ashmore, this logical and unemotional Southerner absolutely refused to let himself be brought into a debate about right and wrong when it came to the issue of segregation. When he had been hired to write editorials in 1945 at the *Charlotte News,* he saw his "first obligation was to try to prepare my readers to cope with a reality most of them refused to recognize—the great, impersonal forces of change that were bringing the region to the day when white southerners, not yet willing to accept blacks as equals, would be confronted by black southerners who were no longer willing to accept anything less."[5]

Indeed, in *Epitaph for Dixie,* published in 1958, Ashmore wrote, "The key to today's dilemma does not lie in attempting to change the white attitude by moral persuasion, but in re-ordering our institutions to accommodate the legitimate demands of the minority group." Change would come as blacks upgraded themselves, but "time in this instance must be measured in generations."[6]

Martin Luther King Jr. and the Southern Moderate

In fact, "the great, impersonal forces of change," would not be impersonal at all. They would consist at least, in part, of a dynamic, fundamentalist Christian faith held by African Americans and their leader Martin Luther King Jr., plus an assortment of black and a very few white men and women possessed also of a belief in nonviolence and a willingness to go to jail for their beliefs. Harry Ashmore was dead wrong. Civil rights for black people became a great moral crusade that would be embraced by many people and no less a white Southerner, if not many of his fellow Southerners, than the president of the United States, Lyndon Baines Johnson. In 1957, however, the kiss of death for the Southern Moderate position, in Little Rock, Arkansas, would have been to argue that segregation was immoral. Even at its strongest, the Southern Moderate position was a convenient whipping boy for Faubus until he and his radical segregationists supporters, as we shall see, finally overplayed their hand in 1959. But for two years Little Rock whites in positions of authority completely miscalculated the power of ordinary white citizens to affect events. All they had needed was some leadership, and with an outsider in the governor's chair, they found the perfect man for the job.

Ashmore, himself, made no apologies for segregation or white supremacy. It could "be defended as a necessary bridge in the Negro's progress from slavery to citizenship."[7] While Ashmore may not have anticipated the form this phase of the civil rights movement would take or feel comfortable with it, he was astute enough to know where history was going, and he felt duty bound to prepare white Southerners for the future. In an interview with Elizabeth Jacoway, Daisy Bates would remember Ashmore as "about the most liberal" white person she knew at the time, but in fact, at heart he was a gradualist who argued in *Epitaph for Dixie* that if the white South as a "absolute incontrovertible fact . . . provided separate but equal facilities [to African Americans]," it would receive a sympathetic hearing that "we have met the stated commitments of citizenship and we may insist that matters involved in the private relationship between the two races, are, and should be, beyond the reach of law." And as if to underscore the paper's position, Ashmore wrote on the editorial page the following: "The members of the Little Rock School Board would without exception qualify as segregationist. Indeed, they felt (as we do) that they were working to preserve the existing pattern of social segregation when they evolved a plan which would, in compliance with the new federal law, result in the admission of only a few, carefully screened Negro students to a single white high school."[8] But even as Ashmore wrote editorials implying he was comfortable with segregation and at most a gradualist, he was also, as he described his employer, J. N. Heiskell, a "civil libertarian." Now that the federal court had approved a token plan of desegregation, he acted behind the scenes to help tokenism come to fruition. In her memoir Daisy Bates wrote that Ashmore, Edwin Dunaway, and Woodrow Mann, the lame duck mayor of Little Rock, tried unsuccessfully on Sunday, September 22, to persuade the federal government to provide protection for the Little Rock Nine who would be attempting to enter Central the next day.

Daisy Bates had her own view of the Byzantine events of this period. According to Ashmore, she told Edwin Dunaway, "He's [Faubus] against you and the people in the Heights, and I'm going to have to pay for it."[9] There are many people today, and Daisy Bates was one of them, who considered Orval Faubus's actions in this period to have been guided strictly by his calculation of what he needed to do to win a third term. After an initial period of demonizing Orval Faubus, recent historians, as indicated, paint a much more complex picture of the governor's motives. Roy Reed, who spent six years on his biography of Faubus and interviewed him numerous times, wrote that Faubus "appears still in my mind, even after his death, as an insoluble mixture of cynicism and compassion, of guile and grace, of wickedness and goodness. I have observed his life off and on for over forty years, and I don't know whether he was good or evil, or even whether those were the choices. There was a time when I knew. But that was long ago and I was young."[10] The motives of the governor may always remain a mystery.

Daisy Bates Front and Center

In the last frantic nine-day period in August 1957 when a number of lawsuits, in addition to the one filed by

Margaret Thompson, were being filed in Little Rock, Daisy Bates became the media conduit for the plaintiffs in the litigation and particularly for those students who would become known as the Little Rock Nine. While there is some controversy among the Nine over the degree to which she became their mentor during the 1957 crisis, there is no doubt about the commitment of either Daisy or L. C. Bates to the goals of the national office of the NAACP and its desire to see that the Nine finish the school year despite their sadistic and cruel treatment throughout. The devotion and dedication of both Daisy and L. C. Bates to this mission never wavered, despite their own continuous harassment. While the Bateses became financially dependent on the national office of the NAACP to continue the operation of the *State Press* until it closed in 1959, the national office of the NAACP through its executive director, Roy Wilkins, was equally dependent on Daisy Bates in particular to continue the fight for school integration at Central High. Throughout this period and beyond, no one ever doubted the courage of either L. C. or Daisy Bates. Cool under fire, Daisy Bates, as the saying goes, never let her enemies see her sweat. At times the stress was unbearable, but she never let on in public how difficult the struggle was. If she and L. C. Bates were sometimes abrasive and arrogant in dealing with the black community in Little Rock, the other side of the coin was that they were strong enough to stand up to the constant hostility shown them by the white community and to the criticism from certain blacks, as well.

No black students tried to enter Central High School Tuesday morning after Faubus's speech the night before. The Little Rock School District had requested that no efforts be made to do so until the legality of his actions had been resolved. What would have awaited them would have been a terrifying sight. A crowd estimated at between three and four hundred whites stood across from the main entrance to Central and had been gathering since six in the morning. They were passing out leaflets, some of which were entitled,

"What Lincoln Said about Segregation." In fact, Lincoln's campaign speech had dealt with his commitment to white supremacy. Throughout the day it was not clear what action Faubus would take now that the National Guard was in place. One statement from the governor's office said the troops were not there to prevent "integration," but then during a press conference he said, "I doubt it," when a reporter asked if the troops would allow the black students to enter.[11]

The Little Rock School District fully expected Judge Davies to order it to proceed with its plan to enroll the students the next morning, and Virgil Blossom hastily called a meeting of the parents of the children and leaders in the black community. While Blossom omitted Daisy Bates from the list, others told her, and she went anyway. What occurred at the meeting illustrated how the white supremacy of the era influenced the behavior of both communities even at a moment of supreme distrust. Blossom told the parents that it would be easier to insure the children's safety if the parents did not accompany them to Central the next morning. "If violence breaks out, it will be easier to protect the children if the adults aren't there."

There could not have been a parent in the room whose blood did not chill at the thought of leaving their children at the mercy of whites whom they had no reason whatsoever to trust. As Daisy Bates wrote in her memoir, "As we left the building, I was aware how deeply worried the parents were, although they did not voice their fears."[12] Nor did Daisy Bates herself apparently protest despite her own knowledge that she could not rely on a single word out of the mouth of Virgil Blossom. As she later told Elizabeth Jacoway, Blossom, in explaining his desegregation plan repeatedly at countless civic meetings, "was saying one thing to whites . . . and one thing to Negroes." Jacoway writes, "Several white leaders, who have asked not to be identified, have corroborated this charge" of "Blossom's duplicity."[13] But here again was the power of white supremacy in 1957. If some white authority figure told a black person what to do, it was nigh impossible to resist or even to protest, no matter how distasteful or dangerous. It was a question of power. If a white person in a position of authority said that he could make something happen, the overwhelming tendency was to accept it even if it went against every nerve fiber in one's body.

As anticipated, the hearing in Judge Davies's courtroom was short, and his order was to the point. The Little Rock School District's plan to admit however many blacks that showed up was to go forward.

Ministers Who Dared

One group of whites who were obviously troubled by what was about to occur at Central was a group of sixteen white ministers who issued a statement earlier in the evening in which they protested Faubus's actions and called on "every citizen to pray for a 'right example' for every child in the community."[14] In fact, the sixteen who signed were ministers of some of the elite Christian churches in Little Rock, including Second Presbyterian, Trinity Episcopal, Second Baptist, Immanuel Baptist, Pulaski Heights Methodist, and Central Presbyterian Church, whose minister was Dunbar Ogden Jr., president of the recently formed Interracial Ministerial Alliance.[15] With black children determined to enroll the next morning and a mob expected to greet them, according to her memoir, it occurred to Daisy Bates to call Dunbar Ogden and suggest to him that since no parents were going to accompany the children to Central that a group of interracial ministers might serve as an escort for them. Ogden was noncommittal but said he would get back to her. When he did call her back later in the night, he had apparently not been able to persuade a single one of his colleagues but said he would keep calling others and "God willing, I'll be there."[16]

Before going to bed after 2:30 in the morning, Bates arranged for a police car to meet the children at the corner of Twelfth and Park where they would meet the ministers, if any of them did show up. She was unable to contact

Elizabeth Eckford, whose family did not have a telephone, and she forgot to arrange to get a message to her.

Early the next morning an interracial group that included ministers and others met at the Dunbar Community Center to plan the effort to enter Central. As it developed, four whites, including Reverend Ogden, his twenty-one-year-old son David, George A. Chauncey (minister of the First Presbyterian Church in Monticello in South Arkansas), and Will Campbell, an activist from the National Council of Churches, walked in front of the students; black ministers Reverend Harry Bass and Reverend Z. Z. Dryver walked behind them. The group of black students included six of those who would become known as the Little Rock Nine: Jefferson Thomas, Carlotta Walls, Gloria Ray, Ernest Green, Thelma Mothershed, and Minnijean Brown. One black student, Jane Hill, walked with the students but did not enroll at Central.

Elizabeth Eckford

As Daisy and L. C. Bates drove to Central High that morning, they heard on the radio that one of the black students was being mobbed at Central High. Because Daisy Bates had forgotten to contact Elizabeth Eckford and tell her to meet the students, she had proceeded all alone without anyone to accompany her. L. C. Bates jumped out of the car and ran to see about her. A picture taken of Elizabeth Eckford that morning sitting on a bench at Fourteenth and Park Streets by herself after having been turned away twice from Central by the National Guard would become one of the most famous photographs of the civil rights movement. According to an *Arkansas Gazette* reporter, Eckford spent thirty-five minutes at Fourteenth and Park enduring the taunts of the mob. When members of the mob got too close, an officer from the National Guard told them to "move back from the bench."[17] At one point Grace Lorch, a white member of the Little Rock NAACP and wife of Little Rock NAACP activist Lee Lorch, stood between Eckford and the assembled mob. Eckford was helped onto a city bus by Lorch. Though the presence of the Arkansas National Guard likely saved Elizabeth Eckford from injury or even death that morning, Eckford, though able to work at full-time employment, experienced post-traumatic stress disorder from which she has never fully recovered.[18]

The experience of the other students was not as tumultuous. According to an affidavit given to the FBI that day by Harry Bass, Arkansas National Guard colonel Johnson said to the students, "This school is off limits to Negro students and Negro schools are off limits to white students."[19] In order to go forward with the litigation in federal court, the students had to establish they had been denied admission, and this was achieved.

"Arkansas Hate"

Instantly, the morning events in Little Rock became a national and international news story as photographs of the howling mob were transmitted around the world. "Arkansas Hate!" read the front-page caption of the *St. Louis Argus,* a black newspaper.[20] However Faubus justified his actions, the refusal of the National Guard to admit black students to Central immediately became the most important constitutional crisis of the first half of the twentieth century. As the world's important democracy, the United States was suddenly on trial in the court of public opinion to determine its capacity to vindicate individual civil rights that had been adjudicated in the federal courts. For many years America's enemies and even friends had excoriated the hypocrisy of a country that held itself out to the rest of the world as a beacon of justice while at the same time allowing a large section of the country to deny equal rights and opportunities to millions of its citizens. The explanation had always been to one and all alike that the United States is a country ruled by law, not by men, and that federal law is supreme. In its wisdom, the Supreme Court had once permitted the doctrine of "separate but equal" in the field of public education, and until it changed its mind or until a constitutional amendment rolled back its decision in *Plessy v. Ferguson,* its decision must and would be respected. Now that the Supreme Court had changed its mind and ruled that black and white children must receive together the same educational services and opportunities, would this actually occur?

The response of the Little Rock School Board to the pressure that was beginning to swarm all sides was to file a motion requesting a delay of its plans to desegregate Central. There was, of course, no going back for the black plaintiffs in *Aaron v. Cooper.* Over the weekend of September 8, Thurgood Marshall flew in to Little Rock for the hearing on Monday before Judge Davies to stay at the house of Daisy and L. C. Bates and found it an armed camp.

If there was any new justification for a delay at the hearing on Monday, it was not apparent to Judge Davies, who responded to the petition and evidence presented by saying, "The testimony and arguments this morning were, in my judgment as anemic as the petition itself."[21]

The President and a Southern Governor

With so much at stake, Brooks Hays, Arkansas's congressman from the second district, which included Little Rock, felt with justification that he could play a constructive role in resolving the crisis between his beloved state and the federal government. Though he had no choice politically but to identify himself as a segregationist, Hays was no fire-eater. Described by Roy Reed as "one of Arkansas's most liberal politicians," Hays had strong ties to Washington and telephoned his friend presidential assistant Sherman Adams to arrange a meeting between Eisenhower and Faubus. Taking place on September 14 at Newport, Rhode Island, the meeting for the president proved a "fiasco." Roy Reed writes, "Faubus, the sometime integrationist, almost persuaded Ike, the would-be segregationist, that he should order the whole process stalled. 'Give us a little more time. Ten days, a few weeks.' The old general saw nothing wrong with that. His lawyer [Herbert] Brownell, spoke up firmly and told him that he couldn't give Little Rock anything. 'Even a president is not above a court order,' he said."[22] The meeting ended with the president, after meeting privately with Faubus for approximately twenty minutes, announcing to Brownell "that Faubus had agreed to let the black children in the high school. Just as flat as that. And Faubus was standing there."[23]

In fact, Faubus returned to Arkansas the next day and immediately announced that he was standing by what he had done. The National Guard troops would remain; no black children would be permitted to enter Central. Either he had lied to the president of the United States, or he had gone back on his word immediately. Neither interpretation brought honor to the reputation of the state of Arkansas. Though his decision would result in his immediate reelection and for years to come, his lack of integrity in dealing with the president was a disgrace to his office and to the state, but, in the immediate future, he would repeatedly top this performance.

Thus, despite a federal court ruling, troops still surrounded Central High School on September 20. Judge Davies held another hearing and at its conclusion ordered the governor of Arkansas not to interfere with the Little Rock School District's plans to desegregate Central High School. Either Faubus would comply or he would undoubtedly be held in contempt of court. He capitulated immediately and three hours later ordered the troops withdrawn, and then despite all his many words about his duty to preserve law and order, he inexcusably left Little Rock in total turmoil the next day to attend the Southern Governors' Conference in Sea Island, Georgia. In explaining this total dereliction of his duty as governor, the only conclusion to be drawn is that Faubus did not want to give any ammunition to his future political opponents that he had assisted school integration in any way by taking responsibility for providing protection for the students. What occurred on September 23 would again shame the entire state of Arkansas in the eyes of the world, but in keeping with long tradition, most white Arkansans would blame the victims of the violence.

The Violence on September 23

Without the National Guard in place, the decision to again try to enroll the students at Central on the twenty-third was risky from the beginning. The crowds at Central were ugly and big and were clearly spoiling for a fight whenever black students should dare to enroll. Though Daisy Bates would later recall that, with the assistance of Edwin Dunaway and Harry Ashmore, she had tried to obtain the help of the Justice Department in Washington for Monday's effort to enter Central, none was forthcoming. A question that has never been satisfactorily answered is why neither the Little Rock School District nor the attorneys for the plaintiffs ever filed a petition asking for the assistance of the federal government as was done so successfully in the Hoxie case. It can only be assumed that by the third week of September the members of the Little Rock School Board felt under too much pressure from whites in the community to risk doing anything that would have been interpreted as aiding blacks in their efforts to desegregate Central High School.

In light of the fact that just days earlier Daisy Bates had given the possibility of danger as a reason why the students had not again tried to enter Central, what had changed now to convince her to go forward? One surmises that she felt under pressure from the NAACP in New York to complete the process now that Faubus had stepped aside. Too, the Little Rock Police Department was saying it could provide adequate security. As difficult as some whites made life for Daisy and L. C. Bates, it would have been infinitely harder had it not been for the evenhanded treatment they and other blacks received from Officer Gene Smith, who would eventually become chief of police in Little Rock.

The lack of adequate security on September 23 can also be placed at the feet of Little Rock's mayor Woodrow Mann, who apparently put his hatred of Orval Faubus ahead of an opportunity to provide additional security by using National Guard troops. Lieutenant Governor Nathan Gordon would have made them available had Mann been willing to put the request for their assistance in writing. Though state policemen supplemented the ranks of Little Rock policemen at Central High, there were not enough law enforcement personnel to make a difference. Mann's failure to ask for help appears inexcusable.

Though the group that became known as the Little Rock Nine made it into Central High without violence early on the morning of the twenty-third, it was only because the crowd was diverted by the appearance of journalists and photographers who were chased and beaten by the mob. Alex Wilson, editor of the black-owned and operated *Memphis Tri-State Defender,* was horribly beaten and severely injured. Earl Davy, who took photographs for the *Arkansas State Press,* was beaten as well as northern white reporters from the staff of *Life,* a popular national magazine. Francis Miller, a photographer for *Life,* said, "He was evidently arrested for striking a man's fist with his head."[24] Inside Central there was no violence. Thanks to Edwin Dunaway, who had agreed to take her calls, Daisy Bates kept up with what was occurring at the school. In the early afternoon she telephoned Gloster Current, an official of the national NAACP, and said, in part, the following: "The students are nice, the teachers are nice. For the most part, everyone was nice. But the mob on the outside is building up and building up and building up." Bates was right to worry. An early afternoon edition of the *Arkansas Democrat* described the scene as a "howling, shrieking, violent mob of more than 1,000 [which was] hurling rocks and bottles indiscriminately at passing cars."[25]

Blacks who lived near Central and were old enough to remember had to be wondering if white mobs were about to go off on them as they had during the John Carter lynching thirty years earlier. Then, mob violence directed against blacks had ruled the streets of Little Rock and seemed on the verge of getting out of control again. Assistant police chief Gene Smith spoke with Superintendent Blossom and made the decision to get the nine students out of the school. Rushed out a back entrance, they escaped physical injury. Upon hearing the news, the mob began to drift away from the school, but the danger was not over. Press reports indicate that at one point during the night police stopped "a caravan of about 100 cars" as they headed east on High Street. A search of the first few cars turned up no weapons, and police sent the vehicles in different directions. Though it appears that a caravan of cars was headed toward the Bates home before it was broken up, news accounts do not confirm her story in *The Long Shadow of Little Rock* that law enforcement confiscated quantities of weapons and dynamite that night.[26] All nine of the children's homes were provided police protection the night of the twenty-third. L. C. and Daisy Bates, their friends, reporters, and others stood guard all night for an attack that fortunately never materialized.

Daisy Bates and Clarence Laws, an employee of the national NAACP who was requested by Daisy Bates to come to Little Rock to assist her, prepared a statement whose message was that the NAACP "deplores violence or vandalism whether committed by white or Negro persons" and "called on all Negroes" to desist from any such acts.[27] In a telephone call between New York and Little Rock the next morning, Gloster Current suggested that the statement be distributed by means of flyers in the community to implore blacks to remain nonviolent and that meetings be held in the community to spread the message. Surely, not one of the Little Rock Nine could have dreamed that night what was about to occur the next day. Suddenly, the story was much larger. It was now the State of Arkansas versus the United States Government.

The Worst Fire Ever

Nothing illustrated Orval Faubus's cynical use of race than his behavior during the aftermath of the worst fire until that point in the history of Arkansas.[28] On March 5, 1959, at approximately four in the morning, a fire swept through a boys dormitory at the Negro Boys Industrial School (NBIS) killing twenty-one children, aged thirteen to seventeen. Situated on 2,600 acres of farm land approximately twelve miles southeast of Little Rock and two miles from the community of Wrightsville, from its infancy the NBIS epitomized neglected and under-funded Jim Crow institutions in Arkansas that existed during the "separate but equal" era.[29] Created by an act of the legislature in 1917, the NBIS eventually found a permanent home in 1936 outside of the community of Wrightsville as primarily a prison farm, not unlike the notorious Arkansas state institution where prisoners were routinely terrorized well into the 1960s.[30] Indeed, a 1956 master's thesis on the NBIS by sociologist Gordon Morgan, now a tenured professor at the University of Arkansas, states that "during a substantial part of the school's history there was not [an] organized educational program of any sort. The 'boys' . . . worked long hours in the field under the supervision of armed 'whipping bosses.'"[31] While "armed whipping bosses" were no longer employed by the school by 1956, conditions at the NBIS in 1956 resembled a tableau straight out of the Dark Ages. Morgan writes, "Many boys go for days with only rags for clothes. More than half of them wear neither socks nor underwear during [the] winter of 1955–56 while this study was in progress." Each boy was provided a single sheet to use that was to last for most of the entire winter. "Pillows and pillow cases are almost non-existent luxuries in the boys' living quarters. In winter baths are seldom required of the inmates, it being not uncommon to see youths going for weeks without bathing or changing clothes." Such squalor was undoubtedly enhanced by the fact that there was but a single thirty-gallon hot water tank in the one shower facility that served the entire school.[32]

Perhaps even more problematic than these conditions was the water supply, a problem that had once been called to the personal attention of Governor Francis Cherry during a visit by him in the summer of 1953.[33] Morgan noted the water the boys drank "was reddish in color. . . . At any rate the staff does not drink this water, but secure their drinking water, in jugs, from another source." Staff explained that the water "will not hurt the boys because they are accustomed to drinking it."[34] Structures and equipment were visibly deteriorating. Morgan noted that "all buildings . . . are in need of extensive repairs, particularly the boys' living quarters."[35] It would be the older boys' dormitory that would burn. The deterioration of the entire physical plant stemmed from the fact that the legislature was determined to treat the NBIS as much as possible as a self-sustaining enterprise. The NBIS grew most of its food and slaughtered stock for meat. There were thirty-five buildings, including a sawmill, a blacksmith shop, and a cotton gin as well as barns to maintain. The typical amount appropriated by the legislature in the 1950s, excluding salaries to run the NBIS, which was home from roughly seventy to over a hundred boys, was around twenty-five thousand dollars annually.[36] In return for accepting salaries that didn't even average two thousand dollars a person, its all-black staff was given housing and food. Even by the 1950s there was little pretense of rehabilitation. A report by the Arkansas director of public welfare in 1952 noted,

> One of the greatest problems of this School has been the large acreage which is in cultivation and which necessitates the boys working long hours during a number of months of the year. During the farming season there would be no time for them to attend school. We asked the Superintendent about this and he said the present plan is to continue the big majority of land.[37]

Gordon Morgan writes of the facility, "Vocational education suffers greatly at the school. There is no adequate shop only a few old tools which can be used. Some agriculture and wood-working is taught but most of the training is in the form of practical work."[38] In comparison, the biennial reports, "Acts of Arkansas," and newspaper accounts of the (white) Arkansas Boys Industrial School in Pine Bluff describe a much greater commitment to providing vocational and academic education and demonstrate that the facility received more money for repairs and maintenance. For example, the 1940 biennial report to the governor lists the following vocational trades provided to the white boys' facility in Pine Bluff: "carpentry and joining, cabinet work, glazing, painting, cement work, brick laying, wood and metal lathe operation, blacksmithing, acetylene welding, plastering, tailoring and shoe mending." In this same report, the NBIS is mentioned only in passing: the white trade school operation turned out 156 mattresses for the NBIS.[39]

In 1953 apparently in an attempt to create an advocate for the NBIS the legislature saw fit to create a separate board for the NBIS, one that required the appointment of two blacks on a five-person board appointed by the governor. It does not seem to have made much of a difference.[40] An article in the *Arkansas Gazette* on March 8, 1959, highlighted some of the differences in the safety features of the all-white Arkansas Boys Industrial School in Pine Bluff and the Negro Boys Industrial School in Wrightsville: according to the white superintendent, "Two one-story fireproof buildings at the Pine Bluff school . . . house 62 boys. . . . Mr. and Mrs. Tony Bucalis, house parents in the building, never leave the dormitory at night." At the NBIS one person was regularly assigned night duty. Further at the white school, "Doors in the dormitory are never locked . . . and the windows are not barred or covered with heavy wire. . . . Electricians make periodic inspection of all wiring in the building."[41] In contrast, the NBIS served as a under-supervised prison firetrap with locked doors and heavy mesh screens.

The Governor and the Fire

Within moments of arriving at the scene of the fire at six in the morning, Orval Faubus found a scapegoat in order to deflect attention from his three administrations' failure to pay adequate attention to the NBIS. Superintendent Lester R. Gaines, a graduate of Arkansas AM&N, who census records show had worked at the school in 1930, immediately became the governor's target. Acting as a self-appointed prosecutor, Faubus told reporters that he would conduct his own investigation "to find the guilty in the tragedy as well as to absolve the innocent" and appointed the board of the NBIS to interview all staff. "There's absolutely no reason for this to happen the way it did except because of negligence of someone."[42]

The "someone" Faubus claimed was negligent at this press conference that morning was Superintendent Gaines who he said had inexcusably failed to maintain adequate supervision over the boys' dormitory the night of the fire. Boys had been locked in for the night and the

> Negro superintendent had not entrusted [the boy] on duty with the keys to the locked doors. He had to break out of the main building and run for help. By this time it was too late for any of the boys to escape through the door. Those who escaped got out and escaped through the windows.[43]

What actually happened was far different than what the governor said, but immediately both the *Arkansas Gazette* and the *Arkansas Democrat* took their cues from the governor and ran stories that made Gaines appear criminally negligent.[44]

On March 7 the governor's own board received unanimous testimony from employees at the NBIS that exculpated Gaines. Every employee who testified supported Gaines's account that due to the hospitalization of a Mr. Banks, whose duty it was to sleep at the dormitory and make periodic bed checks with keys in hand, he had made arrangements with two other employees to perform those duties. Gaines had assigned Lee Austin, the livestock supervisor, to be on duty that night in the dormitory, but because Austin had worked all day, he had also instructed Wilson Hall, the farm manager, to check on Austin at 11 p.m. and 3 a.m. to make sure he was awake. Austin claimed, however, that because the storm that night had knocked out the lights in the dorm, he had gone to his house to search for a flashlight when the fire had started. On the last page of the transcript, three NBIS board members arrived at the following recommendation:

> Based upon the facts brought out at this investigation, this Board is of the unanimous opinion that this tragedy could not have been prevented, that everyone concerned had attempted to carry his duty, and that the person directly charged with the supervision of the building in question, be severely reprimanded.[45]

Clearly, the board was suspicious of Austin's excuse that he had gone to his house to get a flashlight, perhaps believing that he had gone home to sleep in his own bed after Hall had made his 3 a.m. check to make sure he was still awake. At the very least, Hall should have given the fourteen-year-old "sergeant" then in charge his key. Whatever the negligence of Austin, unwittingly his own board had presented Faubus with an extremely embarrassing problem because when asked if "any hazardous condition [had] been reported to you in connection with this dorm" Gaines replied in the affirmative. He said there was "bad wiring in the caretakers room; and the floors are bad."

This information was significant because the fire marshal could not rule out wiring as a cause of the fire. Gaines said that he had known of the condition six months earlier and had gotten his "maintenance man" to correct the problem as "far as he was able," but "to correct the whole situation would require rewiring the entire building." Gaines then testified that he didn't have the funds for repairs but had appeared before the legislative council to request funding and contended that he had "copies of the report presented to the Council." In fact, the minutes of the 1958 legislative council do reflect that Gaines had appeared before it on November 18 and had told the council "that the dormitories, dining hall and personnel living quarters were all badly run down, and the additional request was badly needed. Mr. Gaines said the school has 96 boys at the present time."[46] Not only had the superintendent not been negligent during the fire, he had brought attention to the problem to the one body who could deal with it.

Not surprisingly during Orval Faubus's tenure as governor, the board's March 7 investigative report was suddenly unavailable to the public or the press, and the governor wasn't stopping there. The media was also denied requests to see minutes of the NBIS board prior to the fire. The media did get information that I. S. McClinton, a black supporter of Faubus whose appointment had run out but who could still attend meetings until a replacement had been found, was no longer even being notified of the meetings.[47] There was also another vacancy on the board that had not been filled. Faubus, of course, still had his ace in the hole. He ordered the state police to conduct an investigation, secret, of course. This report has never been located and the results never disclosed, but his NBIS board would soon get the message. On March 25 the governor said he would "recommend" that Superintendent Gaines and three other employees be fired. The principal reason, according to Faubus, was that two unidentified employees of the NBIS had been escorted to the governor's mansion the previous Sunday to recant their testimony. Gaines, these mysterious visitors claimed, had leaned on employees to "fix up" a story to tell investigators.[48]

What Faubus hadn't counted on was that there was still one newspaper in the state that hadn't thrown in the towel. Undoubtedly, L. C. and Daisy Bates smelled the rat in the governor's story from the beginning. As far back as 1953 Daisy Bates had toured the NBIS with two hundred other black women accompanied by Governor Cherry, so she knew of the horrific conditions firsthand. On April 3, in an editorial that was written by L. C. Bates entitled, "Is Governor Faubus Using NBIS Personnel For One of His Escape Holes?" the *State Press* threw down the gauntlet and virtually called the governor a liar.

> Those of us who know the governor's tactics, cannot take too seriously any statement the governor makes. His blame on the personnel of the school for the tragic happenings, could easily be one of his "holes" that the governor boasts about to make his escape when trapping appears evident.[49]

To back up the editorial, the *State Press* ran a statement signed by eleven employees of the NBIS that refuted the governor's statement that two employees had recanted their statements given to the board for the March 7 investigation. It is not known whether the statement was the idea of L. C. Bates or the employees, but it confronted Faubus in a way few dared at the time. In his initial press conference the day of the fire the governor had released a statement intended to cover himself by saying he had accompanied the superintendent on an inspection tour a year earlier and had seen no fire hazards. L. C. Bates turned this statement on its head by including in his editorial the following:

> When the Governor made his "unannounced" visit to the school a little over a year ago, the same "inexcusable conditions" which were so "deplorable" then still e[x]ist. Did Mr. Faubus recommend then that finance [*sic*] be appropriated to correct any of these "deplorable" conditions?[50]

While the statement made by the employees did not keep Gaines and the employees from being fired because of the governor's influence, the impact of L. C. Bates's editorials and the willingness of NBIS employees to confront Faubus would be felt almost a year later. In the meantime, expressing their solidarity with Gaines, all the employees submitted their resignations.

Faubus had wanted Gaines criminally indicted as well as fired. Instead, almost a year to the day of the fire on March 4, 1960, the public institutions committee of the Pulaski County grand jury recommended that no one be indicted criminally for the fire. In part, the report stated:

> The blame can be placed on lots of shoulders for the tragedy: the Board of Directors, to a certain extent, who might have pointed out through newspaper and other publicity the extreme hazards and plight of the school; the Superintendent and his staff, who perhaps continued to do the best they could in a resigned fashion when they had nothing to do with; the State Administration, one right after another through the past years, who allowed conditions to remain so disreputable; the General Assembly of the State of Arkansas, who should have been so ashamed of conditions that they would have previously allowed sufficient money to have these conditions corrected; and finally on the people of Arkansas, who did nothing about it.[51]

As unique and important as this apology was, it, of course, was far from any recognition that government-sponsored segregation was immoral both in principle and practice, nor did it hurt Orval Faubus, who on May 22, 1960, used the occasion of the dedication of a new dormitory and other improvements at the NBIS to campaign for black support. Far from acknowledging any responsibility for the fire, he took credit for the improvements and told his mostly black audience of approximately four hundred people, "These things we did by working together, not by fighting, not by yielding to the agitators of whatever race or creed."[52]

Tucked away in the governor's files were approximately thirty letters and telegrams from Americans from other states who had written him immediately after the fire. Typical of almost all of them all was the following telegram:

> WE HOLD YOU AND THE JIM CROW SYSTEM OF THE SOUTH JUST AS RESPONSIBLE FOR THE BURNING OF THE NEGRO CHILDREN IN LITTLE ROCK AS IF YOU HAD STRUCK THE MATCH WE PLEDGE TO FIGHT UNTIL YOU AND THE SUBHUMAN RACIALISM YOU REPRESENT ARE THROWN INTO THE GARBAGE DUMP OF HISTORY DETROIT PROTEST RALLY GREATER KING SOLOMON BAPTIST CHURCH SPONSORED BY TRADE

UNION LEADERSHIP COUNCIL AND COMMITTEE TO COMBAT RA[C]IAL INJUSTICE[53]

Only one Arkansan wrote the governor to criticize him. Held fast in the grip of white supremacy and their governor's continued ability to convince voters of both races that they were somehow victims of the federal government and "agitators," Arkansans both black and white continued to elect Faubus again and again. Even after the passage of the Civil Rights Act of 1964, the legislature balked at abolishing separate "reform" schools. It would take litigation by civil rights attorney John Walker in 1967 to win this victory. On March 20, 1959, the *State Press* had run a lonely editorial about the fire entitled, "IS Segregation Worth This?" Given the history of the NBIS and the fire, the last two paragraphs seem particularly apt:

> We wonder if the white man in the South who has set the pattern for the Negro to live by, can find any consolation for the irreparable damage that his system has caused.
>
> We also wonder if the Negro who joins the white man and boastingly admits that segregation is what the Negro wants, can sleep soundly at night?[54]

An Alternative View of the Little Rock Crisis

In 2007 Elizabeth Jacoway, a major scholar of the 1957 school desegregation crisis, published *Turn Away Thy Son Little Rock: The Crisis that Shocked the Nation.* Indeed, Jacoway's comprehensive research of the crisis is unsurpassed. Jacoway challenges at several points the prevailing interpretation of the events in Little Rock during this era.[55] In her treatment of the appeal of the Little Rock School Board to the U.S. Supreme Court in *Cooper v. Aaron,* she appears to argue that school board attorney Richard Butler offered a legally sufficient and compelling justification for a delay. Butler claimed in his legal argument to the court that the Little Rock School District was, in fact, wrestling with the issue of "educational quality." In other words, the Little Rock School District should be accorded a delay in order to deal with the issue of how to educate "black children from schools that were admittedly inferior without impairing the standards of education being offered to white children."[56]

The substance of Jacoway's argument seems to be that white Southerners had legitimate concerns about how school desegregation should be accomplished under the *Brown* decisions. Thus, rather than a test of federal versus state authority, the Little Rock crisis should have been dealt with by the federal judiciary as a societal issue that would have been best resolved had the Little Rock School District been allowed to take into consideration "educational quality" from the beginning.

Was it, in fact, "educational quality" that concerned Southerners in the 1950s, or was "educational quality" simply an argument to justify delaying integration of the public schools? Repeatedly, Little Rock School Board members to a man, including the administration, insisted that their goal was to have as little integration as possible for as long as possible. One must remember the district fought tooth and nail when black school teachers in Little Rock in the 1940s had gone to court and fought for equal salaries and had demonstrated no perceptible interest in upgrading the educational quality provided to its black students. Had Arkansas whites, including the Little Rock School District, ever demonstrated a commitment to equal funding for black education, Butler's arguments would not sound today so hollow. In 1957, there was no commitment to maintain "educational quality" for all Arkansans, only white Arkansans.

CHAPTER 14

The Student Non-violent Coordinating Committee Years

A hint of what the 1960s was to bring came to Daisy Bates in a letter after she had spoken on January 1 in an Emancipation Day speech at the Second Baptist Church in Chattanooga, Tennessee. After what she had been through the last three years, Bates had grown increasingly militant. She refused to join in singing the national anthem, explaining to her audience of adults and young people "she felt great sadness" each time it was played, for the United States was not yet "the land of the free." Typically, her harshest words were reserved for blacks themselves as she reprised familiar themes from years of *State Press* editorials. "We must stop the Uncle Toms from running down town saying, 'we have the Negro vote in our back pocket.'" On black ministers: routinely she received letters from the church asking if she had "paid her pledge," but never once had she gotten a letter from a minister asking if she were a registered voter. Ministers should "demand" that members vote. On black leadership: "The day is past when we need a white man to speak for us."

By 1960 Bates was an old hand at raising money for the NAACP, and she would have had no particular reason to think the response to this speech would be any different than normal: enthusiastic applause, contributions to the cause, and then on to the next speech. But a letter sent to her home in Little Rock dated February 26 from a black high school senior named Bettye Williams must have pleased her deeply.

> I'm sure that by now you know what has happened here. Some of the students at Howard School have been conducting "sit-down" demonstrations at different Department stores down town. It began Friday, February 20, 1960. We decided we were tired of waiting for the adults to do something about this matter. So we went to three stores Friday.

Williams described how she had participated and then added,

> I wonder, if you hadn't given such an effective speech that day what would we have done? I have learned from different people that your speech was what gave them so much inspiration and courage to take the steps we have taken. If they do integrate schools, I will apply at the University of Chattanooga this fall.[1]

Williams's letter, in fact, is an artifact of the new phase of the civil rights movement that began on February 1, 1960 when four black freshmen from North Carolina Agricultural and Technical College in Greensboro, North Carolina, sat down at the segregated lunch counter at Woolworth's and requested service and were refused. In turn, the students refused to leave immediately but departed at closing time. Neatly dressed, polite, nonviolent, the students were confronting segregation as a moral issue. When more students came back the next day, the United Press International wire service picked up the story, and during the next fourteen days, sit-ins occurred in fifteen cities in five Southern states.[2]

The Sit-Ins in Little Rock

Soon, Little Rock would be one of them. Ironically, the sit-ins in Little Rock would mark the beginning of the end of an effective leadership role by the NAACP in Arkansas. Part of the reason was financial and tactical. Since the day in 1957 the Little Rock Nine had tried to enroll at Central, the national office of the NAACP had made the support of the *Aaron v. Cooper* litigation a priority. This had involved supporting the Bateses and the Arkansas NAACP leadership through subsidies of the organization and the *State Press*. Though now L. C. Bates had been hired by the national office to be the new paid field secretary for the NAACP in Arkansas and Daisy Bates continued as president of state conference of branches, support of the student sit-ins in Arkansas did not receive the financial support of the national office in the way the school desegregation litigation had. Because of their legal significance and symbolic importance, the national NAACP had even paid for the college educations of the Little Rock Nine. Now, the Arkansas NAACP was no longer to be singled out for special attention by the national office and would have to raise its own funds.

In a letter to Roy Wilkins dated February 23, 1960, Daisy Bates wrote,

> Some of the students from Philander Smith College contacted me Sunday—they are ready to move in on the downtown eating places. They asked for advice on how to proceed, etc. I told them to wait until we had checked and/or interpreted Arkansas's recently passed law concerning sit-down protests and crowds assembled for this purpose.[3]

These would be questions that had no easy answers. Though on February 23 the U.S. Supreme Court in a unanimous decision had ruled that the right to "freedom of association" was more important than any pretext government might have for requiring the disclosure of the names of NAACP members, the victory may have seemed hollow in light of the NAACP's decimated membership. The total amount in the Arkansas NAACP account was one hundred dollars. As important as it had been for the Little Rock Nine and the NAACP to demonstrate the ability to withstand the attacks of their enemies in Arkansas, no mass civil rights movement in Arkansas emerged. By 1960 the NAACP was barely hanging on in Arkansas.

The Student Movement in Arkansas

On March 10 approximately fifty black students from Philander Smith entered Woolworth's five-and-dime, some of whom occupied seats at the lunch counter in the "whites only" section.[4] The police were called and police chief Eugene Smith ordered the managers to close the store. The leader of the students was Frank James, a twenty-one-year-old Air Force veteran and math major from Oklahoma City. In the tradition of civil rights activists who had and would serve in the military, James posed the question always asked by black American veterans, "If we can fight and die our country, why are we now treated as inferior beings?"[5] In addition to James, four other students, including Arkansans Chester Briggs from Hot Springs, Vernon Mott from Little Rock, Ledridge Davis from Malvern, and Charles Parker from St. Louis, were arrested when they refused to leave the store. Each posted bond of one hundred dollars, which according to the press was supplied "by the local NAACP." They were initially charged under a statute that made it illegal to refuse to leave a building when requested. To deter future sit-ins attorney general Bruce Bennett suggested to local authorities that they add two other charges. Act 17 of 1958 made it a misdemeanor to enter a public building to create a disturbance; Act 226 made the act of a sit-in demonstration a crime. For either offense one could receive a fine of five hundred dollars and a six-month jail sentence.[6]

As a chain store, Woolworth's was a target, but it also had special meaning for blacks. Almost fifty years later, nationally syndicated columnist Deborah Mathis recalled her own anger in Little Rock as a ten-year-old upon seeing the look on her eight-year-old sister's face watching a white customer sitting at the lunch counter eating a banana split. "I was good and mad that day, finally taking Sandra's hand and leading her away. Neither of us knew the word 'discrimination' then, but we sure knew what it felt like."[7]

What advice Daisy Bates gave Philander Smith students

before their initial sit-in is not recorded in her papers, but a pattern was set that lasted throughout the year. If students were bound and determined to try to challenge segregation, whites tried to make them pay such a steep price they would ultimately have to give up. There was no pretense of judicial fairness. Municipal judge Quinn Glover refused to rule on the constitutionality of the statutes, judicial behavior that flouted all ethical norms judges are sworn to uphold. After all, as prosecutor J. Frank Holt explained, the behavior of the students was "a deliberate attempt . . . to disturb the peace of the community."[8] The Arkansas "good ole boy" legal network worked together as if they were all members of the same family. No, the judge would not grant a continuance asked by the defense. Yes, he would grant the prosecutor's request of a trial date in one week. He did have advice for Harold Anderson: advise your clients to hold no more demonstrations.

The fledging student movement got its first dose of Little Rock justice with Glover's ruling on the seventeenth. Each student received a $250 fine and a thirty-day jail sentence. George Howard Jr. and Harold Anderson filed an immediate appeal, and thereafter, some efforts, not always successful, were made to avoid giving the police a reason to arrest the students. The same day Glover issued his finding of guilt and passed sentence, "an estimated 25 to 40 blacks peacefully sat-in at lunch counters on Main Street in Little Rock, then went to the state capitol steps and sang 'God Bless America' and 'The Star Spangled Banner.'" On neither occasion did L. C. nor Daisy Bates participate in these events. L. C. Bates had talked to the press afterwards on March 10, and his comments revealed the ambivalence of the NAACP both nationally and locally. Clearly intending to avoid giving the Little Rock police a reason to arrest either one of them, he said that his wife advocated no position either for or against the sit-ins.

This admission revealed a stunning weakness and confusion in the one organization in Little Rock that for decades had spoken up for the rights of blacks.[9] Despite the NAACP's difficulties, absolutely crucial to the civil rights movement was its separately organized Legal Defense Fund (LDF). As LDF lawyers, Wiley Branton, George Howard Jr., Harold Anderson, later John Walker, and others provided indispensable legal services to students, staff members, and blacks generally in discrimination and criminal cases.[10] Nor was there support in the spring of 1960 from Philander Smith president M. Lafayette Harris, who, though ill and in the hospital, warned students and faculty away from involvement with "mass action."[11]

The Birth of SNCC

It was not just in Arkansas where students realized how reluctant and ill-prepared existing civil rights organizations were to demand an end to Jim Crow. This vacuum throughout the South created the need for a new structure of leadership. Thus, the Student Non-violent Coordinating Committee (SNCC) was born at meetings April 15–17, 1960, at Shaw University in Raleigh, North Carolina. Composed of about fifteen student leaders and observers such as Martin Luther King Jr., James Lawson, and Ella Baker, the group included no Arkansans. It is worth here pausing a moment to briefly discuss the principles of SNCC and modus operandi since it played such a significant role in civil rights activities in the South. The interracial group, though mostly black, adopted a statement of purpose that read in the very first paragraph:

> We affirm the philosophical or religious ideal of nonviolence as the foundation of our purpose, the presupposition of our faith, and the manner of our action. Nonviolence as it grows from Judaic-Christians seeks a social order of justice permeated by love.[12]

SNCC's significance and ultimate impact in Arkansas in breaking down the barriers of Jim Crow and attacking white supremacy is still a matter of debate among historians, members of SNCC, and local blacks where it was active. Story Matkin-Rawn states that "local people [where SNCC was active in Arkansas] see it as one step in a continuum" of civil rights activity that began in the 1940s.[13] It is this view of SNCC as part of a continuum of civil rights activity that works best in understanding the organization in Arkansas, for SNCC itself nationally and in the state was very much a work in progress throughout its existence. Though it is tempting to see the burst of student activity in the 1960s as something radically new and to view the overall history of SNCC as being primarily at loggerheads with organizations such as the NAACP, often it was not, and more importantly, as the letter from Bettye Williams to Daisy Bates indicates so clearly, students drew their inspiration from figures like her, whatever their institutional label.

The Failure of the NAACP

While Daisy and L. C. Bates may have been indecisive about their next move, the pace of change nationally seemed to leave them few options but to try to become more active. Vanderbilt divinity student James Lawson, a passionate supporter of nonviolent passive resistance who had just been expelled for participating in the Nashville sit-ins and who gave the keynote address one week later in Raleigh, spoke in Little Rock at the Dunbar Community Center on April 9. Lawson's words and example put pressure on the Arkansas NAACP and obviously led to the effort on April 15 by Daisy and L. C. Bates to spearhead a protest downtown of about twenty college and high school students. Apparently, it seemed too risky to lead the students in a sit-in; however, the students

> set up picket lines in front of three Main Street stores . . . parading with placards protesting segregated lunchrooms. . . . Mrs. Bates appeared at all three stores and for a brief time wore a sign.[14]

The three stores were Pfeiffers of Arkansas, McClellan's Variety Store, and the Gus Blass Company. Though Daisy Bates told reporters that "picketing will continue indefinitely until the conscience of the community is made to realize that Negroes are being refused service in these places," it was not resumed the next day or afterwards.[15]

Neither this effort nor subsequent ones by the NAACP to desegregate the downtown stores were successful in this period. On April 22 a letter signed by Daisy Bates went out to NAACP members asking for contributions to pay the legal expenses for the thirteen students who now had been arrested. Signed, as well, by J. C. Crenchaw, still president of the Little Rock NAACP branch, and Garman Freeman, Bates's next-door neighbor and now chairman of the Little Rock branch's executive committee, the letter urged members to boycott the stores downtown that served lunch to whites only. In his year-end report to the NAACP in New York, L. C. Bates admitted that the efforts of the NAACP to work with others, including ministers and a "citizens group," had come to nothing. No money had been raised; "there has not been one thing accomplished by the group."[16]

The city of Little Rock had continued to ratchet up the pressure with great success. After hearing the appeal of the first five students, circuit judge William Kirby doubled their sentences to sixty days and fines to five hundred dollars. For another six defendants whose appeals were heard on May 31, he also gave them sixty days in jail and the maximum fine of five hundred dollars. Finally, on June 17 he gave two other students each ninety days in jail and a fine of $418. All the defendants appealed, but with students out on vacation and scattered, their civil rights activity ceased, though resuming in the fall.

SNCC Comes to Arkansas and the Departure of Daisy Bates

The national office of SNCC in Atlanta was eager for involvement by Arkansans and in June invited Frank James to come in August to learn about SNCC. "Our excitement over having a real life contact in Arkansas is great."[17] Sent train fare of $31.50, James arrived in Atlanta and while there meeting with SNCC officials also heard Martin Luther King Jr. Though James returned with great enthusiasm to Arkansas for the fall semester and organized a chapter of SNCC, it accomplished little for two years. Randy Finley writes that "for twenty months, from October 1960 to October 1962, Arkansas members of the newly formed organization remained remarkably moribund."[18] It was during 1960 that John W. Walker, then working as a student for the Arkansas Council on Human Relations in Little Rock, observed in a report, "Negro leadership is virtually nil."[19] It is worth a moment here to consider why the NAACP was not more successful in this period when only two years before, Daisy Bates, in her role as president of the NAACP, had been the unchallenged leader in the black community. As suggested earlier, the enemies of the NAACP and the Bateses had accomplished exactly what they had intended. Though L. C. Bates had found new employment with the NAACP, they were walking advertisements of what happened to people who took the organization too seriously. With strains appearing in the marriage and with a book to write about her life, Daisy Bates found an apartment in New York and kept it for the next two years. There were those in Little Rock who would not miss her decision-making process. Recalled Ozell Sutton, who became one of the black civil rights leaders in Little Rock after her departure, "Daisy Bates was a leader for the Negroes in the contending forces concerned with integration, but there was definite disagreement within the Negro community over her tactics and personality."[20] His view also was that the personality of L. C. Bates was better suited to being an advocate for civil rights as a crusading journalist and editor than as a field organizer. More conservative than his contemporaries in the civil rights movement, he was never comfortable with the idea of nonviolent protest. Over the next few years Bates increasingly found himself at odds with the organization he had loved. Forced to adopt a more militant posture in order to compete successfully with organizations such as SNCC, the NAACP was trying to change with the times. Its field secretary in Arkansas was not at all certain it needed to do so.

The Freedom Riders Come to Little Rock

A report by the Arkansas Council on Human Relations characterized the situation as a lack of "coordinated support from the adult community which is showing its usual fragmentation and divisiveness."[21] Yet this lull in activity did not mean that the civil rights movement was not gaining steam elsewhere. On July 10, 1961, Little Rock received its first "Freedom Riders" whose mission it was to test bus terminal desegregation in the South. Whites had attacked these nonviolent civil rights advocates in Anniston, Alabama, Birmingham, and Montgomery, though in other parts of the South there had been relatively few incidents. The group arriving in Little Rock had begun their journey in St. Louis and had encountered no trouble or discrimination at bus stops in Arkansas. The group included three blacks and two whites. At the bus terminal they were met by four hundred whites who jeered them as they got off the bus and went into the waiting rooms, one of which had a sign for "White Intra-state" passengers. Here, the Freedom Riders were arrested for violating Act 226 and accused of "threatening to breach the peace."

What happened afterwards showed the sensitivity that authorities in Little Rock had developed since the bad publicity of 1957. First, Glover held a trial the next day and imposed the maximum sentence of six months in jail and the maximum fine of five hundred dollars. However, to get the Freedom Riders out of Little Rock he suspended their sentences on condition that they "leave the state of Arkansas and proceed to their respective homes." The Freedom Riders accepted these terms, not realizing Glover had meant his words literally. The Freedom Riders had been planning on going to Louisiana. When they realized he had meant for them to go immediately to their homes, they announced they could not accept these terms and were rearrested. The media was about to have a field day as Rev. Ben Cox announced publicly that he would "much rather be dead and in my grave" than be a "slave to segregation."

With Little Rock about to receive a fresh blast of unwelcome publicity, thirteen business leaders decided they had had enough and met at the First National Bank to discuss what they viewed as a totally unnecessary martyrdom. Doubtless, some behind-the-scenes arm-twisting transpired, and the next day Glover admitted his authority to prevent the Freedom Riders from continuing their journey was nonexistent. The judge averred he was turning "the other cheek in this matter, hoping it to be for the good of all," though he said he was doing it "very, very reluctantly."[22]

The manner in which the entire episode was handled by the whites in authority illustrated the internal weakness of African Americans in Little Rock who showed little support for the Freedom Riders. Whites had feared they could not control the damage that would result from the publicity given to the Freedom Riders, and so they had leaned hard on the judge. But it was as if local blacks did not even exist. At this point whites knew how disorganized they were and did not take them seriously.

Blacks Come Together

John Kirk maintains that the civil rights activity by outsiders involved in the Freedom Rides "did act as a catalyst for a significant new black community initiative."[23] That initiative, formed in 1961, was the Council on Community Affairs (COCA), which became for a time a highly organized steering committee that had authority to speak for all the diverse interests in the black community. Its president was William H. Townsend, who probably because of his genial, mild temperament has until recently been somewhat underrated by some historians of the Arkansas civil rights movement, but his easy-going personality was just what the doctor ordered to bring blacks together in Little Rock. A number of the founders of COCA, including Townsend, had been members of the executive committee of the Little Rock branch of the NAACP when it had functioned so effectively in the early 1950s, but now the NAACP was just one among a number of groups that was brought under one umbrella. Like Townsend, a number of influential blacks in Little Rock belonged to a host of organizations, but John Kirk contends that it was "Townsend's ability to mediate between various factions in the black community and to negotiate effectively with the white community [that] made him a key figure in efforts to end segregation [in Little Rock]."[24] Born in 1914 in West Point, Mississippi, and the oldest of eleven children, Townsend had moved with his family to Earle in Crittenden County. He managed to get not only a high school diploma but also a bachelor of science degree in agriculture from Tuskegee Institute in 1941. He spent the next forty-six months in the army, most of them outside the United States. In 1950 he graduated from the Northern Illinois College of Optometry and in the same year opened an office in Little Rock, making him the first black to obtain an optometrist license in Arkansas. Besides serving on the boards of the NAACP, the Little Rock Urban League, and the Arkansas Council on Human Relations, Townsend was a member of the Pi Lambda Chapter of Alpha Phi Alpha fraternity, a thirty-second degree Mason, a member of Mount Zion Baptist Church, and member of the American Legion.[25]

Others also with medical backgrounds helped make up COCA's leadership positions, including Dr. Maurice A. Jackson and husband and wife dentists Garman Freeman and Evangeline Upshur. With Townsend, in the 1960s they opened up medical offices on Wright Avenue in Little Rock. Another dentist, Jerry Jewell, would also have a role in COCA affairs: Jerry Jewell had grown up a sharecropper's son in Crittenden County but had graduated from Meharry in Nashville. He opened his practice in North Little Rock in 1961 and later became president of the NAACP state conference of branches.[26] In their roles in COCA they were joined by Ozell Sutton, the first black reporter to be hired by the *Arkansas Democrat* in 1948. A graduate of Philander Smith, Sutton had left the paper to go to work for Winthrop Rockefeller. In June 1962 Sutton became associate director of the Arkansas Council on Human Relations. All of these individuals owed a deep and lasting debt to both L. C. and Daisy Bates, but, in fact, as leaders in a younger and better educated generation they had a more inclusive and at the same time more pragmatic view of their roles than their mentors. Finally, there were important representatives in COCA from the black religious community. Negail Riley, then thirty-two and pastor of Wesley Chapel, the Methodist church on the campus of Philander Smith, represented a totally new breed of minister in the black community. From Oklahoma City, he had been one of the first blacks to attend the prestigious Perkins School of Theology at Southern Methodist University in Dallas. From there he had studied at Boston University, and in the structure of the United Methodist Church had been sent to Wesley where he served as pastor and worked on his doctoral dissertation in theology. Riley was balanced by Reverend Rufus K. Young, then fifty-two and pastor of Bethel AME, who had been in the center of the 1957 school desegregation crisis and had deep roots in Arkansas.

Initially, the Little Rock business community did not take seriously overtures from COCA to negotiate desegregation in downtown Little Rock. Accustomed to dealing with a fragmented and disorganized group of blacks who clearly were not together, the leaders saw no reason at first to engage with COCA and continually put the group off. The white leadership in Little Rock felt comfortable, too, that it could delay, as well, desegregation of the schools by one device or another. Prevented by the federal courts from closing the public schools and creating private schools with public money, the Little Rock School District turned to its Pupil Placement Act, which the federal court found unconstitutional based on its application in actual situations in March 1961. As long as the courts and federal government permitted them, school districts in Arkansas were committed to tokenism. In 1962 and 1963, despite the declared unconstitutionality of the Pupil Assignment Act, there were no efforts being made to desegregate the elementary schools in Little Rock. In fact, there were only a total of seventy-seven blacks who had started the school year in the Little Rock school district in white schools, all in junior high and high school. A threatened boycott of the schools by COCA yielded a promise to desegregate all twelve grades, but it was an empty commitment.[27] The damage done by *Brown II* was never more clear than by the end of the school year 1963–64. During that year only 390 blacks in the entire state were attending school with whites and only 13 of 228 school districts with students of both races having any desegregation at all.[28] Rather than face the loss of federal aid, nearly all school districts chose to comply on paper, but all they were obligated to do was to submit desegregation plans for approval.[29]

Jim Crow, Sex, and Music

White supremacy still ruled the day, and in the early 1960s white males still dealt contemptuously with black males especially in the area of sex. It only took a little alcohol to bring this anxiety out into the open. Pioneer music promoter Jim Porter of Little Rock, who was inducted into the Arkansas Entertainers Hall of Fame in 2005, recalled the sign at Club 70 near Prothro Junction in North Little Rock during the 1960s that read "Black musicians cannot talk to white women." Club 70 had "chicken wire strung across the bandstand to protect the musicians from flying beer bottles.[30]

Whites who dared to cross the color line in any fashion could be met with police reprisal in short order. In a 2005 article for the *Pulaski County Historical Review* Jim Porter remembers the August night in 1961 when Ray Charles performed before a large crowd at Robinson Auditorium. Porter's effort to find a seat in the black section resulted in an arrest by a Little Rock policeman. Asked the charge, he was told, "You're attempting to incite a riot." Asked how, the policeman responded, "You're trying to sit in the colored section." To prove he was serious, the policeman escorted him out of the rear of the building, put him in a police car, and drove him to the municipal jail.[31]

Illustrative of the power differential between blacks and whites that has always existed in Arkansas was Porter's one phone call to Jack Holt Sr., who was then Arkansas attorney general. The call brought an apology from the policeman who said he had made a "mistake." The policeman had made a "mistake" only because he had picked on the wrong person, a form of "white profiling" that backfired. Though it was generally the state police that provided the heavy lifting during the Faubus "Police State" era, garden-variety law enforcement took their cues from a variety of sources, nearly all of which endorsed white supremacy and looked the other way while these policies were being enforced in such a way that the recipients would get the message. They had been treating blacks in the same manner but worse since the "Slave Patrols." And thus they would harass whites working in the civil rights movement in Arkansas so long as they were outsiders, which almost all were. What made Jim Porter unique was that not only was he a businessman who was trying to make his living bringing top flight music to the central Arkansas era but also saw nothing wrong with racial integration. The difficulty was that while a Frank Holt could get him out of jail, much of the politics of white supremacy was handled at a different level. Thus, any change in the policy of segregated seating at Robinson Auditorium had to come from the top. Meanwhile, Arkansas was missing out on some great entertainment because of the policy. In effect the national NAACP declared Robinson Auditorium off-limits to blacks, and the ban was respected. Porter and his associates received a telegram five days before a major concert. "Duke Ellington refuses to play Little Rock on the basis of segregation law." While it was not the "law," it might as well have been. Porter remembers, "When we met with their [the Robinson Auditorium] board regarding the matter, they would only say, 'It's our policy.' I pleaded with them, stating it would soon be the law of the land. The reply from one of the members was 'It may soon be the law of the land, but it will NEVER be the law of Robinson Auditorium.'"[32] This "I'll take my stand in Dixie" response had been heard before and would be again, but it was fast becoming the exception rather than the rule. The humiliation it caused blacks was irrelevant. Deborah Mathis recalls her school teacher mother's experience of taking a class of black first-graders to Robinson for a performance of *The Nutcracker* and being forced to sit in the balcony where her children could not see over the railing.

> Mama said she had been grateful for the darkness in the concert hall because it had allowed her to hide her tears. That's the way grown-up's often dealt with the blows of discrimination in those days—hiding their anger and pain from the children, lest we become afraid, embittered and hopeless. Still, my mother vowed never to take another class to the auditorium until equal rights and fair play found its footing.[33]

After the fiasco with Duke Ellington, the George Shearing Quintet was scheduled to play Robinson. Shearing had a clause in the contract with Porter that read, "It is mutually agreed between all parties concerned, that the artist has the prerogative of canceling this contract if the audience is segregated because of race or color. Furthermore, the artist will be paid in full." According to Porter, this language, known as the "The Little Rock Clause," was used all through the South. Porter ran the risk and was rewarded when enough blacks showed up for the concert "but not enough to bother the auditorium management."[34]

Not willing to continue to fight the battle with Robinson Auditorium, Porter began to book his musical acts in a few selected hotel ballrooms in Little Rock after he had "established a firm understanding with the hotel management that our functions would be integrated. We sold seats at tables to blacks and whites, a number of which brought a 'brown bag' of their favorite cocktails." In this way, Porter brought in such talent as "Lionel Hampton, Errol Garner, Ramsey Lewis, Dizzy Gillespie, Al Hirt, Pete Fountain, the Four Freshmen, Count Basie, Maynard Ferguson, Buddy Rich, Woody Herman and Stan Kenton."[35]

Smoke and Mirrors: Downtown Little Rock

Despite all the brave words by whites about "Dixie now, Dixie forever," as early as 1961 the white business community had appointed a secret committee to try to negotiate as quietly as possible the desegregation of downtown Little Rock. Businessman and community leader Grainger Williams, who favored integration, remembered,

> I don't know whether it was formed by the Chamber of Commerce or who formed it, but somebody called me and asked me if I'd serve on this committee . . . and I said certainly. I think they wanted it secret 'cause they didn't want anybody to know they were working on it. They just wanted it to occur.[36]

Taking place was a recognition of how financially disastrous it would be to again invite the ruinous publicity of the 1957 crisis on the business community. At the same time, however, the last thing businessmen wanted was to be known as appeasers of the civil rights movement. For most it went deeply against the grain of white supremacy, which was essential to their personal identity. By forming a secret committee the question, at least for some downtown businessmen, was how to save face and not incur the wrath of their friends and fellow businessmen. Thus, these men felt they could save some dignity by forcing blacks to file a lawsuit they were certain of winning to desegregate public facilities in Little Rock, and that is exactly what happened. Though COCA had begun meeting with the Little Rock city board as early as July 21, 1961, it took litigation filed in federal court on March 8, 1962, to bring about integration of public facilities in Little Rock.

A more delicate issue for Little Rock downtown businessmen was how to save face among their fellow whites in desegregating lunch counters, restrooms in department stores, restaurants, hotels, and private theaters because, after all, there was no law to make them do it. The public accommodations section of the Civil Rights Act would not be passed until July 1964. It now appears that the desegregation of downtown Little Rock involved more smoke than fire as a way to make it seem that downtown merchants were forced into desegregating their facilities by the threat of protracted demonstrations, when, in fact, they were actually willing to do so, if only it could appear they were forced into it.

Until this point, though favoring integration, the Arkansas Council on Human Relations had generally tried in the past to play the role of the honest broker in facilitating dialogue and communication between whites and blacks in Little Rock but without a great deal of tangible success. Its failure had little to do with lack of effort, but by October 1962 ACHR director Nat Griswold was convinced that the downtown businessmen were ready to proceed with desegregation and only needed a push to get over the hump. To accomplish this he sent a telegram to SNCC in Atlanta asking for help.[37] SNCC responded by sending William Hansen, a twenty-three-year-old white activist who arrived in Little Rock on October 24. By this time the SNCC was composed of battle-tested veterans of the civil rights movement. Absolutely faithful to the principles and practice of nonviolent tactics in breaking down the walls of segregation, members of SNCC, both black and white, put their bodies on the line repeatedly as they helped register blacks to vote and conducted sit-ins and demonstrations. One forgets that it was only after being confronted by SNCC that Martin Luther King Jr. began to encounter the risks inherent in Southern jails. Hansen already was a legend in SNCC circles before he came to Little Rock. Before joining SNCC he had been a "Freedom Rider" from his hometown of Cincinnati to Montgomery with a ninety-day stop in a Mississippi jail. After helping to organize sit-ins in Maryland, he joined SNCC and worked in the South in Virginia and Georgia, where he was thrown into jail. There, white occupants of the jail shattered his jaw and broke several ribs. After a long recuperation in New York, he was at SNCC headquarters in Atlanta when Julian Bond received the telegram from Nat Griswold asking SNCC to send someone to Little Rock.[38]

By that afternoon Hansen was visiting with Worth Long who took him to a meeting at Philander Smith. The extent of SNCC's inactivity on the campus was evident when only seven people showed up. Hansen remembered there was no "ground-swell of enthusiasm."[39]

Nobody illustrated the "direct action" approach to civil rights activity more clearly than William Hansen, who the next afternoon accompanied by Philander Smith SNCC chairman William E. Bush took a seat at Woolworth's. The waitress refused to serve Bush, but instead of calling the police the manager was willing to discuss the matter. He told the men his refusal to serve Bush was a matter of city policy, not the policy of Woolworth's. In a report about the encounter Hansen noted the "absolute lack of tension at the counter while Bush was sitting there." The contrast between what had occurred in other places in the South and Little Rock was obvious. Taking into account everything that had occurred, "the whole incident gives an indication that there would be no widespread consternation among the white community if Negroes were served at the lunch counters."[40] As a result, initially, Hansen advised students against demonstrations, fearing a backlash. Perhaps store managers would be persuaded to desegregate. It would not be as easy as this, and it would require sit-ins, the glare of unwanted publicity, and intense negotiations. Under strong SNCC leadership, Philander Smith students showed quickly they were willing to engage in protracted demonstrations. Later, when Hansen and Worth Long were arrested in November for refusing to leave Walgreen's, COCA immediately put up a thousand-dollar bond for their release. The black community was clearly united in a way it was not in 1960. On the other side, as previously mentioned, the business community saw no advantage in risking another publicity fiasco as occurred in 1957. Led by James Penick, president of Worthen Bank and Trust, the Downtown Negotiating Committee (DNC) was composed of such heavyweights as B. Finley Vinson, president of First National Bank, and Will Mitchell, who had been a key leader in organizing the STOP committee. Vinson and his group negotiated with, among others, Philander Smith student leader Worth Long and COCA leader Ozell Sutton. The DNC wanted to delay complete integration of downtown stores for years, which, of course, was unacceptable to the blacks on the other side of the table. Keeping the pressure on, Hansen coordinated more sit-ins by Philander students in December, including a march on Main Street with over one hundred Philander Smith students. On January 2, 1963, four downtown stores, Woolworth's, McClellan, Walgreen's, and Blass, opened their lunch counters to blacks in exchange for the termination of demonstrations. To thwart Amis Guthridge, who led a small group of Capital Citizens Council members in picketing the stores, white supporters of the DNC's position packed the lunch counters at these establishments. Even the media conspired with the agreement. It was not until January 20 that a Pine Bluff paper reported the news of what was going on in downtown Little Rock. The successful desegregation of these four major businesses opened the way for the others. By the end of January, smaller businesses, along with major hotels and motels, had followed suit. And at year's end, according to John Kirk,

"Little Rock had desegregated most of its public and some of its private facilities."[41]

It is worth speculating here upon the significance of a white male who apparently had such an impact on both the black and white community and certainly invites the question of how Arkansans in 1963 in responded to issues of leadership. Clearly, both races took William Hansen very seriously from the beginning. Doubtless he had unsurpassed credentials and courage to back him up, but there would soon come a time when some blacks in SNCC would question the value of having whites in the organization at all and would bring issues of white leadership to a head. The question of why SNCC in Little Rock lay "moribund" almost two years after its initial formation at Philander Smith and then with the appearance of a single white male become active is still a question. Within two years, the separatist implications of the black power movement overshadowed more fundamental issues of grass-roots participation in the civil rights movement in Arkansas. In any event the process of desegregating downtown Little Rock, then the main shopping area for the city, can be considered in the nature of a choreographed event. The next stop, Pine Buff would not.

CHAPTER 15

Brothers against Brothers

With such a ready-made base of college students to draw from at Arkansas AM&N and a large black population in Jefferson County in 1960 (about 43 percent), the base of SNCC operations shifted to Pine Bluff, some forty-odd miles southeast of Little Rock, where sit-ins began at Woolworth's on February 1, 1963, exactly three years to the day after the first sit-in by students in Greensboro, North Carolina. Thirteen Arkansas AM&N students, dressed as if for church, occupied the lunch counter at 2 p.m. Immediately a waitress turned off the lights and closed the counter for business. Robert Whitfield, a junior from Little Rock, spoke with store manager T. W. Harper in his office, but after Harper announced the store was closing two hours early, the students left.

Painful Choices in Pine Bluff

In the spring issue of the 2007 *Arkansas Historical Quarterly,* Holly Y. McGee[1] traces in part the painful conflicts within the black community in Pine Bluff caused by the commitment to end segregation. Until recently, historians have displayed little interest or appreciation for the extraordinary cohesiveness of historical black institutions, whether within churches, high schools, or black colleges in the state. But as McGee demonstrates, the Arkansas AM&N "family" was torn apart and deeply scarred by the overwhelming pressures white authorities put on the institution during the winter of 1963. Within days, as the Pine Bluff Student Movement

(PBSM) continued with its sit-ins, Arkansas AM&N president Lawrence A. Davis faced a choice no college head should have had to make: expel members of the PBSM for fighting for their civil rights or face possible funding cuts by the Arkansas legislature, which was then in session, and in the process jeopardize his own career. It was an agonizing time for Davis who had incurred the wrath of the legislature once before by inviting Martin Luther King Jr. to be the commencement speaker in 1958.[2] Joanna Edwards, one of the students whom he expelled, recalled hearing him say that his bags were packed and he would leave the school before he would "suspend a student for participating in the sit-in-demonstration."[3] After this pledge, however, he did suspend and expel fifteen AM&N students for their participation in the Pine Bluff movement. The sense of betrayal was never forgotten. As Joanna Edwards remembered, "The thing that was so tragic for most of us was that we *loved* [emphasis in original] this man. We called him 'Prexy,' fondly, we just loved him to death."[4] McGee helps make clear that no one in the black community was immune to the firestorm caused by the decision to take on white supremacy in Pine Bluff and, by implication, anywhere in Arkansas.

The pressure on students by blacks themselves to drop out of the protests in Pine Bluff was intense, and many did. Before the suspensions took place, close to a hundred students, including high school students, participated in the sit-ins. After Davis announced that those who participated in sit-ins beginning February 11 would be suspended, "only 10 students went downtown to the Woolworth's lunch counter."[5] Five more would join them and be suspended, as well. "According to interview participants, some of the same student leaders who spoke out against the suspended students [had] sat beside them during the first days of protest." Of course it was not only the administration and fellow students exerting pressure, but it was relatives, as well. McGee makes a point easily forgotten when it comes time to celebrate the courage of the Little Rock Nine: many other black

Arkansans paid a significant price, too, for standing up for themselves in the face of overwhelming pressure. For example, Joanna Edwards who had a double major (mathematics and art) gave up a full academic scholarship. Ruth Buffington, a second-semester senior, was told by her great aunt that if she continued her participation in the sit-ins, she could not continue to live in her house. Adults in high places counseled against what was going on in Pine Bluff. I. S. McClinton, still the long-time president of the segregated Arkansas Democratic Voters Association, the black counterpart of the Arkansas Democratic Party organization, criticized the students by complaining that demonstrations by Negroes "are not helping the principles of American Democracy at home or abroad."[6]

In retrospect, one minimizes the conflicts and emotional pain among black people during this period at the risk of not understanding the difficulties involved in the decision to participate in the sit-ins and demonstrations in Pine Bluff. Students and their leaders often took opposite sides after the suspensions. James Dorsey, president of the AM&N student government, actively supported President Davis's decision to suspend the fifteen students.[7] On the other side, community leader Rev. Arthur Robinson criticized Davis, arguing the chancellor "owes it to his people to defend them."[8]

The Pine Bluff Movement

The expulsion of college students in Pine Bluff did not stop the movement that now expanded and now called itself the "Pine Bluff Movement" (PBM). Robert Whitfield, James Jones, Janet Broome, Joanna Edwards, William Whitfield, and Mildred Neal, six of the original students, formed the group and

> encouraged a type of organizational solidarity in other groups in the Black Community. Even the city's NAACP chapter, previously hidden in the folds of "good race relations" decided to take a chance on activism and

> mobilized to boycott two separate downtown stores, much to the chagrin of business leaders who dismissed the original protests in February as only a fad.[9]

McGee notes that student status at Arkansas AM&N had provided protection inasmuch as no students were arrested while they were in school, but now that demonstrations were continuing, arrests began to be made. On March 26 six former students were arrested for refusing to leave the Pines Motel after having not been allowed to check in. Some of the men had taken off their shoes and socks and had stretched out on recliners in the lobby of the motel in an obvious attempt to provoke the manager. The six refused to make bail and claimed they would remain in jail until they were tried or the charges dropped. Arrests quadrupled within a week. The PBM sought admission to the white section of the Saenger Theater, resulting in twenty-seven arrests on one day including nineteen females and eight males, "mostly high school age." This was followed by the arrest of sixteen more. Randy Finley writes,

> Their freedom songs resonated six blocks from the jail. The next mass meeting drew 1000 participants, followed by a march on downtown Pine Bluff that covered twenty-five blocks and engaged nearly 500 protesters. By the first day of June, there were 44 protestors in jail (five had accepted bail). When the jail refused to feed the protestors, Helen Hughes Jackson, one of the mothers of the jailed young people (Leon Jackson) took over this responsibility which was agreed to by jail administrators.[10]

Helen Hughes Jackson, a self-employed hairdresser in Pine Bluff, also allowed her house to become a meeting place for the group. Without her son's involvement, she admitted that as a black woman and a widow she would not have participated otherwise.[11] It was by this kind of grassroots activity and much more that women such as Jackson played a role in the civil rights movement in Arkansas.

On March 5, the PBM achieved its first victory. The local

Holiday Inn served four blacks. By mid-March negotiations had achieved integration at Woolworth's, Walgreen's, and Keesee's Restaurant. And then it was on to boycott Jefferson Square Shopping Center.[12]

Finley notes that whites set off several fire bombs at St. James Methodist Church, the gathering point for demonstrators. Windows of the church were blown out. An excited crowd of whites threw ammonia and bricks at protesters as they marched downtown. "Police tried to control and defuse the tense situation, arresting whites who violently attacked demonstrators."[13]

In April 1963 approximately five hundred blacks heard James Farmer, national director of CORE (Congress on Racial Equality), exhort them to continue their boycott of Pine Bluff merchants and urged them to stick together.[14] In the next several months a number of important persons in the civil rights movement appeared in Pine Bluff, including national SNCC chairman John Lewis, James Bevel, and comedian Dick Gregory. In August Ben Grinage reported to SNCC headquarters in Atlanta,

> all lunch counters desegregated in May, and as of July 27, all theaters, including two drive-ins will be desegregated in the area. Two private restaurants have opened to all customers. In a five week period . . . we have registered 970 new Negro voters.[15]

After the summer vacation Ben Grinage from Louisville became head of SNCC when Robert Whitfield returned to the University of Arkansas. Wiley Branton, with the Voter Education Project out of Atlanta but then working out of an office in Little Rock, gave twelve hundred dollars to encourage voter registration in Jefferson and Lincoln counties. Eight hundred of this amount was made contingent on the PBM's cessation of demonstrations while the grant money was spent. According to Randy Finley, this 1963 drive increased added 2,200 new voters to the Pine Bluff voting rolls and 400 in Lincoln County.[16]

The Roles of Kennedy and Johnson

Though much of what was occurring in Arkansas during this era was being motivated by black organizations such as SNCC, black Arkansans derived hope from signals from the white power structure outside the South. The death of John F. Kennedy was a grievous blow to many blacks in Arkansas. Janis Kearney, in her memoir *Cotton Field of Dreams,* recalls the emotion of her elders.

> Witnessing my usually stoic parents' open expressions of grief taught us what words couldn't—that John F. Kennedy evoked a rare hope in America. For James and Ethel Kearney, President Kennedy's death threatened that fragile hope.[17]

And yet it was dyed-in-the-wool Southerner Lyndon Baines Johnson who used every bit of his political skill as president to pass and implement into law the hopes that blacks had for change. Time and time again Johnson emphasized morality as a basis for action. It was the issue of right and wrong that, as president, Johnson hammered home. In signing the Civil Rights Act of 1964 on July 2, Johnson said to America,

> The reasons for racial discrimination . . . are deeply embedded in history, tradition, and the nature of man. . . . But it cannot continue. The Constitution, the principles of freedom and morality all forbid such unequal treatment.[18]

Where President Johnson was going as a Southerner, few, and none in politics, had gone before. Not only did Johnson characterize race as a moral issue, but he was also willing to confront the demons that all but a few white Southerners had avoided. In a commencement speech delivered at Howard University on June 4, 2005, entitled "To Fulfill these Rights," he said that the causes of black poverty were "the devastating heritage of long years of slavery; and a century of oppression, hatred and injustice." Their poverty could only remind blacks "of their oppression. For the white they are a constant reminder of guilt."[19]

SNCC's Fight in the Delta—Helena–West Helena

Organizing to fight segregation in urban areas such as Little Rock, Pine Bluff, and Hot Springs was easy compared to the small towns of the Delta, but SNCC had no intention of avoiding the part of Arkansas most like Mississippi.[20] Within SNCC nationally and locally there were debates about whether "direct action" tactics of confrontation were more productive than a more "grass-roots" approach of letting local leaders set the agenda, in which case they might choose to concentrate on registering blacks to vote and developing "community centers" for education. In Arkansas both approaches were tried, usually depending on the desires of the particular SNCC leaders in charge at the time. In Mississippi, for example, Bob Moses became known and revered by fellow activists for his efforts to register voters as well as his refusal to insist on a personal agenda.

Jayme Stone argues that SNCC, unlike other civil rights organizations, provided local leadership opportunities to women in the sense that SNCC staff were open to working with strong local women and helping them develop and sustain grass-roots programs that strengthened the black community in ways that survive today. Black women had a tradition of civil rights activism in Arkansas that extended all the way back to the nineteenth century.[21] The initial step for SNCC workers was deceptively simple: Stone quotes Marvell (Phillips County) resident Gertrude Jackson.

> The first thing the civil rights workers from the north wanted to do in my community is talk to a few people and tell them what it is about. They came to my house and we would have eight or ten people there and they would explain to them. . . . Then we would spread it to the whole community after a few key people.[22]

In particular, Stone identifies and focuses on the work of "movement mamas," whom she calls "the backbone of the African American communities and activism in the Arkansas Delta." While Stone identifies sixty-five-year-old Carrie Dilworth in Gould and Ruth Buffington in Pine Bluff in particular, she documents the work of other women, some nameless. For example, an unidentified woman in Pine Bluff on Bell Street provided a "Freedom House," saying, "I got a house out there empty and I got four bedrooms here and I'll put all my children in one room and I will give the other two rooms to the girls, whatever they need. I will take them in right here."[23] Stone shows that black women pressured their ministers to support the "freedom work" and "fed, housed, counseled, and supported the young activists."[24] Stone contends that all of this activity fit into the philosophy of SNCC because, in fact, "SNCC was founded on the principles of grass-roots activism, not to direct but to coordinate the local organizations and activities of local people in order to maximize their potential for effecting change." She contends that "women, in particular African American women, were central to SNCC's efforts in the Arkansas Delta."[25]

One can understand the mixed feelings that greeted SNCC activists. From one perspective it was easy for activists to come in and stir up trouble. They would raise hell and then one day go home, leaving native blacks with few options with which to contend with whites who could take it out on those left behind. That deep but understandable ambivalence over brash newcomers showing up in town and challenging the established order is part of the civil rights story that sometimes is minimized in the celebratory accounts of SNCC and other civil rights organizations. Local blacks had to make a hard choice about whether they were ready to join them or not.

Randy Finley summarizes the initial reactions to SNCC's appearance in Helena:

> Activists John Bradford, Bruce Jordan, and Noah Washington arrived in Helena in late October 1963, after cotton-picking season. . . . Rochester Johnson, secretary of the International Woodworkers of America local, whose membership was 20 percent black, was not nearly as enthusiastic as the activists hoped. By contrast, when they met at a local barbershop with Bobby O'Neale, a

> twenty-six year-old with a pregnant wife, the activists found a man who wanted to be in the first march down the main street of town. Several black businessmen and professionals greeted them warmly. George Miller, a twenty-five-year old black teacher and Michigan State graduate who owned the movie house, twenty rent houses, a café, and a barbershop, provided their principal support. He said that he is ready, when we are ready, Bradford reported. Frank Jordan, funeral home director, would contribute bail for those arrested. Two local dentists named Miller and Profitt and a pair of physicians, a Dr. Douglass and a Dr. Connor, supported the movement, though only behind the scenes.[26]

Yet the black church was deeply split. "The preachers are holding us back," lamented Bradford in a report to national headquarters. Finley writes that several leading black ministers in Helena, in fact, opposed SNCC's activities and told their congregations to avoid SNCC protests. On the other hand, Rev. J. H. Price of Allen Temple AME opened his church to SNCC rallies as did also Rev. Raymond Lyles, pastor of the Pettis Memorial Christian Methodist Episcopal Church.[27]

Of course, any adult black of a certain age who had lived in Phillips County his whole life had fears that the average SNCC member could never have fully appreciated. As mentioned previously, the Elaine Race Massacres of 1919 may have held the record for the most blacks slaughtered by whites in the United States, but outside of Arkansas it was an unknown event. White authority figures in Arkansas remembered. When news of SNCC's efforts to organize in Helena reached attorney general Bruce Bennett, he said, "Whoever is pulling the strings that make William Hansen jump, does not know the facts of life of Helena or Phillips County. I remember my father telling me about the Elaine incident."[28]

Bennett's comments had to be taken as a warning to blacks of what could happen again and how the Elaine Massacres had been understood by whites in Phillips County.

Of course, what had occurred more than decades earlier was not just old news. Lynchings, whether they were called that or not, still occurred in the Delta. In July 1963 a white posse ran down and murdered an unarmed black teenager near Marion in Crittenden County after a white woman had said he had tried to rape her eight-year-old daughter. Shot in the leg, he bled to death before he was treated. An all-white coroner's jury of nineteen men ruled that the killing was justifiable homicide. A white doctor testified the youth was bleeding too badly for him to treat him, so he sent him to a hospital in West Memphis where he was pronounced dead.[29] More common in the 1960s was simple assault. When five white teenagers were finally arrested in 1962 in Lake Village in Chicot County for randomly hitting about a dozen blacks in their faces with their fists with no provocation, one of them gave as their reason, "We just wanted to."[30]

The idea that the First Amendment applied in Phillips County to African Americans was a foreign concept. Finley documents that

> Helena police chief Roy Ross warned SNCC workers that "whenever you come across that Phillips County line, we've got you. Take that station wagon, that literature and all that SNICK stuff and get out of here if you know what's good for you. Be sure to tell your buddy Hansen that everything I've told you goes for him."[31]

Finley contends that SNCC was a success story in the sense that the risks it took as an organization raised the bar for local blacks as to what was possible. But as he points out, from the point of view of economics and politics, what did the average black Arkansan in the Delta have to lose?

> Less than one-fourth of those registered to vote [in Phillips County] in 1963 were black. Sixty-five percent of the black population had less than a sixth-grade education, compared to only fourteen percent of whites. Three percent of blacks had high school diplomas, while twenty-eight percent of whites did.

Out of 25,308 blacks in Phillips County (57.5 of the population), only 147 black households in the county earned more than $5,000 in 1960. Even more disheartening was the fact that "1,923 black households [reported] earning less than $1,000 in 1960."[32] Despite their fears, blacks began to protest against discrimination in white-owned stores in Helena in November 1963. Thirty demonstrators seeking to desegregate Habib's Cafeteria and Henry Drug Store were arrested and jailed. Leaders William Hansen, John Bradford, Bruce Jordan, and Rev. Raymond Lyles were charged with "inciting to riot." The legal argument that the U.S. Constitution protected free speech and the right to peaceful assembly for the petition of grievances fell on deaf ears in Helena municipal court.

Again, one forgets how much courage it took for African Americans in the Arkansas Delta to assert their constitutional rights after generations of murder and intimidation. William Hansen testified before the Arkansas advisory committee of the U.S. Commission on Civil Rights in January 1964 that "a general systematic aura of fear permeates the county." SNCC organizer James Jones pointed out the obvious to the commission: "Helena is very much a Mississippi type of town. . . . When we first came to Helena people were completely afraid of anything that was connected or related to freedom."[33] Helena, of course, was no different from any other Arkansas Delta town in its determination to intimidate blacks into resuming their customary obedience and deference to whites. One of the principal differences in 1963 was the likelihood the glare of national publicity could once again shine on Arkansas, which in fact was considered a relatively unimportant state for the national civil rights movement. The focus would rightly be on Mississippi right across the river, but in 1963 there was little difference concerning attitudes in the Delta, whether it was the Magnolia State or the "Land of Opportunity." It was essential for whites to deny there were any problems that were not being caused by outsiders. In Phillips County and Helena race relations were simply "wonderful" according to E. C. "Tock" Gathings, congressman for

Phillips County's congressional district. "The lot of the southern negro isn't as bad as it is sometimes painted," he told the House Rules Committee in 1964. "The Negro in the South is a happy person. He enjoys the life he lives. He understands the members of the white race, and they understand him."[34] Leaning against a water fountain marked "White Only," a Helena service station operator told an *Arkansas Gazette* reporter in 1964 who was investigating SNCC's reception, "Right or wrong, our niggers are satisfied with things the way they are." Blacks in Phillips County declined to give their names for the article.[35]

SNCC's earliest efforts to organize in Helena were met with arrests, arbitrary justice, and sermons from the bench. When two of its organizers, Bruce Jordan and John Bradford, were arrested while sitting in a car in a driveway, the police chief admitted they had not breached the peace but that they were arrested for "planning to breach the peace."[36] Addressing two SNCC workers as he was fining them, municipal judge D. S. Heslep said,

> The trouble in this situation is that they [blacks] don't all come educated and neatly dressed like you. These people need help. They need people to teach them to think, talk and act like human beings. I'd like to see organizations like yours teaching these people the desirability of bathing regularly, respecting the sanctity of marriage and settling their differences without reverting to the law of the jungle.[37]

If Pine Bluff was difficult to organize, Helena at times seemed impossible. Local blacks were terribly afraid of retaliation by whites, making it extremely difficult for SNCC to have even a mailing address. It did not take long for blacks to get the message. Finley records that "Cornelius Perkins, a black employee at the City Water Company, lost his job when he housed SNCC workers."[38] James Jones said, "I get the impression that nobody wants us to have an office near them." Jones and Wright could not find a place to sleep two nights in a row. Finley writes, "The duo slept from house to house as no one considered it safe to permanently lodge them."[39]

As mentioned, though SNCC was able to open a "Freedom House," whites harassed its occupants, driving around it continuously. In retrospect it is amazing there were no SNCC workers killed. At one point "[a] mob of 150 whites gathered at the Helena Freedom House in early 1964 and forced SNCC workers to spend the night in a cornfield."[40] SNCC workers were not safe anywhere in Helena. "Whites peppered a young black SNCC female house with shot five times. Two whites firebombed another dwelling in West Helena that housed SNCC workers."[41]

Despite the harassment, SNCC and local blacks continued their efforts in Helena, and they finally began to bear fruit. In June three SNCC workers, including Thomas Allen, an Arkansas AM&N student, and Ellis Ford, a student from the black high school, peacefully integrated the public library and were then served in the "whites only" section of Habib's cafeteria. Trailed by police chief Ross, the three were arrested by him when they attempted to integrate the swimming pool.[42] Though it was a tortured process, SNCC's influence was felt in the public schools, as well. SNCC workers James Jones and Joseph Wright urged black parents to enroll their children in previously all-white schools. Thirty-five students had registered by mid-April to attend school in August.[43]

Pine Bluff, 1964

Meanwhile in Pine Bluff, early in 1964 fourteen retail stores, among them J. C. Penney, Sears, Shainberg, Sterling, and Woolworth's, arrived at an agreement with leaders of the Pine Bluff Movement in which management agreed to hire some blacks for clerical positions and non-menial jobs in exchange for the boycott ending against them. When activist Dick Gregory and William Hansen were arrested on February 17 at Ray's Truck Stop and Barbecue in Pine Bluff, the attention of the entire civil rights movement briefly focused on Pine Bluff. Instantly demonstrations composed of mostly high school students began at the truck stop. Police took into custody nearly one hundred students. One could hear their freedom songs three blocks from the jail.[44] From Little Rock Governor Faubus could not resist the publicity. "We don't intend to let any group of demonstrators take over any place of business on the streets of any town in Arkansas."[45] Twelve state patrol cars raced around the city at the request of Sheriff Norton.

Unwilling to let the governor make the same political hay out of Pine Bluff that he had in Little Rock, the Retail Merchants Committee representing fifty store owners petitioned Governor Faubus that his riot-control measures were excessive. Pine Bluff business leaders including the mayor, president of the chamber of commerce, and state representative all urged that the community remain calm. A deal was worked out, and the students were released. Years after Faubus had caused the business slump in Little Rock, its lesson was still being heeded.[46]

As always, some local whites, who out of conscience or religious faith took a stand in favor of integration, paid dearly. Pine Bluff Methodist minister Edward W. Harris incurred the almost total wrath of the First Methodist Church when he preached that the doors of the church should be open to blacks. Secure in the knowledge that he had support of his bishop, in anticipation of "Race Relations Sunday" in February 1964 Harris preached a sermon in which he called upon his church

> to change those community patterns in which racial segregation appears, including education, housing, voting, employment and the use of public facilities. . . . To exempt the church from the same requirements is to be guilty of absurdity as well as sin.[47]

Instead of support from his bishop in the Methodist Church, the official response was total silence. His wife remembers,

> The congregation heard his words . . . and reacted swiftly and furiously. . . . Parishioners who had previously been close and generous to us turned quickly against us, and some did not hesitate to say why.[48]

After the media made Harris's stand public, the White Citizens Council smelled blood. "The parsonage telephone began to ring off the wall. We could not allow our young daughter to answer it, for so many of the callers threatened our lives."[49] Though "a small minority" continued "in quiet ways" to support them, Ed and Mabel Harris became instant pariahs in a church where they had once felt loved. The Methodist hierarchy showed its own contempt for them by transferring Harris in May to Ferguson Methodist Church in St. Louis with only a week's notice. Curiously, after six years, Harris was transferred back to Little Rock to serve another church where he "discovered a written policy still on the books in 1970: 'No Blacks.' . . . Shocked at the continuance of such a policy, he stayed only two years."[50] Obviously disillusioned, he ended his career as a church pastor by taking a low-paying and unrewarding non-pastoral position as director of the Christian Civic Foundation of Arkansas.

A New Ally Emerges in Little Rock

Officially, the state was still committed to a policy of segregation. Five COCA members who tried to integrate the pool at War Memorial Park were turned away in 1963 and again in 1964. Still there was no litigation, perhaps because COCA believed the city would make good on its promise to close the pools and drain them, which is exactly what the city did on June 16, 1964. Besides criticism from interracial groups such as the Arkansas Council on Human Relations and the Catholic Interracial Council, there was a strong reaction from the *Arkansas Gazette* that was rapidly moving from its celebrated "Southern Moderate" position to that of "Liberal Queen," although as late as 1964 the paper still carried a separate obituary column for blacks. James O. Powell, who took Harry Ashmore's place as editor of the editorial page in 1960, remembers that the change in the *Gazette's* position was a matter of "evolution," for

> it was in that period [1964] that the *Gazette* was moving into the advocacy not only of desegregation and integration as a point of principle and morality and not just as a matter of following the national law. . . . When we evolved, we became stout advocates of desegregation and integration and full opportunity under the law. Even and including affirmative action, the whole and entire repertoire of the liberal position.[51]

Partially due to the *Gazette's* pressure, the pools were not sold and later were reopened on an integrated basis in 1965. Besides its significant influence on the people and institutions of Arkansas, a major contribution of the paper was its thorough coverage of the civil rights movement in the state. Despite its traditional emphasis on national and international news during this period, the *Gazette* consistently reported civil rights stories in the South and in Arkansas.

Paul Greenberg, editor of the *Pine Bluff Commercial,* also won a Pulitzer Prize for his editorials in 1968 urging equal rights for blacks. The *Commercial* specifically urged, among other measures, desegregating the public schools, integrating the city's civil service commission, hiring more black policemen for an almost all-white police force, and supporting a black candidate for the city council.[52]

Out of Sight, Out of Mind

In areas of Arkansas where there was no SNCC presence the civil rights ferment of the 1960s typically seemed to make no impression on most whites, who accepted the terror experienced by blacks as normal. There were exceptions. David McDonald, who grew up in DeWitt in Arkansas County, remembers a neighbor, Miss Hattie Boone, who "had a black man that worked for her. He was referred to only as 'my house nigger' or 'Monkey' which explains the way he was treated." When young McDonald, a child of eleven or twelve, asked the man if he could pick up some bottles from the trash to sell them,

> A look of panic came across his face. He quickly looked down to avoid eye contact with me and would not face me directly. He said that if he were to give me the bottles, he could lose his job. Even as a child, I understood this event. This man was terrified of what could happen to him if he gave me a few Coke bottles that were going to be thrown away. His employer had complete control of this man's destiny, due only to the color of his skin.[53]

He recalled his father telling him that once a black man had unintentionally gone to the side door of a neighbor's house.

> A black person was always to go to the back door. His father answered the door to find the black man standing there and flew into a rage. He stormed out of the house, hitting the man, knocking him down. Cursing and yelling, he went back into the house to get a gun. Fortunately, the black man was able to run away, but if my friend's father had succeeded in killing the man, there would have been no serious consequences.[54]

Everyone, black and white, knew the rules of behavior, and the consequences to blacks for breaking those rules could be deadly. The rule had been broken unintentionally but that was of no importance.

As David McDonald explains,

> In the Arkansas of 1963, it was too dangerous for blacks to speak out in favor of civil rights. My peers would frequently tell how their parents had asked their black servants what they thought of civil rights, or desegregation, as it was called then. The answer was always the same. "You treat me and my family good. I don't like this desegregation, it ain't right. We like to be to ourselves." Blacks who answered in this manner, and they all did, were referred to as "good niggers."[55]

When John F. Kennedy was killed, McDonald, who was in the eighth grade in DeWitt, remembers a student "walking up and down the hall, in celebration yelling, 'They finally got that nigger lover.'" One of his brothers told him that when the announcement was made over the school intercom, students in his class cheered.[56]

David McDonald's father was reassigned to the DeWitt Methodist Church in May of 1964, and on May 24 he announced his reappointment to the congregation. Rereading the notes of his father's sermon that day, McDonald writes that his words today seem mild, but in 1964 in south Arkansas they were courageous. "Several times he repeated his belief that Jesus would welcome all people into any place of worship. My father's profound belief that the church was for all people was the theme throughout his sermon."[57]

When his father finished, he did not end with a benediction or prayer. He said, "You're dismissed," and then for the first time in forty-five years as a minister he walked out.

> People sat in the pews, stunned and confused. It seemed like an eternity before people stood and began to leave the church. Few spoke and no one was standing at the doors as the people left. Everyone went to their cars and drove away.

Later, one of his brothers found their father supporting himself against a desk. "When one of the adults came into the study and found him, Daddy said he was terrified."[58] For a white Arkansan the act of personally and publicly confronting the immorality of racism in the 1960s was simply overwhelming, for it meant not only going against much of one's previous identity but often against the present values and beliefs of one's family, friends, colleagues, and acquaintances, not to mention it could end one's employment.

Testing the 1964 Civil Rights Act

The 1964 Civil Rights Act signed by President Lyndon Johnson on July 2 was truly a landmark event for the South. Among other measures, the act prohibited racial discrimination not only in the administration of government-funded programs but also in public accommodations. This latter section was immediately tested in Arkansas and met with mixed results. Blacks in El Dorado were locked out of a dairy bar but were admitted to a drive-in. In Forrest City where SNCC attracted major publicity in 1965, blacks integrated a bowling alley, a movie theater, and skating rinks within days after the 1964 Civil Rights Act became law. At Texarkana blacks tried to integrate Lake Texarkana and were arrested after a fight broke out between blacks and whites. In Fort Smith on the Oklahoma border two restaurants served blacks, but a third refused. In Helena, Randy Finley writes that when activists

> Wright, Allen, Ford, Robert Blockum, and Larry Siegal, a New Yorker, tested the Civil Rights Act of 1964 within days of its becoming law . . . [w]hite business owners seemed unsure of what to do. Some refused service one day but offered it the next. . . . No whites acted violently, however, and no blood was shed.[59]

Once more subjecting Arkansas to ridicule, Bruce Bennett, still the attorney general, called on Arkansans to act as if the Civil Rights Act of 1964 had never been passed, on the absurd legal theory that until the courts upheld it the law need not be obeyed. The extremely elementary principle that laws are always presumed to be constitutional until courts say otherwise apparently did not apply in Arkansas. Remembering 1957 and the turmoil that followed, the governing body of the Arkansas Bar Association urged compliance until the law was changed or ruled unconstitutional. The Little Rock Chamber of Commerce also called for compliance.

Though Orval Faubus had as early as 1962 found it expedient not to campaign directly on the racial issue and even agreed at the behest of L. C. Bates to hire a number of blacks through the state Employment Security Division, he stubbornly refused to allow blacks to eat at the state capitol cafeteria. Instead of setting an example after the Civil Rights Act of 1964 was passed, he had the cafeteria made a private club. This degrading effort by Faubus was simply the price the state had to pay, since, in the mind of the governor, "if you give in to them on this, there will be something else." The pretext for making the cafeteria private was that it would somehow facilitate service for state employees. It was a ready-made issue for SNCC and its allies. When whites testified in federal court that they ate there and were not checked for membership and were not state employees, the court, after hearing testimony of a black secretary, Barbara Leary, declared the scheme as nothing more than an effort to discriminate against blacks. Even as state-sponsored segregation was being dismantled, Faubus insisted on humiliating African Americans for political gain.

SNCC's Arkansas Freedom Summer

SNCC moved its headquarters back to Little Rock in January 1965, using as its headquarters a former drug store in the black community at 700 West Ninth Street. In June SNCC workers held orientation for its "Arkansas Summer Project" at Ferncliff, a camp outside Little Rock owned by the Presbyterian church. At one point SNCC met at St. John's Seminary and St. Phillip's Episcopal Church in Little Rock, both of which revealed a radically different attitude on the part of some churches in Arkansas. Twenty-four males and six females made up the group. Half were black.

According to Jayme Stone, with the training of the summer volunteers came an important new grass-roots emphasis. Stone writes that prior to the training of the new volunteers, the new Arkansas project director "Jim Jones and the ArkSNCC staffers invited over fifty grassroots leaders from outside the Delta to establish the agenda for the Summer

Project based on 'what the people want and are concerned with.'"[60] Grass-roots advocates from the Delta chose to emphasize voter registration, school desegregation, and establishing community centers. Continued protests against Jim Crow policies were also a concern, but clearly there was a shift in priorities. Stone sees this strategy as establishing a much needed link between younger black activists and adults and leading to a more unified community stand. It also signaled a shift of the spotlight from William Hansen, whose self-described "gunslinger" persona gave way to more collaborative approaches. According to Stone, Hansen's "celebrity status . . . detracted from the message," and by early 1965 Hansen was functioning as a project codirector with Benjamin Grinage and James Jones. In any event,

> the establishment of Community Centers in Forrest City, Gould [Lincoln County] and Forrest City [*sic*] and a massive voter registration effort became the two key objectives with the issue of public accommodation being the secondary objective.[61]

In 1965 SNCC began to focus on Forrest City as six volunteers began to pound on doors of blacks in the spring and summer. It had begun work there early in 1964 and, as had happened in Phillips County, encountered resistance from some in the black community.[62] However, by June 1965 a local group called the St. Francis County Achievement Committee, which included SNCC activists, began to picket businesses that refused to hire blacks, but it was over the condition of the black school in Forrest City that SNCC found a hot-button issue. Whatever its original intent, the "freedom of choice" plan in the middle sixties approved by the courts was even more of a disaster in Forrest City than elsewhere. Randy Finley writes that the handful of blacks in 1965 who chose to enter the

> previously all-white junior high school . . . were forced to eat lunch in a separate room. School officials insisted this deterred violence, but many blacks believed it but a

> façade for continued segregation. Other black parents vehemently protested the inferior facilities assigned to predominantly black schools. They charged that schools were rat infested and lacked inadequate science laboratories and libraries. Over 1,000 students and 500 parents petitioned black principal C. T. Cobb demanding better facilities. After the principal stonewalled, a boycott of schools began in mid-September, 90 percent of the black students participating.[63]

On September 16, 1965, 198 black demonstrators were arrested for disturbing the peace on school property as they protested conditions at the black school and urged desegregation of their high school. Within a few days 105 more blacks were arrested for still more demonstrations.[64] Throughout this period there was an ongoing battle between white authorities in the South who sought to use the local law enforcement and judicial procedures to limit and suppress civil and constitutional rights and civil rights lawyers who sought the intervention of the federal courts to protect rights. Unless a federal judge acted quickly to intervene and prohibit the enforcement of an ordinance or order forbidding demonstrations, the fact that a decision could be appealed meant little to the demonstrator who faced arrest. Confronted with jail, many blacks were afraid to challenge an unconstitutional ordinance or official act and decided to forego these constitutionally protected activities. Had John Walker been successful in his effort to remove the cases of the demonstrators to federal court, perhaps many more demonstrations would have likely taken place in Forrest City, the Arkansas Delta, and elsewhere in the South, but federal judge Gordon Young declined to exercise jurisdiction over the cases.

Most interestingly, it was NAACP field representative L. C. Bates, once feared by whites as uncompromisingly militant, who played the role of middleman along with Dr. Earl Evans of the state Office of Economic Opportunity who finally negotiated a deal between the school board and black parents. The board promised to investigate the complaints brought by blacks and dropped all charges.[65]

Gould 1965

It was not just in the strip of eastern counties where SNCC flourished as a grass-roots organization. In southeast Arkansas, in tiny Gould in Lincoln County, sixty-five-year-old Carrie Dilworth became, in effect, a role model for the type of the Delta black female community and civil rights activist that Jayme Stone describes. With her background as a former secretary in the Southern Tenant Farmers' Union, Dilworth was already a woman committed to the struggle. She remembered distributing leaflets for the STFU calling for a strike. "You'd pick up speed and that'd just make things go flying all over the yards. . . . White folks thought it was a plane that distributed flyers."[66] Dilworth moved from Mississippi to Gould, a town of less than two thousand in Lincoln County, in her twenties with her parents who were able to purchase land and grew cotton, rice and soybeans. Her parents "raised [her] in an egalitarian tradition that stressed the importance of community and the expansive notion of family . . . holding that every man and woman . . . is entitled to some regard."[67] Thus, her participation in the STFU was a natural progression.

Much later in her life when SNCC activists approached her, she opened her home to them. With a friend, she established the Gould Citizens for Progress, an organization that she led in demonstrations in July 1965 in Star City outside the Lincoln County Courthouse, protesting the closing of the voter registration office in Gould. But it was her leadership in trying to force the Gould School District to integrate that would be her most sustained effort. Sixty-five black students were allowed to attend the white schools in September 1965, but forty were prohibited from transferring because of "overcrowding," a decision that was upheld by the federal Department of Education and sustained by the federal judiciary. After the school district obtained an order prohibiting SNCC from "holding demonstrations or meeting within a block of the school," SNCC activists announced that students denied a transfer would boycott the all-black

Fields school, which had outdoor toilets, a library that had thirty books, rats, and no science laboratories. Testimony in federal court further showed that the school had no vocational program, no hot lunch program, and black teachers were paid six hundred dollars less than white teachers. Working with SNCC activists, Dilworth led fifty blacks to Little Rock and marched and sang in front of the federal courthouse, protesting conditions at the black school and the school desegregation plan of the Gould School Board. Eventually a lawsuit filed against the Gould School Board and consolidated with two others went to the U.S. Supreme Court and ended the so-called "freedom of choice" method of desegregating public schools in 1968. Whites then abandoned the Gould schools and sent their children to school in Star City.

During this period Dilworth provided a building across from Fields High School for SNCC activities. Called "the Hall," the building was an old two-story wooden building that opened in the summer of 1965. SNCC activists Laura Foner, from New York, and Bob Cableton, a black Arkansan raised in Mississippi, taught classes in "African American history, art, typing, French and voter registration." The school continued operating in the fall of 1965, providing classes after school let out in the afternoon. The hall burned "mysteriously" on January 12, 1966, in a midnight fire six months after it was opened. SNCC suspected arson by "the Ku Klux Klan and some other of their black hencemen [*sic*]."[68] As usual there was a significant cost for local blacks who chose to exercise their constitutional rights. Finley notes that seven black teachers were not rehired at Lincoln County High School after they participated in SNCC voter registration drives.[69] It was almost impossible for black SNCC–backed candidates to win elections in Gould and Helena despite a black population of 82 percent and 56 percent, respectively. Of the thirty black candidates who ran for school boards on September 28, 1965, Finley writes,

> Rampant voter fraud revealed whites' fears that blacks would at long last win. Policemen, often accompanied

> by dogs, used excessive force in monitoring black voting precincts. At Forrest City, according to a SNCC report, a white man marked ballots for illiterate blacks, casting their votes for the white candidate regardless of blacks' preferences. Temporary deputies in West Helena warned blacks not to vote for SNCC-backed candidates.[70]

The Shifting Priorities of SNCC

Stone notes again another swing in SNCC's direction after Jim Jones resigned. She documents that Ben Grinage and William Hansen "again brought significant energy and focus to activities involving direct action." These involved integrating restaurants throughout towns in eastern Arkansas, challenging the governing body of the community action agency in Lincoln County, protesting the "freedom of choice" route being taken by school districts seeking ways to delay full implementation of *Brown v. Board of Education,* and picketing Cohen's Department Store in Forrest City as part of a selective buying campaign. According to Stone these activities "all began to stress the fragile unity Jim Jones had crafted between the youth and the adults."[71] Stone argues that Grinage further undermined grass-roots decisions made by the "people's conference in May 1965 by rejecting funds offered ArkSNCC in March 1966 by the Voter Education Project."[72]

Randy Finley paints a somber picture of SNCC's work in Gould, noting that in 1966 Carrie Dilworth ran for mayor but lost to a white candidate. He writes that Bob Cableton, still a SNCC activist in Gould in January 1967,

> observed that the defeat of [Carrie Dilworth] had further demoralized the spirit of the movement. Since 82% of the town's voters were black, large numbers of blacks had voted for her white opponent. He urged more political education classes and reported that they had distributed clothes and toys to the few need families he could help. Icy weather reflected the gloomy spirits of SNCC workers in the death rattle days of SNCC in Arkansas.[73]

In fact, SNCC was beginning to implode. The defeat of the national SNCC chairman John Lewis and the rise of the black power ideology eventually would end SNCC's work in Arkansas, but the immediate reactions of SNCC workers within the state were not to follow the new leadership. In May 1966 Stokely Carmichael, the new national SNCC chairman, announced publicly that racial integration was "irrelevant" and that SNCC would in the future work toward the goal of black political supremacy in black areas. SNCC had begun with the same goals that other traditional civil rights movement had espoused. But within SNCC it was felt that whites were too dominant within the organization. Usually better educated and accustomed to leading, the idealistic whites who belonged to SNCC eventually came under fire by blacks who insisted that a civil rights organization that had as its purpose the advancement of blacks should be run by blacks. Despite the national reversal of goals, within Arkansas SNCC was devoted to remaining within the mainstream of the civil rights movement. Ben Grinage, then SNCC project director for Arkansas after Jim Jones resigned to return to school, in May 1966 issued a statement refuting the position of the new leadership. He said, in part, "We do not feel that integration is irrelevant but is vital if this country is concerned with showing the rest of the world that peaceful coexistence is really what we are trying to achieve."[74] William Hansen criticized Carmichael and supported Grinage's leadership by saying, "I don't consider Ben any less militant than Stokely Carmichael. I don't think Carmichael used good judgment."[75]

What Carmichael and those that supported him in the black power movement may have liked the least was Grinage's irrefutable observation that the idea of a third party for blacks in Arkansas was absurd since only 22 percent (and declining) of the state was black. With the Arkansas SNCC leadership in open revolt, Carmichael came to Arkansas and consolidated his power. Attacking Grinage's financial management of SNCC, he also blasted Hansen and Grinage for their statements to the press. Grinage resigned, and soon both he and Hansen were gone. With donations to SNCC drying up, the organization struggled on in Arkansas with a few volunteers, at one point organizing a seven-week boycott of the black school in Marvell in Phillips County that was so effective that at one point approximately 1,500 out of a total of 1,800 black students participated. The object of the boycott was to protest the failure of the school authorities to issue "freedom of choice" forms to black students and to comply with the new federal desegregation guidelines. The boycott ended with about a hundred blacks choosing to go to the white school.[76]

There are perhaps two ways to look at the contributions of SNCC's work in Arkansas. Randy Finley writes, "Although SNCC ended its work in Arkansas not with a bang but a whimper, it instigated staggering changes."[77] Finley is, of course, referring to the totality of changes that occurred in the state between 1960 and 1967. Had it not been for SNCC and its student brigades pushing the more middle-class organizations, such as the NAACP and the Southern Christian Leadership Conference and the politicians in Washington, it is difficult to imagine the degree of change that occurred in this period. As much as the young activists infuriated the Kennedy and Johnson administrations, SNCC with its student brigades and "movement mamas" were living and dying proof of the commitment to first-class citizenship. No one can forget the horrific murder in June 1964 in Neshoba County, Mississippi, of Andrew Goodman, James Chaney, and Michael Schwerner.

Another way to view the contributions of SNCC is to understand it as an organization that helped empower local people at the grass-roots level, like Carrie Dilworth who once said very simply about the SNCC activists, "They're a big help to the people down here. I've been living here 65 years and I ain't had no one help no like that." Her granddaughter, Annette Cox, twelve in 1965 and a plaintiff in the Gould school litigation, remembers that SNCC "helped us and motivated us and sold us dreams that really weren't dreams it was just the way that things should have been."[78]

According to Jayme Stone, SNCC's influence can still be seen today in organizations in the Delta such as the Boys, Girls and Adult Community Development Center in Marvell.[79]

Black Pride and Black Insecurity

As Arkansas blacks struggled to integrate the white world in the 1960s, despite celebrating "black pride," they continued to wrestle with their own feelings about their blackness. For all the taunts of whites, Janis Kearney recalls that black children unleashed upon each other assaults, as well. "Tar baby, tar baby . . . black as tar, slick as snot! You'll never get to heaven on a slop jar top!" "You so black we have to turn the light on to even see you during the day." Kearney saw her father "take special pains to instill . . . self-confidence" in his darkest skinned child, Jo Ann, for he knew what she encountered. As Kearney said, "Negro children of a darker hue simply endured more humiliation than Negro children with a lighter complexion. This came not only from whites, but also from fellow Negroes, as well."[80] It mattered little that Kearney's father would demand that his children cease tormenting each other, pointing out, "It's just plain crazy for you to be thinking you better than somebody else 'cause you one shade lighter." But color mattered. These "were hurtful words that sometimes stung whether we showed it or not and were often internalized by children on the receiving end," Kearney observes.[81] While in public blacks demanded a colorblind society that at the same time celebrated color and racial pride, others struggled to be proud even as many white Arkansans began to moderate their views on race.

Finally, the emotional devastation of racism generally and Jim Crow in particular in the 1960s in Arkansas on black children and their families is captured by former Arkansas resident and columnist Deborah Mathis in her 2002 book *Yet a Stranger: Why Black Americans Still Don't Feel at Home*. As a child, she, her siblings, and her father traveled to Fayetteville in the spring of 1964 to watch her mother receive a master's degree in education from the University of Arkansas. Her father had made reservations at the Holiday Inn, but when they arrived to check-in, her father was turned away. The desk clerk had not been able to tell by his voice that he was black. Getting back in the car, her father was silent until her mother asked what had happened.

> None of us kids asked any questions but tried to distract our parents and recover the merriment. I led my siblings in a silly song, hoping our folks would assume we hadn't caught on to what had transpired. It was something that I learned over the years; that the thing that stings black people the most about discrimination is what it does to their children. What I remember now is how fervently we kids wanted to protect our parents against that self-same sting.[82]

CHAPTER 16

The Impact of the Death of Martin Luther King Jr.

The black power movement and the urban riots that began to sweep the black ghetto beginning with Watts in Los Angeles in 1965 were a firestorm that rocked the nation and seemed to have no end. By the end of 1966 "forty-three disorders and riots had been reported across the country."[1] In Chicago police arrested 533 people, including 155 juveniles. Three blacks were killed by stray bullets. A week later riots broke out in the Hough section of Cleveland that left four blacks dead. During the summer of 1967 there were riots in such places as Tampa, Cincinnati, Atlanta, and Newark. The worst was in Detroit where forty-three people were killed, thirty-three of them black. More than 7,200 were arrested. The national commission appointed by President Johnson attributed the massive unrest to "police practices, unemployment, inadequate housing, inadequate education, poor recreation facilities and programs."[2] But the commission also found that

> militant organizations, local and national, and individual agitators, who repeatedly forecast and called for violence were active in the spring and summer of 1967. We believe that they sought to encourage violence, and that they helped to create an atmosphere that contributed to the outbreak of disorder.[3]

The Comparative Calm in Arkansas.

At the same time these clashes were occurring in the rest of the country, Arkansas was reporting no mass violence by African Americans. In fact, the riots seemed to have little visible effect on black Arkansans in central Arkansas as old barriers to creating a just society continued to be chipped away due to the pressure of the federal government. In early 1965 Governor Faubus announced he would not stand in the way of state agencies that agreed to sign a statement pledging compliance with the 1964 Civil Rights Act in order to continue receiving federal funds. If these agencies wanted to "acquiesce," as Faubus called their decision, then he would permit them to do so.

There were other ways to achieve desegregation, of course, than the withdrawal of federal funds. In early 1965 a suit filed by the federal government named defendants in Pine Bluff, West Memphis, Blytheville, and Hope in Hempstead County because of discrimination against blacks in hospital wards, restrooms, cafeterias, and other facilities.[4] In the spring of 1966 blacks filed successful suits to desegregate the state sanitarium and state reformatories.[5]

Other politicians in central Arkansas besides Faubus were now balancing the risks of appearing to be pro-integration with the political benefits of attracting black voters. Prosecuting attorney–elect of the sixth judicial district (Little Rock) Richard B. Atkinson, who later became chief justice of the Arkansas Supreme Court, appointed Christopher Mercer, former NAACP aide to Daisy Bates, as the first black—possibly in modern times—in the South as a deputy prosecutor. Faulkner County state senator Guy H. "Mutt" Jones, later convicted of income tax evasion and expelled from the senate, announced two black students as senate pages from the black high school in Conway.

In eastern and southern Arkansas it was of course a different story. In the period after the passage of the Voting Rights Act of 1965, SNCC workers claimed in February 1966 that although blacks could vote in the Delta election practices made their votes worthless.[6] In April 1966 Little Rock attorney John H. Haley, director of the Election Research Council, confirmed in part their allegations by testifying before the Arkansas advisory committee of the U.S. Commission on Civil Rights that he had found evidence of massive misuse of the absentee ballot in Poinsett and Phillips Counties.[7]

Other white Arkansans also began to pay attention to SNCC, most notably Ted Lamb, who continued his advocacy of civil rights while he was in law school after having lost his advertising business due to his views on integration. Now as chairman of the advisory committee on civil rights in Arkansas, Lamb agreed to hear allegations made by SNCC in eastern Arkansas. Meeting in Forrest City, the committee took sworn testimony from numerous blacks about discrimination in all areas. For example, a black undertaker from Marianna, Lacy Kennedy, testified that in the downtown area, excepting two federal agencies, blacks held no jobs.[8] There was other similar testimony, and Lamb's group submitted an advisory report to the civil rights commission that recommended that federal funds be withheld from several school districts in eastern Arkansas for failure to comply with the 1964 Civil Rights Act. Additionally, it recommended that all federal contracts be suspended with the Mohawk Rubber Company in West Helena because of alleged discrimination in hiring policies. When the report was released by the commission, several changes had been made.

> The final report recommended only that further studies be made into school desegregation and hiring practices in Crittenden, Lee, St. Francis and Phillips Counties. The revised report did not mention the school districts or the company by name.[9]

After Lamb harshly criticized the revised report, he was not appointed again as chairman of the Arkansas advisory committee, thus ending the public life of one of the very few white Arkansans outside of ministers who took a strong public stand against discrimination on moral grounds in this period.[10] Lamb did leave legacies of vigorous leadership, one which was carried forward by his successors.

The Education of Winthrop Rockefeller

In retrospect, it seems incredible as Jim Ranchino noted in his book, *From Faubus to Bumpers,* that Faubus got 86 percent of the black vote against Republican Winthrop Rockefeller in 1964.[11] If in 1964 Arkansas blacks still were allowing themselves to be manipulated into voting for a man who had so viciously exploited them, a valid question was raised about the sort of leadership that was being exercised in the black community throughout the state. Ranchino noted that apparently blacks had not yet learned to split their ticket since they voted overwhelmingly for Lyndon Johnson over Republican Barry Goldwater for president. According to Ranchino, the refusal of Winthrop Rockefeller to support the 1964 Civil Rights Act and the endorsement by Faubus of the Johnson-Humphrey ticket were other factors that determined the lopsided victory by Faubus over Rockefeller in 1964.[12]

Winthrop Rockefeller learned a great deal from his defeat by Orval Faubus, and one of the most obvious lessons was that simply because his last name was Rockefeller did not mean that blacks would not automatically vote for him. He would have to campaign hard for their votes to win an election as a Republican in a state whose loyalty to the Democratic Party was then the match of any state in the country. Beaten by Faubus in 1964, Rockefeller was anxious to try him again, but Faubus decided not to run, and Rockefeller faced one of the few candidates he could have beaten in 1966, arch-racist Jim Johnson. Such was the bankruptcy of the Democratic Party in Arkansas as the reign of Orval Faubus ended. Johnson ran such a negative and racist campaign as the Democratic nominee that many individuals, normally ardent Democrats, felt they had no choice but to vote for Rockefeller. White Arkansans living outside eastern and southern Arkansas were increasingly sensitive to how the state appeared to the rest of the country, and not wanting to be categorized as either "hillbillies" or "rednecks," they found it too difficult to accept as their official spokesman and representative a man who was as vituperative and overtly racist as Johnson. The days when most Arkansans were happy to have a clone of Jeff Davis in the governor's mansion were now in the past.

Helped by increasing black awareness and his expensive but effective campaign to register blacks, Rockefeller was also aided by Johnson's reported refusal even to shake hands with African Americans.[13] Election day found Rockefeller with 71 percent of the black vote, a far cry from the result two years earlier. An inarticulate, transplanted Yankee millionaire with a suspect last name, running as a Republican in a staunchly Democratic state, won by sixty-three thousand votes, which, as Jim Ranchino noted, was "roughly the number of blacks who voted for the Republican [Rockefeller]."[14] Ranchino also pointed out how crucial the black vote was in Rockefeller's margin of victory two years later against another undistinguished "Old Guard" Democrat, Marion Crank. Although the Democratic Party began to make serious efforts to improve its image racially (and Crank tried to attract black votes), Rockefeller still squeaked by with a margin of twenty-six thousand votes in 1968 with blacks giving him 91 percent of their ballots. An unknown attorney named Dale Bumpers watching him from the hills in western Arkansas learned the valuable lesson that most Arkansans were ready to respond to a positive image. Running an upbeat campaign in 1970 after gaining the Democratic nomination over Faubus in a runoff, Bumpers trounced Rockefeller badly.

In the past, white Arkansans had helplessly watched as white and black coalitions crumbled under the cry of "nigger lover." Had Arkansans changed so much that such coalitions were now possible when they had failed so miserably in the past? The main difference now was that the federal government had forced so much change on white Arkansans that there was no political advantage to be gained by one Arkansas politician calling his colleague "nigger lover" except to a minority of voters, because almost all white Arkansans of all political stripes at one time or another had resisted civil rights legislation whether it was Faubus, the Southern Moderate, or Winthrop Rockefeller. The federal government, first through the courts and then through the executive and legislative branches, had prevailed against the South, and white Arkansas politicians, along with their brethren in other states, had lost in battle after battle. Blacks as a political force were here to stay because the federal government had decided again to guarantee their existence. Once Southern politicians realized and accepted this fact, expediency dictated that blacks be accepted and courted at election time.

Yet Winthrop Rockefeller went far beyond personal expediency. As governor, he genuinely made a conscious effort to change the atmosphere surrounding race relations within the state. Beside finding jobs for blacks in state government, his main contribution was that he, as governor, made the notion of equality respectable, though not necessarily accepted, inside Arkansas. While a man of the caliber of Faubus spent part of his administration trying to keep blacks from being allowed to eat in the employees' cafeteria, Rockefeller, during his first term, had lunch with Roy Wilkins, still the head of the NAACP nationally, and then had him flown in his private plane to El Dorado for the state meeting of the NAACP held at Magnolia in Columbia County.[15] At one point in Rockefeller's administration in 1967 Arkansas was near the top of the nation in the number and percentage of blacks on local draft boards. Faubus had not appointed a single African American to any draft board in the state. Still, the powers of an Arkansas governor were quite limited. Although he would exert as much influence as he could muster to control situations or at least contain them, the violence that was coming was often out of his jurisdiction, and the power to persuade was all he had.

Black Militancy after the Death of Martin Luther King Jr.

Before the assassination of Martin Luther King Jr. there had been practically no violence on a mass scale by black Arkansans. What violence there had been before King's death—and it was relatively little compared to the atrocities in places like Birmingham or in Mississippi—was almost always perpetrated by whites against blacks. Most white Arkansans never made the effort to comprehend what Martin Luther King Jr. meant to blacks. In the minds of many he was just another troublemaker like Daisy Bates, only infinitely more powerful. After his murder in April 1968, blacks rioted in Arkansas in Pine Bluff and Hot Springs, causing an estimated property damage of $210,000.[16] His death and the initial violence that followed seemed to act as a catalyst, releasing a new militancy by blacks inside the state. Peaceful demonstrations and memorials following King's death were held in different parts of the state, but the largest was held in Little Rock where more than three thousand persons estimated at two-thirds black participated in a memorial service that was ended with Governor Rockefeller and his wife Jeanette's joining hands with blacks and singing the anthem of the civil rights movement, "We Shall Overcome." The tone of the service was sorrowful, but it was also angry as black leaders called for immediate action. When Rockefeller called for an end to discrimination in all areas of life, the mood of blacks was most clearly articulated by black minister, Cecil W. Cone. "Let's wait a day," Cone told the crowd. "If you can be assured that the powers that be really mean what they say, you can wait a day. The dream of Martin Luther King must become a reality and it must become a reality today after tomorrow."[17]

Over a century of official and unofficial prejudice in Arkansas could not be wiped away overnight, and an example of the gulf between black and white was illustrated in Little Rock at a meeting between approximately forty black leaders and the mayor and city manager to discuss community relations within a day after the memorial service. During the meeting one of the young blacks spoke up and objected to the term "colored," which had been used in the opening remarks to the group. Mayor Martin Borchert responded by saying he had lived in the community all his life and had never known that blacks resented being called "colored." After promising in the future to say "Negro," he pronounced it in typical Southern white male fashion as "nigra" and was corrected again. The meeting was reported as "tense," with younger blacks warning of possible violence and older blacks cautioning against it. For its part, the city of Little Rock through the mayor and city manager promised money for more parks in black areas and stated that an attempt would be made to hire blacks.

Rockefeller ordered a survey by the state that showed of 13,189 state jobs, blacks held only 489 of them, and about two-thirds of these were jobs for custodial, kitchen, or laundry workers. In the twelve years that Faubus was governor, 265 blacks were hired, and in the year and a quarter of the Rockefeller administration, 168 blacks had already gone to work for the state.

The Little Rock Riot

Any hope of averting violence in the city of Little Rock was short-lived. In August what began as a protest demonstration in Little Rock against the death of a black youth at the county penal farm turned into a rock- and bottle-throwing mob that necessitated the calling of five hundred National Guardsmen into the city and the imposition of a curfew that lasted three nights.[18] The incident that touched off the violence was a direct result of a condition that had existed for years but which white authorities had not seen fit to correct. An eighteen-year-old teenager, Curtis Ingram Jr. of Little Rock, had been sent to the county farm to serve a six-month sentence and had been ordered to pay $110 fine for violation of the state's drug-control law. The county penal farm, typical of Arkansas prisons, worked through the trusty system, and the official version was that after Ingram had attacked a trusty he had been killed in self-defense. But on the black radio station, KOKY, Bob Broadwater, the same young man who had corrected the mayor at the meeting in Little Rock following King's assassination, broadcast a program in which two anonymous ex-inmates of the county farm stated that Ingram had complained he was sick and had asked to leave the fields and return to the barracks. A supervisor had told a trusty to give him a whipping. The broadcast enflamed the black community. The leaders of a new militant group called Black United Youth (BUY) of which Broadwater was a part organized first a memorial service and then what was supposed to be a peaceful demonstration.[19] In the ensuing riot there were injuries and property damage, but there was no loss of life. After the curfew was lifted and the situation had calmed, the Pulaski County grand jury was called into session to investigate the county farm. Thirteen blacks, ranging from the conservative I. S. McClinton to Bobby Brown, a forty-five-dollar-a-week worker for the county's economic opportunity agency and also head of BUY, filed a lawsuit challenging the constitutionality of the racial makeup of the grand jury.[20] Warned by the federal judge in open court that the grand jury could not withstand a legal challenge, the members of the grand jury met no more. Undoubtedly, under these circumstances, county officials were only too happy not to have to make a report on the conditions of the county farm.

Trouble in Forrest City

Though resentment in black communities festered throughout the year after King's murder, it was not until 1969 that black anger over past wrongs reached full boil outside of Little Rock. The most extended civil rights activity in 1969 occurred at Forrest City, where SNCC had once been active four years earlier. Fiercely dedicated to changing hearts and minds, SNCC workers and their supporters in Arkansas had almost always stayed nonviolent, whatever the provocation. Now, although blacks remained for the most part nonviolent, the philosophy of nonviolence was no longer for them an indispensable element in the effort to achieve equality.

King's murder seemed to transform many black Arkansans from docile, fear-ridden individuals into sometimes openly hostile and occasionally destructive forces who now demanded jobs and fair treatment. In March 1969 between one and two hundred students at all-black Lincoln School in Forrest City went on a rampage, smashing nearly every window in the building and destroying thousands of dollars of school property. Their anger had suddenly boiled over in protest at the firing of a black social science teacher, J. F. Cooley, who, among other civil rights activities, had organized some low-key boycotts and picketing among the students.[21] Cooley had encouraged picketing at a grocery store across the street from the school because the owner had controlled the number of blacks who could be in the store at one time.[22] The reaction to the school riot was predictable. With no hint of understanding, the editor of the local white-owned paper wailed, "There is no reason . . . no logic in this type of action. It's one of those awful things that has always happened somewhere else . . . never here at home . . . not in Forrest City where race relations have always been so good."[23]

A long, hot summer was in store for both blacks and whites in Forrest City. Within the white community in these small Delta towns, opinions were not as uniform as one might have supposed. In Forrest City, then a town of approximately ten thousand evenly divided between blacks and whites, the John Birch Society, which had begun in 1964, had between four and five hundred members in 1968. Headed by Dr. Norman R. Saliba, a school board member, the Birchers disseminated literature that described the civil rights movement as a tool of Communism.[24] Active and influential, the Birchers and similar organizations created the climate for a white backlash that erupted in open violence in Forrest City in September 1969. At the same time, a more moderate element sought to resist the Birchers and their supporters' efforts to defy federal guidelines and return to "freedom of choice" in the schools and to block an urban renewal program.

The Committee for Peaceful Coexistence, the black organization that led the boycotts, pickets, and demonstrations throughout the summer of 1969 in Forrest City, perhaps invited unnecessary trouble for itself and the community by requesting a group called the "Memphis Invaders" to help them organize. The leader of this group, Lance Watson, called himself "Sweet Willie Wine." This group and its leader in no way fit the image of nonviolent protesters and, in fact, were a public-relations nightmare, unless their goal was to whip whites into a frenzy of fear that would lead to an inevitable backlash. Watson's police record was rumored to go beyond the civil rights movement. Not unexpectedly, the Forrest City NAACP refused to become involved with the picketing in Forrest City.[25]

Within the black leadership in Forrest City, there was rivalry between Cato Brooks and J. F. Cooley, the teacher whose dismissal provoked the riot at the school. Cooley had moved to Little Rock, courtesy of Charles Bernard, a wealthy white planter and former Republican senatorial candidate from Earle who had contributed enough money to Shorter College in Little Rock to give Cooley a job there. Cooley and Brooks overcame their differences to propose a march from West Memphis to Little Rock to protest conditions in eastern Arkansas, but Governor Rockefeller, by promising more jobs for blacks, was able to convince the leaders to postpone the march. Watson went ahead with his own "March Against Fear" and produced the only comic relief in what soon became a very tragic situation in the history of Forrest City.

In anticipation of the invasion of Watson's army, the mayor of Hazen ordered barricades and rice combines manned by men with helmets and shotguns to be placed at entrances to city streets so "Sweet Willie Wine" and his men would not be tempted to leave Highway 70 and go into Hazen and rape and pillage. City officials imposed a curfew and evacuated women and children as the white men of Hazen bravely set about to protect their little town against the expected hoards.[26] What finally passed by Hazen was "Sweet Willie Wine" and a handful of unarmed "Invaders" surrounded by state police and reporters. The mayor, Jerry Screeton, allowed that the "city may have been left looking a little silly" but blamed the press.[27]

As could have been predicted, events quickly turned sour after the invaders and their leader returned to Forrest City. A white crowd estimated between five hundred and a thousand beat not only Watson but also tore the clothes from the back of Bonner McCollum, the editor of the *Forrest City Times Herald* who was accused of printing "nigger news."[28] Both incidents occurred in the wake of the jailing of two blacks accused of raping white women. The angry mob, fueled by the alleged rapes, had seized two convenient targets in order to give vent to their frustration after a tormented summer of boycotts and demonstrations. The two blacks were later found guilty, but their convictions were overturned because of jury discrimination. The Forrest City police had rescued Watson from the mob but were unable to control the situation. Chief Marvin Gunn, in fact, was praised for his fairness by Cato Brooks, which undoubtedly added fuel to the fire. With the situation escalating out of control the governor dispatched National Guard troops to seal off a section of the city. A curfew was essential as blacks and whites at one point lined up on opposite sides of an intersection and cursed and screamed at each other.[29]

Ultra-conservative whites adopted blacks' picketing tactics and marched in front of city hall and the police station. In early September an estimated crowd of more than seven hundred whites turned out for a rally at which speakers denounced city officials, the news media, and outside black influence. Dr. George McPhail claimed the *Arkansas Gazette* was "Communist controlled" and said, "You can rough up a few Sweet Willies and be within the law."[30] The Forrest City School Board voted to close the white high school indefinitely after some white girls claimed that they had been threatened by Negro students and after white students and their parents had picketed the school. The high school reopened shortly after the more moderate element in the community banded together to complain about the closing, claiming that reports by more conservative whites had been exaggerated. [31] Sue Saunders, a local correspondent for the *Arkansas Gazette,* was physically assaulted by an irate woman as she attempted to cover a story dealing with the racial situation. She had been called a "Communist" and "nigger lover" and frequently had been cursed by incensed white conservatives for her efforts to cover news stories involving race relations in Forrest City. After her attack, she said, "I've never seen such hate. I didn't know it existed."[32] Rockefeller attempted to mediate throughout the conflict, but most whites felt there was nothing to resolve. An example of the hopelessness of the situation was evident from the remarks of the president of the Forrest City Chamber of Commerce, Francis Vandiver, who said in response to a question about the first change needed to improve race relations in Forrest City, "I have no idea of any change we need to make."[33] A black member of the newly formed biracial council with Vandiver was John Clark, who was director of the East Central Arkansas Equal Opportunities Council. Clark said that the first thing that had to be discussed was respect and courtesy and then employment. Although blacks comprised half the population, there were none employed by the city except for three city policemen.

The most eloquent attempt made by a black person to make whites understand what blacks were trying to achieve came from Dr. Charles J. Latimer, a wealthy, highly educated man who began to take out advertisements in the local paper to get through to whites.

> I wish I could tell you that Forest City is a city where democracy prevails and that justice is just around the corner but I can't. I wish I could tell you that Forrest City is a city where though one's lips are thick, his hair kinky, and his skin black, in a business institution he is treated with courtesy and is more often than not referred to as Mr. or Mrs., but I can't. I wish I could tell you that Forrest City is a city where all of the white college graduates know that the o in Negro is a long one, that the word is not pronounced nigguh nor nigger but I can't. . . .

When asked why he took out advertisements, he said, "How else is the white man going to know how the black man feels? No one asks me to speak to the Rotary Club, the Lion's Club. . ."[34]

Civil Rights Protests throughout the State

Forrest City was a prime example of delayed civil rights activity that began to appear in many small towns in Arkansas where there was a substantial black population after the death of Martin Luther King Jr. While black residents in Forrest City and in other parts of the Delta may well have been inspired by the work done by SNCC, protests took place far beyond the Delta and in places SNCC had never been. Even before King's assassination, approximately 350 blacks had marched in the streets of El Dorado in Union County to protest the shooting death of a black seventeen-year-old by a white who was acquitted by an all-white jury.[35]

Black anger continued to spark in central Arkansas in 1969. In August in predominantly black areas of Little Rock, rock-throwing, fire-bombing, and other incidents were reported, prompting the chamber of commerce to condemn "hoodlum attempts" aimed at destroying a "sound relationship between blacks and whites in the city.[36] Black United Youth chapters were organized in North Little Rock, Arkadelphia, and Benton. In Hot Springs a group called the

Council for the Liberation of Blacks was formed. Called CLOB, the ominous-sounding organization received publicity for picketing the Miss Arkansas pageant because there were no blacks in the contest, such was its integrationist bent.

Black students in Texarkana in November staged a walkout, giving as reasons the playing of "Dixie," the lack of respect, and lack of representation in school activities.[37] In December blacks in Cotton Plant in Woodruff County contacted the U.S. Commission on Civil Rights about investigating the shooting death of a black by the town police chief. A grand jury had returned no indictment.[38]

1970

The new assertiveness continued unabated into 1970 as blacks at Blytheville in January appeared before the city council saying that serious racial problems were on the horizon and demanded street and drainage improvements.[39] Also in January between two and three hundred black students in Pine Bluff walked out of the high school, demanding that Martin Luther King Jr.'s birthday be made a national holiday, while students in the Carthage School District in Dallas County complained of unequal disciplinary procedures.[40] At Strong in Union County approximately two hundred students walked out in April to protest the dismissal of a science teacher, Bernard Snowden, who claimed he was fired for discussing racial issues at the school.[41]

Though no statewide civil rights leader emerged, it was inevitable that blacks tried to form larger civil rights organizations than existed in each community. Cato Brooks, who had been instrumental as a leader in Forrest City, Roy Laird of Cotton Plant, and Lawrence Swain of North Little Rock became leaders of a group called "Community Organization Methods Build Absolute Teamwork" (COMBAT) and announced marches by poor people in the communities of Cotton Plant, Augusta, and McCrory (Woodruff County) as well as in Strong in May 1970.[42] COMBAT's efforts, which among other issues centered around jobs, had hardly gotten off the ground when at Strong the three leaders were arrested for attempting to lead a march of approximately 225 persons without a parade permit. At Cotton Plant the three had been arrested on charges of possessing an illegal weapon.[43] Seventy-one marchers were arrested at Strong and Cotton Plant.[44]

A black group at Stuttgart in Arkansas County named BOYS (Black Organized Youth) sought a state boycott of Kroger stores because of employment discrimination. The boycott was lifted in Stuttgart a little over a month later as blacks gained concessions from the Kroger chain in hiring practices.[45] Voter registration was still a goal very much on the minds of the leaders of COMBAT who sponsored a "March against Fear" across Woodruff County in June 1970. Approximately forty blacks accompanied a flat-bed wagon drawn by a mule that carried a sign stating, "I'm not registered to vote because I'm an ass—what's your excuse?"

In Hot Springs CLOB leaders John Paschal and Ernest Scott were sentenced and fined in municipal court on charges of malicious mischief in connection with an outburst by blacks in which five windows in downtown businesses were broken after whites had burned crosses on West Mountain in view of a party sponsored by CLOB. Four white youths were fined in the cross-burning incident, as well.[46] On August 11, 1970, an incident in Hot Springs involving a white policeman who shot and wounded a black touched off a disturbance in which thirty-four blacks were charged with unlawful assembly after some windows in businesses were broken.

Also in August in Blytheville a black man, Carter Williams, was shot and killed by two white men as he picketed a grocery store. The two whites were said to be involved in the ownership and management of the store. Fire bombings occurred in the predominantly black section of town after Williams's funeral, and several blacks were arrested for curfew violations. COMBAT and BUY members marched in the funeral procession. One white man, Ernest Ray, was found guilty of manslaughter but never served a day in prison after the jury recommended a suspended sentence because of his health problems. The other white was found innocent.[47] Later, the grocery store was mysteriously burned prompting a move to Little Rock by the two men where juries later found them liable to the deceased's family in a total amount of $31,309.[48]

At Earle in Crittenden County a major confrontation between blacks and whites on the night of September 10, 1970, developed as blacks claimed that state police and Earle officials fired shots over their heads during a march. The blacks were led by Ezra Greer, a veteran of civil rights marches outside Arkansas. Greer had previously led a successful effort in 1969 to remove a garbage dump from the black community. The confrontation in 1970 grew out of an earlier boycott by black students. The white superintendent, Sam I. Bratton, had admitted at a federal hearing that no whites were assigned to classes where whites would be in the minority, and with a few exceptions, no blacks were assigned to teach integrated classes. The school system had 65 percent black enrollment and had recently switched from "freedom of choice" to a supposedly unitary system. A federal judge ordered the segregation within the school to be discontinued.

In October 1970 all 350 of the students at the all-black school in Wabbaseka in Jefferson County, incidentally the boyhood home of one-time revolutionary Eldridge Cleaver, began a boycott that lasted three months until blacks gained control of the school board, at which time a mass suspension of two hundred blacks was withdrawn and the boycott ended. The walkout had occurred over the dismissal of two black teachers.[49]

"Many Voices" and Respect, Inc.

Since lasting and tangible achievements of this post–Martin Luther King Jr. grass-roots civil rights movement in Arkansas were often problematic at best, one forgets how militant the black consciousness of this era was at the time. The most important vehicle for black expression at this time was the publication *Many Voices* produced by the Delta civil rights group Respect, Inc., which was founded in May 1970 by four white former VISTA volunteers who had worked in the area. Respect, Inc. was incorporated in July 1970, its two goals being the organization of a newspaper written for and by the blacks and the poor of eastern Arkansas and the establishment of a community information center in West Memphis. Respect, Inc. was run by a board of directors composed of members from eight counties in the Delta. Though the staff was primarily made up of whites, the board was composed of individuals "elected or appointed by the members of three organizations known by Respect, Inc. to be working in each of the counties."[50] Earl Anthes remembers,

> The reason some of us started *Many Voices* is because . . . we saw things were bubbling up in individual communities but there was no way they were talking to each other. They all thought they were working in isolation.[51]

Not only did *Many Voices* report on civil rights activity in the black community, they documented white violence. Throughout this turbulent period of civil rights activity by blacks some whites continued to react by resorting to tried and true measures of the past. In such an atmosphere it was not surprising that the Ku Klux Klan resurfaced in Arkansas. In April 1970 Ku Klux Klan "Imperial Wizard" Robert Shelton appeared at a rally that drew an estimated crowd of five hundred whites in St. Francis County near Forrest City. Shelton apologized for the length of his speech by saying, "When I get a group of white folks together and don't have to look at niggers all day, I can't help it."[52]

Whatever the influence of Shelton, at Parkin in September 1970 authorities arrested thirteen whites, some of whom had Ku Klux Klan membership cards, and charged them with the crime of nightriding.[53] In Madison, near Forrest City, there was evidence of Klan activity over several months in 1971. As usual, information about its organization was sketchy. Klan chapters were believed to have been organized at Texarkana, El Dorado, Strong, and Pine Bluff before 1965. This latest version of the Klan, unlike the Klan that was so popular back in the 1920s, had difficulty gaining respectability. White Arkansans were much more likely to rally behind someone more socially acceptable who could persuasively articulate the belief that whites were victims of a conspiracy concocted by the federal government and international Communism.

While the Klan had its own share of problems, it still was capable of doling out misery to black activists in at least one case with the assistance of local authorities. The *Many Voices* lead story in the August 25, 1971, issue reported an attack on black family members shortly after they were released from jail after a family disturbance.

> Mrs. Juanita Shelton, wife of Forrest City activist Everett Shelton, and four members of the Cochran family of 105 East Midway were assaulted and beaten by KKK members as they were released from jail about 10 pm Monday August 23rd. . . . According to Mrs. Shelton, upon their release after posting bond, they were met by a group of 150 to 200 Klansmen who then attacked them. 'I was hit by bricks, beaten with a water-hose, and kicked in the back,' said Mrs. Shelton. Both Frank Cochran Jr. and Sr. were beaten and hospitalized.

According to Frank Cochran Sr., his family had been told by a jailer that someone was waiting to see them outside the jail. Photographs of the Cochran family swathed in bandages accompany the story.[54]

Depending primarily on activist African Americans themselves to provide the news, the staff of *Many Voices* made no pretense of presenting a nuanced picture of events in the Delta. Like the *State Press* under L. C and Daisy Bates, the biweekly was a call to action. In doing so, *Many Voices* provided specific information about the demands of blacks, which were usually briefly summarized. The paper was careful to detail the specific demands of the black community in the Delta, which invariably called for inclusion of African Americans into the commercial, political, and educational activities of the towns in which protests were taking place. For example, the July 28–August 10, 1971, issue listed demands the black community organization (COMBAT) made in Brinkley in Woodruff County that had to be met before a buying boycott would be called off. Demands ranged from the vague ("More blacks be hired in county and city positions") to the specific ("No black students be expelled from school without a hearing in the presence of their parents.") A photograph of COMBAT leader Rev. Roy Laird accompanied the story.

After a year in operation *Many Voices* had much to report in its anniversary issue dated October 27–November 9, 1971. Headline stories on the front page included "Earle, Brinkley Schools Again Hit by Protest," "Forty Students Suspended for [West Memphis] Walkout," [Forrest City] Judge Hears Testimony About Madison Shootout," and "Final Plans Announced for Delta Rights Hearing."

An editorial for the issue highlighted not the continuing protests and violence in the Delta but the Achilles' heel of the civil rights movement in the Delta—the failure of local blacks to effectively mobilize politically. It concluded that an evaluation of the elections in 1970

> would perhaps show that: Black political organizations lagged in their efforts. Many qualified citizens were never called upon to register. Little effort to secure absentee ballot applications for the elderly and shut-ins was made. . . . Most Black candidates failed to reach the people and failed to produce a platform that would sell to the people. . . . Many politicians failed to organize their campaigns prior to filing for an office. . . . Voting turn-out was poor in almost every election. . . . People were uneducated on how to vote in a primary election. . . . Most Black candidates running for a position on their school board ballot lost.

Though in hearings before the civil rights commission blacks claimed intimidation and fraud by whites had cost them elections, the *Many Voices* editorial put the responsibility for the poor showing on blacks themselves:

> In 1972 Black politics must take a new face. There must be strength and undivided Black political motivation locally, state and nation-wide. . . . The idea that there is no certain Black man who acts as the Black people's "wheeler and dealer" must get around to the white suppressors and the white political world that intends to remain in control over Black people.

Significantly, the anniversary issue of *Many Voices* carried a poem by a reader from Marianna named Gloria Williams. Entitled "Stop Killing Your Brother" Williams wrote, in part,

> You kill, steal, murder me, And then you can me "Brother." You fight, bite, call yourself right. . . . You holler, "Man, give me five." But I don't take that jive, When you go around killing your color. You say to me, "Right on, Man," then turn right around to cut my throat. We know we're cool so quit being a fool. Why don't you quit killing your Brother, Cause we're all the same color.

As relentlessly aggressive as *Many Voices* was in its denunciation of white supremacy, there was also the recognition that often blacks' worst enemy in the community was staring back at them in the mirror each morning.

1971

The year 1971 would be no let up in civil rights activity in Arkansas. In addition to the above, at Brinkley in Monroe County a fight broke out in January 1971 between blacks and whites at the high school. A group of white students had celebrated the birthday of Robert E. Lee in response to the celebration of Martin Luther King Jr.'s birthday earlier. When two blacks were suspended from the high school, which had a 46 percent black enrollment, approximately 240 blacks walked out.[55] Blacks demanded that "Dixie" no longer be played at school functions and that a black principal and a black basketball coach be hired.

At Star City in Lincoln County racial tensions quickly developed after a black male, Carnell Russ, was killed inside the jail by a city marshal while the man's family waited outside in the car after he had been arrested for speeding.[56] After the shooting, fifty to sixty blacks gathered at the courthouse. A Lincoln County grand jury returned an indictment of voluntary manslaughter. Trouble returned to Blytheville as black junior and senior high students demonstrated, protesting the lack of representation by blacks in the school. Approximately three hundred whites out of a total of nine hundred briefly boycotted in retaliation for the amnesty granted to the blacks.[57]

Black anger seemed to be growing in Little Rock. In August 1971 a white reporter, Bob Stover, was beaten by blacks at the Dunbar Community Center. Stover, a reporter for the *Arkansas Gazette,* was trying to cover a story on police brutality.[58] At Hall High School in Little Rock, which had avoided substantial desegregation for many years, approximately seventy-five blacks broke eight windows after a white teacher refused to withdraw assault and battery charges against a black student.[59]

There was a mood of increasing hopelessness about race relations in the state as the decade of the seventies began. If Little Rock seemed a racial powder keg at times, it did not compare to the growing tenseness in the Arkansas Delta, where pressure had been building for years.[60]

CHAPTER 17

Marianna

Marianna in Lee County in the heart of the Delta epitomized the racial problems of the state in the late 1960s and early 1970s. In many ways this small, forgotten town of less than five thousand, about equally divided between whites and blacks, proved to have the right ingredients for the "perfect storm." But it was not just a racial confrontation that was about to occur. Through the vision and political skills of a Southern president, racial injustice and poverty (both white and black) were deemed no longer acceptable in a nation as rich and powerful as the United States. It was Lyndon Johnson who at the height of his power in 1964 insisted in a speech in May at the University of Michigan that America must create a "Great Society" whose goal was to create opportunities for the poor so that they might lift themselves out of poverty.

Volunteers in Service to America

With the passage of the Economic Opportunity Act of 1964 federal programs proliferated, including the creation of Volunteers in Service to America (VISTA), a domestic Peace Corps in which volunteers, usually college-age young men and women, were trained and often assigned to "community action agencies" throughout the poorest areas of the country. Perhaps the most radical notion of the "war on poverty" was that the local poor themselves would have a voice in governing these entities. It was this self-governing feature that caused such consternation. Whites in the South had become accustomed to receiving federal aid with its onerous red tape, but it made sure the federal largess went to the "right" people as had occurred, for example, during the Great Depression. As discussed, investigations showed Arkansas had been exhibit A of this practice as the local farm bureaucracies intervened to make certain that planters and not their tenants benefited from the federal programs. But now, with the passage of the economic opportunity act and its regulations, the poor were actually included on the governing boards that administered these programs. Their allies in insuring their actual participation in Lee County were out-of-state VISTA volunteers who began to arrive in Lee County in early 1969. Assigned to the East Central Arkansas Economic Opportunity Agency in Forrest City in adjoining St. Francis County, VISTA volunteers trained as "health advocates" and began to hold meetings with "neighborhood action committees" in Marianna and at least three other rural communities in Lee County. The volunteers could not help but think they had stepped back in time. Dr. Dan Blumenthal, the first VISTA physician in the nation, writes of Lee County:

> We viewed a scene archetypical of rural poverty in the cotton South. Outside of town [Marianna] there were scattered plantation houses owned by white gentlemen farmers. Down the road was, typically, a collection of tumbledown wooden shacks inhabited by black field hands. Living in similar shacks were elderly blacks and poor whites too old to farm and too unschooled to do anything else, who lived on social security checks or on food stamps, or on seemingly nothing at all. Typically, their houses were located on dirt roads that became impassable when it rained.[1]

The health needs were obvious. Blumenthal writes that the

> The lack of health care . . . the people receive in an area such as this leads to an early death. . . . It's an early death following a lifetime of frustration and hopelessness. . . . People suspect, I'm sure, that they're dying younger than they need to. . . . It's a hopeless feeling.[2]

Though blacks composed half the town and were much in evidence as maids, cooks, laundresses, yardmen, and delivery men, they addressed children as "Mister" and "Miss" and were in turn called by their first names. As late as 1962 members of the senior class at the white high school in Marianna (some dressed in black face) performed a minstrel and made fun of blacks to a full house.[3] The Civil Rights Act of 1964 seemed to make little difference. Waiting rooms were still segregated in 1969.[4] Blumenthal remembered, "Dr. Dwight Gray taught me what Lee County was all about. He leveled with me as a fellow southern doctor, one of the clan, and said he had segregated waiting rooms because that's what the colored folks wanted, and he winked."[5]

When whites in authority in Lee County realized that the federal government was serious about providing healthcare to its poor, they reacted by mobilizing their resources to oppose change and, when that was not successful, to try to co-opt the changes they could not prevent. First, the five-person Lee County Medical Society denied that it was not treating the poor. However, the board voted to deny Dr. Blumenthal's application to join it, meaning he could not admit his patients to the hospital in Marianna. It took a federal lawsuit to change this result. There is little doubt that the physicians were worried that Blumenthal was going to cost them business, just as private lawyers were futilely resisting federally funded lawyers for the poor. One of the most urgent needs identified by poor people in Lee County was a place to treat people, and this need was the genesis for the idea for a health clinic. When he first arrived in Marianna, Blumenthal used his own vehicle to travel to people's homes.[6]

Despite growing opposition from Lee County whites in positions of authority, support for a health clinic for the poor was coming forth from the federal government. Though doctors and pharmacists in Lee County obtained the help of Arkansas senator John McClellan to try to block the initial federal funding of forty thousand dollars for a health clinic, he was unsuccessful. Much had changed since the days when powerful whites in the Delta backed down Washington. From Little Rock the *Arkansas Gazette* weighed in with the view that denying privileges to a federal government physician to use the facilities of a hospital built with federal funds was "an outrageous situation."[7] Unlike federal agricultural officials during the 1930s, federal Office of Economic Opportunity officials in the 1960s had no intention of giving in to the Delta. Marvin Schwartz documents the unwillingness of federal officials to buckle under to pressure.

> Joe Bruch [program officer for the Southwest region and Arkansas], in a June 1970 OEO memo, wrote, I will not back off from calling any and all of the so-called establishment of Lee County involved in this matter racists of the worst order.

At a more local level, though vulnerable to pressure, John Clark, who was head of the east-central Economic Opportunity Agency, ran interference for VISTA volunteers and also had to sign off on the clinic. No ordinary bureaucrat, Clark's "strongest selling point to the board was the specialty training the VISTAS had received and their ability to do things that no one else in the area could do." According to Marvin Schwatz, "He finally overcame their hesitancy to approve the program by reminding them they could always have the Volunteers removed." [8]

Black Leadership in Marianna before the Movement

The Delta and, in particular, Marianna had long been accustomed to a much different kind of leadership from the

African American community than it would have in the late 1960s. *In Marianna: a Sociological Essay on an Eastern Arkansas Town* Gordon D. Morgan has described the light-skinned leadership that for decades served as literally a pale imitation of the white community. "It was difficult to tell many of the upper class blacks from affluent whites either in terms of color or style of living."[9]

While the black power movement in the 1960s would bring the slogan "black is beautiful" to life throughout the United States, Morgan asserts the opposite was true for much of the South's existence. He has written:

> Colorism permeated southern life to such an extent that very many citizens thought and acted in terms of a hierarchy ranging from low status dark to high status white. . . . In Marianna the color leaders more or less accepted the facts of mass black poverty and did not try very hard to function against or undermine the official discrimination of the period.[10]

Like others writing about Marianna in the Jim Crow era, he acknowledges the role of a strong woman leader.

> School people like Dr. Anna M. P. Strong practically ran the black community through charisma and with the support of the town government. By being directly responsible to the town authorities, Mrs. Strong and her teachers could do little more than what they were told by their employers. . . . Dr. Strong held the community together until the mid-fifties with Moton School serving as the nucleus. The literally hundreds of former Moton students who were working successfully in schools and professions mainly outside Arkansas served to sensitize the Marianna blacks as to what was possible.[11]

Dr. Strong did more than hold the black community together. She was revered in the black community for her strength and commitment to the thousands of students who passed through black schools in Marianna. Her positive influence was legendary. In an interview in 1992 Olly Neal

Jr. pointed to a photograph of her in his office and admitted that even his impossibly strong-willed and "mouthy" mother had been intimidated by her aura.[12]

Morgan comments,

> With the death of Dr. Strong in the mid-sixties, the era of indirect rule of the blacks in Marianna community through appointed local leaders came to an end. The mulatto aristocracy fell onto hard times and retained only private symbols of former wealth and power. Those who remained became more uncertain of their roles as black emphasis burst upon the scene in the early sixties, culminating in the riots in the ghettoes of the nation during the middle third of that decade.[13]

Olly Neal Jr. Returns to Marianna

Black submissiveness was about to change with the return of Olly Neal Jr. to Marianna. Neal would come to seem a black devil incarnate to many of Marianna's whites, but in fact Neal is the first to admit that much of his early success as administrator of the desperately needed health clinic came as a result of his willingness to cooperate with whites. The difference was that the whites Neal depended on were from VISTA and outside the Marianna power structure themselves. And it was VISTA volunteers Jan Wrede, a teacher, and Corrine Cass, a nurse, who conceived the idea for the clinic, which has become one of the genuine success stories in the Arkansas Delta. Neal has said,

> As long as Jan was here, I relied heavily, and this will shock a lot of people, on her to help me figure out who I needed to communicate with to make things happen. For the first three months I was here, all the letters with my signature probably came from Jan and Corrine. . . . I know many times in the early 1970's when I was talking strong, raising hell, my palms were sweating and my heart was about to jump out of chest. I was scared as hell, too.[14]

Neal was talking about the insecurity that all blacks had to overcome when dealing with whites in the Arkansas Delta. In many ways, even in the early 1970s, Lee County was a place that was singularly untouched by the civil rights movement even though, as Jayme Stone documents, SNCC had once been active there. The clinic was to receive federal funds for expansion in 1972 of over a million dollars for construction and operating expenses, and, as Neal explained, the white community was putting out the story, "You got that crook in there, Olly Neal. Matter of fact they put out the word that I had an FBI record as long as your arm." Once Neal was able to get his FBI file, he distributed "copies in the county to everybody in the county that I could run in to."[15] According to Neal, the file revealed that Neal had been a civil rights activist of the first magnitude and that in the 1960s he had been arrested multiple times, as were many activists in that era, but there was nothing in his record that would impinge upon his ability to administer a non-profit corporation.

At stake was the principle of white supremacy itself. According to whites, blacks could not manage the money; they would steal it or mismanage it. If that kind of money was going to flow into Lee County, whites who had always been running the county should at least be on the board to oversee the project to keep blacks from running off with everything that was not nailed down. In Neal's mind the turning point for the clinic was the meeting he and some members of his staff and board had with Governor Bumpers at the mansion in Little Rock on a Sunday afternoon. Though it was federal money, under the Office of Economic Opportunity regulations Bumpers had to review and sign off on the project. If he vetoed it, Washington had the power to override the veto.[16] One can appreciate the contrast of what occurred that afternoon. A half-century earlier, Charles Hillman Brough, Arkansas's most educated governor and devoted student of race relations, turned over the entire investigation of perhaps the worst race massacre in the history of the country to a self-appointed group of white planters and politicians (the "Committee of Seven") in exchange for a promise that there would be "no lynchings" in Phillips County; less than a decade earlier governor Orval Faubus had refused to let blacks be served with whites in the cafeteria at the capitol; Dale Bumpers invited into his official residence on a Sunday afternoon for tea and cookies a group of poor blacks from the Delta to hear their side of a dispute over the funding of a proposed expansion of a health center. Nearly as important as the close attention that the governor gave to the matter was the gracious hospitality shown by both Betty and Dale Bumpers, who had learned the names of the delegation and treated them with dignity and respect. Neal would remember Bumpers as "an extremely graceful, beautiful guy," but he would also remember that Bumpers listened carefully not just to him but to others on his board.[17] Bumpers had nothing to gain politically. Blacks in the Delta had begun to run for political office as Republicans, and whites in the Delta had not yet become Republicans, so Bumpers was acting against his own political interest by signing the next day the documents okaying the expansion of the health clinic.

Inevitably, the clinic and its staff acted as a consciousness-raising mechanism for other areas besides healthcare. Two victories by Republican Winthrop Rockefeller had naturally made many blacks particularly in the Arkansas Delta rethink their allegiance to the Arkansas Democratic Party as they dared to think that they might run black candidates and actually have a chance to win in counties still securely in the hands of whites devoted to white supremacy. Nowhere did this make sense to blacks as in Lee County because of the success they had in organizing the Lee County health clinic. As Olly Neal explained, "If we could organize around health care, why not other parts of our lives?"[18]

In Olly Neal blacks in Lee County had an undeniable leader. From Lee County, where he had graduated from Robert R. Moton High School in 1958, Neal had been part of the student sit-in movement in Memphis in the sixties, but he had also been a letter carrier in Chicago where he had been drafted to serve in Vietnam. At Lane, a black college in Jackson, Tennessee, he was convicted of "disorderly conduct and inciting a riot" following an explosion of the school's science lab. Fined fifty-three dollars, he was expelled from school. As a result of his military background, his militant reputation, his imposing physical stature, and his bullhorn voice, he had been a leading suspect of the bombing of the school.[19] Returning to Memphis, he was supervising a feeding program in a poor neighborhood through St. Jude's Hospital when he learned on a visit home that VISTA was putting together Marianna's new health clinic. Soon he was named as administrator when the clinic began operation in March 1970. Only an organization completely independent of the Delta power structure could have gotten away with hiring a man like Olly Neal. As a dark-skinned, militant black male who seemed totally unafraid of anyone, initially Neal was the worst nightmare many of either race could imagine, for he soon displayed no intention of confining his leadership role to improving the health of the poor. From this point forward whites first saw Neal as the leader in a battle for control of Lee County. As we shall see in the remaining chapters, the career of Olly Neal would later exemplify the possibilities for cooperation in the Delta, but no black male was as feared and detested as Neal in the early 1970s.

The Marianna Boycott

In June 1971 blacks in Marianna began a boycott that was to have devastating consequences both directly and indirectly for that racially divided community. The boycott against white merchants in the downtown area highlighted the fact that in Arkansas in the 1970s nonviolence was a tactic that, in certain places, no longer applied. At least one of the reasons for the effectiveness of the boycott was the willingness of blacks to use violence. As William Adler writes,

> Defiance of the boycott was not tolerated. A minister who preached opposition awoke one night to find his

> house engulfed in flames; someone had firebombed it. One retailer complained that "all my good colored customers out in the country, they've been threatened so bad they're scared to even come to town to pay what they owe me, much less buy anything."[20]

Since no blacks were ever charged during this period, we know nothing of Olly Neal's involvement. On the other hand, there appears to be nothing that has been made public to suggest he did anything to stop intimidation and violence either.

In the summer of 1971 the situation in Marianna came to a head when Rabon Cheeks and Olly Neal's brother Prentiss Neal, two of the leaders of the boycott, charged that county judge Haskell Adams tried to run them down as they stood on a downtown street corner distributing leaflets. The two blacks could not get either the police chief or the sheriff to file charges. When they appeared at the county courthouse, Adams pulled his pistol at them and reportedly said, "You niggers, get out of here. I run the courthouse. I will kill the whole pack of you lying sons of bitches."[21] Adams later claimed his brakes had jammed, causing his truck to slide. In fact, Adams could have been charged with attempted murder. Cheeks and Neal went to the prosecuting attorney who only allowed them to file charges against Adams of assault and carrying a concealed weapon. A week before Adams's trial, three downtown stores were burned.

Adams avoided a trial by pleading no contest, entering in effect a plea of guilty. He was fined a mere one hundred dollars.[22] With blacks angry over the easy treatment of Adams and whites angry over the boycott and now forming groups to offer protection to blacks who would dare to shop downtown in defiance of it, violence was inevitable. When fights began to break out between whites and blacks, Governor Bumpers sent in the National Guard, and a curfew was imposed that lasted several days.[23] By 1972 whites in Marianna were offering rewards totaling ten thousand dollars for information leading to the arrests of persons involved in ten specified incidents, some of which involved the arson of blacks' homes who had not been sympathetic to the boycott.[24]

The demands of blacks in Marianna were similar to the demands they had made elsewhere. They revolved mainly around specific jobs in the private and public sector, but they also included ultimatums for the resignation of certain public officials.[25] A sit-in at the high school by approximately 250 black students in January 1972 developed into a school boycott after the police were called and blacks ran from the school, some of whom were injured in the melee.[26] Many of the students were suspended, and white officials decided to prosecute the students who had participated in the sit-in. Governor Bumpers appointed a statewide commission of three blacks and three whites to mediate, but the group had no success. A biracial committee from the state education department had previously investigated the situation and had urged that blacks drop their demand that the principal and superintendent be fired and that charges be dropped against the black students.[27] With a private white academy in full swing, blacks composed 80 percent of the student population, although in the county blacks were only a slight majority.[28] The state education committee stated in its report that it was "quite clear" that intimidation was a factor in the effectiveness of the school boycott.[29]

Over a year after it started, the group that called itself the Lee County Concerned Citizens formally ended the economic boycott, although it had begun to die months earlier. A study published in the *Arkansas Business and Economic Review* estimated that as much as five million dollars were lost to the economy as a result of the boycott.[30]

The emotional cost was not measurable, but it would affect permanently the consciousness of every person living in Lee County. Many whites in Marianna saw the kind of black activism exhibited in this era as nothing but deliberate racial hatred. School board president Lon Mann, an influential planter and participant in this period in Marianna who to the consternation of many blacks saw himself as a promoter of racial harmony, targeted the newspaper *Many*

Voices. In a December 21, 1971, letter to Arkansas attorney general Ray Thornton in which Mann asked for an investigation, he called the paper "one of the strongest forces at work today in Eastern Arkansas . . . in setting race against race and spreading hatred." The basis for his requested investigation was in part "the grounds that it is attempting to incite riots with its poems and 'history' lessons."[31] For example, one of the "history" pieces dealt with "the sexual exploitation of Black women [that] was inherent in the slavery system."[32] According to the story in *Many Voices* Mann said "he believed in freedom of the press but only 'when it tells the truth.'" Said Mann,

> You all [the staff of *Many Voices*] contributed to the continued boycott of the Marianna schools by not asking black parents to send their children back to school. Your whole pitch is trying to get the people against each other. You all could do a good job if you didn't print all that hate.

The real difficulty for Mann and other whites like him was that blacks and their allies in the Delta for the first time were insisting on telling own version of history.

The Bid for Political Power in Marianna

In the Delta the benefits to blacks running as Republicans seemed obvious: even as Governor Rockefeller was going down in flames in 1970 to Democrat Dale Bumpers, Republican Rockefeller had carried Lee County. His victory there was no accident since 60 percent of the voters were black. As Republicans, blacks were entitled to their own poll watchers and having one election official out of three counting the ballots, though the Democrats as majority party would have two. Not insignificantly, they could also set the filing fees lower. Thus, in the summer of 1972, serious discussion began among blacks about making a concerted challenge to this aspect of white supremacy in the Delta. The decision was not undertaken lightly. Sterling King Jr., who had served in the Peace Corps and worked in the civil rights movement in Mississippi registering voters, recalled that initially, "We had to meet in peoples' homes because of the fear of meeting in public places."[33] With Thomas Ishmael running at the top of the ticket for county judge, the top administrative post, blacks ran for a full slate but lost. Ishmael was defeated by eight hundred votes.

Blacks claimed that voters had been intimidated, arguing that "at some precincts, sheriff's deputies wearing guns looked over the shoulder of black voters At one polling place, a white police officer listed the license plates of cars driven by blacks."[34] The defeat for the black community was significant if only because, according to an interview with Neal in 1992, "it was the biggest election turnout in Lee County either before or sense. . . . It crushed me. . . . I was sick for three or four days."[35] The election results throughout 1972 were terribly discouraging to the black community. *Many Voices* did nothing to hide its disappointment. The headline in March 18, 1972, read: "One Black Wins School Position in Delta." Of all the black candidates that ran for school board, only J. C. Moore of Lexa-Barton won over two white candidates in the Phillips County school district. A later recount gave one seat to a black in Mississippi County. As the paper said, "The March 14 school board elections provided disappointment after disappointment due to generally inadequate turnout." In Marianna, for example, both black candidates for school board lost by almost a thousand votes.

Continuation of Black Racial Violence in 1972

In 1972 black violence again erupted in other parts of Arkansas as approximately forty black students at Arkadelphia in March were reported attacking white teachers and students and throwing chairs through windows. The rioting left twelve whites injured.[36] Several blacks and two white students were convicted on misdemeanor charges. Leaders of the group of blacks who picketed the jail demanding the release of those who had been arrested were convicted of the crime of inciting a riot.[37] Also in March, a severe racial disturbance developed at a college basketball game in which predominantly black Arkansas AM&N was one of the teams. According to the article, most of the responsibility for the fights which broke out was placed on AM&N students who had been transformed into a militant force in opposition to a proposed merger with the University of Arkansas.[38] The black students feared a merger would cause a further loss of their identity. Hundreds of AM&N students had demonstrated and boycotted in Pine Bluff and also went to the state capitol in Little Rock to voice futile opposition to the merger.[39] It appeared that a portion of the violence that occurred in this troubled period was unprovoked attacks by blacks against whites. However, blacks might have sought to justify their actions, the record in this period indicated that they were just as capable of violence as whites. By the end of 1972, however, demonstrations, picketing, boycotts, and most racial incidents had sharply tailed off in the state, and a sullen, uneasy peace took its place. Employment and housing discrimination seemed intractable, and with the spectacular growth of private schools in Arkansas, an uncertain future presented itself.

The Burden of School Desegregation before Busing

By 1970, according to an *Arkansas Gazette* survey, there were fifteen private all-white schools in the state, four of which were sponsored by Baptist churches. White parents had gotten together money for schools at Marvell and West Helena in Phillips County, England in Lonoke County, Bellaire in Chicot County, McGehee in Desha County, Wheatley in St. Francis County, Warren in Bradley County, and Gould in Lincoln County. There were two church-sponsored schools in West Memphis in Crittenden County and one each in Forrest City and Sherwood, a suburb of the metropolitan area of Little Rock.

At the same time, in those instances where school districts were beginning to desegregate in order to retain federal funds, black administrators and teachers paid the price. W. Fitzhugh Brundage writes: "Between 1963 and 1971 the number of black principals in Arkansas shrank from 134 to 14."[40] Black teachers were not immune either. Though no statistics are available for Arkansas, Brundage notes, "A 1970 study estimated that integration had resulted in the termination of more than 31,000 black teachers and principals."[41]

The requirement by the U.S. Supreme Court that all dual systems be abolished did not end discrimination in Arkansas. As Michael Dougan observes,

> As a result of the dismantling of dual systems, it was usually the black school that was closed and the black teachers and administrators that suffered. By one estimate, three-fourths of the black administrators lost their jobs. Only seven black superintendents remained in 1989, located mostly in overwhelmingly black districts.[42]

The abolishment of dual systems also resulted in the end of black teachers separate organizational identity when the Arkansas Teachers Association merged with the Arkansas Education Association.

Athletics and the University of Arkansas at Fayetteville

The decade of the 1960s closed in Arkansas with an event in December that attracted a sitting president and a nationwide television audience: the University of Arkansas–University of Texas football game on December 6, 1969. With the possible exception of the election of Bill Clinton as president, for almost the last half-century nothing in Arkansas has ever been bigger than the Razorback athletic program, which serves as an important mechanism to boost its citizens' self-esteem as well as to entertain and divert the masses from more pressing issues. Consistently ranked at the bottom end of so many national statistics, in third-world fashion the state of Arkansas has poured hundreds of millions of dollars, both public and private, into athletic programs. As the most prominent example, the colossal sports complex covering acres and acres of land at the University of Arkansas in Fayetteville is arguably the equal of any in the nation and is an undeniable recruitment tool for athletes, some students, and faculty alike. For students of race relations, 1969 would be the last time two college teams competed for a national championship in football with solely white players. White Arkansans of a certain age remember the game in which Texas beat Arkansas 15-to-14 for the national championship as one of the most memorable events of their lives. Indeed, the game was attended by Richard Nixon, and the invocation was given by world-famous evangelist Billy Graham.

None of the above would have likely occurred without the hiring of Frank Broyles as football coach in 1958. As football coach at Missouri the previous year, Broyles had recruited Missouri's first black scholarship athletes. That was not to happen for years at Arkansas. Terry Frei writes,

> Broyles long has said the state board [at the University] informally made it clear to him when he arrived at Arkansas that he could not recruit black athletes but that he felt integration was inevitable and right.[43]

After Southern Methodist University successfully recruited Jerry Levias who became the first black varsity football player in the southwest conference in 1966, the taboo on recruiting African Americans was broken. However, Arkansas did not have a black scholarship athlete on its freshman football team until the fall of 1969. Running back Jon Richardson had been student body president of Horace Mann High School in Little Rock and lettered for the Razorbacks from 1970 to 1972. The basketball's first black scholarship basketball player letterman was Almer Lee in 1969.[44] Black athletes, of course, quickly changed college athletics in Arkansas.[45]

Though the playing field in Razorback Stadium in Fayetteville on December 6, 1969, was lily white, the campus was not without its tensions, which stemmed from hostility to the Vietnam War and the Razorback band's playing

"Dixie." Freshman law student Eugene Hunt, one of only three blacks enrolled in law school, was a leader in Black Americans for Democracy (BAD) on campus. Hunt, now a lawyer in Pine Bluff, recalled,

> "Dixie" was seen as a racist call to arms, and I don't think I can put it any better than that. We felt the university was very insensitive when it countenanced the playing of "Dixie" at the pep rallies.[46]

It was not only "Dixie" that concerned BAD. As mentioned, there was a single African American professor on the campus. Gordon Morgan, who had gotten a doctorate in sociology from Washington State, had only been hired in the fall of 1969. During the fall semester of 1969

> BAD also demanded more black faculty members and students, more financial aid to black students, a black culture center in the planned new student union, and the hiring of a black campus police officer.[47]

BAD made enough noise to get their point across about "Dixie." It would not be played by the Razorback band again, but blacks in the coming years would not see enough change to feel that Fayetteville was a hospitable place. Writer E. Lynn Harris remembered his freshman year in Fayetteville in 1973. Blacks made up less than 2 percent of the student body.

> The three hundred or so black students formed a community within the university community. When I arrived at the campus, my heart skipped a beat of job whenever I saw another person of color.[48]

The arrival of thirty black football players at one time would begin to change collegiate sports forever at the University of Arkansas, but the influx of black athletes did not necessarily make it easier to be a black on campus. The small number and low percentage of blacks on campus have remained contentious issues into the present and, ironically, has hurt recruitment of black athletes.

CHAPTER 18

The Seventies: No Rest for Those Weary of Race

Before discussing the changes that began to occur in the racial demographics of Arkansas during the 1970s, it is appropriate here to note perhaps the most important statistic that has affected race relations in the state of Arkansas. Donald Holley, author of *The Mechanical Cotton Picker, Black Migration, and How They Shaped the Modern South* writes that reliable estimates

> suggest that Arkansas lost over 1.2 million people between 1920 and 1970. . . . The migrants were predominantly white, totaling one in five white residents between 1940 and 1960; but black migration was proportionately heavier, consisting of as much as a third of the statewide black population in the 1940s and 1950s, and almost as much again in the 1960s. These numbers are staggering. If those people had remained in the state, Arkansas's population might be as high as 3.9 million today instead of the 2.7 million counted in 2000.[1]

One can only speculate about the talent that left Arkansas for greener pastures. While lack of opportunities for both whites and blacks were apparently responsible for migration to other states before the end of the decade, beginning in the 1970s pressure from the federal government to integrate public schools began to have an impact on where white and black Arkansans chose to live *within* the state. The political mileage to be gained by attempting to defy the federal government on the issue of school integration by politicians produced fewer and fewer dividends. Thus, after 1968 when the Supreme Court announced it would no longer tolerate delays by school districts in converting to unitary systems, "freedom of choice" candidates in Arkansas were still being elected but in fewer numbers. The most notorious example was the Watson Chapel School District in Jefferson County whose school board fired its lawyer and hired John Norman Warnock from Camden whose counsel was to defy the orders of federal district judge Oren Harris. A head-on collision was avoided after the Court told the board members they faced heavy fines if they did not comply with his order to create a unitary school system. Additionally, the judge in effect imposed a gag order on Warnock. After a great deal of publicity which further inflamed passions in the community, the board complied.[2]

Integrating the Little Rock School District

As set out in Chapter 11, whites in authority in Pulaski County before the 1960s had no trouble implementing policies of racial apartheid. Blacks lived in certain areas and sent their children to schools according to plans that were acceptable to whites. There was little blacks could do but accept the situation. By the late 1960s, however, the Supreme Court signaled that it would no longer tolerate the subterfuges to avoid meaningful integration employed by school districts since *Brown I* and *II*. With its decision in *Green v. New Kent County* in 1968 the Supreme Court decreed that school segregation now had to be "eliminated, root and branch." In *Swann v. Charlotte–Mecklenburg Board of Education* in 1971, the Supreme Court specified the methods by which school integration could be accomplished, including busing of students to obtain a racial balance. Though busing would be deemed a failure, according to historian Frye Gaillard, for a number of years it proved successful in Charlotte, North Carolina, because of the community efforts to make it work. Gaillard writes, "For a decade or more, Charlotte was fundamentally changed. By almost any measure, the schools were working well. Test scores rose; white flight was minor; parental involvement was high."[3]

Though in 1957 the city of Little Rock had epitomized racial hatred because of Central High, despite all its substantial difficulties, controversies, and endless litigation, the Little Rock School District beginning in the 1970s became the poster child for public school integration in the state of Arkansas. With the steady support of the *Arkansas Gazette,* the Little Rock School Board began to embrace policies that signaled a commitment to school integration that was unmatched in the state of Arkansas by school districts that had a significant minority population. Cross-town busing and pairing of schools became the order of the day. However, from the beginning, there was a "do as I say, not as I do" attitude on the part of some school board members. Philip Reese, a reporter for the *Arkansas Democrat-Gazette,* notes

> By September 1971, five of the seven board members had children in private schools, many of which had recently opened. That same month, board member Charles A. Brown told the *Arkansas Democrat* that safety concerns spurred him to enroll his two oldest daughters in Pulaski Academy, saying, "The fear of injury to our children—I just cannot take a chance on it."

To civil rights attorney John Walker, the difficulty in integrating schools in Little Rock was rooted elsewhere. In October 1971 Walker said the following,

> The real problem is that we live apart—not only black apart from white, but rich from middle class and middle class from poor. It is necessary to reunite the city, just as the schools are reunited. Housing integration is the answer to elimination of busing [which is an] . . . artificial tool at best.[4]

Walker analyzed the problem as one in which the groups that ran the city and influenced its growth patterns—such as the Little Rock Chamber of Commerce, "Fifty for the Future" (an elite business organization), and those who controlled the financial institutions—were working to divide Little Rock into two separate communities: the expanding western section and the eastern part that contained blacks and poor whites. A strong commitment by these groups to the development of western Little Rock would result in allowing wealthier whites to escape racial problems, especially if they could afford the newly created Pulaski Academy.

Implicit in Walker's message was that public and private policy in Little Rock should merge into a vision of the future that was strongly influenced by racial integration. And at the very least, pubic policy should not be placed in the service of those who stood to enrich themselves by avoiding integration through fleeing central Little Rock and creating new neighborhoods out west. This same argument was made later in a different form by the white activist Jim Lynch and others who argued that the city's development policy tilted sharply against existing neighborhoods. Resources that should be going to stabilizing existing areas instead went to providing infrastructure and services out west. As noted in Chapter 11, whites in authority since the 1950s had implemented policies whose net effect was to segregate along racial lines the city of Little Rock through decisions of planning commissions, housing authorities, and private interests. There was nothing subtle about many of these maneuvers, and there was much at stake. By 1970 there was no doubt that the Little Rock real estate industry was going to enjoy boom times out west. Still an activist after she had convened into action the Women's Emergency Committee, Adolphine Terry complained,

> When new people come to town and are looking for homes, his [William F. Rector's real estate] agents take them to additions in the far west and assure them "there will never be a nigger in the schools your children will attend."[5]

Blacks who move to the city were steered to black areas. Albert Porter, who became a community activist, recalled being steered in 1966 to a housing development in Granite Mountain located near Gillam Park. According to John Kirk, "When Porter asked to see housing in another part of the city, he was told, 'This is where blacks live.'"[6]

The power of business persons in Little Rock who profited directly or indirectly from development out west was not to be denied. John Kirk writes, "In the 1960s and 1970s, 41,000 whites moved from east to west Little Rock while 17,000 blacks moved—or were moved—in the opposite direction."[7]

By definition, real estate and financial interests in Little Rock had always seen immediate financial gain in growth, no matter how wasteful or unnecessary one could argue it was. Playing on racial fears to stimulate sales and growth was common in the 1970s, whether or not there was an overarching intention to divide Little Rock into two communities based on race.[8] If blacks were coming in into the neighborhood, the assumption, true or not, was that property values would go down, and for many whites their homes were their principal investment. In fact, the drive to move the center of Little Rock out west had been going on long before the 1950s with the creation of the first shopping mall at the corner of Hays, now University, and Asher.[9] Though race was a motive in the minds of many who moved out west, there were other factors at work, including the American love for the automobile and what was once assumed to be an inexhaustible supply of cheap oil. The path of least resistance was through the heart of the once vibrant black business community on Ninth Street straight west. Still known as the "Wilbur Mills Freeway" due to the influence of the powerful Arkansas Ways and Means Committee chairman Wilbur Mills, federal funds poured in to create an east-west corridor identified as I-630 that, in turn, generated further highway development out west (I-430). In fact, where there was money to be made, had it been only poor whites that lived in the Ninth Street corridor, the results would likely have been the same. Though the grass-roots, populist group ACORN (Arkansas Community Organizations for Reform Now) was able to delay the construction of the Wilbur Mills Freeway by forcing the government to carry out the required environmental impact statement, the result was that it merely added to the final costs of construction but did not stop the financial and real estate interests from accomplishing their goal.[10]

Yet, according to Berna J. Love, "Many blacks felt like there was a 'master plan' or 'plot' to rid the city of the West Ninth Street black business district."[11] Whatever the intentions, Love documents that Ninth Street as a black business community began to die in 1960 as it was changed to a one-way street that ran east. By 1979 a reporter for the *Arkansas Gazette* called West Ninth Street an "eyesore." Once alive with businesses, now it was "a desolate street . . . that stands out like dirty litter in a new home." It was now a place of crime, drugs, and prostitution. Raymond Holoman, who managed Bob and Orin's Rebuilders Service, was quoted as saying, "Ninety-five percent of blacks are scared to come down here after dark."[12]

Subtle and not so subtle forms of blockbusting began to appear in the early 1970s in the formerly all-white neighborhood of Oak Forest and Pine Forest in Little Rock. Real estate agents began to solicit in these neighborhoods with letters, some of which said, "I specialize in the sale of real estate in areas that are undergoing change." The U.S. Department of Justice filed a complaint against Ming Realty Company for soliciting customers in such a manner, alleging a violation of the 1968 Housing Act.[13] Without admitting liability, Ming signed an agreement in April 1972 that regulated its activities in the area. This slap on the wrist by the Justice Department may have encouraged other real estate agents in Oak Forest, immediately west of Pine Forest, to get around the Housing Act of 1968 by flooding the neighborhood with solicitations, making no reference to the changing racial composition. Repeated solicitations were as effective in creating panic as more blatant representations. The Justice Department apparently had little interest in trying to prove more subtle cases, and a local neighborhood group in Oak Forest sponsored by ACORN was unsuccessful in its efforts to convince the city to address itself to the problem. Blockbusting in certain areas of the city was not the only tactic realtors used to avoid the law. Many whites were desperate to keep blacks out of their neighborhoods, whether they rented or were buying. And as long as they were willing to cooperate with real estate agents, it was easy to circumvent the federal law prohibiting discrimination in the renting and purchasing of property.[14]

Busing and White Flight

The timing of these efforts to panic whites was not by accident. In her dissertation concerning school desegregation efforts in Pulaski County, Mary Caroline Proctor has traced the white flight that began occurring when the Little Rock School District began busing students in an attempt to fully desegregate its schools and comply with federal court orders. In the 1971–72 school year the total enrollment in the district was 26,265. The ratio of white to black students was three to two. In ways the district could not control, Proctor notes that efforts to integrate the schools were complicated by the fact that "between 1960 and 1980, the black population in Little Rock had grown 110 percent, while the white population had only increased by 23 percent."[15]

As in almost every jurisdiction that used busing to desegregate its schools, it was wildly unpopular, especially with whites who had other options. Though an Arkansas poll was not needed to confirm the results, a 1971 survey found that 99.74 percent of those who responded were opposed to busing.[16] Busing was counterproductive from the start. Proctor found that "crosstown busing of high school students during the 1971–72 school year coincided with a decrease of 1,256 in white enrollment and an increase of 218 in black enrollment."[17] But the harder the Little Rock School District tried to integrate its schools through busing, the more distant the goal became. When during the next school year the district began to bus intermediate students, it lost 1,487 white students but gained 95 black students. Where were whites going? Some remained in Pulaski County but sent their children to private Catholic schools that began to experience record enrollments. By the 1988–89 school year, 8,961 white children were attending private schools in the county. The minority enrollment of these schools was 484. But whites who had been in the Little Rock School District were moving outside Pulaski County. For example, Conway in Faulkner County and Bryant in Saline County began to mushroom. When whites were facing a move to central Arkansas, in increasing numbers they chose to live outside Pulaski County and commute into the city.

Though proponents of integration pointed out that children had been riding buses to get to school for generations, blacks themselves found it difficult to send their children across town to attend school with children of a different race. Even such a stalwart of integration such as Daisy Bates commented about busing, "Of course, I don't want it. But if they didn't have busing [as an excuse], they'd have some other reason."[18] In an interview in 2003, Art Gillum, a white parent who served on the school board in the 1970s, remembered, "The more we tried to desegregate, the more white people we lost," he said. "We did everything we possibly could do, and we continually lost white students."

Regardless of the fact that children had always ridden buses, doing so to achieve racial balance simply did not make sense to people. "I don't think this is a racial issue," North Little Rock resident Jo Ann Platt told an Associated Press reporter in 1974. She now sent her children to Catholic schools. "The boys have always gone to school with blacks. But I don't like busing."

As white parents pulled out of the public system, they left behind schools with black majorities. The school board found itself running a shell game, attempting to achieve racial parity by switching black and white students from school to school, further upsetting parents who wanted stability. "We had to keep the schools balanced for a federal mandate," Gillum recalled. "If you lost a bunch of white students, next year, you have to move a bunch of kids to balance it."

Left unsaid in interviews was that whites did not want their children being taught by blacks. A lifetime of racist conditioning had convinced many whites that blacks were stupid and incompetent. Never before had whites worried whether black teachers were adequate in the classroom, but real integration as was occurring in the Little Rock School District meant black teachers and principals, as well. Suddenly quality was a real concern for white parents who had always put up with "bad" white teachers. Those blacks whose grammar was deficient were particular targets for private discussion among whites who, if they chose, could easily remember former teachers in white schools who did not speak the King's English either. And so what happened? As previously discussed, it was black teachers and black principals who paid for integration with their jobs.

The lure of private schools also had to do with issues of safety and discipline. Though blacks who had integrated white schools had been picked on and harassed by whites for well more than a decade, whites showed little toleration for this behavior when it was their children who came home with stories of intimidation.

According to Art Gillum, the quality of public education was threatened as the Little Rock School District struggled to obtain funding from an alienated voter base. For example, in 1976 Little Rock voters rejected a four-mill property tax increase for schools. The next year they passed a smaller increase. These quality issues, whether real or perceived, further drove parents to private schools, as did concerns about safety and discipline, according to newspaper interviews with parents during the 1970s. The debate surrounding corporal punishment, which by the mid-1970s was being curtailed in public schools, added to those concerns, and it was private schools that had no or few restrictions on paddling children who were the beneficiaries.

One Giant School District?

As white flight continued through the decade of the seventies, Little Rock's superintendent Paul Masem was eyeing the 80 percent white enrollment of the Pulaski County Special District and concluding the only way to desegregate the Little Rock School District now was to expand its district into the white neighborhoods of its sister district. This would ultimately involve a lawsuit. His attorney Hershel Friday was pessimistic about the outcome of undertaking such litigation, cautioning the school board that it "would take several years to resolve, could cost hundreds of thousands of dollars and [didn't] have great chances of success."[19] Hershel Friday knew firsthand about being on the losing end of school litigation, and there was something ironic about the fact that he was representing a Little Rock School Board that was so committed to school integration. The Friday firm had not so long ago been known as Smith, Eldredge Friday and Clark. Smith had been none other than Orval Faubus's executive secretary during the era when Faubus had pronounced blacks and the civil rights movement as tools of the Communists. As a reward for his services, Faubus saw to it that the state of Arkansas had rewarded the Smith firm with lucrative bond business and in the process had helped made Smith's partner Hershel Friday a rich man. For twenty years the Friday firm had defended school districts seeking to avoid integration in cases which were routinely reversed on appeal in the Eighth Circuit Court of Appeals.[20]

As white flight continued, a revised strategy was necessary. The Little Rock School District also considered suing the North Little Rock School District in addition to Pulaski County Special District. But because the Friday firm represented the North Little Rock School District, new counsel had to be found. Now that the state's first integrated law firm of Walker, Rotenberry, Kaplan, Lavey, and Hollingsworth had broken up, the Little Rock School District hired as lead counsel Philip Kaplan who had years of experience in civil rights cases on the plaintiff side. In the view of the lawyers for the plaintiffs, the best practical legal remedy in terms of racial integration was the consolidation of the three school districts. As it so happened, the Little Rock School District drew as the federal judge in the case Henry Woods, who once had been the law partner of governor Sidney McMath and an astute advisor to the Women's Emergency Committee. If successful, the new school district would be composed of over fifty-six thousand students and cover the entire borders of Pulaski County. Before filing suit, the Little Rock School District also decided to name the state Board of Education of Arkansas as a defendant, for it was the state that had mandated segregation, and Orval Faubus as governor who had used the offices of the state as a vehicle for resisting lawful desegregation of the Little Rock School District. The pockets of the state, of course, were much deeper than individual school districts.

At trial there were a number of factual questions that were resolved in the Little Rock School District's favor, not the least of which was the fact that plaintiffs' attorneys showed that otherwise experienced school board members in the other two districts lacked basic information about the desegregation orders that governed their districts. For example, in one instance board members were

> unaware that a biracial committee had been called for, or that two blacks were to have been appointed to serve as ex-officio members. Board members were unable to testify as to the percentage of black and white students or teachers in the district.[21]

Fatal to the defendants, the court found,

> The housing authorities, lending institutions, realtors and others had acted in collusion to create segregated neighborhoods with the major impact of steering blacks to Little Rock and North Little Rock and steering whites to the Pulaski County School District.[22]
>
> The existence and location of the housing projects, the location of other government-subsidized housing units,

> the failure to build projects within the geographic boundaries of the county district, and the private and public steering and redlining practices are major contributing factors to the residential segregation in Pulaski County which exists today.[23]

Judge Woods found for the plaintiffs in April 1983, ordered consolidation of the three districts, and as part of the remedy found that the state of Arkansas had liability, as well, and would have to help pay for the costs involved with consolidation. Fortunately for the parties involved, he delayed implementation of his order while the defendants appealed to the Eighth Circuit Court of Appeals. In November 1895 the court unanimously rejected consolidation as a remedy, primarily saying it could be imposed only as a last resort. In remanding the case back to Judge Woods for further consideration, the court of appeals made several important rulings, but one of the principal findings was that the state of Arkansas had financial liability in the case, a decision that lead to the basis for the case being settled by the parties. The eighth circuit

> assigned the state varying degrees of financial responsibility for the magnet and specialty schools, voluntary interdistrict transportation costs, and the costs of providing compensatory, remedial and quality education programs for black students.

In ways almost too obvious to mention, the decision of the court that the state of Arkansas bore financial responsibility gave the Little Rock School District a wish list for its integration efforts. As Proctor notes, "The Little Rock plan was designed on the assumption that the state would pick up the cost."[24] Ultimately, according to Proctor, the plan proposed by the Little Rock School District would cost an additional $554 million over the next ten years.[25] In response, the Arkansas House of Representatives overwhelmingly approved a resolution that read in part, "The plan reflects selfishness and reckless disregard for the quality of education anywhere outside of the Little Rock School District."[26]

It must be said that this era was the heyday of school litigation in which federal courts, primarily in the South but in many other states, as well, involved themselves in the minutiae of complicated and costly plans to achieve integration of students and teachers. Additionally, federal courts began to require state governments to earmark revenue for school districts where the issue of state liability was successfully raised in a school desegregation case. In Arkansas, which had legally sanctioned segregation through the passage of state law as far back as the 1860s, in theory the state could be forced to pay out enormous sums of money to every school district that had discriminated against blacks and had not yet provided an adequate remedy by fully integrating its schools. While this sounded like justice to black plaintiffs, Arkansas legislators were understandably outraged when they were forced to take money from their own districts' schools to fund desegregations in the Little Rock School District. Yet because of a legal precedent that had been set in Missouri, which is part of the eighth circuit, the legislature swallowed hard and entered into a financial settlement to fund desegregation costs, knowing that if the case went to trial the state's liability could be much worse.

The Clash of Cultures

The experience of both races involved in the efforts to desegregate the Little Rock School District was painful as cultures clashed from the onset. In 1981 the *Arkansas Gazette* in a three-part series entitled "Turmoil in the Schools" examined the increasing racial imbalance in the Little Rock School District. The district had dropped from a high of 17,654 in white enrollment in 1963–64 to just 6,740 in 1981–82. In that same time the percentage of black enrollment had risen from 29 percent to 66 percent.[27] As one unidentified black parent complained:

> It seems that we have come full circle and are back where we started, still having to fight for something as

> basic as an education for our children, still hassling over something so trivial as the color of one's skin.[28]

Many white Arkansans did not see the problems of school integration so simply. In 1975 the principal of Dunbar Junior High School for four years, Dr. Harold D. Algee, gave as the major reason for leaving the district and taking another job in Mountain View the inability to demand and expect discipline from black students at Dunbar who composed 66 percent of the enrollment. "It seems that black students don't respect the limits that you can verbally request of them." In discussing the number of blacks who were suspended from Dunbar, Dr. Algee gave poor attendance as a reason and then added:

> But there have been quite a few suspensions for either threatening or striking another student, or making threatening remarks to students or teachers. Student relationships between blacks and whites did improve this year, but there still are too many instances where blacks have intimidated whites to the point of asking for money.

Algee noted in his four years at Dunbar he had not known of an instance where white students had made intimidating or threatening statements to blacks or asked for money. Thus far in the semester, 84 percent of all suspensions in the district had been black.

In a memoir entitled *What Becomes of the Brokenhearted* E. Lynn Harris documents his experiences in 1968 at West Side Junior High, which was then 70 percent black as whites began to transfer to Pulaski Heights and Southwest Junior High. "To prove yourself, you either had to bully other kids or challenge authority—which at West Side meant testing the mostly white teaching staff. I welcomed it."[29] Harris recalled it did not take long before he was in trouble. "I had become such a terror in the school's library that the librarian, Miss Lowery, had me permanently banned for always talking too loud and then ignoring her when she asked me to be quiet."

But that was nothing compared to his problems with his white math teacher. Told to put away a comic book, Harris recalled he told his teacher, "I will when I finish.

"'Now!' Mr. Ask shouted at the top of his lungs . . . The class giggles turned to laughter . . ."

> Finally, the teacher snatched the comic book from Harris.
>
> Without thinking, I took my heavy math book and fired it at Mr. Ask, hitting him right above the left eye. I couldn't believe what I had done. Neither could my classmates. They started to laugh and clap, and several were banging their desks with balled fists. . . . I felt powerful. Other than my sisters and a cousin here and there, I had never hit anyone, and now I had hit a grown man—and a white man at that.[30]

Harris recalls his enraged teacher literally dragged him to the principal's office, but in those days an entirely different standard of discipline prevailed. Instead of being expelled from school and charged with assault in juvenile court, Harris only received a three-day suspension and was told he would have to bring a parent to be reinstated. Since his mother was a single parent who left for her factory job each morning before dawn and did not return until six, Harris managed to avoid telling her and stayed home for forty-three days, and only then returned because a truant officer showed up at his mother's factory job. Again, procedures were quite different in this era. Instead of automatically expelling him for truancy, his white principal, Weldon Faulk, allowed Harris, whose brilliance and potential were obvious to all as a result of his performance on standardized tests, to finish the eighth grade without going to summer school. The next year, his white teacher, a Mrs. Adams, selected him as one of two black students to be on the staff of the *Bear Chat,* though warning him that he had absolutely no margin for misbehavior. Though his path as a gay, black man was never smooth after that, the rest is history as Harris has become a bestselling novelist and for several years was a visiting writer at the University of Arkansas at Fayetteville.

This kind of fairy tale ending would, of course, never have been possible for the average black child and would never have happened in a later era when the Little Rock School District was fighting so desperately to retain every white student it could. In the *Gazette* articles in 1981, the unidentified black parent quoted above, a divorced woman with three children in the public schools, said as she was fighting back tears that she viewed the movement of white students out of the district as another way of telling blacks "you're not good enough to associate with us. It doesn't matter if you're a doctor, lawyer or garbage man, whites view you as some inferior being with animalistic tendencies." She talked about the prejudice that she had encountered and said that she had thought her sons would not have to go through it.

> I've tried to raise my sons to believe in the good of all people, no matter the color. Then, I have to explain to one of them why a neighbor no longer allows her son to play with him and why the child has been placed in a private school. You try to make them believe that such things are isolated incidents, but they aren't dumb. They see what's happening in the schools.

She rejected the charge that black students were responsible for the trouble in the schools. "White parents never consider that the fights they're so concerned about are caused by the things they've taught their children."[31]

The racial disturbances of the late 1960s and early 1970s never totally ceased, though after 1972 there were only isolated incidents throughout the state. The most severe eruption occurred in 1976 in Eudora in Chicot County. On April 19 more than a third of Eudora High School students were involved in stone-throwing incidents and fistfights. After violence broke out again two days later, the board voted to cancel school for the rest of the year. When blacks sued to reopen the school, white parents sued for an order requiring black parents to control their children. Federal judge Oren Harris refused to order the school to be reopened after being informed that students would get credit even though a month of school would be missed.

The Klan Resurfaces

In the spring and summer of 1979 the Ku Klux Klan briefly resurfaced in Arkansas and the South. Though rallies were held in Rogers, Hamburg, Fort Smith, Ashdown, Texarkana, and Little Rock, the Klan no longer seemed as threatening as it had in the recent past, perhaps because its activities seemed limited to speeches by leaders who were clearly on the defensive. Randy Howard, the state organizer for the Knights of the KKK in Arkansas, complained, "The minorities have lots of organizations for them but how many are working for white people? If you are white and proud to be white, then people call you a racist."[32] The largest rally was the first one in Rogers, attracting over three hundred people. Subsequent rallies attracted smaller crowds and were met with protests from both blacks and whites. Perhaps a measure of progress was that the new voice of the Klan sometimes sounded like a whine rather than a threat.

Black Politics in the 1970s

In 1972 the first African Americans served in the Arkansas legislature since the 1890s. They were Representatives William H. Townsend, Richard Mays, and Jerry Jewell, all from Pulaski County. By the mid-1970s, much on the surface had changed in central Arkansas. The National Black Political Convention even chose Little Rock as their convention city in March 1974 but could agree on nothing except to honor the principals of the 1957 crisis, giving Daisy Bates a standing ovation that reduced her to tears. But old problems remained. In December 1974 an extensive police brutality trial brought by blacks began in federal court in Little Rock. Several white officers took the Fifth Amendment in response to the question of whether any of the officers had firsthand knowledge of any instance of physical and verbal abuse or deprivation of rights by police officers. A great deal of testimony was offered by blacks who had been victims of police brutality.[33] Though Judge G. Thomas Eisele ruled that plaintiffs had not shown a sufficient pattern and practice of police brutality to meet the existing legal standard of municipal liability, he found considerable merit in as much as one-third of about thirty-five instances of police conduct.

For some members of the black community, there had to be some irony as a result of the timing of this trial. Earlier in the year Charles Bussey, an African American member of the city board of directors, had arranged for Erma Cunningham, representing the black Greater Little Rock Baptist Pastors Conference, to present an award to Little Rock police chief Gayle F. Weeks in appreciation for the efforts of the police in the black community.[34] In fact, the other black city director, Perlesta "Les" Hollingsworth, himself a civil rights attorney, objected to the procedure used by Bussey in getting the ceremony on the agenda. A white member of the board of directors, A. M. "Sandy" Keith, said about Chief Weeks, "There is no question that Weeks is a racist. I am too, about half-way."[35]

Going on here was a skirmish between old- and new-style black politicians. First elected to the Little Rock city board in 1968, Bussey was regarded by many observers as an ally of white conservative business interests that spared no effort in seeing that "Charlie" Bussey had a place on some government payroll. Bussey himself claimed in 1971, "I've done more for the black community than Mr. Rockefeller. After all the good I've done in this community and the people I've helped, if I don't merit someone getting a job for, it's all for naught."[36] Bussey claimed not to understand what the excitement was all about in 1974 when it was revealed that W. F. "Billy" Rector, who had worked for segregation for years and who had financial interests at stake in many of the zoning interests that came before the city board, was behind a fundraising effort to honor him, sponsored by Model Cities residents in Little Rock. A three-thousand-dollar cash gift was promised to Bussey at the reception in his honor. Rector had written a letter to his business friends asking for a minimum of fifty dollars each in appreciation "for the many things he [Bussey] has done, not only for the residents of the Model Cities Area, but for the entire city of Little Rock."[37]

Bussey, increasingly sensitive to the charge of being an "Uncle Tom," would himself play the race card when it suited him.[38] Yet some observers felt he had spent much of his career in the black community playing the old-fashioned Negro political boss, periodically given something to distribute in the black community so he could retain prestige and assert how much he had done for blacks and yet all the while actively assisting white conservative business interests. In 1981 Charles Bussey was finally elected mayor by his fellow board members.[39]

L. C. Bates had spent much of the last half of his life railing against black politicians like Bussey, and he continued to criticize his own race in ways no other black Arkansan ever dared to do. In an interview with Bill Lewis of the *Arkansas Gazette* in 1972, Bates said, "The average Negro, you see, instead of trying to improve himself, is standing around begging and complaining. I have never been to seek popularity. I'd rather be what I term right any time. That's the way it is with me." Bates said one of the greatest difficulties was in

> facing the fact that the Negro has more prejudices than the white man. Any time a Negro makes good, he's got to be superhuman, because not only does he have to fight opposition from the other side, but opposition from his own race. That makes him pretty hard. So Negroes are jealous—and they shouldn't be.[40]

Little Rock Interracial Couples in the 1970s

In 1976 in interviews for an article entitled "Mixed Couples" in the *Arkansas Times,* David Glenn took the emotional temperature of interracial relationships in Little Rock, beginning with the unwillingness of couples to allow their full names to be used for the article. All the couples he interviewed agreed upon the obvious: their reception by their fellow citizens depended upon whether the male of the couple was black. Lucy, a twenty-six-year-old white woman married to a black musician, told Glenn,

> After all, white men used to regularly have sex with black women when they were slaves. It's culturally more acceptable for a white man to claim a black woman, but if a black man takes a white woman that's a whole different picture. Then they are raping our Daisy Maes.[41]

Yet at the same time, at least in Little Rock for "Edward," a black man, the anecdotal evidence was that in his experience interracial dating was more acceptable than it had been even four year earlier. Comments, stares, and threats "don't happen very often now. I think society is finally coming around to the idea of mixed dating and marriage. It doesn't seem to be as big a deal anymore."[42] Lucy, who married a black male, claimed that white women

> think of me as the whore and him as the stud and that we spend all day in bed together. A white mechanic who was fixing his car came up to "William," also white, and said, you know, I wish I could have me a nigger woman.[43]

It is one's family in Arkansas, of course, that matter the most. As Lucy told Glenn, when she finally told her mother she was marrying a black man, "I kept it a secret from her all that time for fear she'd explode. Well, she did. She said she would have a heart attack, and she practically disowned me on the spot." Yet, later, when her mother got to know him, "she felt a lot of affection" for her husband.[44]

Difficulty in accepting relationships is not limited to whites. "Gloria" was of the opinion that other black women viewed her marriage to a white male as a "little ego trip. Specifically, [they think] I married him because he was a good catch, that I am now some sort of affluent 'Oreo Cookie'"[45]

In retrospect the 1970s in Arkansas ended state-sponsored segregation and began the era of privatization that so marks the present era. At the same time there seemed to be a growing bitterness and frustration that was finding expression in the black community in the state even as progress in the political area was beginning to be made and some racial attitudes in the white community were changing.

CHAPTER 19

The Eighties and Nineties: So Far to Go

At the beginning of the 1980s blacks in Arkansas seemed stuck politically. As Lamar Keels, president of the NAACP State Conference of Branches, noted in 1981, "Across the state, there are extreme difficulties in getting blacks on school boards, city councils, county commissions and other board appointments. Blacks do not really have a handle on the political system."[1] Keels was referring primarily to the fact that of the five legislative districts in eastern Arkansas where blacks represented upward of 55 percent of the voting population blacks in the state legislature, with the exception of Henry Wilkins from Pine Bluff, were all from Pulaski County. William "Sonny" Walker, formerly an Office of Economic Opportunity official in Little Rock and in 1980 director of the southeast region of the federal Community Services Administration in Atlanta, returned to the state to address a voting registration campaign rally of 250 people and told the group that blacks had made fewer gains than in any other southern state, pointing out that 36 percent of Arkansas's 392,000 blacks still lived below the poverty line.

By 1980 blacks only composed slightly more than sixteen percent of the state's population, a significant decline from over 22 percent in 1950. In 1982 one step forward seemed to guarantee two steps backward. In West Memphis, where blacks were 33 percent of the population, African American Leo Chitman became mayor with a plurality of the votes in a six-man field that featured no runoff. Suddenly, that system of electing mayors with no runoff was not good enough any longer, and the Arkansas legislature, over the fierce objections of the NAACP, in the first session after the election changed the law to require majority elections in all city and county races.

Yet help for blacks was on the way. Jay Barth notes that the federal Voting Rights Act of 1982 and federal voting rights lawsuits made a major difference locally in the electoral landscape, "promoting the shift from at-large elections to ward or district elections that maximize the opportunity for African Americans to gain office."[2] To understand how this occurred, it is necessary to appreciate the importance of federal law and federal judges in this era. In *Jeffers v. Tucker,* a 1994 decision, Judge Richard Arnold summarized recent voting rights law in the state, noting that

> in 1989 . . . a federal court ruled that portions of Arkansas's 1981 state-legislative-redistricting plan violated section 2 of the Voting Rights Act. . . . In 1990, the court ordered the State to remedy these violations by creating black-majority legislative districts. . . . Later that year, we approved . . . the remedial redistricting scheme proposed by the Arkansas Board of Apportionment. . . . It was the scheme which was used in the 1990 elections, under which a total of twelve black persons were elected to the 1991 Arkansas General Assembly—as compared with four in 1980.[3]

Time and time again since the 1950s, the federal government had intervened to create the potential for African Americans to participate in the broader society. As we shall see, some whites began to vote with their feet.

Lee County Race Relations before the Twenty-First Century

From the white perspective in eastern Arkansas, the reason that it took blacks so long to obtain positions in local and county government was not due to roadblocks by whites but to blacks' lack of competence. In 1988 Kenneth Hunter, county judge of Lee County, told an *Arkansas Democrat* reporter, "It's taken a while for them to get people smart enough that they could run the office if they got it."[4] Despite comments like Hunter's, during the 1980s and 1990s the white response in Lee County in public was that race relations were good. Robert Shearon, the editor of the weekly *Courier Index,* gushed in 1994, "The races get along in Marianna better than any place I've ever lived. Marianna is just a friendly small town, and a neat place to live. It's not Mayberry, but it's closer than some might think."[5]

But behind the politeness that characterizes much of the day-to-day life in the Delta, there was a different Marianna if one was black, one that was not so "neat." In the blunt words of the initial 1989 report of the Lower Mississippi Delta Development Commission, "The Delta's economic, social and cultural structure of life has often reinforced tensions between ethnic groups and worsened the economic subjugation of African-Americans."[6]

White Arkansans however have never taken responsibility for the financial condition of blacks and certainly not in the Delta. In his book, *Land of Opportunity: One Family's Quest for the American Dream in the Age of Crack* published in 1995, journalist William Adler reports the view in 1889 of Sherry Benson, the executive director of the Marianna Chamber of Commerce, whom he asked why so many young black males left Lee County for Detroit. She professed not to understand. "It's here for them if they want to find it."[7]

Such obtuseness seemed a deliberate attempt to avoid the reality of the barren nature of life in the Delta for blacks. The bitterness and turmoil of the 1960s and 1970s had never been addressed by whites just as slavery and Jim Crow were never addressed. Perhaps, one could not expect a chamber of commerce representative to say anything that would reflect negatively on white leadership, but in some ways it simply seemed the chickens were coming home to roost. Adler chronicles the completely perverse use of energy, discipline, and hard work of the Chambers brothers, who, finding no opportunities of any kind in Lee County, moved to Detroit in the 1980s and began a crack cocaine empire that grossed at least $55 million yearly at its height and exceeded any legitimate business in the city. Despite being devoted to an enterprise that ultimately dealt in human misery, the entrepreneurial skills and dedication of the Chambers brothers were duly noted and undeniable. Just as energetic, determined whites who were seeking opportunity came to the Delta using slavery as a means to creating wealth regardless of its costs, the energetic, determined Chambers brothers left the Delta and went North, using crack cocaine as a means to creating wealth regardless of its costs. Adler's point is not that crime pays for impoverished blacks; in the case of the Chambers, it did not. The Chambers brothers are in prison. Rather, it is,

> until there are more attractive and practical options for young people mired in urban and rural ghettos, until their life prospects amount to more than serving or cleaning up after other people, it takes little reflection to see that selling drugs and gang-banging will continue to be rational career choices.[8]

Adler points out that perhaps if there had been more legitimate opportunities available to the Chambers brothers a cocaine problem in Marianna might never have developed as it had by March 1989 after they had been arrested and some of their workers had come back to Marianna. Police chief Mark Birchler said, "I got a helluva crack problem down here. And it goes right back to those damn Chambers brothers." In the past year the Marianna Police Department had arrested twelve persons for drug-dealing. "We've never had drug arrests like this before. Two years ago we didn't have any."[9]

If despite the turmoil in the 1970s in Lee County it seemed as if nothing had changed, it was because very little had. Eventually, the judicial system took note of the political subjugation in the Delta. The U.S. Supreme Court in 1986 ruled in *Thornburg v. Gingles* that blacks were entitled to a plan of legislative redistricting if they could show that election laws, practices, or structures interact "with social and historical conditions to cause an inequality in the opportunities enjoyed by black and white voters to elect their preferred representatives."[10]

The changes wrought in the Delta as a result of this decision were of great significance not only in the legislature but also in other elections. In 1992 a federal judge found the method of electing Arkansas judges discriminated against blacks under the Voting Rights Act, and the end result of the litigation was a document signed by the parties and the judge called the Hunt Consent Decree. In this document the state agreed to create judicial subdistricts in which the majority of voters were black.[11] Where there had been no black trial judges elected in Arkansas, now suddenly there were thirteen. An article in the *New York Times* in April 1996 highlighted not only the changes but also the resentment felt by whites in the Delta and their ultimately futile efforts to challenge what was occurring. As discussed, for so long in the Delta blacks in towns with significant African American populations had not run successfully for political office. Now with these changes, black political power in the Delta began to increase. For example, as a result of federal court litigation in 1983 the town of West Helena, with a 40 percent black population that had elected only three African Americans to the city council between 1917 to 1982 under an at-large system, increased the number to four in one year. As Jay Barth points out, however, "The resultant representative democracy has not always been painless," noting that in West Helena the four black members of the city council in 1996 to 1997 engaged in a yearlong boycott to prevent a quorum from voting on a city budget.[12]

Political progress rarely equated with economic progress for blacks in the Delta. Adler provides a racial snapshot of Marianna in Lee County in the mid-1980s.

> The color line still suffused almost every aspect of life. There were no blacks behind the counters at the businesses that rimmed the courthouse square, none in the

> fire department or on the board of the chamber of commerce. No blacks belonged to the Marianna Country Club or the Rotary or Lions Clubs None attended the private Lee Academy. Asked why no blacks were invited to enroll, a parent of Lee Academy students named David Cahoon, a lawyer and former prosecutor, says: "We wanted our kids to go to school with people who bathed every day and who weren't on welfare." . . . When white women drove across town to pick up their black maids, the maids sat in the backseat.[13]

Poverty continued unabated. Lee County was consistently ranked among the poorest in the United States. Adler writes that the official unemployment rate at times topped 20 percent. Worse, 40 percent of young black males were unemployed, but the reality may have been far more bleak. "I can't think of eight black teenagers who are employed," Bill Lewellen, then a Marianna city alderman and later state senator, told Alder in 1988.[14]

Falling Further Behind in Lee County: Why?

As Adler points out, even if jobs for blacks had been available, they would have been bottom of the barrel employment opportunities, for

> only one in five black males in the county was a high school graduate, and half the adult population was functionally illiterate. One of every three public school teachers failed a 1985 statewide basic skills test—the worst rate of any of the state's school districts. . . . Lee County students in two of three grades tested had the state's lowest average achievement test scores.[15]

Though nothing could disguise the depth of the failure of African Americans in Lee County to enjoy the fruits of the American dream, critics differed as to the cause. Was it, as Adler suggested, racism and white supremacy that stunted opportunity at every turn in the Arkansas Delta? The Arkansas NAACP contended that racism was still the number one issue in the black community as it boycotted the fortieth anniversary commemoration of the 1957 school desegregation crisis. Nationally syndicated columnist and director of the *Arkansas Democrat-Gazette* editorial page Paul Greenberg disagreed. Writing in the *Nation,* Greenberg said,

> The great unmentionable in discussions of civil rights today is the mundane observation that racial discrimination is no longer the basis of the most serious problems that beset black Americans. Racism may make a great scapegoat but it is not a cogent explanation for the social pathology raging in black ghettoes. No racist could do what drugs, crime, ignorance and family disorganization have done there.[16]

Even black liberal feminists such as the social critic Bell Hooks agreed with conservatives to some extent. In books like *Rock My Soul: Black People and Self-Esteem,* Hooks points to psychological causes that go far beyond attributing solely to white racism the social devastation seen in the present era in many black families. Unfortunately, there has been little agreement among scholars, scientists, politicians, and social commentators about the ultimate significance of psychosocial causation in the lives of not only African Americans but whites, as well.[17]

Gangs, Schools, Drugs, and Black-on-Black Crime

Beginning March 5, 1995, the *Arkansas Democrat-Gazette* ran a three-part series on gangs. Taken from law enforcement data, the paper reported the astonishing statistic that "about one of every 11 teenagers in Pulaski County belongs to a gang. . . . The ratio in public schools could be closer to one in eight."[18] The typical image of a gang member is not a public-school student, and perhaps it was the stereotype of the street-wise punk who hung out on a street corner all day that allowed public school officials to keep the problem under wraps for as long as they did; however, gangs were then everywhere in the schools and were increasingly at war with each other. The lid seemed to come off in January 1995 after fights broke out in four different schools. Twenty-three students attending Hall High, J A. Fair High, McClellan High, and Mabelvale Junior High were arrested. According to Little Rock police captain Sam Williams, "the fights were gang related." Williams added, "There is a gang presence in every junior high school and high school in this city. And anybody who tells you differently is lying." Gangs in Pulaski County presented their own special racial problems for the schools. The image of black gangs in the schools was bad enough publicity, but the reality was more complicated. Though most gang members were black and had their own customers for crack cocaine within specific neighborhoods, authorities pointed out that "white gangs such as the Southwest Kings" were on the rise and "more likely to sell LSD and crystal methamphetamine to a more disparate clientele, spread over a larger area."

Regardless of the growing drug problem in public schools, "source after source attributed fights, especially at the beginning of the year [1995], to youngsters being bused to schools in areas dominated by rival gangs." Originating in Los Angeles and Chicago, "Crips," "Bloods," "Folks," and "Vice Lords" fought turf battles in Pulaski County to control the drug trade. The drug of choice for black gangs, authorities said, was crack cocaine. The question of how many individuals at any time were gang members and which territory their organizations controlled was very much a guessing game that varied day to day, but the fights that were occurring in the schools were devastating.

African Americans in Little Rock, themselves the victims of most of the crime and murders, were deeply troubled by the most recent spike in killings. While being interviewed for the Dunbar Project in 1994, Christabel Graham Eatmon volunteered, "We are very spiritual people, and that spirit now has been broken and I think that has contributed to a lot of the crimes and the meanness and all this killing and stuff that's going on in our community."[19]

As have others, nationally and locally, Paul Greenberg notes in the *Nation* that "black America has become a two-tiered community, and that where education, family, the work ethic and the black church have played their part, black Americans are thriving."[20]

Historians, however, such as John Kirk have noted a connection between the historic policies of the city of Little Rock regarding slum clearance, urban redevelopment, and segregation and the plight of much of the black community. Citing a 1992 study conducted by the city's racial and cultural diversity commission, Kirk contends that the impact of "the city's race-driven urban development plans since the 1950s" have been "profound." With the 1992 study documenting that ten census tracts in the eastern part of the city had a 90 percent black population housing 46 percent of the entire black population of the city, the effort to segregate blacks into certain residential areas has been successful. Though Kirk does not state overtly that residential segregation and black poverty and crime are related, he notes that statistics from the 1992 study revealed that the rate of unemployment for blacks was 153 percent greater than for whites and that 68 percent of those below the poverty line in Little Rock were black. Kirk observes, as well:

> Although blacks made up approximately one-third of the city population, black people accounted for over 50 percent of those arrested by the Little Rock police Department. 97 percent of the suspects for violent crime and 80 percent of the victims of violent crimes were black.[21]

Shocking as these statistics were, no specific solutions seemed on the horizon. As he had years earlier, John Walker bemoaned the lack of black leadership. "What is lacking today," he said in 1987, "is a cadre of younger people willing to push for more change."[22]

Important Breakthroughs

Despite the lack of blacks in leadership positions on a local level, in 1982 a candidate for governor commanded an overwhelming percentage of the black community's vote and relied upon it as an important voting block. The candidate, of course, was Bill Clinton, whose rapport with black Arkansans was quite unlike that of any politician, before or since. Clinton's phenomenal political ride to the top was important to black Arkansans, for he appointed them to crucial positions not only in Arkansas but in the White House, as well. As president, his appointments of Rodney Slater from Marianna as secretary of transportation and Dr. Jocelyn Elders from Little Rock as surgeon general were much more than symbolic, empty gestures.

Bill Clinton was not alone in his efforts to make black Arkansans part of the larger society. In 1980 George Howard Jr. became the first black federal judge in Arkansas, Lencola Sullivan was crowned "Miss Arkansas," and Mahlon Martin was named city manager of Little Rock. In the fall of 1982 Frank Neely was selected over four white applicants for the job of commanding a forty-two person police force in Jacksonville. A telling statistic was that except for Neely the police force was all white. Nolan Richardson became the head basketball coach of the Arkansas Razorbacks in 1985.

Though racial discrimination continued to exist in employment, in June 1980 Timex and black plaintiffs signed a consent decree that resulted in more than six thousand present and former employees sharing in a settlement of $150,000. More importantly, Timex, by the time the case was settled, had improved its hiring practices to the point where the percentage of blacks in its workforce was higher than the percentage of blacks in the community. Since its inception Title 7 of the Civil Rights Act of 1964 has been a major weapon in black Arkansans efforts to achieve equality. Though it is impossible to judge its exact impact on hiring and promotion practices, certainly the impact of Title 7 has been profound. A number of employment discrimination suits filed in the 1970s generally resulted in gains for blacks in the 1980s against corporate employers including Arkansas Power & Light, Montgomery Ward, Missouri Pacific Lines, and International Paper Company as well as local employers such as Harris Hospital in Newport. [23]

The Price of Integration

Just as the black community paid the price for integrating schools, in the view of some observers it also began to pay a more subtle price for the integration of society at large. In *Bitters in the Honey: Tales of Hope and Disappointment across Divides of Race and Time,* interviews in the 1990s conducted of Arkansas black residents by the author, sociologist Beth Roy revealed significant hidden costs to the black community that were just becoming apparent. Though discrimination against blacks in the rental and sale of housing remained, many of the black elite had found their way out of their old neighborhoods. Mahlon Martin, who had successful careers as the first black city manager of Little Rock, as the executive director of the Winthrop Rockefeller Foundation, and as Bill Clinton's director of the Arkansas Department of Finance and Administration, was one of those who left. Dying of lung cancer shortly after the interview with Roy, Martin was speaking shortly after Little Rock had become known for a time (1993) as the murder and gang capital of the United States. Martin told Roy that the gains made by blacks in accessing better housing had an unexpected negative consequence.

> I think equal housing and the results of it have been good generally, but I think in the minority community what it has done is take out of the neighborhoods many of the leaders that were there years ago that provided leadership, that set moral standards, that set ethical standards for the neighborhood.[24]

Martin said that he had begun to question whether integration had been a good thing for the black community, a heretical position at one time but now no longer. "I know a lot of people wouldn't have said that five years who are now beginning to really discuss it and wonder about it." Martin said that with the exception of the black church, blacks had been absorbed "into a larger community" but at the cost of giving up black institutions, mainly the schools that blacks had once controlled and had set ethical and moral standards. As a result of integration, "we've taken the moral leadership out of—in large part, not completely, but out of the minority community. It's kind of like creaming; I mean, those can afford to get out, get out."[25] Unintentionally, according to Martin, what integration accomplished was "to pull out of those neighborhoods those things that made them strong." Speaking in the context of a multicultural approach in schools, Martin felt that what had occurred with school integration

> was an abandonment of black culture, and, albeit, not conscious, an attempt to force blacks to become part of the white culture. The more they were successful, the more they undid the black folks and regrettably everybody wasn't able to make that transition.[26]

Martin said that he had not seen the benefits of integration for his own children who were attending Central.

> I sensed that there was as much segregation within the school as there was when I went to school with two separate schools. Clearly, they associated primarily with kids of their own color.

In his view, school was as polarized as the rest of society: "I have yet to see either one of them bring a white kid home."[27] As an individual who had achieved in his life the utmost respect from both black and white communities in Little Rock and state government for his competence and fairness, Martin admitted, "I guess my frustration as an individual centers around how much effort and how many people we've put through that process, only to sit in a room rather than really to enter into a relationship." Martin told Roy that he had come to the conclusion he had badly underestimated the time the process of integrating the schools would take.

> I recall thinking that this experiment would probably at least cause us to lose a generation, a large part of a

> generation, because it would take that long to really work things out. . . . Clearly, I now think I was wrong when I thought one generation would do it.[28]

Misgivings about *Brown* in this era can be seen in the interviews of the Dunbar project. Though the question was not asked, Jewell Scott Mayes volunteered,

> Even though I was 100 percent for integration, I didn't realize [what] we was [*sic*] going to do to the black children. . . . And they're not being taught the way we were taught. They don't have that individual attention. It's just a lot of things they don't have that we had.[29]

Roy also interviewed a number of whites who were students at Central during the 1957 crisis. According to Roy, the whites she interviewed often scapegoat blacks. Disappointed near the end of their working lives that they did not face an easy retirement and worried about their children's future, they blamed blacks for the feelings of insecurity they face. They blamed crime even though they had never been victims of black crime themselves. Commenting on their racial attitudes, Roy writes,

> Not only do they not feel responsible for racism past, but they feel victimized themselves. If they can't believe the American system of meritocracy has failed, if they can't believe they themselves were inadequate, then what is left is to demonize those they believe to have gotten the rewards they themselves deserve.[30]

Fortieth Anniversary Celebration of the Central High Crisis

Despite the reaction of the Arkansas NAACP, the fortieth anniversary celebration of the Central High crisis in 1997 was notable in several ways. Nothing imaginable could match the symbolism of the president of the United States, the governor of Arkansas, and the mayor of Little Rock holding open the doors of Central High for the Little Rock Nine as they entered the building before a cheering crowd of 7,500. But as important as the symbolism of the moment, nothing that was said on the occasion was more important than the words of Governor Mike Huckabee. "We come here today to say once and for all that what happened here forty years ago was simply wrong. It was evil and we renounce it."[31] This willingness to confront the moral aspects of the behavior of white Arkansans in an event that attracted nationwide attention was a unique moment in the history of the state. For if what happened at Central was wrong, what about slavery, peonage, lynching, race massacres, racial expulsion, and other features of racism that have been part of Arkansas for its entire history?

The acknowledgement of past racism during the Central High crisis by the governor had no effect on the demographics of Little Rock as whites not only left the school district but began to leave the city. From 1990 to 2000, the white population in Little Rock declined from 113,707 to 100,848, a drop of more than 9 percent. During the same period the black population in Little Rock increased from 59,742 to 74,003, a gain of over 6 percent. In contrast, for example, during the previous two decades, the white population of Little Rock had increased.[32]

Exodus in the Delta

It was in the Delta that the racial future seemed bleakest. The exodus of whites seriously began in the 1980s. In an essay about the region in 1995 *Arkansas Democrat-Gazette* reporter Michael Leahy focused on the southeast town of Dumas in Desha County. According to the 1990 census Dumas lost 17 percent of its white population in the 1980s and now was 52 percent black. Its population was now 5,520. According to Michael Jones, president and CEO of the Farmers and Merchants Bank of Dumas,

> In the last three years or so, white flight has undeniably been going on. . . . Certainly, there is a lingering bigotry here, but I believe that involves an isolated few. What you have mostly in this is fear—fear that our town is dangerous, fear that our schools are dangerous

> . . . fears that, I think, are based 90 percent of the time on nothing more than rumor. . . . But then something real happens and people think that all the rumors are true. It's frustrating.[33]

But it was not just Dumas that was experiencing white flight. In Dermot, a black majority town in Chicot County, there was a 38 percent drop in the white enrollment between 1989 and 1994; in Eudora in Chicot County there was a 50 percent drop in the number of white students in the last five years. The Delta was in free fall. An unidentified businessman in Monticello, only twenty-five miles from Dumas, but light years in other ways, said,

> The typical white guy who is moving to our town from the Delta, does it to get away from the Delta. Race enters into it about 100 percent of the time. But there are other things going on. That area is becoming too depressing for people. No one wants to be from some of those towns with all their problems.[34]

What Monticello had done to remain viable economically and racially was to attract industry as far back as the late 1940s and depend less on agriculture to sustain it. In 1995 Monticello had a school system still 63 percent white.

The Odyssey of Olly Neal Jr.

One can make a case that the Arkansas Delta in this era was a scene of hopelessness and without hope. Yet there were indications that despite the bitterness of the past, racial accommodation was possible. People did not remain static. Though many left, others stayed to try to work things out. If Arkansans of both races in the Delta since the turmoil in the 1960s and early 1970s wished to have optimism for race relations for the future, they could point to the amazing career and life of Olly Neal Jr., who will be the first to tell an interviewer of either race that he has mellowed with age. Neal makes no efforts to hide his warts, indeed, he can not resist telling about them, but by the end of the twentieth century

Neal had come about as far as any politician, black or white, could be expected to in the Delta in dealing with the racial divide. We pick up his life story after the bitter disappointment of the elections in 1972. What occurred in the coming years was transformational in its nature. Some whites learned that they could trust Olly Neal, and he learned he could trust them. Here he is in 1992 on J. B. Smith, former state representative from Marianna.

> J. B. and I are good friends and I have more confidence in J. B. than I had in many of my much more liberal friends. J. B. has never lied to me. As I look back, I can't think of anything. When he opposed me, he opposed me vigorously. He tried his best to get us [the Clinic] shut down, to block the money and everything else. When he decided it was all right, he was helpful. When I asked him about some business deal, he gives it his best shot. When I asked him who did I need to contact, he says, "Let me call him for you and get him lined up."[35]

In an e-mail in 2006 Smith had the following to say about Neal.

> Back in the early 70s we didn't agree with Olly Neal, but now Olly Neal is a real close friend of mine. He did an excellent job as prosecuting attorney and I supported him for that position. . . . We have worked together to do what was best for Lee County.[36]

Whites who could bring themselves to look past Neal's militant stance during the civil rights era saw a man who was helping Arkansans, whatever their color. One of Neal's physicians, Dr. Irvin Redlene, at the clinic convinced him that Delta residents had so many of their health problems as a result of sewage problems. Neal got involved with a program called the National Demonstration Water Project and helped get federal programs to change their rules to aid rural counties. Mississippi County judge "Shug" Banks gave him support as did Representative John Miller. The result was that Arkansas changed its laws to take advantage of these programs.

What makes Neal stand out as a figure in that era and the present is not only his degree of commitment to eastern Arkansas but also his willingness to engage racial issues directly. In 1973 he took a leave of absence from the clinic to run against Paul Benham of Marianna for state senator and was beaten soundly. Remaining in the Delta was his passage from a civil rights activist to a lawyer, politician, and businessman who worked hard to convince both races that there was room in the Delta for both. In so doing, absolutely no one would claim Olly Neal became an "Uncle Tom" in the process. He began law school in 1974 and commuted from Marianna to Little Rock for four years in the night program at the University of Arkansas at Little Rock. As an attorney in private practice in Lee County he represented criminal defendants and stayed involved in politics. He was elected to serve on the school board in Marianna from 1979 to 1981 and held the office of president for part of that period. He ran and lost in 1982 to incumbent Robert Donovan for city attorney. He ran again in 1984 for municipal judge, losing to Dan Felton III, who was also an incumbent.

In 1990 he paid part of the filing fee for Dan Dane, a white attorney, to run for prosecuting attorney for the first judicial district. Dane won. He needed a deputy prosecutor and selected Neal, who served as deputy prosecuting attorney until 1991. Neal was appointed prosecuting attorney by acting governor Jim Guy Tucker in 1991 where he served to January 1, 1993. He served as circuit judge from 1993 to 1995. In 1996 he was appointed by Tucker to the Arkansas Court of Appeals and in 2000 ran unopposed for a different seat on the court of appeals. Neal explained his efforts to hold office in a speech to the Arkansas Advisory Committee on Civil Rights in Helena in 1990. He pointed out that in the first judicial district, which comprised Phillips, St. Francis, Monroe, Woodruff, Cross, and Lee counties with a population that was 43.7 African American, there was not a single black county judge, sheriff, circuit clerk, county clerk, tax assessor, or county treasurer. Thus, of thirty six constitutional offices not one was held by an African American. He said,

> And many of my white friends are perplexed that we consider [race] as essential in selecting candidates we support in political races. . . . The Delta will not move forward until we all do what we should do. And for my white friends, that is to insist upon a sharing and not just a sharing of a few jobs, but a sharing of the ownership and control and a sharing of the political leadership. . . . And that is, where African Americans participate in this government in the activities of our community in every way that you participate.[37]

As a prosecuting attorney, Neal saw firsthand the self-destructiveness that was running rampant in the African American community in the Delta. In his speech to the advisory commission, he said that,

> the most frustrating thing about this job to me is I hear about all the kids who shoot each other. . . . I know that I've got on the docket right now close to a dozen homicides in this six county district. . . . I know that in St. Francis County down the road in the last eighteen months we've had nine young men to kill young men, where both the killer and the killer is under twenty-one years of age.

As prosecuting attorney Neal let the chips fall where they may. Acknowledging that he upset some in the black community, Neal asked for the death penalty for the brutal murders of two whites by a black male. After a mistrial was declared in the first trial, Neal tried the case himself and got a murder conviction but the assailant escaped the death penalty. One assumes that Neal's subsequent political career as both a trial and appellate judge says something about his trustworthiness by the voters of his district and by those whites who have aided him. The point is not only that men and women like Olly Neal represent the future in the Delta but also that the passage of time heals many wounds and opens doors once thought closed forever.[38]

CHAPTER 20

Race Relations in the Twenty-First Century

Nothing symbolizes the changes in Arkansas race relations than the morning of August 30, 2005, when the Little Rock Nine unveiled life-size statutes of themselves on the grounds of the Arkansas State Capitol. Funded by the Winthrop Rockefeller Foundation, the Arkansas legislature, and the Little Rock Nine Foundation, the civil rights monument, proposed and created by Little Rock artist John Deering and his wife, Cathy, depicts the Nine with school books in hand. Depending on one's mood, their facial expressions seem determined or apprehensive or sometimes both. The placement of the exhibit at the state capitol has great historical and symbolic importance, not the least of which is that it is the first civil rights memorial of its kind to be placed at a state capitol anywhere in the South.[1] But before describing the present era, we must acknowledge the influences and attitudes about race that drive our choices on how to view the present. Once so isolated and in the grip of a white supremacy so encompassing that perhaps the worst race massacre in the history of the United States took place with barely a blip on the national consciousness, Arkansans, like everyone else, now live in a fishbowl of instant communication. A half-century ago they learned the painful lesson that the world was watching in horror at the naked display of hatred and bigotry. Today, white and black Arkansans, like other Americans, are driven by a political correctness that in public masks their real feelings about race.

The Glass Half Full

If one takes the long view of race relations, one sees the possibility of progress that often seems impossible in the present. Gone forever is the paternalism of the slave and Jim Crow era. The civil rights era of the 1960s and early 1970s banished forever the overt display of racial superiority displayed by whites in their dealings with blacks. Though the civil rights protest movement in this era accomplished little immediately in the way of tangible economic advancement for blacks, the demonstrations, confrontations, and boycotts were watershed events because they demonstrated that no longer would most blacks allow themselves to be treated overtly and publicly as second-class citizens. On some level most whites understood they could no longer treat blacks publicly as they had in the past. None of this ended racial discrimination as whites insisted on maintaining supremacy in the 1960s in their dealings with blacks. The glass half full or half empty is an unavoidable metaphor, sometimes depending on one's race. Before discussing the most intransigent issues that characterize the present era, it is crucial to acknowledge how far race relations have come in Arkansas. Viewing the glass as half full, it would be folly not to appreciate how much progress has been made in our public behavior, especially when one takes the long view. Exactly a century ago governor and then senator Jeff Davis chilled the blood of black Arkansans with his racist rants; racial expulsion in towns in northern Arkansas was common, and lynching was on the rise in the Delta. Jim Crow, with all its discrimination, intimidation, and economic exploitation was in full swing, and blacks had no political voice. Still to come were the Elaine Race Massacres of 1919 and the appalling spectacles of the last lynching in Little Rock in 1927 and, of course, the 1957 crisis at Central High School with its violence on display for the rest of the world.

However, unlike most Southern states, while not relinquishing white supremacy as an operating principle, Arkansas, under pressure from federal court decisions in the

1940s, began token desegregation in higher educational programs at the University of Arkansas in Fayetteville and at the medical school in Little Rock. After judicial pressure blacks were also welcomed to participate in the Democratic Party. In Little Rock in the early 1950s carefully controlled exceptions were made to the dictates of segregation at, for example, the Little Rock library and zoo. After the *Brown* decision in 1954 a handful of school districts with few black students and outside of the Arkansas Delta desegregated their school systems. Though under increasing pressure from die-hard segregationists, the Little Rock School District and the North Little Rock School District were prepared to begin token desegregation in 1957.

In Little Rock in particular, under pressure business leaders eventually agreed to negotiate an end to Jim Crow practices without the mass acts of violence in the face of protests and demonstrations that took place in Deep South states. Within Arkansas in the mid-1960s a substantial number of whites turned away from the crude racist appeals of candidates such as Jim Johnson and with the decisive swing vote of black voters elected Winthrop Rockefeller as governor, who began a tradition of racial moderation at the state level that was continued by Democratic governors Dale Bumpers and David Pryor. In the almost six administrations of Governor Bill Clinton black Arkansans held significant and numerous posts in state government, a tradition that carried over to the Clinton presidency. As a political force, black Arkansans continued in the twenty-first century to receive attention on a state level as evidenced by the pronouncements on race and the political appointments by Republican Mike Huckabee and Democratic governor Mike Beebe. In 2007 there were fifteen African Americans serving in the state legislature, including four in the senate.

Despite criticism that Central High School caters to students with exceptional academic skills, its selection in 2006 as the twentieth-best high school in the country out of the nation's top thousand was an undeniable achievement in a school district that despite often harsh criticism from both communities has remained committed since the 1970s to school integration.[2]

UALR—an Urban University

At the college level within the state, the University of Arkansas at Little Rock holds itself out as an urban university and appears to have made an authentic commitment to racial diversity. In 2005, 29.1 percent of its student body was African American.[3] Other minorities totaled 4.3 percent. Like most universities in the South, UALR has difficulty in competing for doctorate-level African American faculty: in 2003 only 5.3 percent of its full-time faculty was African American. Directly confronting the racial problems in Arkansas, UALR chancellor Dr. Joel Anderson said in his inaugural speech in 2003, "Race, particularly white-black race relations, has been a major problem, indeed the major problem, the biggest obstacle to progress, in our state since it was founded in 1836." As part of the UALR commitment to deal with the issue of race within the area it primarily serves (Pulaski County), since 2004 its Institute of Government has expended considerable resources and effort annually to survey with maximum statistical accuracy racial attitudes in Pulaski County, some of which is summarized in this chapter. As a university that accepts many first-generation, lower-income college students who work and thus attend part-time or rely heavily on financial aid, UALR, like other educational institutions that serve the community, is constantly struggling to improve graduation rates. With a six-year graduation rate (1999–2005) of only 21.1 percent overall, it is in institutions like UALR where the battle to provide successful higher educational experiences for black Arkansans is waged on a daily basis. Despite the allocation of considerable resources to assist its minority students in successfully negotiating the university experience, the graduation rate for black males (1999–2005) was a shocking 8.8 percent.

The Black Middle Class

The most optimistic way to view race relations in Arkansas in the first decade of the twenty-first century is to see life from the eyes of three financially and professionally successful black couples who live and work in different parts of the state. Though all have tales of racism to tell, each individual cautiously professes some degree of hope for the future. As well-educated black Arkansans they expect to encounter a certain amount of prejudice not only from whites but also to some extent from less fortunate blacks in their daily lives, but none of them appears to be defeated or overly dismayed in the slightest. Profiled in the February 3, 2005, issue of the *Arkansas Times,* the six, despite some feelings of ambivalence, generally seemed to find a balance in race relations that gives hope for the future.

Northwest Arkansas

Dana and Shanna Ammons, both thirty-two and from Little Rock, pulled no punches about what they expected to find in northwest Arkansas. "The reputation within the state is that the area is racist," said Shanna Ammons in her Rogers home. "We knew Harrison was the headquarters for the Ku Klux Klan. No one wanted to come here for college, because this area of the state always had bad connotations." Yet outside of a meal their first week back in Arkansas when their first waitress would not serve them at the Cracker Barrel restaurant in Springdale, they claimed not to have encountered significant problems since moving from Atlanta three years earlier. Ammons explained,

> We are always the only black couple or only black family in a restaurant, and we get looks. But they are looks of surprise, not "why are you here." People are refreshingly honest. They say, "We are glad to see you," or "We have never seen an African-American family here." One

> time an older couple came up to us at AQ [restaurant] and said "You are a beautiful family, and we are glad there are black people living in the area." So, it's more positive than not.

Clearly, their experiences were generally good because of their financial status and class. "There is no economic diversity among blacks here," Dana Ammons said. "Almost all have full-time jobs, are college educated and are doing well."[4] In fact, according to Ammons, despite its reputation for "Sundown towns," the northwest part of the state

> represents the biggest potential for growth for blacks. . . . Folks in central Arkansas are naïve about what is happening here—not racially, just in general. A lot of people just out of college looking for jobs in Central Arkansas ruled out Northwest Arkansas. But there are jobs here! They can't find enough people up here. People are always asking, "How do we get more diversity in the office?" And they don't get talent from in-state which is a shame, because there are opportunities here. As the area grows, the issue of being . . . African-American in Northwest Arkansas will minimize.[5]

Perhaps more revealing than the experiences of one African American couple in northwest Arkansas was the reaction of over a thousand presumably white residents of Harrison who in 2006 signed a public petition in the *Harrison Daily Times* rejecting the "blatant racism and bigotry" of certain residents in the area in favor of "respect, harmony and acceptance of all people." The petition campaign had originated after a letter to the editor from a resident of nearby Omaha had written to object to the photograph of the marriage of an interracial couple involving a white woman whose parents were from Harrison. The petition continued,

> We do not want the fine city of Harrison, Arkansas, and its citizens to continue to be known worldwide as tolerant of hatred, racism and bigotry. By signing, we declare that we will remain SILENT NO MORE on this

> issue and will continue to speak out and take action to change the perception of our town.[6]

The Delta

Willard Gatewood observes, "The Delta today still presents the basic paradox of human want amidst abundance, of some of the nation's poorest people living on some of the nation's richest land."[7] In 2000 Forrest City, in the heart of the Delta, was still almost evenly divided between blacks and whites, but not everything seemed filtered through the lens of race as was Dion Wilson's hometown of Helena. Speaking of his hometown, Wilson said,

> I come from a place where *race* is the order of the day. Every move you make in Phillips County is *that*. We got involved early in boycotts, sit-ins. I saw racism at its ugliest, right at the end of the bitterness between blacks and whites, with white people spitting on us, throwing things at us. I saw the white flight from the public schools. . . . White kids who were with us in junior high, by high school they were already in private school. [8]

It was not as if Forrest City did not have its own share of racism. A certified public accountant in practice by herself with 70 percent of her clients African American, Sharon Wilson had originally found work with a firm in Forrest City as its first black CPA, but "they had to ask clients if it was OK for a black CPA to work on their stuff. Some of the clients said they were stupid for asking, but they also didn't give me some clients because they knew [the clients] wouldn't like it."[9] When they moved to Forrest City five years ago, they looked for a house in a "neighborhood [that] was predominantly white," said Sharon Wilson. They were able to get a good price for it, but found out later that "a group of neighbors had visited [the seller] to discourage her from talking to us."[10]

Yet both Wilsons understood some of what occurs in Forrest City that could be interpreted racially had more to do with class. Sharon Wilson gave her own experience of having gone into a bank in sweats to ask about an interest rate. "The woman ran me down, asking where I worked, what kind of work did I do, before she would give me the rate. I was offended. People shouldn't have to go through that. I can just imagine how people who don't fit the bill get treated . . . [but] I think it's class, not race." [11]

A lawyer with his own practice, Dion Wilson, the son of Phillips County firebrand Jimmy Wilson, was hardly the type who lets himself get pushed around by whites, but he and his wife welcome friendships in both communities. "I know who I am, and I know the ins and outs of racism. . . . I don't let anyone treat me or my kids as second-class citizens. But that doesn't mean I don't open myself to have friends or camaraderie with white people.

"Our daughter [Haley, a third grader] had a sleepover, and all of her friends came, black and white. This astonished our friend, a black woman who grew up here. She couldn't believe the white parents let their kids come over. She could see things are changing," said Sharon Wilson.

The test, as both races know, will come later. Dion Wilson added, "What I would like to see, what would give me hope, would be for Haley to have those same friends when she is in the 12th grade, and not somewhere along the way, they get separated. . . . Right now, they don't see color. I see them calling each other on the phone, getting together at community programs, getting out of the car in the morning and walking into school together. I just hope they won't get separated during their adolescent years like I did."[12]

The Wilsons were not unaware they are paying a price for their openness. Sharon Wilson commented,

> Sometimes you feel the racism is 75–25 . . . with 25 percent coming from your own people. Because you worked hard, studied hard, had opportunities—not more than they had—they have a preconceived idea we think we are better, and they decide they don't like us.

Yet they persevere, knowing that at least racial issues in Forrest City are "not in your face" everyday as they were in Helena. Generally, they see racial progress within their own generation, having maintained most of their friendships with whites they made in school in Fayetteville, and according to Dion Wilson, in that regard "our age is doing a lot better than the generation before us." It is, of course, in Forrest City where they see the biggest challenge. Wilson argues,

> If we don't extend an olive branch to each other, then our towns won't ever be like the Jonesboros, Conways, Springdales—communities that can prosper with business and industry. . . . I want to help take Forrest City to that place.

Sharon Wilson expressed her commitment to better race relations in Forrest City as part of her faith.

> I am mindful that there are still barriers here, but I don't let the barriers keep me from being open. I believe that what God has given to me, no one can take it away. That's where we get our strength from. I know that things can change, and I want to be used to help that change happen.

Change was hard though. Even though the Wilsons lived in an integrated neighborhood, their interaction with whites came mainly through their children. Haley, a third grader, goes to "racially mixed" Central Elementary while Kobe is in kindergarten at Stewart Elementary, which is predominantly black. Dion Wilson said, "I don't meet anyone different unless they have their kids in activities. If not for the kids, and their activities, our paths may never cross. They are teaching us."[13]

Central Arkansas

Dr. Ramona Davis is the first black ophthalmologist to come out of the University of Arkansas for Medical Sciences (UAMS). Raised in Louisiana, she attended a predominantly white high school and had numerous white friends but attended predominantly black Dillard University in New Orleans. Dillard felt like home. "Throughout my childhood, I was always conscious of having large lips and a big nose, as compared to my Caucasian friends. At Dillard, no one commented on that. It was very much a pleasant surprise."[14]

It so happened that her future husband Lamar Davis attended Dillard, as well. Growing up in North Little Rock, Davis in 2005, a thirty-three-year-old lawyer with the attorney general's office, related that "most of his friends were white until college." It was not that Davis did not know he was black. "I was always conscious of race. It came out when we played, with kids calling us names, using the n-word. At that age, it is very hurtful, because you don't fully understand it."[15]

After working in other jobs, each attended professional schools in Little Rock, where issues of race surfaced. "On more than one occasion, there were unpleasant experiences," said Ramona Davis, now on staff at UAMS and the veterans hospital. "There are patients at the VA who are outspoken about their unwillingness to be seen by a black physician."[16]

For Lamar Davis, who enrolled in UALR law school in 1995, there was an absence of black role models. Though black males served as adjuncts, which he also was doing at UALR at the time of the interview, there were no black male professors nor did the prospects after law school seem particularly inviting.

> After Dillard, I was even more conscious of not seeing African-Americans in leadership positions. I recall being in law school and contemplating employment opportunities in Little Rock. There were certain places that, as African-Americans students, we didn't apply to. We didn't see many African-American lawyers anywhere.

Yet despite his trepidation, Davis had a "great experience" clerking for the all-white firm of Jack, Lyon and Jones. He also worked for African American court of appeals judge

Wendell Griffen and Pulaski County circuit judge Marion Humphrey before going to work in the attorney general's office where he was assigned to the consumer protection division. "Race is still a factor," said Davis.

> I am always conscious when in the courtroom, or dealing with the public, that I am an African-American lawyer. You're conscious that people may perceive you differently. Sometimes, when I'm talking to people on the phone, because they can't tell that I'm black from my voice, they make politically incorrect statements about black preachers or ebonics. You constantly get reminders that race is still a factor in society.[17]

Of course, as Lamar and Ramona Davis acknowledged, some of those reminders come from African Americans themselves. Ramona Davis said,

> It's frowned upon when two [black] professionals tend to change circles. . . . They might move to the suburbs, or send their kids to private schools. People will call them "Cosby-like," which they may say instead of "uppity." I don't tell people what I do unless I'm asked, and then, if it is a direct inquiry, I'll just say "I work at UAMS." I'm not ashamed, but people treat me differently if they know I'm a doctor. Like they start changing the way they speak, completing sentences.[18]

Working as a black professional in Arkansas does not come easy, but Dr. Davis sees a growing awareness at UAMS that the administration must respond actively if it seriously wants to address the problems involved in educating minority health workers, including physicians, in the state of Arkansas. She commends the efforts of UAMS to institutionalize a culture that recognizes the necessity of diversity throughout its system and looks for ways to achieve it. Whether the program is window dressing or is real remains to be seen.

Personal Friendships

Since the end of Jim Crow in the last fifty years significant numbers of white and black Arkansans have formed and remain open to genuine friendships of varying intimacy that have nothing in common with the relationships characterized by paternalism and condescension that existed in earlier eras. In the 2006 annual survey by UALR of racial attitudes in Pulaski County, "Eight (8) in 10 blacks and 7 in 10 whites reported that they socialize regularly with members of another race. Reported rates of interracial socializing increased by 15 to 20 percentage points from previous years."[19] According to the survey,

> out of the respondents who said they socialized regularly with friends of another race, more than 80 percent indicated that they had either visited one another's homes or gone to places of entertainment with a black or white friend within the past year.[20]

Most whites raised after the civil rights movement in Arkansas have experienced different kinds of racial issues but have dealt with an entirely different black Arkansan since the death of Martin Luther King Jr. On at least a surface level, respectful behavior is expected and given. Even when not forming friendships or acquaintances, the inbred politeness of Southerners, both black and white, compel most Arkansans in the present to observe a basic and respectful etiquette in public that was often unimaginable during Jim Crow and before.

The Political Process

In a state that still appears toward the bottom in many national statistics, one can easily overlook positive political change. Jay Barth reminds us,

> Until recently, the hallmarks of traditional Arkansas politics were a nonparticipatory public, a corrupted and unrepresentative electoral process; absolute domination

> by one political party; issueless campaigns; the deliberate subordination of the black race. . . . By the early twenty-first century, voter registration and participation in Arkansas occasionally exceeded national norms, elections were honest tests of a much larger and more representative electorate. . . . Moreover, African Americans and women were legitimate political participants slowly expanding their spheres of influence.[21]

Though no black Arkansan has ever been elected to statewide or national office, it is likely that individuals with the talent and charisma of, for example, former state representative Joyce Elliot or Rodney Slater, former Clinton aide and secretary of transportation, will emerge in the near future as candidates who have statewide appeal.

Criminal Justice System

Without question there has been a sea change in the commitment of the whites in positions of authority to provide a trial process that is increasingly fair to African Americans accused of serious crime. Returning to the case mentioned in the introduction involving the beating death of an elderly white woman in a nursing home in Fordyce in southern Arkansas, had this crime occurred in the first third of the twentieth century, both black women accused of this crime would have been lynched. At the very most their defense would have been perfunctory, and each would have been executed. What actually occurred in Fordyce was an example of the Arkansas public defender system at its best and an example of how much white Arkansans have changed in their willingness to follow the law regarding black criminal defendants. Briefly, two black nurse's aides were charged in the beating death of eighty-one-year-old Willie Mae Ryan, who was suffering from dementia. Shermika Rainey pled guilty to conspiracy to commit first-degree murder and received a thirty-year sentence in exchange for her testimony against Gayla Smith Wilson that the older woman had beaten Ryan to death with brass knuckles for "disrespecting" her. Rainey, then seventeen, allegedly held the victim down during the beating that caused her death. In two separate trials predominantly white juries mostly voted for acquittal, resulting in two mistrials. In the second of the two trials, there were two blacks and ten whites on the jury. It was revealed after the trial that ten members of the jury had voted for acquittal, one for conviction, and one undecided. Public defenders Katherine Street and Teri Chambers called twelve witnesses over the week-long trial in their successful effort to discredit the testimony of Shermika Wilson. When one contrasts their aggressive representation with, for example, the negligible efforts of the defense bar in Helena who represented the Elaine Twelve in 1919, the difference is night and day. This is not to say perfect justice has been achieved, since there should have been more blacks than two on a jury in Union County, which was 32 percent black in 2000.

One can see significant progress in the judicial administration of the criminal justice system in other parts of the state, especially in comparison with even the not-so-distant past. As referenced in chapter 14 the closing of an investigation of the shooting death of an unarmed black teenager in Crittenden County in 1963 within twenty-four hours of its occurrence stands in stark contrast to the thorough investigation of the shooting death of twelve-year-old DeAunta Farrow in Crittenden County in June 2007. In the latter incident Crittenden County prosecuting attorney Brent Davis referred the matter for investigation to prosecutors from Faulkner and Saline County, who compiled an eight-hundred-page report that concluded that the police officer acted within departmental guidelines in using deadly force. Additionally, the matter was also investigated by the Department of Justice and the Arkansas State Police, which have both reached the same conclusion.

While an investigation of this magnitude by independent prosecutors represents progress in the criminal justice system, it no longer satisfies the African American community, which sees the case as just one more example of whites escaping justice when a black person is involved. Indeed, no criminal case in Arkansas racial history has divided a community so bitterly for as long as the death of DeAunta Farrow. The case has become the perfect racial storm insofar as it has brought conflict to the town of West Memphis on a number of fronts.[22] On the Internet anonymous bloggers of both races have used the case as a vehicle for giving vent to their most virulent prejudices. Outsiders such as Al Sharpton and others have made repeated visits to West Memphis to call attention to the shooting. Black members of the West Memphis City Council have unsuccessfully demanded the resignation of the city's white chief of police, Bob Paudert, who called them "a group of vigilantes." The judicial district's one black judge, Victor Hill, was prohibited by the Arkansas Supreme Court from calling a grand jury to investigate the shooting. In his petition to the court, Hill, among other contentions, criticized the city attorney and assistant chief of police for filing "a series of frivolous and racially motivated complaints" against him in order "to attempt to publicly undermine the authority and dignity of the court for no other reason than that a black man occupied the position." A civil trial of the matter for damages was expected to take place in 2008.

Athletics

As every Arkansan knows, despite well-known problems, it is in the area of athletics that race has proved most often to be a unifying factor. Because of the great importance of success on the athletic field to the psyches of many Arkansans, one need not be a sports fan to realize that superstar black athletes have attained almost iconic status. At one time or another, for example, over the last thirty-odd years the names of Sidney Moncrief, Corliss Williamson, and Scottie Pippin and more recently Darren McFadden and world-champion boxer Jermain Taylor, who in 2006 turned out a huge crowd for a parade in Little Rock that included many whites, have become household words.

Successful Institutions in the Delta

Earl Anthes, the former VISTA volunteer who now lives in the Delta with his wife Chari and runs his own Forrest City–based consulting business, Community Systems Consultants, describes two highly successful and important examples of what he terms "institution building" in the Delta. The Lee County Cooperative Clinic, once so controversial, is now the major healthcare provider not just for Lee County but also for most of St. Francis County. Anthes says simply, "It's like walking into any good health care professional center."[23] Still community run with a board of local persons, it is staffed by skilled administrators and healthcare professionals.

In addition, Anthes cites the Arkansas Land and Farm Development Corporation headquartered as "now a major institution." Located at Fargo north of Brinkley, the corporation has a "business incubator" at Forrest City. According to Anthes, John Clark's economic development ideas back in the 1960s eventually set in motion the East Arkansas Vegetable Marketing Association that evolved into the Arkansas Land and Farm Development Corporation.

One of the brightest spots in the Delta is the Knowledge is Power Program (KIPP) charter school in Helena, which is officially known as Delta College Preparatory School. By 2005 the average student at Delta was said to have increased scores 41 percent in reading, 61 percent in mathematics, and 47 percent in language, as measured by the SAT10, a nationally administered normative test. Given the conflicting data about the charter school movement, it is too early to proclaim it a success, but it bears watching.

Problems in the Present Era

While one needs to do no more than drive around the city of Little Rock in order to observe racial and class separation, the annual 2006 UALR survey tells much about how black residents in Pulaski County feel about not only about whites but also themselves. Summarizing the results, the "data showed whites were more than twice as likely as blacks to say, 'Most people can be trusted' and three out of four blacks agreed, 'You can't be too careful in dealing with people.'"[24] The survey shows a massive degree of distrust of whites by blacks in Pulaski County. For example, almost one-quarter of whites in Little Rock trust blacks "a lot" while only five percent of Little Rock blacks trust whites "a lot."

Not surprisingly, the survey concludes that in Pulaski County *"Blacks and whites have enormous differences in perceptions about whether blacks are treated the same as whites. Blacks are much more likely to perceive inequitable treatment"* [emphasis in original]. This difference in attitude doubtlessly arises, in part, from the perception of many blacks that they are either regularly suspected of dishonestly or victims of racial profiling. For example, when asked specifically about treatment in a store while shopping; at work; in a "restaurant or bar, theater, or other entertainment place; in dealing with the police, such as traffic accidents; [or] getting healthcare," the survey reports *"around 2 in 10 blacks reported having experienced what they perceived to be unfair treatment due to racism in the last 30 days."* [emphasis in original].[25]

But what is perhaps most revealing is the lack of trust this survey showed blacks have of anyone, including other blacks. "Fewer than 2 in 10 blacks have a lot of trust in any of the other groups mentioned—neighbors, co-workers, people in stores, black people, white people or Hispanics." Conversely, "approximately one-half of whites have a lot of trust in people in their neighborhoods . . . and people they work with."[26]

The survey demonstrates wide differences between the

races in personal satisfaction in a number of areas including family life, health, financial, community, housing, safety, and education. It concludes that "*whites were significantly more satisfied than blacks in every aspect of their lives addressed in the survey*" [emphasis in original].[27] What emerges from the survey is that for varied reasons many blacks in Pulaski County presently experience life with a great deal more insecurities than whites.

Segregation in the Schools

It has long been a given that most whites who remain in the Arkansas Delta and can afford it have abandoned the public school system for private academies. A comprehensive three-piece series in the *Arkansas Democrat-Gazette* in 2003 demonstrates in detail the degree of abandonment by whites of the public school system in Little Rock. The statistics reported in the series are sobering: slightly more than 48 percent of white kindergarten-through-twelfth-grade students went to private schools in 2000. Only 4 percent of black students in Little Rock attended private schools. Nationwide statistics showed that 13 percent of white K–12 students were attending private schools in 2000, compared with 6 percent of blacks. From 1970 to 2000, white public school enrollment dropped 53 percent while private school enrollment in Little Rock climbed 157 percent. In 2000, about 6,400 white K–12 students in Little Rock attended private school compared to about 6,800 who attended public school, according to the U.S. Census Bureau. Among the 250 largest cities in the nation, Little Rock ranked ninth for the highest percentage of white children in private school. The trend continued. Since the 2000 census the Little Rock School District had lost almost 600 more white children by the time of the articles in the paper in 2003.

Private Attitudes at the University of Arkansas at Fayetteville

Though former University of Arkansas basketball coach Nolan Richardson was not successful in 2004 in a racial discrimination lawsuit against his former employers for wrongful termination of his contract and violation of his constitutional rights, the trial brought to light a number of facts that bear on present-day race relations in Arkansas. In his lengthy opinion, which was upheld by the eighth circuit, federal judge Bill Wilson has written:

> There was troubling testimony from witnesses about racism in the higher ranks of UAF. A former member of the Board of Trustees (and former board chair), and a current board member admitted, during examination by Plaintiff's counsel, that they still use the word "nigger" and tell racial and ethnic jokes. . . . Most troubling to me was that neither of these witnesses seemed abashed by their admissions. . . . Former University of Arkansas Board trustee chairman Bill Clark admitted in testimony that he had made "racial statements, including use of 'the n word,' more than once or twice a year in the past five to seven seasons."[28]

If the contempt expressed above reflects the private attitudes of some of the highly influential guardians of the flagship university in the state, one need not guess at the mindset of many white Arkansans. That these attitudes, expressed publicly or not, adversely affect the thing many white Arkansans seem to care about the most—the success of the football and basketball teams at the University of Arkansas in Fayetteville—is the ultimate irony, but the effects go beyond athletics. As it did in 1957, the effects of racism extend beyond the immediate concern of attitudes in higher education circles. Just as business and growth were severely hampered in the years after 1957 in Little Rock, the efforts of the UAF administration to compete in the national education arena for high quality professors and the research grants they attract are inevitably affected by a redneck reputation of its highly visible board of trustees. With diversity and globalism the current buzzwords of the twenty-first century, the failure of the university to attract and retain African Americans, both as students and faculty, do not go unnoticed by those individuals whom the university wishes most to recruit, especially as often and as loud as African Americans have protested in recent years. The evidence at Richardson's trial showed that the black alumni society at Fayetteville had been complaining to Fayetteville since 1989 about the "lack of African-American presence and diversity within the Athletic Department."

The failure to create diversity within the university is a serious problem. At Fayetteville, in the fall of 2001, black students constituted only 6.2 percent of the total enrollment; the faculty was 3 percent black. Richardson's firing in 2002 brought to light chancellor John White's efforts on behalf of diversity since he was hired in June 1997. Though the faculty was only 3 percent black in 2001, he had brought the percentage of African American administrative hires to more than 10 percent. Statistics in the university's office of affirmative action showed that in 2002 19 out of 181 people who were listed as executives were African American.[29] By 2006 the percentage of African American students had slipped to 5.2 percent of the total enrollment of 17,821. A 2000 doctoral thesis revealed the depth of the alienation that black students felt. In a survey taken by the author, 114 blacks, 48 percent of those responding, reported that they "had experienced some form of discrimination or racism at the UAF."[30] The university launched a $300,000 advertising campaign in 2006 to attract more blacks and Hispanics to the campus.[31] Another indication that the University of Arkansas at Fayetteville was sincere in creating a more diverse faculty and administration was the elevation of a black woman in 2006 to the deanship of the law school. Professor Cynthia Nance was given a two-year appointment after a national search resulted in the failure to find a candidate suitable to the faculty to replace

Richard B. Atkinson who had died in 2005. At the grass-roots level was the successful recruitment of African American law students. According to *U.S. News and World Report,* "in 2006 the law school at Fayetteville 'had the fifth highest percentage of African American students of all law schools rated' by the magazine."[32]

Desire of Blacks to Return to Separate but Equal

As mentioned, former city manager Mahlon Martin forcefully and articulately questioned in the 1990s whether school integration was in the best interest of blacks. A decade later his criticism is echoed by other members of his generation who had attended Scipio A. Jones High School in North Little Rock. Artis Webb-Boykin, president of the school's active alumnae association, told Helaine Freeman of the *Arkansas Democrat-Gazette* that she "would welcome a return to 'separate but equal' . . . that is, if the schools for black children were truly equal."[33] Freeman reported that the black committee members planning their next reunion told her that "the education they received was far superior to that available to their children and grandchildren." The point made by the group was that in the past teachers had been more accountable.

> Our teachers lived in our communities. We all attended the same churches. And so there was a . . . sense of urgency to take what they had and make it much better [and] teach us from that. Today's children don't have that. The teachers come into the neighborhood, make their day, and go right back out [of] the neighborhood.

Behind these comments, in part, is the unspoken recognition that fifty years after *Brown* and after primarily having carried the burden of school integration, most black students are still not doing as well academically as their white counterparts. Whatever the reasons, blacks continue to lag behind whites on standardized tests.[34]

The Test-Score Debate

Viewed from one perspective, what have blacks gained by all they have been through to desegregate the schools for the last fifty years if equality of results, in fact, is not the goal? In *Brown* the Supreme Court accepted the proposition that requiring blacks to attend separate schools, in and of itself, violated the Fourteenth Amendment because discrimination itself affected the ability of black children to learn. Though left unsaid, the assumption was that at some point genuine integration would result in blacks being able to perform as well academically as whites. Fifty years later standardized test scores in the Little Rock School District showed how problematic this assumption was. For example, on the Iowa Test of Basic Skills for 2004–2005, African American students in the third grade scored in the following percentiles: 41st in reading, 38th in math concepts, and 36th in math problems. Caucasian students scored in the 78th, 77th, and 73rd, respectively.

Though nearly all student scores on standardized tests in Arkansas improved in 2006, some significantly, the gap between blacks and whites remained. "For example," noted the *Arkansas Democrat-Gazette,* "on the third grade literacy exam, 64 percent of 23,436 white students scored at proficient or above, while only 35 percent of the 7,914 black students who took the same test scored at proficient or above." Ken James, state education commissioner, while noting that scores had improved across the board, said that the achievement gap between blacks and whites remained nearly the same as before. "Our goal is to see that gap narrow in the future while maintaining increased performance for all."

Control of the Little Rock School District

It seems appropriate that the statues of the Little Rock Nine are facing the state capitol, for it is there the debate also continues to rage over public school integration in the

Little Rock School District and its soaring costs. In a legislative hearing on November 10, 2005, the desegregation litigation oversight subcommittee heard a report that since 1989 the state had paid out $660 million as part of the court settlement in the litigation involving Little Rock, North Little Rock, and Pulaski County Special School districts.

"Does it ever end?" a legislator asked.

In fact, no one could answer the question, for the parties to the litigation had signed an agreement in 2001 that, at minimum, payments would continue through June 30, 2008 and possibly longer. On that date the state will have the legal right to petition the court to discontinue payments.

Attorney John Walker told the subcommittee,

> This case will continue to last until Little Rock seriously addresses the remediation of the academic achievement disparity between African-American students and white students. You're looking at these figures, and you're asking where did all this money go. You'd at least be expecting some results. It's our position black children are not being taught, and white students are being taught.[35]

Ron Heller, attorney for the school board, replied that "it was 'completely ridiculous' to say teachers aren't teaching black students." Heller said such a statement would particularly offend black educators, who make up half of the teachers and administrators in the Little Rock district.

During its now decades-long effort to get out from under the jurisdiction of the federal court, the district had gone through numerous superintendents, white and black, and was then in the hands of Roy Brooks, a black educator who quickly put his stamp on the district by reorganizing the administrative staff in such a way that, according to him, made more resources available for actual instruction. In October 2006, a coalition of the Little Rock Classroom Teachers Association, Pulaski County ACORN, and attorney John Walker gave the Little Rock School District its first ever black majority school board with the runoff election of Dianne Curry. Walker commented, "It's a majority-black school district; why shouldn't it be a black majority School Board?" Though Charles Armstrong, an African American elected to the board in September, said, "It's not a black-white issue at all," the debate among members of the Little Rock School Board over the performance of Roy Brooks soon began to take on serious racial overtones.[36] Though on February 23, 2007, federal district judge Bill Wilson issued an opinion that the Little Rock School District is "completely unitary in all aspects of its operations" and terminated court jurisdiction over the case after decades of judicial oversight,[37] the school board began voting along strict racial lines as the black majority used its power to buy out the superintendent's contract.

Observers have noted that for some time demographic trends suggest that in time, and sooner rather than later, Little Rock may become a majority-black city.[38] The impact of such a development can only be surmised. If the discord in the Delta is any guide, present racial problems will seem mild by comparison.

Central High School Fifty Years after the Crisis

Fifty years after the 1957 crisis, reflecting the widespread distrust between blacks and whites in Little Rock, Central High School in large part remains divided along racial lines. In a widely disseminated essay written by Central High senior and student body president Brandon Love for Vanderbilt University, first printed in April 2007 by the Texas-based Intercultural Development Research Association, this talented African American student has captured the stark racial divisions at Central from the black perspective. Though acknowledging the nationally recognized academic success of the school, Love points to the "other" Central, "the Central that is filled with gang activity, the Central with obvious racism, and the Central divided by an imaginary line better known as Advanced Placement."

As an African American at Central who is often the only black student in the Advanced Placement (AP) classes, he writes, "The greater part of my world consists of a predominantly white Central pervaded by prejudice and stereotypes." Officially, of course, there is no discrimination. Love experiences mockery he deems subtle but real all the same. Perhaps most disturbing is the sense of alienation that Love experiences in both worlds. "The majority of my lifelong friends are now affiliated with gangs. Most students at this Central couldn't care less about completing homework assignments, let alone attending college."

In this world, to excel academically is to betray. "For my friends at this Central, the term Advanced Placement is synonymous with white. To these students, enrolling in Advanced Placement courses makes you a sellout." At the same time he claims that blacks are not encouraged to take AP courses. In taking eleven AP courses while at Central, Brandon recalls a total of twenty black classmates. Central's administration has become extremely sensitive to the charge made by Brandon Love and points to recent progress. According to Principal Nancy Rousseau and Leslie Kearney, chair of Central's guidance department, "African American enrollment in AP classes has risen from 274 students in 2004–05 to 357 students in 2006–07, a 30 percent increase in just two years."

In the year that Central High School once again occupied the national spotlight, it fell to the student body president to state the obvious: "After almost 50 years of struggle and confusion, my school has yet to integrate." According to Love, while Central "boasts vast diversity, injustice reigns."[39]

Black Crime and White Fears

Whether whites admit it or not, they fear poor blacks in Little Rock and stay out of low-income black areas if possible. One need only drive into a poor black neighborhood and experience mostly black males, but young black women, too, deliberately walking in the path of a car driven by whites in order to sense their contempt and hostility. One does not have to think consciously how to avoid the black underclass. It is as much a part of daily life today for whites as the days when blacks got off the sidewalk during Jim Crow. Yet, just as whites fear going into a poor black neighborhood, every black knows he or she is watched and encounters racial profiling by not only law enforcement but by whites themselves in white areas and stores.

Ominously in 2006, Little Rock was for the first half of the year on its way to setting a new record for murders. Most of the victims were again African Americans who were killed by African Americans in their own neighborhoods. A *Democrat-Gazette* editorial captured the sense of dread the pace of killings stirred up with an editorial called "Killings R Us."

> Every time somebody is killed on the streets of Little Rock, whether it affects you or your family directly, the whole community is wounded. The intangible but very real tone of the state changes becomes coarser, more fearful.

Still, given the racial and class divisions that exist in most of Little Rock, so long as the murders remained confined to poor black neighborhoods, there was no sense of outrage in the white community that the situation was running out of control. The *Democrat-Gazette* courageously confronted the unspoken issue for its white readers: "After all and for the most part, it's just Them killing Them. Why should those of us in the 'burbs care, let alone in Lonoke County or Magnolia?"[40]

Despite the progress in the criminal justice system at the trial level, it is the administration of the criminal justice system where white supremacy retains its most racist grip in Arkansas. While the three couples mentioned at the first of the chapter have some ability to redress racial grievances, blacks at the bottom of the socioeconomic scale are at the most risk of racial violence against them in the prisons and jails throughout the state. One only needs to read back issues of hometown and statewide newspapers to realize how often blacks in custody are injured or killed in encounters with white police officers.

Politics in the Twenty-First Century

Jay Barth points out that despite the

> relative openness of opportunity compared to the past, blacks have not made substantial gains overall. Only a handful of African Americans have been elected to any of the numerous executive offices in any of Arkansas's seventy-five counties since Reconstruction (five held such positions as of 2002).[41]

Even when blacks have been successful in taking office, whites and white-owned businesses have often voted with their feet in the Delta. In Pine Bluff since the election in 2004 of Carl Redus Jr., its first black mayor, the *Democrat-Gazette* reported that "Flowers Baking Co., Hood Packaging Corp., Rich Products Co, and VP Buildings have announced layoffs and plant closures."[42]

Earl Anthes calls race the "unspeakable issue," not just in Forrest City or in the Delta, "but it may be in all of America." He added, "You can make a whole room get quiet by bringing up race."[43] When it was mentioned that during the late sixties and early seventies race was all anyone talked about, Anthes said those discussions in that era were made in the context of "opposing sides." Now in the present, "It's not proper to admit we're still on two sides. You don't bring it up at all." Candidates make promises to represent "everybody," but they only campaign among their own race. The tradition of candidates speaking in one venue at one time to seek votes from the community at large does not apply in Forrest City. "Race," Anthes says, "is still behind all that is," but political correctness makes it a taboo subject.[44]

Conclusions and Observations

In order to discuss race relations in any meaningful way, there can be no avoiding opinions and findings that cause pain and anxiety. One of the more constructive approaches comes from the sociologist Beth Roy whose 1999 book *Bitters in the Honey: Tales of Hope and Disappointment across Divides of Race and Time* traces in the 1990s the racial attitudes of both whites and blacks in Little Rock who were involved in the Central High crisis. She concludes: "One finding of my study in Little Rock is that white racist attitudes continue unabated, their forms and codes changed since the fifties, but not their intensity."[45] This opinion by a white-trained observer with no axe to grind is not one whites prefer to hear, but Roy does not condemn the whites she interviewed as unregenerate bigots. Far from condemning those she labels as "racist," she sees them as "good people" who "mistakenly and vehemently blame fellow Americans of color for all sorts of improbable things."[46] Interviewing whites who went to Central during 1957, she finds a bitterness whose causes, as suggested earlier, have perhaps more to do with disappointment with their experiences with the free enterprise system than actual harm caused to them by African Americans. Whether one agrees with Roy or not, any white Arkansan who has read this far would have to agree that the vast majority of people who have suffered harm as a result of relations between the races have been African American.

A Moral Obligation?

In an article published in the *Arkansas Times* during black history month in 2008, I characterized the racial conflict in West Memphis over the shooting of a twelve-year-old African American by a white police officer as an "endless night" that marks present race relations in the Arkansas Delta. Coupled with the open racial split within the Little Rock School Board in 2007 and present demographic trends that Little Rock may well be on its way to becoming a majority-minority city, an observer might well ask what happened to the portrait of Arkansas, and particularly of Little Rock, as "moderate" before the crisis at Central High, as painted by not only historians but also black and white Arkansans themselves. Or to put it another way, can we continue to blame Orval Faubus for the racial ills that have seemingly befallen the state since 1957, or did he merely exploit events and help collapse a shaky foundation that no leaders since then, however well-intentioned and sincere, have been able to shore up? Some may take the view that this discussion is no longer relevant, or more bluntly put, that it is time to get over race. A review of our entire racial past suggests to me that Arkansans have not yet come to terms emotionally with the damage done through our historic commitment to the polices of white supremacy.

Whether race relations in Arkansas are viewed as a glass half full or half empty matters less than the challenge to all Arkansans to understand that they do no service to themselves and those who come after them if they remain in denial about their past and the present. What does their racial history mean for Arkansans in the twenty-first century? For white Arkansans it means coming to terms with more than a century of racial oppression that at times has been brutal and exploitative beyond description. Though white Arkansans did not react as violently toward blacks during the civil rights era in the 1950s and 1960s as did other Southern states with greater black populations, their behavior was largely determined by simple pragmatism and perceived self-interest. As important as it was to avoid a repetition of the economic dislocations that occurred, for example, in Little Rock in 1957, one must ask if part of the solution to the racial divide in Arkansas is not more complicated than an economic calculus.

For present and future generations it behooves white Arkansans to consider their past behavior and contemplate whether a different approach to race relations is in order—

one that factors in a consideration of whether pragmatism and self-interest are enough in achieving the kind of society in which we want to raise our children. Certainly, the approach they have taken beginning with slavery, Jim Crow, the civil rights movement, and the post–civil rights era have not resulted in peace of mind or prosperity of which anyone can be proud. In the twenty-first century, no one can read the history of race relations in Arkansas from slavery to the present without being appalled by so much violence and exploitation. What does one do with this knowledge? The initial test for Arkansans, both white and black, is to assimilate their difficult history with open minds and open hearts.[47] It is impossible to avoid the conclusion that in light of the past white Arkansans have a moral obligation to African Americans to understand their racial history and to be fully engaged physically, emotionally, and intellectually in racial issues in the present and future. Since many African Americans have apparently become so disillusioned that they can not even trust each other, how can they be asked to risk trusting whites? The answer is that neither whites nor blacks have a choice if they want to avoid the violence, nihilism, and despair that characterize so many polarized societies. If two one-time enemies such as Olly Neal and J. B. Smith can take such steps, the way is open to all Arkansans. In light of this knowledge of our past, perhaps the real key to long-term racial harmony in Arkansas is to make the effort to build bridges of trust between black and white individuals one relationship at a time.

NOTES

Introduction

1. Donald Holly in *The Second Great Emancipation: The Mechanical Cotton Picker, Black Migration, and How They Shaped the Modern South* argues that much migration had already occurred before mechanization took hold (Fayetteville: University of Arkansas Press, 2000).

2. Steven Hahn, *A Nation Under Our Feet: Black Political Struggles in the Rural South from Slavery to the Great Migration* (Cambridge, MA: Belknap Press of Harvard University Press, 2003), 1. For all Arkansans of the time Hahn describes, geography, of course, was destiny within the context of the Southern experience. Numerous Arkansas historians have pointed out the frontier qualities that made Arkansas unique as part of the Old South. As a frontier state of the Old South, timing was everything. As we shall see, when the nation burst apart in 1861, Arkansas was just beginning the process of becoming a major slave state. Its distinct geography, divided diagonally into fertile lowlands and highlands, made the state like and at the same time quite unlike, for example, Mississippi. When war came, Arkansas's location in the west made the state, much to its leaders' chagrin, an afterthought instead of a major player in the Civil War. As important as the Reconstruction era was in giving opportunities to blacks within the state—an unsurpassed record twenty blacks were elected in 1873 to serve in the legislature—their leadership roles were limited in comparison, for example, to Mississippi where 226 blacks held public office. Relatively soon after the war ended, once again geography dictated the state's racial composition for blacks from the older cotton states such as Georgia, Alabama, and Mississippi, lured by labor contractors, poured into the state seeking greater freedom and opportunities. By the 1890s lynching was on the rise, and Arkansas soon joined the rest of the Old South in passing Jim Crow legislation and measures to disfranchise its black citizens. For most of the first half of the twentieth century, the state's commitment to white supremacy made it indistinguishable from the rest of the Old South. By the late 1940s a change had begun, and Arkansas distinguished itself from other Old South states by admitting a few blacks into graduate schools.

3. For example, see Donald P. McNeilly, *The Old South Frontier: Cotton Plantations and the Formation of Arkansas Society, 1819–1961* (Fayetteville: University of Arkansas Press, 2000), 1. "Geography was a central force in the historical development of Arkansas."

4. According to Jason Phillips, "At least 226 black Mississippians held public office during Reconstruction, compared to only 46 blacks in Arkansas and 20 in Tennessee. Mississippi sent the first two (and only) black senators of this period to Congress." "Reconstruction in Mississippi, 1865–1876," *Mississippi History Now*, Mississippi Historical Society, http://mshistory.k12.ms.us/index.php?id=204 (accessed July 13, 2007).

5. Willard B. Gatewood writes that the "few issues were more emotion-laden in the black community than relating to the color prejudices and preferences of blacks themselves . . . multiple color lines allegedly existed in the black community." *Aristocrats of Color: The Black Elite, 1880–1920 (Bloomington:* Indiana University Press, 1990), 151.

6. *Arkansas Democrat-Gazette,* December 8, 2004.

7. *Arkansas Democrat-Gazette,* December 17, 2004.

8. *Arkansas Democrat-Gazette,* August 23, 2004.

9. *Arkansas Democrat-Gazette,* July 9, 2004.

10. *Arkansas Times,* February 3, 2005.

11. *Arkansas Times*, February 3, 2005.

12. W. Avery Brundage, *The Southern Past: A Clash of Race and Memory* (New York: Belknap Press of Harvard University, 2005), 122. In the late twentieth century, the Arkansas History Commission required that African American history be included in its collection efforts, creating a black history advisory committee. The commission also employs a coordinator of African American history.

13. William M. Adler, *Land of Opportunity: One Family's Quest for the American Dream in the Age of Crack* (New York: Atlantic Monthly Press, 1995), 21.

14. Brundage, *The Southern Past,* 121.

15. Brundage, *The Southern Past,* 119.

16. While I have no quarrel with the increasingly widespread view among academics that race is a "social construct" and has no scientific meaning, for the purpose of discussing past and present relationships between whites and African Americans in Arkansas I have chosen to characterize the events in this history as having a racial significance simply because that is how most Arkansans, white and black, have viewed "race" relations and still, in fact, view them.

Chapter 1

1. George E. Lankford, ed., *Bearing Witness: Memories of Arkansas Slavery Narratives from the 1930s WPA Collection* (Fayetteville: University of Arkansas Press, 2003); "Ten More Voices: A Supplement to *Bearing Witness," Arkansas Historical Quarterly* 63 (Autumn 2004). The complete interviews are now in a 2006 edition. Readers interested in the history of the compilation of the Arkansas narratives may read Lankford's thorough introduction in which he assesses the trustworthiness of the inter-

views. Readers may access the slave narratives online by state or volume number at http://memory.loc.gov/ammen/snhtml/snhome.html.

2. Carl Moneyhon, *The Impact of the Civil War and Reconstruction on Arkansas: Persistence in the Midst of Ruin* (Baton Rouge: Louisiana State University Press, 1994), 217.

3. Randy Finley, *From Slavery to Uncertain Freedom: The Freedman's Bureau in Arkansas 1865–1869* (Fayetteville: University of Arkansas Press, 1996), 145.

4. Lankford, *Bearing Witness,* 136, 137.

5. Lankford, *Bearing Witness,* 245.

6. Lankford, *Bearing Witness,* 102.

7. Lankford, *Bearing Witness,* 102.

8. Lankford, *Bearing Witness,* 262.

9. Lankford, *Bearing Witness,* 143.

10. Lankford, *Bearing Witness,* 260.

11. Lankford, *Bearing Witness,* 148.

12. Lankford, *Bearing Witness,* 14.

13. Lankford, *Bearing Witness,* 217.

14. Lankford, *Bearing Witness,* 311.

15. Lankford, *Bearing Witness,* 48.

16. Lankford, *Bearing Witness,* 72.

17. Lankford, *Bearing Witness,* 143.

18. Lankford, *Bearing Witness,* 262.

19. Lankford, *Bearing Witness,* 308. S. Charles Bolton writes that the "average [Arkansas] escapee was a male in his mid-twenties whose goal it was to win concessions from his owner, to visit relatives in places not too far away, or to make his way to a city." S. Charles Bolton, *Fugitives from Injustice: The Underground Railroad in Arkansas,* report to the National Park Service, 2006, 83.

20. Lankford, *Bearing Witness,* 207.

21. Lankford, *Bearing Witness,* 50.

22. Lankford, *Bearing Witness,* 50.

23. Lankford, *Bearing Witness,* 62.

24. Lankford, *Bearing Witness,* 127.

25. Lankford, *Bearing Witness,* 266.

26. Lankford, *Bearing Witness,* 282.

27. Lankford, *Bearing Witness,* 258.

28. Lankford, *Bearing Witness,* 136, 137.

29. Lankford, *Bearing Witness,* 66, 67.

30. Lankford, *Bearing Witness,* 147.

31. Lankford, *Bearing Witness,* 344.

32. Lankford, *Bearing Witness,* 249.

33. Lankford, *Bearing Witness,* 145, 146.

34. Lankford, *Bearing Witness,* 411.

35. Lankford, *Bearing Witness,* 336.

36. Lankford, *Bearing Witness,* 297.

37. Lankford, *Bearing Witness,* 337.

38. Lankford, *Bearing Witness,* 384.
39. Lankford, *Bearing Witness,* 388, 389.
40. Lankford, *Bearing Witness,* 389, 390.
41. Lankford, *Bearing Witness,* 245.
42. Lankford, *Bearing Witness,* 250.
43. Lankford, *Bearing Witness,* 250.
44. Lankford, *Bearing Witness,* 402.
45. Lankford, *Bearing Witness,* 227.
46. Lankford, *Bearing Witness,* 258, 259.
47. Lankford, *Bearing Witness,* 165.
48. Lankford, *Bearing Witness,* 343, 344.
49. Lankford, *Bearing Witness,* 102.
50. Lankford, *Bearing Witness,* 248.
51. John Hugh Reynolds, *Makers of Arkansas History* (New York: Silver, Burdett and Company, 1905), 178–80.
52. Carl Moneyhon, *Impact of the Civil War,* 70.
53. Carl Moneyhon, *Impact of the Civil War,* 70.
54. Lawrence W. Levine, *Black Culture and Black Consciousness* (New York: Oxford University Press, 1978), 122.
55. McNeilly, *Old South Frontier,* 146.
56. Quoted in McNeilly, *Old South Frontier,* 146.

Chapter 2

1. For an understanding of the distant past in Arkansas, the reader should consult Morris S. Arnold, *The Rumble of a Distant Drum* (Fayetteville: University of Arkansas Press, 2000); *Unequal Laws Unto a Savage Race: European Legal Traditions in Arkansas 1686–1836* (Fayetteville: University of Arkansas Press, 1985).
2. *Ewell v. Tidwell,* 20 Ark. 136, 144 (1859).
3. Quoted in Kenneth M. Stampp, *The Era of Reconstruction, 1865–1877* (New York: Knopf, 1965), 32, 33.
4. Ark. Const. of 1836 art. VII, sec. 1.
5. L. Scott Stafford, "Slavery and the Arkansas Supreme Court," *University of Arkansas at Little Rock Law Journal* 19 (1997): 441.
6. Stafford, "Slavery," 441.
7. Stafford, "Slavery," 441.
8. Stafford, 441. "Slavery," quoting *Hervey v. Armstrong,* 15 Ark. 162 (1854).
9. Stafford, "Slavery," 418.
10. Quoted in Stafford. "Slavery," 441.
11. Quoted in Stafford, "Slavery," 441.
12. Stafford discusses cases in which slaves were acquitted of attempted rape on appeal but notes the reason for the acquittals often appeared to be as likely protection of the slave owner's financial interest as it was the right of the slave not to be accused falsely (422–28).

The Arkansas constitution afforded slaves the right to be appointed counsel in criminal cases.

13. Robert S. Shafer, "White Persons Held to Racial Slavery in Antebellum Arkansas," *Arkansas Historical Quarterly* 44 (1985): 134, 151. Stafford also analyzes the *Guy and Stevenson* cases in "Slavery" (458–62).

14. Stafford, "Slavery," 417.

15. Michael B. Dougan, *Arkansas Odyssey: The Saga of Arkansas from Prehistoric Times to Present* (Little Rock: Rose, 1994), 167.

16. Dougan, *Arkansas Odyssey*, 167.

17. Moneyhon, *Impact of the Civil War*, 67.

18. McNeilly, *Old South Frontier*, 9.

19. Orville W. Taylor, *Negro Slavery in Arkansas* (Fayetteville: University of Arkansas Press, 2000), 158. Taylor's book was first published by Duke University Press in 1958.

20. Taylor, *Negro Slavery in Arkansas*, 151.

21. Taylor, *Negro Slavery in Arkansas*, 151.

22. Taylor, *Negro Slavery in Arkansas*, 151.

23. Quoted in McNeilly, *Old South Frontier*, 51.

24. Quoted in Taylor, *Negro Slavery in Arkansas*, 104.

25. McNeilly, *Old South Frontier*, 9.

26. Quoted in S. Charles Bolton, "Slavery and the Defining of Arkansas," *Arkansas Historical Quarterly* 58 (1999): 8.

27. Lankford, Bearing Witness, 337.

28. Bolton, "Slavery and the Defining of Arkansas," 8.

29. Billy Higgins notes that Arkansas may well have copied its legislation from Virginia. *A Stranger and a Sojourner: Peter Caulder, Free Black Frontiersman in Antebellum Arkansas* (Fayetteville: University of Arkansas Press, 2004), 196.

30. Taylor, *Negro Slavery in Arkansas*, 253.

31. Quoted in Taylor, *Negro Slavery in Arkansas*, 246.

32. Higgins, *A Stranger and a Sojourner*, xiii.

33. Higgins, *A Stranger and a Sojourner*, 192, 193.

34. Higgins, *A Stranger and a Sojourner*, 197.

35. Stafford, "Slavery," 450.

36. Quoted in Taylor, *Negro Slavery in Arkansas*, 174.

37. Quoted at Taylor, *Negro Slavery in Arkansas*, 169.

38. Walter N. Vernon, *Methodism in Arkansas, 1816–1976*, (Nashville: Parthenon Press, 1976), 85.

39. Taylor, *Negro Slavery in Arkansas*, 175.

40. P. Horace Jewell, *History of Methodism in Arkansas* (Little Rock Press Printing Company, 1892), 133.

41. Quoted in McNeilly, *Old South Frontier*, 83.

42. Quoted in Dougan, *Arkansas Odyssey*, 176.

43. Thomas A. DeBlack, *With Fire and Sword: Arkansas, 1861–1874* (Fayetteville: University of Arkansas Press, 2003), 2.

44. Quoted in McNeilly, *Old South Frontier*, 78.

45. Kenneth C. Barnes, *Who Killed John Clayton? Political Violence and the Emergence of the New South 1861–1893* (Durham: Duke University Press, 1998), 15.

46. Ralph Wooster, *Arkansas Historical Quarterly* 13 (1954): 177.

47. Gary Battershell, "The Socioeconomic Role of Slavery in the Arkansas Upcountry," *Arkansas Historical Quarterly* 48 (1999): 49.

48. *Confederate Imprints 1861–1865,* Research Publications, Inc. Reel 34, p. 44. Arkansas History Commission.

49. Barnes, *Who Killed John Clayton?,* 13.

Chapter 3

1. Jeannie M. Whayne, ed., *Arkansas: A Narrative History* (Fayetteville: University of Arkansas, 2002), 166.

2. Whayne, *Arkansas,* 168.

3. Quoted in Whayne, *Arkansas,* 168.

4. Quoted in Moneyhon, *Impact of the Civil War,* 141.

5. Moneyhon, *Impact of the Civil War,* 140.

6. Bobby Lovett, "African Americans, Civil War, and Aftermath in Arkansas," *Arkansas Historical Quarterly* 54 (1995): 311.

7. Quoted in Carl Moneyhon, "From Slaves to Free Labor," *Arkansas Historical Quarterly* 57 (1994): 138.

8. Lovett, "African Americans, Civil War," 314.

9. Quoted in Moneyhon, *Impact of the Civil War,* 140.

10. Randy Finley, "In War's Wake: Health Care and Arkansas Freedmen, 1863–1868," *Arkansas Historical Quarterly* 51 (1992): 137.

11. Finley, "In War's Wake," 138.

12. Lovett, "African Americans, Civil War," 315.

13. Moneyhon, "From Slaves to Free Labor," 154.

14. Moneyhon, "From Slaves to Free Labor," 148. "Investigations indicated widespread fraud. Leaseholders cheated their workers by overcharging for clothing and other supplies. . . . Colonel Samuel Thomas reported incidents in which leaseholders drove the freedmen back into government camps by cutting rations, provoking quarrels, or creating guerrilla scares, then refusing to settle with the workers because they had not stuck with their work. According to Thomas, leaseholders forgot their contracts in an instant. Freedmen reported abuses but found little help in securing redress."

15. Lankford, *Bearing Witness,* 289.

16. Melissa Langley Biegart, "Legacy of Resistance: Uncovering the History of Collective Action by Black Agricultural Workers in Central East Arkansas From the 1860s to the 1930s," *Journal of Social History* 164 (Fall 1998). Biegart argues that this extract from the WPA narratives suggests that the freedmen were capable of and did organize themselves to resist their exploitation by planters in Arkansas as far back as 1865. She contends that if it were possible to research local his-

tories sufficiently they might well reveal that Bryant Singfield's effort to organize blacks was not an isolated event but occurred routinely, and she argues that historians might well find a history of labor organization that went on into the 1930s with the Southern Tenant Farmers' Union. Whatever the extent of black organizational efforts what has been documented is the unremitting violence of white Arkansans at times and places of their own choosing.

17. Ronnie Nichols, "The Changing Role of Blacks in the Civil War," in *All Cut to Pieces and Gone to Hell: The Civil War, Race Relations, and the Battle of Poison Spring,* ed. Mark Christ, 71 (Little Rock: August House, 2003). For the figure of 5,000, see Ronnie Nichols, e-mail message to author, May 2, 2007, Grif Stockley Papers, Butler Center for Arkansas Studies, Little Rock. Nichols was expected to publish a book on the subject. See also Dougan, *Arkansas Odyssey,* 227; Bobby L. Lovett, "African Americans, Civil War, and Aftermath in Arkansas," *Arkansas Historical Quarterly* 45 (1995): 320.

18. Mark Christ, ed., *All Cut to Pieces and Gone to Hell: The Civil War, Race Relations, and the Battle of Poison Spring* (Little Rock: August House, 2003), 89.

19. Christ, *All Cut to Pieces,* 89.

20. Christ, *All Cut to Pieces,* 91.

21. Christ, *All Cut to Pieces,* 325. For a comprehensive discussion of blacks in the Civil War in Arkansas, see 322–26.

22. Christ, *All Cut to Pieces,* 112.

23. Christ, *All Cut to Pieces,* 124.

24. Christ, *All Cut to Pieces,* 125

25. Christ, *All Cut to Pieces,* 124.

26. Christ, *All Cut to Pieces,* 126.

27. Quoted in Christ, *All Cut to Pieces,* 129.

28. Christ, *All Cut to Pieces,* 130.

29. Christ, *All Cut to Pieces,* 131.

30. Quoted in Christ, *All Cut to Pieces,* 133.

31. Moneyhon, *Impact of the Civil War,* 189.

32. Quoted in Finley, *From Slavery to Uncertain Freedom: The Freedmen's Bureau in Arkansas, 1865–1869* (Fayetteville: University of Arkansas Press, 1996), 6.

33. Lovett, "African Americans, Civil War," 304, 315. The freedmen's goal of owning land, however, was thwarted by President Johnson, who in 1865 ordered that abandoned lands be returned to their owners.

34. Barnes, *Who Killed John Clayton?,* 7.

35. Barnes, *Who Killed John Clayton?,* 1, 2.

36. Barnes. *Who Killed John Clayton?,* 15.

37. Barnes, *Who Killed John Clayton?,* 18.

38. Finley, *From Slavery to Uncertain Freedom,* 21.

39. Finley, *From Slavery to Uncertain Freedom,* 32.

40. Lankford, *Bearing Witness,* 136.

41. Finley, *From Slavery to Uncertain Freedom,* 32.

42. Quoted in Finley, *From Slavery to Uncertain Freedom,* 36.
43. Finley, *From Slavery to Uncertain Freedom,* 37.
44. Quoted in Dugan, *Arkansas Odyssey,* 243.
45. Quoted in Moneyhon, *Impact of the Civil War,* 152.
46. Finley, *From Slavery to Uncertain Freedom,* 123.
47. Quoted in Moneyhon, *Impact of the Civil War,* 154.
48. Quoted in Moneyhon, *Impact of the Civil War,* 211.
49. Finley, *From Slavery to Uncertain Freedom,* 122.
50. Finley, *From Slavery to Uncertain Freedom,* 129.
51. Finley, *From Slavery to Uncertain Freedom,* 130.
52. Moneyhon, *Impact of the Civil War,* 154.
53. Arkansas Black History Online, from "Negro Teacher Holds Record in Point of Service with Schools," *Arkansas Gazette,* July 2, 1939.
54. Finley, *From Slavery to Uncertain Freedom,* 49. Levine, *Black Culture and Black Consciousness,* 158.
55. Finley, *From Slavery to Uncertain Freedom,* 46.
56. Finley, *From Slavery to Uncertain Freedom,* 47.
57. There is much irony in the fact that the Arkansas Supreme Court in the case of *Rison v. Farr* during the Unionist government struck down the state loyalty oath on the grounds that the 1864 constitution contained no express authority restricting adult male suffrage.
58. Moneyhon, *Impact of the Civil War,* 195.
59. Whayne, *Arkansas,* 208.

Chapter 4

1. Quoted in Finley, *From Slavery to Uncertain Freedom,* 152.
2. Quoted in Finley, *From Slavery to Uncertain Freedom,* 143.
3. Quoted in Finley, *From Slavery to Uncertain Freedom,* 144.
4. Quoted in Finley, *From Slavery to Uncertain Freedom, 145.*
5. Quoted in Finley, *From Slavery to Uncertain Freedom,* 143.
6. Finley, *From Slavery to Uncertain Freedom,* 143.
7. Quoted in Finley, *From Slavery to Uncertain Freedom,* 143.
8. Finley, *From Slavery to Uncertain Freedom,* 147.
9. Moneyhon, *Impact of the Civil War,* 218.
10. Quoted in Moneyhon, *Impact of the Civil War,* 210.
11. Quoted in Moneyhon, *Impact of the Civil War,* 209.
12. Eric Foner, *Forever Free: The Story of Emancipation and Reconstruction* (New York: Knopf, 2005), 92.
13. Quoted in Finley, *From Slavery to Uncertain Freedom,* 144.
14. Quoted in Finley, *From Slavery to Uncertain Freedom,* 144.
15. Finley, *From Slavery to Uncertain Freedom,* 144.
16. Quoted in Finley, *From Slavery to Uncertain Freedom,* 93.
17. Moneyhon, *Impact of the Civil War,* 214.
18. Moneyhon, *Impact of the Civil War,* 215.
19. Quoted in Moneyhon, *Impact of the Civil War,* 217.

20. Quoted in Moneyhon, *Impact of the Civil War,* 220. Unlike almost all of the other states in the Confederacy, Arkansas's legislature in 1866 did not pass "black codes" that imposed a form of quasi-slavery on blacks. For example, a freedman in Florida could be convicted of vagrancy if he did not sign a labor contract and be auctioned off to labor for a white employer who would pay his fine. Why the Arkansas's planter-dominated legislature did not pass this onerous legislation is not clear, but black code or no black code, whites in Arkansas demonstrated the same attitude as their countrymen in the sister states of the south. In August 1867, General C. H. Smith, who had replaced General Ord as head of the Freedmen's Bureau in Arkansas, "reported that planters had found many ways to cheat their tenants" Quoted in Moneyhon, *Impact of the Civil War,* 220. See Foner, *Forever Free,* 95.

21. Quoted in Moneyhon, *Impact of the Civil War,* 220–21.

22. Quoted in Moneyhon, *Impact of the Civil War,* 221.

23. Foner, *Forever Free,* 79.

24. Eric Foner argues that what occurred during congressional Reconstruction was no less than a revolution that changed all of America into an interracial democracy that had never been contemplated by the founding fathers. Before "boundaries of exclusion—essentially, limiting the privileges of citizenship to white men—had been intrinsic to the practice of American democracy. . . . Racism, federalism, and belief in limited government and local autonomy—Reconstruction challenged these deeply rooted elements of nineteenth-century political culture. . . . The underlying principles—that the federal government possessed the power to define and protect citizens' rights and that blacks were equal members of the body politic—represented striking departures in American law" Foner, *Forever Free,* 122–23.

25. Quoted in Moneyhon, *Impact of the Civil War,* 244.

26. DeBlack, *Arkansas,* 214. Carl Moneyhon argues that the Union League was only thoroughly organized around Little Rock and that in rural areas local planters had a good deal of influence over blacks' political behavior. Moneyhon, *Impact of the Civil War,* 244.

27. Finley, *From Slavery to Uncertain Freedom,* 59.

28. Moneyhon, *Impact of the Civil War,* 252.

29. Whayne, *Arkansas,* 214.

30. John Graves, *Town and Country: Race Relations in an Urban-Rural Context, Arkansas, 1865–1905* (Fayetteville: University of Arkansas Press, 1990), 17.

31. Quoted in Joseph M. St. Hilaire, "The Negro Delegates in the Arkansas Constitutional Convention of 1868: A Group Profile," *Arkansas Historical Quarterly* 33 (Spring 1974): 40, 38–69.

32. Quoted in Whayne, *Arkansas* , 214.

33. St. Hilaire, "Negro Delegates," 65.

34. Quoted in St. Hilaire, "Negro Delegates," 47, 48.

35. Quoted in St. Hilaire, "Negro Delegates," 57.

36. St. Hilaire, "Negro Delegates," 62. For information on James W.

Mason, see Jeannie M. Whayne, ed., *Shadows over Sunnyside: An Arkansas Plantation in Transition, 1830–1945* (Fayetteville: University of Arkansas Press, 1993).

37. Graves, *Town and Country,* 11.

38. Whayne, *Arkansas,* 215.

39. Quoted in Finley, *From Slavery to Uncertain Freedom,* 149.

40. Quoted in Finley, *From Slavery to Uncertain Freedom,* 149.

41. Otis A. Singletary, "Militia Disturbances in Arkansas During Reconstruction," *Arkansas Historical Quarterly* 15 (1956): 142.

42. Whayne, *Arkansas,* 220.

43. Whayne, *Arkansas,* 220.

44. Whayne, *Arkansas,* 220.

45. Whayne, *Arkansas,* 221

46. Whayne, *Arkansas,* 224.

47. Barnes, *Who Killed John Clayton?,* 30

48. Singletary, "Militia Disturbances," 144.

49. Singletary, "Militia Disturbances," 144.

50. Whayne, *Arkansas,* 225.

51. Quoted in Whayne, *Arkansas* , 226.

52. Barnes, *Who Killed John Clayton?,* 30.

53. Blake J. Wintory, "African-American Legislators in the Arkansas General Assembly, 1868–1893," *Arkansas Historical Quarterly* 65 (2006): 385. Information on file at the secretary of state's office makes it possible for scholars to identify African Americans who served in the Arkansas legislature. See Blake J. Wintory, e-mail message to author, September 25, 2006, Grif Stockley Papers, Butler Center for Arkansas Studies, Little Rock.

54. Blake Wintory has shown conclusively that previous historians have been in error in stating that Mason was county judge in Chicot County. Records from the secretary of state's office do not list Mason nor does a list obtained from the Chicot County judge's office (*Arkansas Historical Report*) indicate that Mason was a county judge. Mason does appear to have served as sheriff in Chicot County. Nor was Daniel W. Lewis country judge of Crittenden County; however, he did serve as a trial judge, surely a rarity in the 1800s.

55. Acts of Arkansas, 1873, 15–19.

56. Graves, *Town and Country,* 30.

57. Foner, *Forever Free,* 144.

58. Graves, *Town and Country,* 30.

59. St. Hilaire, "Negro Delegates," 75.

60. Graves, *Town and Country,* 76.

61. Graves, *Town and Country,* 78.

62. Todd Everett Lewis, "Racial Politics in Arkansas, 1865–1894: An Overview," undated monograph, Special Collections Division, University of Arkansas Libraries, Fayetteville, 15, 16.

63. Todd Everett Lewis, "Racial Politics in Jefferson County and Phillips Counties: Political Revolution and the Military Construction

Act, 1867–1894," undated monograph, Special Collections Division, University of Arkansas Libraries, Fayetteville, 13.

64. Graves, *Town and Country,* 47.

65. Quoted in Graves, *Town and Country,* 48.

66. Graves, *Town and Country,* 49.

67. Graves, *Town and Country,* 52.

Chapter 5

1. Quoted in Graves, *Town and Country,* 53.

2. Graves, *Town and Country,* 53.

3. Quoted in Barnes, *Who Killed John Clayton?,* 26. Historians once assumed that Reconstruction was immediately followed by Jim Crow. It would be C. Vann Woodward, a historian with Arkansas roots, who stood this conventional view of history on its head with his ground breaking work *The Strange Career of Jim Crow.*

4. Quoted in Fon Gordon, *Caste & Class: The Black Experience in Arkansas, 1880-1920* (Athens: University of Georgia, 1995), 15.

5. Graves, *Town and Country,* 56.

6. Peggy Lloyd, "The Howard County Riot of 1883," *Arkansas Historical Quarterly* 59 (2000): 386.

7. Graves, *Town and Country,* 61.

8. Barnes writes that in the 1880 gubernatorial election "returns showed only ten Republican votes of the 1,654 votes cast in Phillips County, a county with more than 15,000 residents in 1880. Neighboring Lee County recorded only one Republican vote, and Crittenden County, none, even though both counties had large black majorities." *Who Killed John Clayton?,* 32.

9. Graves, *Town and Country,* 54.

10. Kenneth C. Barnes, *Journey of Hope: The Back-to-Africa Movement in Arkansas in the Late 1800s* (Chapel Hill: University of North Carolina Press, 2004), 33.

11. Graves, *Town and Country,* 54.

12. Barnes, *Journey of Hope,* 35.

13. Blake Wintory has uncovered the local historian's penchant in this era for interpreting the actions and motivations of blacks during Reconstruction and its aftermath as less than self-directed. He shows that earlier historians, including the author's maternal grandmother, Effie Allison Wall, portrayed Furbush as an individual who "lent himself to manipulation by the white man and democrat as perhaps no carpet bagger would have done." Wintory demonstrates that Furbush was much more complicated a figure than presented by local historians and "seems like to have possessed a similar [to whites] middle-class consciousness." His portrait of Furbush reminds the reader how important it is to avoid stereotypes of any kind. As he states, the career of Furbush, "highlights the political and class divisions within the

African-American community, the multiple strategies for attaining power by African Americans, and the conflicting opinions over the political path African Americans should follow after emancipation." Perhaps more importantly, Wintory suggests that "the remarkable life of this nearly forgotten individual reminds us of all the histories and lives yet to be pieced together through the reassessment of primary sources and secondary literature." Blake Wintory, "Environmental and Social Change in Lee County Arkansas and the St. Francis River Basin, 1865-1905" (dissertation, University of Arkansas, 2005), 94, 99.

14. Wintory shows that Furbush was born in Kentucky in 1839 and apparently at an early age learned to read and write. He was born a slave, according to two sources, one of which asserts he was able to purchase his freedom. In the early 1860s Furbush was working as a self-employed photographer out of his own studio over a bookstore in Delaware, Ohio. His customers appear to have been Union soldiers and white women. For a while in 1862 he was in Paducah, Kentucky. Wintory then traces his passage on the steamship Kate Adams to Helena, by then under the control of Union forces. Again, he worked as a photographer and perhaps as a barber. He may have worked on ships during this period, as well. He found time to marry Susan Dickey in Ohio in December 1862. Three years later he joined the Union army in Ohio and served as a private in the 42nd United States Colored Infantry. He was honorably discharged as a sergeant in January 1866. By November 1866 Furbush was bound for Liberia and described as a twenty-seven-year-old "photographer of the Presbyterian faith, with a 'good' education, traveling with no family." In that year the American Colonization Society was promising African Americans ten acres of land and financial support to last six months. Eighteen months later with the prospect of better conditions in the United States for blacks, Furbush likely returned to Ohio for two years. In 1870 he appeared in the census in St. Francis Township in Phillips County, working as a photographer, with real estate and personal property valued at $2,500. He was married with two children, Edward and Harry, both born in Ohio. Enough details have emerged about Furbush to suggest that his sense of himself both racially and culturally was that of a man who had little in common with the black masses he would soon represent. In this regard, he was little different from other African Americans who were elected to Southern legislatures, including Arkansas. It is more than a curiosity that Furbush successfully led the legislative fight to carve out of existing counties, including Phillips, a new county named after Robert E. Lee in 1873, one year after his election as Republican representative from Phillips County. He was rewarded for his efforts by being appointed sheriff of newly-formed Lee County by Republican governor Elisha Baxter and would serve in that capacity for six stormy years, most of which were after Reconstruction ended in Arkansas in

1874. Depending on how one wishes to interpret his actions, Furbush can be viewed as the ultimate political opportunist or as an extremely shrewd player of racial politics. By 1878 with the fusion principle at risk in Lee County, Furbush switched sides and became a Democrat and ran successfully for the office of state representative. Wintory explains that "Furbush, it was reported, had 'voluntarily' chosen not to seek reelection as sheriff, so that a 'white man' could be elected." By doing so, Wintory infers that Furbush had given "implicit support [to] the party's coercive tactics. See Blake Wintory, "Environmental and Social Change," 34-104, for a comprehensive discussion of the details summarized in this note.

15. Graves, *Town and Country*, 57.

16. Quoted in Graves, *Town and Country, 125.* For a discussion of the black elite in Little Rock, see Gatewood, *Aristocrats of Color*, 92-95.

17. Graves, *Town and Country,* 126.

18. A. E. Bush and P. L. Dorman, *History of the Mosaic Templars of America—its Founders and Officials* (Little Rock: Central Printing Company, 1924), 81-82.

19. Graves, *Town and Country,* 108.

20. Quoted in Graves, *Town and Country,* 110.

21. William Pickens, *Bursting Bonds: The Autobiography of a "New Negro"* (Bloomington: Indiana University Press, 1991), 18.

22. Graves, *Town and Country,* 32.

23. Berna J. Love, *End of the Line: A History of Little Rock's West Ninth Street* (Little Rock: Center for Arkansas Studies, University of Arkansas at Little Rock, 2003), 2. With the fall of Little Rock in 1863, blacks poured into Little Rock and were settled by the army into "a log cabin shantytown" near what is now Mount Holly Cemetery.

24. Quoted in Gordon, *Caste & Class,* 60.

25. Graves, *Town and Country,* 32, 33.

26. Quoted in Graves, *Town and Country,* 115.

27. Graves, Town and Country, 116.

28. Barnes, *Who Killed John Clayton?,* 128.

29. Quoted in Dougan, *Arkansas Odyssey,* 317.

30. Quoted in Gordon, *Caste & Class,* 2.

31. William Pickens, *Bursting Bonds: The Autobiography of a "New Negro"* (Bloomington: Indiana University Press, 1991), 9.

32. Graves, *Town and Country,* 61.

33. Pickens, *Bursting Bonds,* 9, 10.

34. Adell Patton Jr. "The 'Back-to-Africa' Movement in Arkansas," *Arkansas Historical Quarterly,* 51 (1992): 164–77.

35. Stephen Ward Angell, *Bishop Henry McNeal Turner and African-American Religion in the South* (Knoxville: University of Tennessee Press, 1992), 251.

36. Quoted in Lloyd, "Howard County Riot," 364.

37. Quoted in Lloyd, "Howard County Riot," 353.

38. Lloyd, "Howard County Riot," 378.

39. Ruth Polk Patterson, *The Seed of Sally Good'n: A Black Family of Arkansas, 1833–1953* (Lexington, University Press of Kentucky, 1985), 51.

40. Patterson, *The Seed of Sally Good'n,* 50.

41. As more documentation for Lloyd's statement that the racial climate in post-bellum Arkansas varied markedly between counties and even between communities within the same county, Michael Dougan writes that, for example, in Mississippi County, though blacks served on juries in the county seat of Osceola "despite some criticism," in the western part of the county blacks were forbidden to live there. Thus a "'red line'—" originally a road surveyor's mark—defined where blacks might live" in Mississippi County. Dougan notes also that while "blacks might farm in the White River Valley but could not cross the Cache River to the east." Dougan, *Arkansas Odyssey,* 317.

42. Helen Hoguet, "Protecting the 'Perfect Africa': The Politics of Race and Property in Post-Reconstruction Africa" (master's thesis, University of Wisconsin–Madison, 2004).

Chapter 6

1. Gordon, *Caste & Class,* 15.

2. Steven Hahn, *A Nation Under Our Feet: Black Political Struggles in the Rural South from Slavery to the Great Migration* (Cambridge, MA: Belknap Press of Harvard University, 2003), 415. Farmers were not the only ones to organize in this era. Hahn also documents that the Knights of Labor, a labor union that recruited skilled and unskilled workers "irrespective of party, race, or sex," was active in Arkansas, particularly in Jefferson County and recruited "black tenants and laborers (in racially separate assemblies)."

3. Barnes, *Who Killed John Clayton?,* 52, 53.

4. Barnes, *Who Killed John Clayton?,* 59.

5. Barnes, *Who Killed John Clayton?,* 67.

6. Quoted in Barnes, *Who Killed John Clayton?,* 69.

7. Barnes, *Who Killed John Clayton?,* 69.

8. Barnes, *Who Killed John Clayton?,* 105.

9. Barnes, *Journey of Hope,* 112.

10. Barnes, *Journey of Hope,* 6.

11. Barnes, *Journey of Hope,* 2.

12. Melanie Welch, "Violence and the Decline of Black Politics in St. Francis County," *Arkansas Historical Quarterly* 60 (2001): 360.

13. Welch, "Violence," 363, 364.

14. Welch, "Violence," 370.

15. Welch, "Violence," 375.

16. Welch, "Violence," 382.

17. Welch, "Violence," 385.

18. Quoted in Welch, "Violence," 383, 384.
19. Quoted in Welch, "Violence," 388.
20. Welch, "Violence," 390.
21. Graves, *Town and Country*, 68.
22. Whayne, *Arkansas*, 267.
23. Quoted in Gordon, *Caste & Class*, 31.
24. Quoted in Gordon, *Caste & Class*, 34.
25. Quoted in Gordon, *Caste & Class*, 45.
26. Quoted in Graves, *Town and Country*, 152.
27. Quoted in Graves, *Town and Country*, 153.
28. Gordon, *Caste & Class*, 110.
29. Quoted in Gordon, *Caste & Class*, 111.
30. Quoted in Gordon, *Caste & Class*, 116. John Graves writes that the 1891 protests led by Little Rock's middle-class black leadership, John E. Bush, Mifflin W. Gibbs, Drs. D. B. Gaines and G. W. Hayman, "did not signal the appearance of a sudden new militancy among blacks. Rather, it represented a desperate attempt by essentially conservative leaders to preserve a relatively open status quo, now seriously threatened." Gordon, *Caste & Class*, 223.
31. Graves, *Town and Country*, 166, 167.
32. Graves, *Town and Country*, 169.
33. Graves, *Town and Country*, 172.
34. Graves, *Town and Country*, 173.
35. John Giggie, "'Disband Him from the Church'": African Americans and the Spiritual Politics of Disfranchisement in Post-Reconstruction Arkansas," *Arkansas Historical Quarterly* 60 (2001): 49, 245.
36. Quoted in Giggie, "Disband Him from the Church," 257.
37. Quoted in Giggie, "Disband him from the Church," 261.
38. Quoted in Graves, *Town and Country*, 190.
39. Quoted in Graves, *Town and Country*, 173.
40. Graves, *Town and Country*, 175.
41. Quoted in Grif Stockley, *Blood in their Eyes: The Elaine Race Massacres of 1919* (Fayetteville: University of Arkansas Press, 2000), 21.
42. Barnes, *Who Killed John Clayton?*, 128.
43. William F. Holmes, "The Arkansas Cotton Pickers Strike of 1891 and the Demise of the Colored Farmers' Alliance," *Arkansas Historical Quarterly* 32 (1973): 108-19.
44. "Nine Negroes Lynched," *Chicago Daily Tribune*, October 1, 1891.
45. Vincent Vinikas, "Specters in the Past: The St. Charles, Arkansas, Lynching of 1904 and the Limits of Historical Inquiry," *Journal of Southern History* 55 (1999): 553.
46. Vinikas, "Specters in the Past," 557.
47. Quoted in Vinikas, "Specters in the Past," 540.
48. .Quoted in Barnes, *Journey of Hope*, 87.
49. Quoted in Barnes, *Who Killed John Clayton?*, 128, 129.
50. Quoted in Stockley, *Blood in Their Eyes*, 24.

51. Quoted in Stockley, *Blood in their Eyes,* 24.

52. Joel Williamson, *The Crucible of Race Black White Relations in the American South since Emancipation (*New York: Oxford University Press, 1984), 117.

53. Vinikas, "Specters in the Past," 536.

54. Vinikas, "Specters in the Past," 557.

55. Jacqueline Dowd Hall, *Revolt Against Chivalry: Jessie Daniel Ames and the Women's Campaign Against Lynching* (New York: Panthem Books,1979), 2, quoted in Vinikas, "Specters in the Past," 556.

56. Quoted in Tom Dillard, "Madness with a Past: An Overview of Race Violence in Arkansas History," *Arkansas Review* 32 (2001): 98. In fact, Dillard finds that rural racial cleansing efforts had already begun earlier in the decade when "whites in Van Buren County tried to force black farmers from the north side of the Cadron River. . . . On 30 August 1882, a black man found a warning tacked to a tree on his land: 'Notice is her by giving That I sertify you, Mr. Nigger, just as shore as you locate your Self her—death is your potion, the Cadron is the ded line, your cind cant live on this side a tall.'" Though charges were filed against six whites in federal court, the historical record is unclear as to the disposition of these charges (97).

57. Quoted in Jeannie M. Whayne, "Low Villains and Wickedness in High Places," *Arkansas Review* 32 (2001): 106.

58. *Arkansas Gazette,* March 25, 1899.

Chapter 7

1. Quoted in Gordon, *Caste & Class,* 50.
2. Dillard, "Madness with a Past," 98.
3. Quoted in Gordon, *Caste & Class,* 51.
4. Quoted in Gordon, *Caste & Class,* 108.
5. Quoted in Gordon, *Caste & Class,* 109.
6. Quoted in Gordon, *Caste & Class,* 110.
7. Quoted in Vinikas, "Specters in the Past," 549.
8. Quoted in Vinikas, "Specters in the Past," 50.
9. Quoted in Dougan, *Arkansas Odyssey,* 213.
10. Quoted in Graves, *Town and Country,* 223.
11. Graves, *Town and Country,* 223.
12. Graves, *Town and Country,* 223.
13. Quoted in Stockley, *Blood in their Eyes,* 30, 31.
14. Quoted in Gordon, *Caste & Class,* 59.
15. Gordon, *Caste & Class,* 59.
16. Vinikas, "Specters in the Past," 550.
17. Vinikas, "Specters in the Past, 553.
18. Quoted in Gordon, *Caste & Class,* 51.
19. Dillard, "Madness with a Past," 98.
20. Dougan, *Arkansas Odyssey,* 318.

21. Jacqueline Froelich and David Zimmerman, "Total Eclipse: The Destruction of the African American Community of Harrison, Arkansas in 1905 and 1909," *Arkansas Historical Quarterly* 58 (1999): 158.

22. Judith Kilpatrick, *Arkansas' Early African-American Lawyers: A Pictorial History* (Fayetteville: University of Arkansas School of Law, 2002), 10.

23. Tom Dillard, "Scipio A. Jones," *Arkansas Historical Quarterly* 31 (1972).

24. Gordon, *Caste & Class,* 53.

25. Gordon, *Caste & Class,* 55. For information about the state's black lawyers before 1950, see Kilpatrick, *African-American Lawyers.*

26. Patterson, *The Seed of Sally Good'n,* 77.

27. Patterson, *The Seed of Sally Good'n, 78.*

28. Quoted in Patterson, *The Seed of Sally Good'n,* 82.

29. Quoted in Patterson, *The Seed of Sally Good'n,* 84.

30. Todd Everett Lewis, "Race Relations in Arkansas, 1910-1919" (dissertation, University of Arkansas, 1995), 276-77.

31. Lewis, "Race Relations in Arkansas," 277.

32. Patterson, *The Seed of Sally Good'n,* 87, 88.

33. Lewis, "Race Relations in Arkansas," 159.

34. Randy Finley, "Black Arkansans and World War One," *Arkansas Historical Quarterly* 49 (1990): 250-51.

35. Gordon, *Caste & Class,* 126.

36. Kieran Taylor, "'We Have Just Begun': Black Organizing and White Response in the Arkansas Delta, 1919," *Arkansas Historical Quarterly* 48 (1999): 270.

37. Quoted in Lewis, "Race Relations in Arkansas," 186.

38. Lewis, "Race Relations in Arkansas," 187.

39. Quoted in Lewis, "Race Relations in Arkansas, " 187.

40. Quoted in Lewis, "Race Relations in Arkansas," 187.

41. Quoted in Gordon, *Caste & Class,* 127.

42. Finley "Black Arkansans and World War One," 260.

43. Quoted in Dillard, "Scipio A. Jones," 212.

44. Finley, "Black Arkansans and World War One," 263.

45. Lewis, "Race Relations in Arkansas," 206.

46. Lewis, "Race Relations in Arkansas,"281.

47. Gerard B. Lambert, *All Out of Step: A Personal Chronicle* (Garden City, NY: Doubleday, 1956), 64.

48. Gordon, *Caste & Class,* 124.

49. Quoted in Diane D. Blair and Jay Barth, *Arkansas Politics and Government,* 2nd ed. (Lincoln: University of Nebraska Press, 2005), 312.

Chapter 8

1. Quoted in Charles Orson Cook, "Arkansas's Charles Hillman Brough, 1876-1935: An Interpretation" (dissertation, University of Houston, 1980), 71.

2. Quoted in Cook, "Arkansas's Charles Hillman Brough," 71.

3. Quoted in Foy Lisenby, *Charles Hillman Brough: A Biography* (Fayetteville: University of Arkansas Press, 1996), 75.

4. Quoted in Lisenby, *Charles Hillman Brough,* 72.

5. Quoted in Lisenby, *Charles Hillman Brough,* 75.

6. Quoted in Cook, "Arkansas's Charles Hillman Brough," 79.

7. Charles Hillman Brough, "The Clinton Riot," Publications of the Mississippi Historical Association (1902), 61.

8. Brough, "The Clinton Riot," 63.

9. Quoted in Cook, "Charles Hillman Brough," 122.

10. *Arkansas Gazette,* October 2, 1917.

11. Quoted in Cook, "Charles Hillman Brough," 122.

12. Quoted in Cook, "Charles Hillman Brough," 11.

13. Quoted in Cook, "Charles Hillman Brough," 122.

14. Quoted in Susan E. C. Huntsman, "Race Relations in Phillips County, 1895–1920" (student paper, Grif Stockley Papers, Butler Center for Arkansas Studies, Little Rock), 16.

15. Quoted Taylor, "We Have Just Begun," 279.

16. One can only contrast the fate of this sharecropper union and later the Southern Tenant Farmers' Union with the reception to a strike in Little Rock in 1918 by local no. 36 of the International Laundry Workers Union whose members were overwhelmingly black women. Though their circumstances were much different, at one point the Little Rock Chamber of Commerce had supported the Union's initial position. Suffice it to say that as much racial discrimination as there was in Little Rock, there was still a world of difference between Little Rock and the Delta. See Elizabeth Haiken, "The Lord Helps Those Who Help Themselves: Black Laundresses in Little Rock, Arkansas, 1917–1921," *Arkansas Historical Quarterly* 49 (1990), 20-50.

17. Margaret Jones Bolsterli, *Born in the Delta: Reflections on the Making of a Southern White Sensibility* (Fayetteville: University of Arkansas Press, (2000), 62.

18. Bolsterli, *Born in the Delta,* 61.

19. The affidavits of H. F. Smiddy and T. K. Jones can be found in the abstract and brief (record) of the appellants (86-100) in *Moore et al. v. Dempsey,* 261 U.S. 86 (1923). They are also located at the William H. Bowen School of Law Library/Pulaski County Law Library in Little Rock.

20. Bessie Ferguson, "The Elaine Race Riot" (master's thesis, George Peabody College for Teachers, 1927), 83-84.

21. Walter Brown, interview by John E. Miller, March 18, 1976, Special Collections Division, University of Arkansas Libraries, Fayetteville.

22. Ida B. Wells-Barnett, *The Arkansas Race Riot* (Chicago: Hume Job Print 1920), 18.

23. Wells-Barnett, *The Arkansas Race Riot,* 13, 14.

24. Wells-Barnett, *The Arkansas Race Riot,* 20.

25. Wells-Barnett, *The Arkansas Race Riot,* 20.

26. *Arkansas Gazette,* September 30, 1919.

27. Oscier Bratton, letter to Ulysses Bratton, November 5, 1919, quoted in Stockley, *Blood in their Eyes,* 66. The most recent book about the events in Phillips County in 1919 is by Robert Whitaker, *On the Laps of Gods The Red Summer of 1919 and the Struggle for Justice That Remade a Nation* (Crown Publishing Group, 2008). Whitaker reaches the same conclusion that blacks were massacred in Phillips County.

28. Brown, interview, 14, 15.

29. L. S. Dunaway, *What a Preacher Saw through a Keyhole in Arkansas* (Little Rock: Parke-Harper, 1925), 109.

30. Dunaway, *What a Preacher Saw,* 109.

31. Jeannie M. Whayne, "Low Villains and Wickedness in High Places: Race and Class in the Elaine Riots," *Arkansas Historical Quarterly* 58, no. 5 (1999), 285.

32. Dunaway, *What a Preacher Saw,* 13.

33. Dunaway, *What a Preacher Saw,* 102.

34. Dunaway, *What a Preacher Saw,* 109.

35. Charles Hillman Brough, letter to Dunbar Rowland, October 3, 1919, Charles Hillman Brough Papers, box 4, file 54, Special Collections Division, University of Arkansas Libraries, Fayetteville.

36. Quoted in Dunaway, *What a Preacher Saw,* 109, 110.

37. *Helena World,* October 3, 1919.

38. Quoted in Stockley, *Blood in their* Eyes, 81.

39. *Helena World,* October 3, 1919.

40. As mentioned, outnumbered by blacks in Phillips County, the oldest fear of whites was resurrected that blacks were about to take retribution for their mistreatment. The savage nature that lay buried under the docile nature of every black had come alive just as whites had long believed. And then before the day was out as the stories of outright murder of women and children and barbarism filtered in from Elaine to Helena, the fear was being replaced by denial and shame. The reaction from whites was as always: denial, rationalization, and projection. There was no massacre; whites had no choice but to defend themselves; it was not whites who were bloodthirsty but blacks whose murderous rage could explode in an instant. Psychologist Daniel Goleman shows that to minimize anxiety "much of what group members say to each other to justify a shaky course of action is rationalization, a story line they pool their efforts to concoct and believe. Rationalizations serve to build confidence and reassure the group about the morality, safety, wisdom, or other validity of their decisions" (quoted in Stockley, xviii, xix). The morality of the actions of whites during the events in Elaine was immediately in question, but as Goleman shows, the "group" invariably assumes its actions were justified and right. "These ethical blinders help the group avoid feeling ashamed or guilty about what otherwise might be questionable means or goals" (quoted in Stockley, xix). These patterns of "group think" are clearly played out in the story of the massacres. Group anxiety was

experienced by blacks, as well. Many blacks reacted as they did to any mass acts of violence whether lynchings or racial cleanings: fear of setting off the murderous rage of whites often resulted in denial and repression. Blacks who had lived through it did often never mentioned it to their children just as they said nothing in this period about acts of racial cleansing.

41. For an extended discussion of the evidence of military involvement, see Stockley, *Blood in their Eyes,* 34–60.

42. Lambert, *All Out of Step,* 77.

43. The crucial affidavits of T. K. Jones and H. F. Smiddy are located in the abstract and brief (record) of the appellants (86–100) in *Moore et al. v. Dempsey,* 261 U.S. 86 (1923). A copy is also available at Special Collections, the University of Arkansas at Little Rock, William H. Bowen School of Law/Pulaski County Law Library.

44. Quoted in Stockley, *Blood in their Eyes,* 111.

45. *Helena World,* November 3, 1919.

46. Stockley, *Blood in their Eyes,* 121, 122.

47. *Helena World,* November 5, 1919.

48. Stockley, *Blood in their Eyes,* 131-37.

49. *Arkansas Gazette,* November 25, 1919.

50. *Arkansas Gazette,* November 25, 1919.

Chapter 9

1. Stockley, *Blood in their Eyes,* 92-100.

2. Stockley, *Blood in their Eyes,* 41, 42.

3. Richard C. Cortner *A Mob Intent on Death: The NAACP and the Arkansas Riot Cases* (Middleton, CT: Wesleyan University Press, 1988). Cortner has written an excellent constitutional analysis of the aftermath of the Elaine Race Massacres, including a detailed summary of the efforts to extradite Robert Hill.

4. Quoted in Cortner, *A Mob Intent on Death,* 62.

5. Quoted in Cortner, *A Mob Intent on Death,* 62.

6. James Monroe Cox, letter to William Pickens, Feb 12, 1920, Arthur Ocean Waskow Papers, 1958–1972, Special Collections, Wisconsin State Historical Society, Madison.

7. Quoted in Stockley, *Blood in their Eyes,* 157.

8. Quoted Lewis, "Race Relations in Arkansas," 244 .

9. Quoted in Lewis, "Race Relations in Arkansas," 274.

10. Ralph Ginzburg, *100 Years of Lynchings (*Baltimore: Black Classic Press, 1962).

11. Quoted in Cortner, *A Mob Intent on Death,* 155.

12. Stockley, *Blood in their Eyes,* 216.

13. Charles C. Alexander, "White Robed Reformers: The Ku Klux Klan Comes to Arkansas," *Arkansas Historical Quarterly* 22 (1963): 9.

14. Alexander, "White Robed Reformers," 16.

15. For a more detailed account, see Stockley, *Blood in their Eyes,* 228–32.

16. Quoted in Marcet Haldeman-Julius, *Story of a Lynching: An Explanation of Southern Psychology* (Girard, KS: Haldeman-Julius Publications, 1927), 12.

17. Quoted in Stockley, *Blood in their Eyes,* 231.

18. Quoted in Stockley, *Blood in their Eyes,* 231.

19. Quoted in Stockley, *Blood in their Eyes,* 231.

20. Love, *End of the Line,* 6, 7.

21. Gene Vinzant, "Mirage and Reality: Economic Conditions in Black Little Rock in the 1920s," *Arkansas Historical Quarterly* 63 (2004): 262.

22. Vinzant, "Mirage and Reality," 269.

23. Vinzant, "Mirage and Reality," 276.

24. Mary Gambrell Rolinson, "The Garvey Movement in the Rural South, 1920–1927" (dissertation, Georgia State University, 2002), 51. See also Rolinson's *Grass Roots Garveyism: The Universal Negro Improvement Association in the Rural South, 1920–1927* (Chapel Hill: University of North Carolina Press, 2007).

25. Rolinson, "The Garvey Movement," 250.

26. Rolinson, "The Garvey Movement," 143.

27. Dougan, *Arkansas Odyssey,* 411.

28. Pete Daniel, *Deep'n as It Come: The 1927 Mississippi River Flood* (Fayetteville: University of Arkansas Press, 1996), 154.

29. Daniel, *Deep'n as It Come,* 152.

30. Jeannie M. Whayne, "Robert E. Lee Wilson and the Making of a Post–Civil War Plantation," in *The Southern Elite and Social Change,* ed. Randy Finley and Thomas A. DeBlack (Fayetteville: University of Arkansas Press, 2002), 107.

31. Whayne, "Robert E. Lee Wilson," 107.

32. Whayne, "Robert E. Lee Wilson," 107.

33. Whayne, "Robert E. Lee Wilson," 110.

34. Whayne, "Robert E. Lee Wilson," 109.

35. Whayne, "Robert E. Lee Wilson," 111.

36. John A. Kirk, "Dr. J. M. Robinson, the Arkansas Negro Democratic Association and Black Politics in Little Rock, Arkansas, 1928–1952," *Pulaski County Historical Review* 41 (Spring 1993): 4.

37. Quoted in Kirk, "Dr. J. M. Robinson," 5.

38. Kirk, "Dr. J. M. Robinson," 6.

39. Kirk, "Dr. J. M. Robinson," 2.

40. Charles F. Robinson, "Most Shamefully Common: Arkansas and Miscegenation," *Arkansas Historical Quarterly* 60 (Autumn 2001): 283.

Chapter 10

1. Lankford, *Bearing Witness,* 52.
2. Lankford, *Bearing Witness,* 232.
3. Lankford, *Bearing Witness,* 2.
4. Lankford, *Bearing Witness,* 185.
5. Dougan, *Arkansas Odyssey,* 438.
6. Dougan, *Arkansas Odyssey,* 439.
7. Dougan, *Arkansas Odyssey,* 438.
8. Quoted in Ben Johnson III, *Fierce Solitude: A Life of John Gould Fletcher* (Fayetteville: University of Arkansas Press, 1994), 204.
9. Ben Johnson III, *Arkansas in Modern America: 1930–1999* (Fayetteville: University of Arkansas Press 2000), 11.
10. Johnson, *Arkansas in Modern America,* 12.
11. Quoted in Dougan, *Arkansas Odyssey,* 430.
12. Dougan, *Arkansas Odyssey,* 430.
13. Johnson, *Arkansas in Modern America,* 10.
14. Dougan, *Arkansas Odyssey,* 429.
15. Donald Grubbs, *Cry from the Cotton: The Southern Tennant Farmers' Union and the New Deal* (Chapel Hill: University of North Carolina Press, 1971), 49.
16. Grubbs, *Cry from the Cotton,* 49.
17. Nan Woodruff, *American Congo: The African American Freedom Struggle in the Delta* (Cambridge, MA: Harvard University Press, 2003), 158.
18. Dougan, *American Odyssey,* 433.
19. Woodruff, *American Congo,* 158.
20. Johnson, *Arkansas in Modern America,* 27.
21. Quoted in Biegert, "Legacy of Resistance: Uncovering the History of Collective Action by Black Agricultural Workers in Central East Arkansas From the 1860s to the 1930s," *Journal of Social History* 164 (Fall 1998): 73.
22. Quoted in Rolinson, "The Garvey Movement," 263.
23. Grubbs, *Cry from the Cotton,* 70.
24. Quoted in Grubbs, 70n16.
25. Grubbs, *Cry from the Cotton,* 71.
26. Grubbs, *Cry from the Cotton,* 73.
27. Grubbs, *Cry from the Cotton,* 73.
28. Grubbs, *Cry from the Cotton,* 73.
29. Norman Thomas, as candidate for president on the Socialist ticket, had polled 880,000 votes in 1932. It was he who had suggested to Mitchell and East that they form a sharecropper union.
30. Quoted in Dougan, *Arkansas Odyssey,* 433.
31. Grubbs, *Cry from the Cotton,* 73.
32. Woodruff, *American Congo,* 173.
33. Grubbs, *Cry from the Cotton,* 89.
34. Grubbs, *Cry from the Cotton,* 91.

35. Grubbs, *Cry from the Cotton,* 91.
36. Grubbs, *Cry from the Cotton,* 91.
37. Grubbs, *Cry from the Cotton,* 91.
38. Quoted in Dougan, *Arkansas Odyssey,* 433.
39. Woodruff, *American Congo,* 175, 176.
40. Woodruff, *American Congo,* 175.
41. Dougan, *Arkansas Odyssey,* 433.
42. Grubbs, *Cry from the Cotton,* 107.
43. Grubbs, *Cry from the Cotton,* 122.
44. Dougan, *Arkansas Odyssey,* 434.
45. Grubbs, *Cry from the Cotton,* 113.
46. Dougan, *Arkansas Odyssey,* 434.
47. Grubbs, *Cry from the Cotton,* 113.
48. Grubbs, *Cry from the Cotton,* 117.
49. Grubbs, *Cry from the Cotton,* 115.
50. Quoted in Grubbs, *Cry from the Cotton,* 118.
51. Quoted in Dougan, *Arkansas Odyssey,* 434.
52. Grubbs, *Cry from the Cotton,* 118.
53. Grubbs, *Cry from the Cotton,* 118.
54. Dougan, *Arkansas Odyssey,* 434, 435.
55. Grubbs, *Cry from the Cotton,* 121.
56. Grubbs, *Cry from the Cotton,* 121. For further details see Grubbs, 121–24.
57. Grubbs, *Cry from the Cotton,* 169.
58. Bolsterli, *Born in the Delta,* 7. For a detailed description of slavery-like conditions in the Deep South, see Douglas A. Blackmon, *Slavery by Another Name: The Re-enslavement of Black Americans from the Civil War to World War II* (New York: Doubleday, 2008).

Chapter 11

1. Samuel S. Taylor, "The Negroes of Little Rock," outline, Pulaski County WPA Writer's Project Place Files, Arkansas History Commission, Little Rock, 16. An edited, official version without Taylor's personal observations is contained in Arkansas Writers Project, *Survey of Negroes in Little Rock and North Little Rock* (Little Rock: Urban League of Greater Little Rock, 1941). In the introduction to the published, official survey, Samuel S. Taylor is credited with being the principal writer.
2. John A. Kirk, *Redefining the Color Line: Back Activism in Little Rock, Arkansas 1940–1970* (Gainesville: University Press of Florida, 2002) 14, 15.
3. Taylor, "Pulaski County WPA."
4. Taylor, "Pulaski County WPA," 87.
5. Taylor, "Pulaski County WPA," 21n13.
6. Taylor, "Pulaski County WPA," 19.
7. Taylor, "Pulaski County WPA," 69.

8. Taylor, "Pulaski County WPA," 71.

9. Even later in the 1950s blacks were not necessarily confined to the Dunbar neighborhood. For example, Daisy and L. C. Bates built their "dream house" in the 1950s at 1207 W. Twenty-Eighth Street in Little Rock in a white neighborhood outside the traditional Philander–Smith–Arkansas Baptist College corridor. Rhonda Stewart notes that some whites continued to live adjacent to blacks during this Jim Crow era in Little Rock. What was called the "Dunbar Neighborhood" was bounded on the north by West Ninth Street, on the east by State Street, on the west by High Street—now Dr. Martin Luther King—and on the south by Roosevelt Road—Twenty-Fifth Street). "From twenty-eighth Street coming south to about twenty-ninth . . . from Arch over to Ringo was all White Neighbors." Ruth Ward Evans, interview, April 2, 2005, quoted in Rhonda Stewart, "Every Day Business: A History of Life in Arkansas," Butler Center for Arkansas Studies, Little Rock.

10. Taylor, "Pulaski County WPA," 45.

11. Maya Angelou, *The Collected Autobiographies of Maya Angelou* (New York: Modern Library, 2004), 147.

12. Bolsterli, *Born in the Delta,* 74. Bolsterli's memoir is a must-read for those who wish to learn how whites of a certain class negotiated not only race relations but life in general in the twentieth century before the modern civil rights movement. Her ambivalence about her racial experiences captures the emotional conflicts and guilt of those whites who have tried to come to terms with the white supremacy of the era. In a single paragraph, Bolsterli, who has a doctorate in English, writes about African Americans: "I don't know how they saw us; I am sure their feelings were as mixed about as ours were about them. They had reason to hate us as well as to love us, and I think our family was not as bad to them as some might have been. Everything I have read on the subject written since 1960 leads me to believe they did hate us . . . and yet I cannot entirely believe they all hated us. They must have made exceptions, as we did" (77).

13. Quoted in Kirk, *Redefining the Color Line,* 25.

14. Quoted in Kirk, *Redefining the Color Line,* 26.

15. *Encyclopedia of Arkansas,* s.v. "William Harold Flowers," http://www.encyclopediaofarkansas.net/encyclopedia/media-detail.aspx?mediaid=6821.

16. Quoted in Grif Stockley, *Daisy Bates: Civil Rights Crusader From Arkansas* (Jackson: University Press of Mississippi, 2005), 36.

17. John Kirk writes that this was not the first racial incident involving soldiers in this era. There had already been two ugly racial incidents in Arkansas involving local whites and black soldiers from outside the South who refused to act subservient to whites. *Redefining the Color Line,* 44, 45.

18. Kirk, *Redefining the Color Line,* 44–47.

19. *State Press,* April 3, 1942.

20. The pressure on the federal level did not come, of course, from

the state's congressional delegation In fact, U.S. representative E. C. Gathings, whose district included the black belt in eastern Arkansas, did not think of African Americans as requiring much attention. In response to a concern about the size of the first congressional district, in 1943 he wrote "approximately 30 to 40 percent of this population is negro. By reason of this fact there is not a great increase in the necessary work of my office in representing a larger population." E. C. Gathings, letter to Senator William L. Ward, February 16, 1943, Papers of E. C. Gathings, Special Collections, Dean B. Ellis Library, Arkansas State University, Jonesboro.

21. *Arkansas Gazette,* January 22, 1972.

22. Daisy Bates, *The Long Shadow of Little Rock: A Memoir* (Fayetteville: University of Arkansas Press, 1987), 37.

23. Quoted in Kirk, *Redefining the Color Line,* 41.

24. *Arkansas Gazette,* June 11, 1942.

25. Bates, *Long Shadow,* 38.

26. Guerdon D. Nichols, "Breaking the Color Barrier at the University of Arkansas," *Arkansas Historical Quarterly* 27 (Spring 1968): 3–21. See *Encyclopedia of Arkansas,* s.v. "Silas Hunt," http://www.encyclopediaofarkansas.net/encyclopedia/media-detail.aspx?mediaid=6821.

27. Alex Haley, "The Man Who Wouldn't Quit," *Readers Digest* (March 1963): 54, 55. The author of the piece is Haley's brother, Alex Haley, who wrote the world-famous *Roots*. Conditions for his brother gradually improved over the next two years, and Haley made the *Arkansas Law Review.*

28. For a useful biography of Wiley Branton, see Judith Kilpatrick, *There When We Needed Him: Wiley Austin Branton, Civil Rights Warrior* (Fayetteville: University of Arkansas Press, 2007).

29. Cheryl Nichols, *Historically Black Properties in Little Rock's Dunbar School Neighborhood* (Little Rock: Arkansas Historic Preservation Program, 1999), 4.

30. John A. Kirk, "A Study in Second Class Citizenship: Race, Urban Development, and Little Rock's Gillam Park, 1934–2004," *Arkansas* 64 (Autumn 2005): 262–28.

31. Kirk, "A Study in Second Class Citizenship," 272.

32. Kirk, "A Study in Second Class Citizenship," 275.

33. Kirk, "A Study in Second Class Citizenship," 279.

34. Further documentation of these developments is provided by Little Rock author Cheryl Nichols who also discusses the creation in 1952 a forty-acre area around Dunbar High School that was designated a "slum clearance project" under title I of the Housing Act of 1949. Similarly, in 1955 the area around historically-black Philander Smith College became Little Rock's first "urban renewal project," authorized under provisions of the Housing Act of 1954, and about ten acres were cleared. . . ." Many of the buildings removed by the Dunbar and Philander Smith clearance projects were truly dilapidated, including some that did not have indoor plumbing but others seem merely to

have been in the way of the Little Rock Housing Authority's plans for the neighborhood." *Historically Black Properties,* 5.

35. Quoted in Kirk, "A Study in Second Class Citizenship," 277.

36. Kirk, "A Study in Second Class Citizenship," 283.

37. Kirk, "A Study in Second Class Citizenship," 284.

38. *Little Rock School District v. Pulaski County Special School District et al.,* 584 F. Supp. 328 (1984).

39. *Little Rock School District v. Pulaski County,* 14.

40. *Little Rock School District v. Pulaski County,* 15.

41. Kirk, *Redefining the Color Line,* 68.

42. Kirk, *Redefining the Color Line,* 31.

43. Lester, *A Man for Arkansas,* 162.

44. Georg Iggers File, Special Collections, University of Arkansas Libraries, Little Rock.

45. Kirk, *Redefining the Color Line,* 91.

46. Quoted in John Kirk, "Daisy Bates, the National Association for the Advancement of Colored People, and the 1957 Little Rock Crisis: A Gendered Perspective," in *Gender in the Civil Rights Movement,* ed. Peter J. Ling and Sharon Monteith (New York: Garland, 1999), 28.

47. Georg Iggers, letter to Tony Freyer, September 17, 1980, Georg Iggers File, Special Collections, University of Arkansas Libraries, Little Rock.

48. Griffin Smith Jr., "Localism and Segregation: Racial Patterns in Little Rock, Arkansas, 1945–1954" (master's thesis, Columbia University, 1965), 52–53, 80, 94–95.

49. Taylor Branch, *Parting the Waters: America in the King Years, 1954–1963* (New York: Simon & Schuster, 1988), 213.

50. "West Memphis Schools," *Life,* March 21, 1949, 81. The results of four taxpayer suits to equalize school facilities filed in 1948 and 1949 had created no sense of urgency. Though a suit against the DeWitt School Board had resulted in a ruling in July 1949 by Judge Harry Lemley that the DeWitt School Board must provide "public education facilities substantially equal to those . . . for white children," the judge set no date by which the equalization must occur, saying only it must happen "within a reasonable time." Even more ominous and a sign of the future was a decision by Judge John Miller who dismissed a Fort Smith equalization case in November 1949 on receiving information that since the filing of the suit a new elementary school for blacks had been erected as well as two other buildings, "and that it [the school board] was planning to renovate the high school building." A new national strategy by the NAACP would soon be implemented. Quoted in Stephan Stephan, "Changes in the Status of Negroes in Arkansas, 1948–1950," *Arkansas Historical Quarterly* 9 (1950): 46.

Chapter 12

1. *Brown v. Board of Education,* 347 U.S. 483 (1954). Kevin Hatfield has demonstrated that in the 1940s Madison County permitted an African American child to attend its all-white public school. Kevin Hatfield, "The History of Education in Madison County, Arkansas, 1827–1948" (dissertation, University of Arkansas, 1991), 325-28.

2. .*Southern School News*, September 3, 1954, 2.

3. Quoted in Kirk, *Redefining the Color Line,* 127.

4. Andrew Brill, "*Brown* in Fayetteville: Peaceful Southern School Desegregation in 1954," *Arkansas Historical Quarterly* 65 (Winter 2006): 337–59. While acknowledging that the small number of blacks contributed to the ease with which Fayetteville desegregated its school system, Andrew Brill documents that the pattern of segregation in Fayetteville, a university town with a liberal reputation, was not as rigid as in other parts of Arkansas. For example, according to Brill, there were never segregated restrooms or drinking fountains in Fayetteville.

5. *Brown v. Board of Education,* 349 U.S. 294 (1955).

6. Quoted in Stockley, *Daisy Bates,* 75.

7. *Arkansas Faith,* May 1956.

8. Stockley, *Daisy Bates,* 80.

9. Quoted in Stockley, *Daisy Bates,* 9.

10. *Arkansas Gazette,* May 5, 1956.

11. Arkansas House of Representatives, Bill 324, 1957. In all, four bills were enacted into law, including that created a "State Sovereignty Commission." Only a few whites had the courage to testify against the bill.

12. A number of historians have discussed the issue of class in the Little Rock School Desegregation Crisis. See, for example, C. Fred Williams, "Class, The Central Issue in the 1957 Little Rock School Crisis," *Arkansas Historical Quarterly* 56 (Autumn 1997): 341.

13. Orval Faubus responded in kind. Phoebe Godfrey has written that during the crisis, Orval Faubus "spoke in a language that his chief constituency, Little Rock's working class segregationists, well understood—a racialized language with powerful sexual overtones." Phoebe Godfrey, "Bayonets, Brainwashing, and Bathrooms: The Discourse of Race, Gender, and Sexuality in the Desegregation of Little Rock's Central High," *Arkansas Historical Quarterly* 60 (Spring 2001): 42.

14. Elizabeth Jacoway, *Turn Away Thy Son: Little Rock, The Crisis that Shocked the Nation* (New York: Free Press, 2007), xiii. Jacoway contends that it is the white fear of "race-mixing" or defilement of their culture that makes the race issue intractable and is much more of a factor than "manipulation by greedy or class-conscious whites."

15. Roy Reed, *Faubus: The Life and Times of an American Prodigal* (Fayetteville: University of Arkansas Press, 1997), 197.

16. Orval E. Faubus, "Speech by Governor Orval E. Faubus calling

out the National Guard, September 2, 1957," FBI Investigation Papers, "The 1957 Little Rock School Desegregation Crisis," Special Collections, University of Arkansas Libraries, Little Rock.

17. Reed, *Faubus*, 92. Elizabeth Jacoway has argued that "with characteristic haste and assurance Harry Ashmore immediately suspected Faubus of using race, 'the old black magic,' to further his career." Jacoway, *Turn Away Thy Son,* 27. Jacoway contends that Faubus's motives for calling out the National Guard were much more complicated than political opportunism. Jacoway contends, "His [Ashmore's placing of all the blame on Orval Faubus] was disingenuous and less than fair"(128).

18. Quoted in Jacoway, *Turn Away Thy Son,* 248.

19. Bates, *Long Shadow,* 172.

20. Quoted in Bates, 104.

21. Quoted in Melba Pattillo Beals, *Warriors Don't Cry: A Searing Memoir of the Battle to Integrate Little Rock's Central High* (New York: Washington Square Books, 1994), 122.

22. *New York Post,* April 7, 1958.

23. Daisy Bates, *The Long Shadow of Little Rock* (draft, Daisy Bates Papers, Wisconsin State Historical Society, Madison), 26-27. Ralph Brodie, who was president of the student body at Central in 1957, argues that most students at Central should be commended for quietly going about their routine and notes that a few students showed courage by reaching out to the Nine. Ralph Brodie and Marvin Swartz, *Central in Our Lives: Voices from Little Rock Central High School, 1957–1959* (Little Rock: Butler Center for Arkansas Studies, 2007).

24. George Howard Jr., interview with author, January 9, 2002, Grif Stockley Papers, Butler Center for Arkansas Studies, Little Rock.

25. Daisy Bates, interview by Elizabeth Jacoway, October 11, 1976, Southern Oral History Program, Library of University of North Carolina at Chapel Hill, 18.

26. Reed, *Faubus,* 274.

27. Reed, *Faubus,* 276.

28. FBI File of Daisy Bates, Grif Stockley Papers, Butler Center for Arkansas Studies, Little Rock.

29. *State Press,* October 17, 1958.

30. Quoted in Sondra Gordy, e-mail to author, August 17, 2006.

31. Laura A. Miller, *Fearless: Irene Gaston Samuel and the Life of a Southern Liberal* (Little Rock:Butler Center for Arkansas Studies, 2002), 36.

32. Ben Johnson III, *Arkansas in Modern America,* 146.

33. Daisy Bates, letter to NAACP board members, November 19, 1959, Papers of the NAACP, Library of Congress, Washington.

34. Daisy Bates, letter to NAACP board members.

35. Reed, *Faubus,* 260.

Chapter 13

1. John A. Thompson, "Gentleman Editor: Mr. Heiskell of the Gazette; The Early Years, 1902–1922" (master's thesis, University of Arkansas at Little Rock, 1983).

2. Quoted in Reed, *Faubus,* 205.

3. Quoted in Nathania K. Sawyer, "Harry S. Ashmore: On the Way to Everywhere" (masters Thesis, University of Arkansas at Little Rock, 2001), 74.

4. Quoted in Sawyer, "Harry S. Ashmore," 75.

5. Quoted in Sawyer, "Harry S. Ashmore," 30.

6. Quoted in Harry S. Ashmore, *Epitaph for Dixie* (New York: Norton, 1974), 181.

7. Quoted in Ashmore, *Epitaph for Dixie,* 56.

8. "Crisis in the South: The Little Rock Story," *Arkansas Gazette,* 1959, 20.

9. Reed, *Faubus,* 205.

10. Reed, *Faubus,* xii.

11. *Arkansas Gazette,* September 4, 1957.

12. Bates, *Long Shadow,* 63.

13. Elizabeth Jacoway, "Taken by Surprise: Little Rock Business Leaders and Desegregation," in *Southern Businessmen and Desegregation,* ed. Elizabeth Jacoway and David Colburn (Baton Rouge: Louisiana State University Press, 1982), 21n9.

14. *Arkansas Gazette,* September 4, 1957.

15. As has been mentioned, during slavery Biblical support was central to some Southerners' justification of the institution. Some churches in the north and south had formally split over it. In A *Stone of Hope Prophetic Religion and the Death of Jim Crow* David L. Chappell contrasts the behavior of Southern white clergy and the denominations they served during slavery with their behavior during Jim Crow and has uncovered a striking lack of commitment on the part of most white religious bodies to fight to the death to maintain segregation in the South during the era when blacks were fighting so aggressively to abolish it. Though his argument seems to be undercut by the strident advocacy of Little Rock Baptist minister Wesley Pruden in the summer of 1956, Chappell argues, as others have, that ministers like him who championed segregation were "obscure" preachers in "fringe" churches. He notes that in Little Rock "two days before the crisis erupted at Central High, the Rev. Dale Cowling, a prominent local minister strongly connected with and supported by the SBC [Southern Baptist Convention] preached at Second Baptist Church of Little Rock," a sermon that took dead aim at preachers like Pruden: "Those who base their extreme opposition to integration upon their interpretation of the Scripture . . . are sincere beyond question. They are simply greatly mistaken in their efforts to prove that God marked the Negro race and relegated it to the role of servant." He called the theological effort linking Noah's curse on

Ham as a foundation for a belief that God had mandated blacks to be condemned to the inferior status of servant merely the "conjecture of man. We might as well reason that the Negro is the descendent of any other Old Testament character." Continuing in this vein, Cowling said, "Since the coming of the Savior, the clear insistence of the Word of God is that in Christ there is neither bond nor free, Greek [n]or Hebrew." While Cowling's words may have been news to some of his particular congregation, Chappell points out that shortly after the 1954 *Brown* decision, the Southern Baptist Convention overwhelmingly passed resolutions supporting desegregation and calling on all to comply with it peacefully. Chappell writes, "The significant thing, given that the [Southern] church was probably as racist as the rest of the white South, is that it failed in any meaningful way to join the anti-civil rights movement." David L. Chappell, *A Stone of Hope: Prophetic Religion and the Death of Jim Crow* (Chapel Hill: University of North Carolina Press, 2001), 116.

16. Quoted in Bates, *Long Shadow,* 65.

17. *Arkansas Gazette,* September 5, 1957.

18. Elizabeth Eckford, interview with author, September 4, 2002.

19. W. H. Bass, statement, September 4, 1957, FBI Papers, Special Collections, University of Arkansas Libraries, Little Rock.

20. *St. Louis Argus,* September 13, 1957.

21. Quoted in Stockley, *Daisy Bates,* 133.

22. Quoted in Reed, *Faubus,* 217.

23. Quoted in Reed, *Faubus,* 221. See David A. Nichols, *A Matter of Justice Eisenhower and the Beginning of the Civil Rights Revolution* (New York: Simon & Schuster, 2007). Nichols offers an important reassessment of Dwight D. Eisenhower's contributions in the area of civil rights, and documents that his deeds in this field spoke much louder than his words.

24. Quoted in Bates, *Long Shadow,* 93.

25. *Arkansas Democrat,* September 23, 1957.

26. Stockley, *Daisy Bates,* 146.

27. Clarence Laws, transcript of telephone conversation with Gloster Current, September 23, 1957, Papers of the NAACP, Library of Congress, Washington.

28. An article in the March 6, 1959, *Arkansas Gazette* called the fire the worst in terms of loss of life in the history of the state. On August 9, 1965, fifty-three Titan II missle silo workers burned to death in Arkansas, making it the "worst fire" in the state's history.

29. The notion that children should be treated differently and separately from adult criminals has a long and troubled history in the United States and Arkansas, in particular. In Arkansas the first "reform school" for boys began in 1905. In 1917 the legislature passed Act 67, creating a separate institution for African American boys. According to an article in the *Arkansas Gazette* on March 6, 1959, a group of blacks contributed $3,000 to begin operation of the institution since the act

creating it did no more than authorize the purchase of three hundred acres of land and authorize the construction of a crude barracks. Later legislation would create segregated training schools for girls. In any event, funds to operate the NBIS were deficient from the beginning and would continue to be deficient in absolute terms and in comparison with the school for white boys.

30. In finding prison conditions unconstitutional, Federal judge J. Smith Henley called the Arkansas Cummins prison "a dark and evil world," in the 1971 case of *Hutto v. Finney*.

31. Gordon Morgan, "The Arkansas Negro Boys' Industrial School: A Case Study in Institutional Organization" (master's thesis, University of Arkansas, 1956).

32. Morgan, "Boys' Industrial School," 66.

33. Francis Cherry Papers, 1952–1955, folder 59, Arkansas History Commission, Little Rock.

34. Morgan, "Boys' Industrial School," 30

35. Morgan, "Boys' Industrial School," 30

36. See for example, Act 511 of 1953, Act 310 of 1955, and Act 453 of 1957.

37. Bernice Ratcliffe, letter to Neva Talley, August 25, 1952, Francis Cherry Papers, folder 59, Arkansas History Commission, Little Rock.

38. Morgan, "Boys' Industrial School," 42.

39. "Eleventh Biennial Report Arkansas Boys' Industrial School," June 30, 1940, Phillip G. Back Papers, file 35, Butler Center for Arkansas Studies, Little Rock.

40. Act 52 of 1953.

41. *Arkansas Gazette,* March 8, 1959.

42. *Arkansas Democrat,* March 5, 1959; *Arkansas Gazette,* March 6, 1959.

43. *Arkansas Democrat,* March 5, 1959; *Arkansas Gazette,* March 6, 1959.

44. See, for example, "Gaines Alters Account, Says Door Free," *Arkansas Gazette,* March 6, 1959.

45. Orval Faubus Papers, "Negro Boys Industrial School, Wrightsville, Arkansas" (Confidential Investigation), March 7, 1959, box 302, folder 12, Special Collections Division, University of Arkansas Libraries, Fayetteville.

46. Minutes of the Meeting of the Legislative Council, Secretary of State's Office, November 18, 1958, Grif Stockley Papers, Butler Center for Arkansas Studies, Little Rock.

47. *Arkansas Gazette,* March 10, 1959.

48. *Arkansas Gazette,* March 26, 1959.

49. *State Press,* April 3, 1959.

50. Orval Faubus Papers, "Statement by Employees," box 301, file 20, Special Collections Division, University of Arkansas Libraries, Fayetteville.

51. Report of the Public Institutions Committee of the Pulaski

County Grand Jury, September 1959, Pulaski County Courthouse, Little Rock.

52. *Arkansas Gazette,* May 23, 1960.

53. Committee to Combat Racial Injustice, telegram to Orval E. Faubus, March 7, 1960, Orval Faubus Papers, box 301, folder 12, Special Collections Division, University of Arkansas, Fayetteville.

54. *State Press,* March 20, 1959.

55. Elizabeth Jacoway, *Turn Away Thy Son.* Among other arguments, Jacoway contends that Orval Faubus was betrayed by Superintendent Virgil Blossom and given no support by the federal government in dealing with possible violence that might present itself the opening day of school. Nor was he receiving help from the upper classes in Little Rock who looked down on him and his family. Thus, according to Jacoway, the governor's action in calling out the National Guard was not based on a prior decision to seek a third term as contended by *Gazette* editor Harry Ashmore and many others. While historical certainty on this point seems elusive even fifty years later, Jacoway's point is that the racism displayed by white Southerners during this period was motivated by a fear of miscegenation.

56. Elizabeth Jacoway, "The Little Rock Crisis and the Courts: A Forum Richard C. Butler and the Little Rock School Board: The Quest to Maintain Educational Quality," *Arkansas Historical Quarterly* 65 (Spring 2006): 28.

Chapter 14

1. Bettye Williams, letter to Daisy Bates, February 26, 1960, box 2, file 3, Daisy Bates Papers, Wisconsin State Historical Society, Madison.

2. Howard Zinn, *SNCC: The New Abolitionists* (Boston: Beacon Press, 1964), 16.

3. Daisy Bates, letter to Roy Wilkins, February 23, 1960, Papers of the NAACP, Library of Congress, Washington.

4. Randy Finley, "Crossing the White Line: SNCC in Arkansas, 1960–1967," unpub., Butler Center for Arkansas Studies, Little Rock, 3. This paper on SNCC is an unpublished but more comprehensive version of "Crossing the White Line: SNCC in Three Delta Towns, 1963–1967," *Arkansas Historical Quarterly* 65 (Summer 2006): 117–37, describing SNCC's civil rights activities in the Arkansas Delta. Both articles, as well as the unpublished papers of feminist historian Jayme Stone entitled "The 1960s Civil Rights Work of Carrie Dilworth: Militant, Organized, and Willing to Catch Hell," "Women of the Arkansas Delta: Grassroots Activism and the Student Nonviolent Coordinating Committee (SNCC, 1963–1966)," and "The ARKSNCC Freedom Summer Project: The Civil Rights Movements Other Freedom Summer," are relied upon by the author for the description of SNCC's sojourn in Arkansas.

5. Randy Finley, "SNCC in Arkansas," 3.

6. Stockley, *Daisy Bates,* 143.

7. Deborah Mathis, *Yet A Stranger: Why Black Americans Still Don't Feel at Home* (New York: Warner Books, 2002), 57.

8. Quoted in Kirk, *Redefining the Color Line,* 143.

9. Historians seeking to understand the work of civil rights advocates in Arkansas during the sixties are faced with the task of separating the work of the NAACP and its rivals, SNCC and then COCA. As important as it once had been in the state, by the 1960s the NAACP in Arkansas struggled to remain a major player in the civil rights movement. Since their identities were so invested in the NAACP, it was difficult for either Daisy or L. C. Bates to admit the civil rights movement benefited greatly by other organizations. One can see this as early as 1962 in a letter from Daisy Bates to Wiley Branton that was copied to Roy Wilkins and others. Bates, who was for the most part living in New York as she wrote *The Long Shadow of Little Rock,* was openly critical of Branton for having worked with Ozell Sutton, by that time a leader in COCA. She wrote that there was "a problem that concerned us greatly. It is the attitude of the people here since they have been alerted to the fact that they do not have to come through NAACP channels to file suit against discrimination." She went on to specifically mention that Branton recently had filed suit to desegregate public facilities in Little Rock in the name of blacks who were not members of the NAACP. Branton, who by that time was living in Atlanta and working as the director of the Voter Education Act for the Southern Regional Council, pointed out that neither she nor her husband seemed to be available to do the work that was necessary in bringing litigation as once had been done, but in fact the real reason was that the needs of the civil rights movement were already becoming far beyond the capacity of the NAACP and either Daisy or L. C Bates to meet them.

10. With the backing of the Legal Defense Fund, Walker formed in the 1960s in Little Rock the first interracial law firm in the state with Burl Rotenberry, Philip Kaplan, John Lavey, and Perlesta Hollingsworth. The firm would later dissolve, and as recently as the twenty-first century, former partners Walker and Kaplan, two of the best lawyers in the state, have appeared on opposite sides of civil rights cases.

11. However, unlike what occurred at state-supported Arkansas AM&N in 1963, no students would be expelled for First Amendment activities.

12. Zinn, *The New Abolitionists,* 34.

13. Story Machen-Rawn, e-mail to author, March 16, 2006.

14. *Arkansas Gazette,* April 16, 1960.

15. *Arkansas Democrat,* April 15, 1960.

16. L. C. Bates, December 1960 Annual Report for Gloster Current, December 3, 1960, box 4, older 10, Daisy Bates Papers, Wisconsin State Historical Society, Madison.

17. Quoted in Finley, "SNCC in Arkansas," 5.

18. Quoted in Finley, "SNCC in Arkansas," 5.

19. Quoted in Kirk, *Redefining the Color Line,* 210. Walker became a close personal friend and financial supporter of Daisy Bates in her later years after the death of L. C. Bates.

20. Quoted in Stockley, *Daisy Bates,* 191, 192.

21. Quoted in Kirk, *Redefining the Color Line,* 146.

22. Quoted in Kirk, *Redefining the Color Line,* 150.

23. Kirk, *Redefining the Color Line,* 150.

24. Kirk, *Redefining the Color Line,* 151.

25. Kirk, *Redefining the Color Line,* 150, 151.

26. Randy Finley contends that one of the reasons that SNCC students at Philander Smith were not more effective during this period was that they were "intimidated" by this highly educated and older group of professionals in COCA. "SNCC in Arkansas," 7.

27. It took the passage of the 1964 Civil Rights Act to force the other school districts in Arkansas even to make a promise to desegregate. With the passage of the 1964 Civil Rights Act, the federal government could decide to withhold federal funds to a school district for failure to follow desegregation guidelines that it now had the power to impose.

28. *Arkansas Gazette,* August 24, 1964.

29. The initial guidelines were toughened in 1966, and in those areas where there was a majority of blacks resistance to the guidelines stiffened. For example, Marvell in Phillips County was one of at least four districts that had accepted the 1965 guidelines but refused to comply initially in 1966.

30. Jim Porter, "The Musical Integration of Little Rock," *Pulaski County Historical Review* 53, no. 3 (Fall 2005): 82–88, 87.

31. Quoted in Porter, "Musical Integration," 84.

32. Quoted in Porter, "Musical Integration," 84.

33. Mathis, *Yet A Stranger,* 57.

34. Porter, "Musical Integration," 85.

35. Porter, "Musical Integration," 85.

36. Quoted in Brent Riffel, "In the Storm: William Hansen and the Student Non-Violent Coordinating Committee in Arkansas, 1962–1967," *Arkansas Historical Quarterly* 63 (Winter 2004): 404–19, 408.

37. Riffel, "In the Storm," 407.

38. Nat Griswold, *The Second Reconstruction in Little Rock* (Little Rock: Butler Center for Arkansas Studies, unpub., n.d.), book III,4.

39. Quoted in Kirk, *Redefining the Color Line,* 155.

40. Quoted in Kirk, *Redefining the Color Line,* 155.

41. Quoted in Kirk, *Redefining the Color Line,* 158.

Chapter 15

1. Holly Y. McGee," It Was the Wrong Time, and They Just Weren't Ready: Direct-Action Protest in Pine Bluff, 1963," *Arkansas Historical*

Quarterly 66 (Spring 2007): 18–42. A longer and slightly altered version of McGee's paper is entitled, "Trifling Elaborations: The Memory of the Movement in Arkansas After '57" (master's thesis, University of Wisconsin, Madison, 2004).

2. McGee notes that according to his son Lawrence A. Davis Jr., who also became president of UAPB, his father encountered the wrath of the legislature in 1959 when he appeared to a committee of that body to request funds. In 1963 a bill was introduced that would have created a branch junior college for blacks in northeast Arkansas. McGee writes that "rumors" were circulating that the money for the black junior college was to come from UAPB's budget. "It is certain the body used its financial powers to pressure Davis into indefinitely suspending and later expelling students for participating in the movement." "Trifling Elaborations," 42.

3. McGee, "Trifling Elaborations," 40.

4. McGee, "Trifling Elaborations," 46.

5. McGee, "Trifling Elaborations," 50.

6. *Arkansas Gazette,* July 14, 1963.

7. McGee, "Trifling Elaborations," 49.

8. Quoted in McGee, "Trifling Elaborations," 49.

9. McGee, "Trifling Expectations," 51.

10. Finley, "SNCC in Arkansas," 12.

11. McGee, "Trifling Expectations," 55.

12. Finley, "SNCC in Arkansas," 11, 12.

13. Finley, "SNCC in Arkansas," 11.

14. *Arkansas Gazette,* April 8, 1963.

15. Quoted in Finley, "SNCC in Arkansas," 13. By contrast, in the town of Hot Springs in Garland County, which depended so heavily on the tourist dollar, the power structure wanted no part of demonstrations, and quiet negotiations there resulted in an end to segregation.

16. Finley, "SNCC in Arkansas," 14, 15.

17. Janis Kearney, *Cotton Field of Dreams (*Chicago: Writing Our World Press, 2004), 57.

18. Quoted in Nick Kotz, *Judgment Days Lyndon Baines Johnson, Martin Luther King, Jr. and the Laws that Changed America (*New York: Houghton Mifflin, 2005), 153.

19. Josh Gottheimer, ed., *Ripples of Hope: Great American Civil Rights Speeches* (New York: Basic Civitas Books, 2004), 278.

20. While most of SNCC's work took place in Little Rock, Pine Bluff, Forrest City, Gould, Helena, West Helena, and Marvell, Jayme Stone documents that SNCC activists worked in other places such as Marianna in Lee County. Ironies abound in the Arkansas SNCC story, not the least of which is that NAACP rival L. C. Bates's judgment that SNCC's "direct action" campaigns of demonstrations and boycotts accomplished nothing except to make whites angry and were more harmful than helpful in achieving the progress that all activists desired. As field representative for the NAACP he concentrated on voter registration efforts and jobs, never

professing to understand that many blacks felt they had to confront whites and demand an end to segregation as a way to purge themselves of the sense of powerlessness that came with Jim Crow status. Before he was forced to retire by the NAACP in 1971, he would be considered an "Uncle Tom" by some activists within the Arkansas NAACP.

21. One particularly thinks of Delta black women who "disbanded" their preachers the 1890s.

22. Jayme Stone, "Women of the Arkansas Delta: Grassrootes Activism and the Student Non-violent Coordinating Committee (SNCC), 1963–1966," unpub., Grif Stockley Papers, Butler Center for Arkansas Studies, Little Rock, 4.

23. Stone, "Women of the Delta," 14.

24. Stone, "Women of the Delta," 13.

25. Stone, "Women of the Delta," 4.

26. Finley, "SNCC in Three Delta Towns," 121.

27. Finley, "SNCC in Three Delta Towns," 122.

28. *Arkansas Gazette,* November 19, 1963. William Hansen was a particular target for Bennett. When he married Pine Bluff resident and activist Ruth Buffington in his hometown of Cincinnati on October 12, 1963, Bennett complained after they had returned to Arkansas in November, "This is a deliberate affront and insult to all races of our state. It is a disservice wholly designed to insult the right thinking people of both races." Quoted in Finley, "SNCC in Arkansas," 16. Finley documents several instances of harassment by whites concerning sex in his unpublished paper, 15–16.

29. *Arkansas Gazette,* July 18,19, 1963.

30. *Arkansas Gazette,* February 2, 1962.

31. Finley, "SNCC in Three Delta Towns," 122.

32. Finley, "SNCC in Three Delta Towns," 121.

33. Finley, "SNCC in Three Delta Towns,"123.

34. Quoted in Finley, "SNCC in Arkansas," 1.

35. Quoted in *Arkansas Gazette,* February 2, 1964.

36. *Arkansas Gazette,* December 8, 1963.

37. Quoted in *Arkansas Gazette,* August 19, 1963.

38. Finley, "SNCC in Arkansas," 23.

39. Finley, "SNCC in Arkansas," 22.

40. Finley, "SNCC in Arkansas," 18.

41. Finley, "SNCC in Arkansas," 24.

42. Finley, "SNCC in Arkansas," 24.

43. Finley, "SNCC in Three Delta Towns," 129.

44. Finley, "SNCC in Arkansas," 27.

45. Finley, "SNCC in Arkansas," 28.

46. Finley, "SNCC in Arkansas," 28.

47. Mabel Harris Webb "A Minister's Stand: Pine Bluff, Arkansas, 1964," in *Crisis of Conscience,* ed. James T. Clemons and Kelly Farr (Little Rock: Butler Center for Arkansas Studies, 2007), 188.

48. Webb, "A Minister's Stand," 189.

49. Webb, "A Minister's Stand," 190.

50. Webb, "A Minister's Stand," 191, 192.

51. James O. Powell, interview by JaJuan Johnson, Butler Center for Arkansas Studies, Little Rock, 23.

52. Editorials and commendation, Grif Stockley Papers, Butler Center for Arkansas Studies, Little Rock.

53. David McDonald, "The Burden of Silence," in Clemons and Farr, *Crisis of Conscience,* 164.

54. McDonald, "The Burden of Silence," 164.

55. McDonald, "The Burden of Silence," 164.

56. McDonald, "The Burden of Silence," 165.

57. McDonald, "The Burden of Silence, 166.

58. McDonald, "The Burden of Silence," 166, 167. McDonald notes that the minister following his father did not share his views, and no blacks came to the church. He feels that what his father had said was "meaningless to everyone but my family."

59. Finley, "SNCC in Three Delta Towns," 124.

60. Jayme Stone, "The ArkSNCC Freedom Summer Project: The Civil Rights Movement's Other Freedom Summer," unpub., Grif Stockley Papers, Butler Center for Arkansas Studies, Little Rock, 10.

61. Stone, "The ArkSNCC Summer Project," 18.

62. Finley, "SNCC in Three Delta Towns," 125.

63. Finley, "SNCC in Three Delta Towns," 129.

64. *Arkansas Gazette,* September 18, 23, 24, 25, 1965.

65. Finley, "SNCC in Three Delta Towns," 130.

66. Jayme Stone, "The 1960s Civil Rights Work of Carrie Dilworth: Militant, Organized, and Willing to Catch Hell," unpub., Grif Stockley Papers, Butler Center for Arkansas Studies, Little Rock, 1.

67. Quoted in Stone, "Carrie Dilworth," 1.

68. Stone, "The Arkansas SNCC Summer Project," 30.

69. Finley, "SNCC in Three Delta Towns," 21.

70. Finley, "SNCC in Three Delta Towns," 131.

71. Stone, "The Arkansas SNCC Summer Project,"34.

72. Stone, "The Arkansas SNCC Summer Project," 34.

73. Finley, "SNCC in Arkansas," 48.

74. *Arkansas Gazette,* May 25, 1966.

75. *Arkansas Gazette,* May 29, 1966.

76. See Grif Stockley, "Thank God for Mississippi: Race Relations in Arkansas" (unpublished paper, Butler Center for Arkansas Studies, Little Rock), 136.

77. Finley, "SNCC in Three Delta Towns," 136.

78. Stone, "Carrie Dilworth," 16.

79. Stone, "ArkSNCC Freedom Summer," 33.

80. Quoted in Kearney, *Cotton Field of Dreams,* 233.

81. Kearney, *Cotton Field of Dreams,* 234.

82. Mathis, *Yet a Stranger,* 60, 61.

Chapter 16

1. Barbara Ritchie, ed., *The Riot Report: A Shortened Version of the Report of the National Advisory Commission on Civil Disorders* (New York: Viking, 1969), 30.
2. Richie, *The Riot Report,* 54.
3. Ritchie, *The Riot Report,* 55.
4. *Arkansas Gazette,* February 14, 1965.
5. *Arkansas Gazette,* March 23, 1966, May 6, 1966.
6. *Arkansas Gazette,* February 27, 1966.
7. *Arkansas Gazette,* April 24, 1966.
8. *Arkansas Gazette,* July 27, 1966.
9. *Arkansas Gazette,* January 6, 1966.
10. *Arkansas Gazette,* January 6, 1966.
11. Jim Ranchino, *Faubus to Bumpers: Arkansas Votes, 1960–70* (Arkadelphia, AR: Action Research, Inc., 1972), 37.
12. Ranchino, *Faubus to Bumpers,* 43.
13. Ranchino , *Faubus to Bumpers,* 75.
14. Ranchino , *Faubus to Bumpers,* 75.
15. *Arkansas Gazette,* November 6, 1967.
16. *Arkansas Gazette,* April 16, 1968.
17. *Arkansas Gazette,* April 18, 1968.
18. *Arkansas Gazette,* August 10, 1968.
19. *Arkansas Gazette,* August 13, 1968.
20. Probably fearing a whitewash of the incident because of the racial and economic composition of the jury—white businessmen, and a single black—the suit sought to prevent the grand jury from continuing to meet. Bobby Brown was Minnijean Brown's brother.
21. *Arkansas Gazette,* March 23, 1969.
22. *Arkansas Gazette,* March 21, 1969.
23. *Arkansas Gazette,* March 23, 1969.
24. *Arkansas Gazette,* April 20, 1969.
25. *Arkansas Gazette,* June 26, 1969.
26. *Arkansas Gazette,* August 21, 1969.
27. *Arkansas Gazette,* August 22, 1969.
28. *Arkansas Gazette,* August 27, 1969.
29. *Arkansas Gazette,* August 28, 1969.
30. *Arkansas Gazette,* September 4, 1969.
31. *Arkansas Gazette,* September 20, 1969.
32. *Arkansas Gazette,* September 19, 1969.
33. *Arkansas Gazette,* April 27, 1969.
34. *Arkansas Gazette,* November 19, 1969.
35. *New South,* Spring 1968, 65.
36. *Arkansas Gazette,* August 16, 1969.
37. *Arkansas Gazette,* November 19, 1969.
38. *Arkansas Gazette,* December 9, 1969.
39. *Arkansas Gazette,* January 15, 1970.

40. *Arkansas Gazette,* January 17, 1970, January 23, 1970.
41. *Arkansas Gazette,* April 7, 1970.
42. *Arkansas Gazette,* May 2, 1970.
43. *Arkansas Gazette,* May 5, 1970.
44. *Arkansas Gazette,* May 10, 1970
45. *Arkansas Gazette,* May 10, 1970, June 26, 1970.
46. *Arkansas Gazette,* June 3, 1970.
47. *Arkansas Gazette,* August 29, 1970.
48. *Arkansas Gazette,* October 16, 1971.
49. *Arkansas Gazette,* January 9, 1971.
50. *Many Voices,* September 15–28, 1971, Butler Center for Arkansas Studies, Little Rock.
51. Earl Anthes, interview with author, July 25, 2006.
52. *Arkansas Gazette,* April 12, 1970.
53. *Arkansas Gazette,* September 25, 1990.
54. *Many Voices,* August 25, 1971, Butler Center for Arkansas Studies, Little Rock.
55. *Arkansas Gazette,* January 27, 1971.
56. *Arkansas Gazette,* April 7, 1971.
57. *Arkansas Gazette,* April 24, 1971.
58. *Arkansas Gazette,* August 24, 1971.
59. *Arkansas Gazette,* October 29, 1971.
60. Much work remains to be done on the history of race relations in Arkansas but particularly in the Delta in the 1960s.

Chapter 17

1. Quoted in Marvin Schwartz, *In Service to America: A History of VISTA in Arkansas 1965–1985* (Fayetteville: University of Arkansas Press, 1988), 192.
2. Quoted in Schwartz, *In Service to America,* 240.
3. The author was a senior at T. A. Futrall High School in Marianna in 1962.
4. Schwartz, *In Service to America,* 240.
5. Schwartz, *In Service to America,* 197.
6. Schwartz, *In Service to America,* 197.
7. Quoted in Schwartz, *In Service to America,* 243.
8. Quoted in Schwartz, *In Service to America,* 204.
9. Gordon D. Morgan, *Marianna: A Sociological Essay on an Eastern Arkansas Town* (Jefferson City: New Scholars Press Jefferson City, 1973), 5.
10. Morgan, *Marianna,* 5. Outside of Ruth Polk Patterson and Morgan, both African Americans, no Arkansas academicians who have written about racial issues appear to have dealt at length with the significance of skin color. However, as noted, other African American writers living in or writing about Arkansas have noted its importance.

11. Morgan, *Marianna,* 6.

12. Olly Neal Jr., interview with Robert Korstad, Fall 1992, Butler Center for Arkansas Studies, Little Rock, 15.

13. Morgan, *Marianna,* 7.

14. Quoted in Schwartz, *In Service to America,* 5.

15. Olly Neal Jr., interview, 70.

16. In a 1992 interview with Robert Korstad, Neal said he had a commitment from a bureaucrat in Washington DC that a veto would be overridden but that he could not reveal this pledge to the members of his group at the time they met with Bumpers. 70.

17. Olly Neal Jr., interview, 75.

18. Quoted in Adler, *Land of Opportunity,* 201.

19. Adler, *Land of Opportunity,* 200.

20. Quoted in Adler, *Land of Opportunity,* 204.

21. Quoted in Adler, *Land of Opportunity,* 205.

22. *Arkansas Gazette,* August 6, 1971.

23. *Arkansas Gazette,* August 8, 10, 17, 1971.

24. *Arkansas Gazette,* March 3, 1972.

25. *Arkansas Gazette,* September 12, 1971.

26. *Arkansas Gazette,* January 14, 1972.

27. *Arkansas Gazette,* January 28, 1972.

28. *Arkansas Gazette,* January 28, 1972.

29. *Arkansas Gazette,* February 14, 1972.

30. *Arkansas Gazette,* April 4, 1972.

31. *Many Voices,* March 4, 1972.

32. *Many Voices,* March 18, 1972.

33. Quoted in Adler, *Land of Opportunity,* 201.

34. Quoted in Adler, *Land of Opportunity,* 202.

35. Olly Neal Jr., interview, 69.

36. *Arkansas Gazette,* March 18, 1972.

37. *Arkansas Gazette,* April 21, 27, 1972.

38. *Arkansas Gazette,* March 7, 1972.

39. *Arkansas Gazette,* February 12, 17, 1972.

40. Quoted in Brundage, *The Southern Past,* 276.

41. Quoted in Brundage, *The Southern Past,* 276.

42. Dougan, *Arkansas Odyssey,* 615.

43. Terry Frei, *Horns, Hogs, and Nixon Coming: Texas vs. Arkansas in Dixie's Last Stand* (New York: Simon & Schuster, 2002), 86.

44. Frei, *Horns, Hogs, and Nixon Coming,* 87.

45. After Frank Broyles became athletic director in 1973 and hired Nolan Richardson as the Razorback basketball coach, it was only then that the Razorbacks reached the pinnacle of success with a NCCA championship in 1994. And it was Darren McFadden who carried the Razorbacks in 2006 and 2007 to their most successful seasons in many years.

46. Quoted in Frei, *Horns, Hogs, and Nixon Coming,* 93.

47. Quoted in Frei, *Horns, Hogs, and Nixon Coming,* 93.

48. E. Lynn Harris, *What Becomes of the Brokenhearted* (New York: Doubleday, 2003), 94.

Chapter 18

1. Donald Holley, "Leaving The Land of Opportunity Arkansas and the Great Migration," *Arkansas Historical Quarterly* 64 (2005): 245–61, 249. See also, Donald Holley , *The Second Great Emancipation*. The numerous conclusions that Holley draws from the "Great Migration" have been widely challenged. For example, see Nan Elizabeth Woodruff's review in the May 2003 Journal of Southern History.

2. *Arkansas Gazette,* April 3, 1971.

3. Frye Gaillard, *The Dream Long Deferred: The Landmark Struggle for Desegregation in Charlotte, North Carolina,* 3rd ed. (Columbia: University of South Carolina Press: 2006), xiv.

4. *Arkansas Gazette,* October 21, 1970.

5. Quoted in Kirk, "A Study in Second Class Citizenship," 280.

6. Quoted in Kirk, "A Study in Second Class Citizenship," 281.

7. Quoted in Kirk, "A Study in Second-Class Citizenship," 283.

8. According to Berna J. Love, "Many blacks felt there was a 'master plan' or 'plot' to rid the city of the West Ninth Street black business district."

9. The strip development "Town and Country" was meant to provide easy access shopping for the seven hundred homes being built in Broadmoor by Fausett and Company in 1953. For a discussion of factors other than race in the development of Little Rock, see F. Hampton Roy Sr. and Charles Witsell Jr., *How We Lived: Little Rock As An American City* (Little Rock: August House, 1984), 217–22.

10. Berna J. Love notes that plans had been drawn up that went back to the early 1930s for an east-west corridor that contemplated using the streets "between Seventh and Fourteenth Streets for development as a major thoroughfare.'" *End of the Line,* 85.

11. Love, *End of the Line,* 87.

12. Quoted in Love, *End of the Line,* 91.

13. *Arkansas Gazette,* December 28, 1971.

14. The author was a member of the Oak Forest Property Owners Association and witnessed first-hand the blockbusting tactics of the real estate industry and government's lack of ability or desire to deal with it. See *Arkansas Gazette,* October 22, 23, 1971.

15. Caroline Proctor, "A History and Analysis of Federal Court Decisions in School Desegregation Cases: Implications for Arkansas (dissertation, University of Mississippi, 1992), 124.

16. Dougan, *Arkansas Odyssey,* 617.

17. Proctor, "School Desegregation Cases," 123.

18. Quoted in Stockley, *Daisy Bates,* 289.

19. Proctor, "School Desegregation Cases," 126.

20. Proctor "School Desegregation Cases," 131.

21. Proctor, "School Desegregation Cases," 35. This evidence of board dereliction confirms that the judiciary and lawyers might dictate changes that demand respect for constitutional rights of minorities on paper, but what actually occurred inside the school to guarantee their rights was quite something else again.

22. Quoted in Paul W. Masem, "Resegregation: a Case Study of an Urban School District," (dissertation, George Peabody College, 1986), 147.

23. Quoted in Masem, "Resegregation," 149.

24. Proctor, "School Desegregation Cases," 155.

25. Proctor, "School Desegregation Cases," 157.

26. Quoted in Proctor, "School Desegregation Cases," 159.

27. *Arkansas Gazette,* October 20, 1981.

28. Quoted in *Arkansas Gazette,* October 19, 1981.

29. Quoted in Harris, *What Becomes of the Brokenhearted,* 35, 36.

30. Quoted in Harris, *What Becomes of the Brokenhearted,* 37.

31. Quoted in *Arkansas Gazette,* October 19, 1981.

32. See Stockley, "Thank God for Mississippi," 197n12.

33. *Arkansas Gazette,* December 3, 1974; *Arkansas Gazette,* December 19, 1974.

34. *Arkansas* Gazette, April 23, 1974.

35. Quoted in *Arkansas Times,* February 9, 1977.

36. Quoted in *Arkansas Gazette,* January 3, 1971.

37. *Arkansas Gazette,* September 17, 1974; *Arkansas Gazette,* September 18, 1974.

38. As assistant mayor, Bussey was quoted in August 1981, "If they throw me out, there's only one thing you can say. It's because I'm black. That's all you can say." *Arkansas Democrat-Gazette,* August 16, 1981.

39. *Arkansas Gazette,* November 26, 1991.

40. Quoted in Stockley, *Daisy Bates,* 265.

41. Quoted in *Arkansas Times,* 27.

42. Quoted in *Arkansas Times,* 27.

43. Quoted in *Arkansas Times,* 30.

44. Quoted in *Arkansas Times,* 27.

45. Quoted in *Arkansas Times,* 27.

Chapter 19

1. *Arkansas Gazette,* July 5, 1981.

2. Diane Blair and Jay Barth, *Arkansas Politics and Government* (Lincoln: University Press of Nebraska, 2005), 286, 287.

3. *Jeffers v. Tucker,* 847 F. Supp. 655–657 (E.D. Ark. 1994).

4. Quoted in Adler, *Land of Opportunity,* 212.

5. Quoted in Adler, *Land of Opportunity,* 272.

6. Quoted in Adler, *Land of Opportunity,* 372.
7. Quoted in Adler, *Land of Opportunity,* 372.
8. Quoted in Adler, *Land of Opportunity,* 373.
9. Quoted in Adler, *Land of Opportunity,* 369.
10. *Thornburg v. Gingles,* 478 U.S. 30, 44 (1986).
11. *Hunt v. State of Arkansas,* no. PB-C-89-406 (E.D. 1992).
12. Jay Barth, *Arkansas Democrat,* May 17, 1986.
13. Quoted in Adler, *Land of Opportunity,* 211, 212.
14. Quoted in Adler, *Land of Opportunity,* 215.
15. Quoted in Adler, *Land of Opportunity,* 215.
16. Quoted in Paul Greenberg, *Entirely Personal* (Jackson: University Press of Mississippi, 1992), 167.
17. Bell Hooks, *Rock My Soul: Black People and Self-Esteem* (New York: Washington Square Books, 2004).
18. Quoted in *Arkansas Democrat-Gazette,* March 5, 1995.
19. Christabel Graham Eatmon, interview with Rearl Johnson, October 3, 1994, Dunbar Project, col. A-119, series 2/1, box 1, University of Arkansas, Libraries, Little Rock.
20. Quoted in Greenberg, *Entirely Personal,* 167.
21. Kirk, "A Study in Second Class Citizenship," 282.
22. Quoted in Dougan, *Arkansas Odyssey,* 617.
23. Dougan, *Arkansas Odyssey,* 616.
24. Quoted in Beth Roy, *Bitters in the Honey: Tales of Hope and Disappointment across Divides of Race and Time* (Fayetteville: University of Arkansas Press, 1999), 357.
25. Quoted in Roy, *Bitters in the Honey,* 355, 356.
26. Quoted in Roy, *Bitters in the Honey,* 358.
27. Quoted in Roy, *Bitters in the Honey,* 364.
28. Quoted in Roy, *Bitters in the Honey,* 365.
29. Quoted in Dunbar Project, col. A-119, series 2/1, box 2, file 19, November 2, 1994, University of Arkansas Libraries, Little Rock, 10.
30. Quoted in Roy, *Bitters in the Honey,* 340.
31. Quoted in Blair and Barth, *Arkansas Politics and Government,* 1.
32. "1990 Census Data Compared to 2000 Census Data," telephone interview with Walter Malone, May 3, 2007, Planning Division, City of Little Rock.
33. Quoted in *Arkansas Democrat-Gazette,* December 31, 1995.
34. Quoted in *Arkansas Democrat-Gazette,* December 31, 1995.
35. Olly Neal Jr., interview, 72.
36. J. B. Smith, e-mail to author, 2006, Grif Stockley Papers, Butler Center for Arkansas Studies, Little Rock.
37. Olly Neal Jr., proceedings of the Arkansas Advisory Committee, Helena, Arkansas, March 21–22, 1990, Grif Stockley Papers, Butler Center for Arkansas Studies, Little Rock, 171–72.
38. Neal's remarks to the Arkansas Advisory Committee in 1990 provide the reader with an unusually candid and open discussion of racial problems in the Arkansas Delta from the perspective of an African

American who played a number of key roles from the late 1960s to the present.

Chapter 20

1. The statues were funded, in part, through the passage of Act 1483 of 2005. According to an oral interview with John and Cathy Deering, the placement of the sculpture at the state capitol was not a foregone conclusion. Cathy Deering reveals that it was she who made convincing arguments that the grounds of the state capitol was the appropriate place for the piece whose title is "Testament." John and Kathy Deering, interview with Jajuan Johnson, November 9, 2005, Butler Center for Arkansas Studies, Little Rock.

2. *Arkansas Democrat-Gazette,* May 2, 2006. Pulaski County Special School District's Mills University Studies High ranked fiftieth. The federal administrative agency implementing the massive "No Child Left Behind Law" placed Central on its national "2006 School Improvement List" because of a history of "poor Benchmark and End-of-Course test results" in math and literacy for blacks.

3. Robert Mock, interview with author, October 2006.

4. Quoted in *Arkansas Times,* February 3, 2005, 18.

5. Quoted in *Arkansas Times,* February 3, 2005, 20.

6. Quoted in *Arkansas Democrat-Gazette,* January 29, 2006. It is not so clear to everyone that much in Harrison has changed and that a public relations effort is under way. One observer of the current racial scene in Harrison by the name of George Holcomb told Elliot Jaspin, author of *Buried in the Bitter Waters Hidden History of Racial Cleansing in America* (New York: Basic Books, 2007), 123, "What has really changed? Not very fucking much."

7. Jeannie Whayne and Willard Gatewood, eds., *The Arkansas Delta: Land of Paradox* (Fayetteville: University of Arkansas Press, 1993), 25.

8. Quoted in *Arkansas Times,* February 3, 2005, 14.

9. Quoted in *Arkansas Times,* February 3, 2005, 15.

10. Quoted in *Arkansas Times,* February 3, 2005, 14.

11. Quoted in *Arkansas Times,* February 3, 2005, 15.

12. Quoted in *Arkansas Times,* February 3, 2005, 15.

13. Quoted in *Arkansas Times,* February 3, 2005, 15

14. Quoted in *Arkansas Times,* February 3, 2005, 17.

15. Quoted in *Arkansas Times,* February 3, 2005, 16.

16. Quoted in *Arkansas Times,* February 3, 2005, 17.

17. Quoted in *Arkansas Times,* February 3, 2005, 17.

18. Quoted in *Arkansas Times,* February 3, 2005, 20, 21.

19. Quoted in *Racial Attitudes in Pulaski County,* Institute of Government Perspectives on Community, March 2006, University of Arkansas at Little Rock, 17.

20. *Racial Attitudes in Pulaski County,* 18.

21. Blair and Barth, *Arkansas Politics and Government,* 360, 361.

22. Grif Stockley, "The Perfect Racial Storm," *Arkansas Times,* February 7, 2008, 12.

23. Earl Anthes, interview with author, July 6, 2006, Butler Center for Arkansas Studies, Little Rock.

24. *Racial Attitudes in Pulaski County,* 10.

25. *Racial Attitudes in Pulaski County,* 14.

26. *Racial Attitudes in Pulaski County,* 12.

27. *Racial Attitudes in Pulaski County,* 15.

28. *Arkansas Democrat-Gazette,* July 9, 2004.

29. *Arkansas Democrat-Gazette,* March 24, 2002.

30. Jaquator Hamer, "University of Arkansas' African American Undergraduate Students' Perceptions of the Campus Climate" (dissertation, University of Arkansas, 2000), 72, 73.

31. *Arkansas Democrat-Gazette,* September 9, 2006.

32. "The Arkansas Lawyer," (Spring 2007), 10.

33. *Arkansas Democrat-Gazette,* July 20, 2004.

34. African Americans have always taken great pride in the two high schools in Little Rock and North Little Rock that existed until white supremacy and school integration dictated their demise. The continued vitality of both black high school alumni groups in the present who attended Dunbar in Little Rock and Scipio A. Jones in North Little Rock is a cultural phenomenon. Annual reunions of both schools have attracted and continue to bring hundreds of blacks to Little Rock to celebrate their educational experiences, which they almost uniformly contend was better than what black students receive in the present. Formal interviews of former Dunbar students show that typical of the beliefs blacks held about their education at Dunbar was that the teachers cared deeply about the students and demanded that they perform to the best of their ability. According to a July 6, 2007, article in the *Arkansas Democrat-Gazette* on the results of the Arkansas benchmark and end-of-course exams, "Black students in Arkansas historically have trailed their white peers often by more than 30 percentage points. But in most cases this year, they closed the divide with their white peers by 1 to 5 percentage points."

35. *Arkansas Democrat-Gazette,* November 11, 2005.

36. *Arkansas Democrat-Gazette,* October 11, 2006. In fact, as Katherine Mitchell pointed out, the school board had already begun voting on racial lines. Now president of the board, she told the *Arkansas Times* in September 2007 that "it was never really characterized as voting along racial lines until the majority of the board became African-American—the only two of us on the board [at the time] voted for Dr. [Morris] Holmes. . . . The five who were white voted for Dr. Brooks. No one mentioned we voted along racial lines, but we did. That's not a new issue." *Arkansas Times,* September 20, 2007, 40.

37. Quoted in *Arkansas Democrat-Gazette,* February 24, 2007.

38. For a comprehensive analysis of this trend since 1957, it is

suggested that readers click on the digital collection on the Butler Center for Arkansas Studies website to view maps and read or hear a lecture of Dr. Jay Barth on this subject. http://www.butlercenter.org/index.php.

39. *Arkansas Times,* May 10, 2007, 10.

40. *Arkansas Democrat-Gazette,* March 3, 2006.

41. Blair and Barth, *Arkansas Politics and Government,* 288.

42. *Arkansas Democrat-Gazette,* July 24, 2006.

43. Anthes, interview.

44. Anthes, interview.

45. Roy, *Bitters in the Honey,* 10.

46. Roy, *Bitters in the Honey,* 13.

47. Margaret Jones Bolsterli's account of her life growing up in the Arkansas Delta will strike natives of that region as an honest and very readable attempt to deal with the legacy of the past without wallowing in guilt. While she candidly admits that "racism permeated every aspect of our lives . . . it was part of the air everyone breathed," she treats her fellow white Southerners with genuine dignity, love, and respect. *Born in the Delta,* 126.

SELECTED BIBLIOGRAPHY

In approximately the last fifty years, there has been a transformation in the literature in Arkansas as scholars and others influenced by the civil rights movement and the federal government's commitment to equality in the 1960s begin to reassess the state's racial past. Significant progress has been made to provide a more inclusive and balanced record of the past. Much, however, remains to be done in documenting and interpreting our racial history. With the advent of the digital era, documentation of the past has been made easier but at the same time more complex as the amount of information available increases. Libraries and historical societies all over the country including Arkansas have created online finding aids that allow readers to research manuscripts and documents related to race. Unique in the state is the online *Encyclopedia of Arkansas* at the Butler Center for Arkansas Studies in Little Rock, which contains many entries and references to the materials in this book. Unique, as well, is the Butler Center's digital index that allows researchers to zero in on a specific topic or issue in a recorded interview. What follows is a selected bibliography (excluding Arkansas history text books) of Arkansas race relations between African Americans and whites beginning with slavery. For convenience of the general reader, materials are not grouped into the divisions of primary and secondary sources but under section headings.

Slavery

Arnold, Morris S. *European Legal Traditions in Arkansas, 1686–1836.* Fayetteville: University of Arkansas Press, 1985.

Battershell, Gary. "The Socioeconomic Role of Slavery in the Arkansas Upcountry." *Arkansas Historical Quarterly* 58 (1999).

Bolton, S. Charles. *Arkansas, 1800–1860: Remote and Restless.* Fayetteville: University of Arkansas Press, 1998.

———. "Fugitives from Injustice: Freedom-Seeking Slaves in Arkansas, 1800–1860." Report to the National Park Service, 2006, *www.nps.gov/history/online_books/ugrr/arkansas*.

Higgins, Billy. *A Stranger and a Sojourner: Peter Caulder, Free Black Frontiersman in Antebellum Arkansas.* Fayetteville: University of Arkansas Press, 2004.

Lankford, George E., ed. *Bearing Witness: Memories of Arkansas Slavery*

Narratives from the 1930s WPA Collection. Fayetteville: University of Arkansas Press, 2006.

McNeilly, Donald P. *The Old South Frontier: Cotton Plantations and the Formation of Arkansas Society, 1819–1861.* Fayetteville: University of Arkansas Press, 2000.

Moneyhon, Carl. *The Impact of the Civil War and Reconstruction on Arkansas: Persistence in the Midst of Ruin.* Baton Rouge: Louisiana State University Press, 1994.

Patterson, Ruth. *The Seed of Sally Good'n: A Black Family of Arkansas, 1833–1953.* Lexington: University Press of Kentucky, 1985.

Stafford, L. Scott. "Slavery and the Arkansas Supreme Court." *University of Arkansas at Little Rock Law Journal* 19 (1997).

Taylor, Orville W. *Negro Slavery in Arkansas.* Fayetteville: University of Arkansas Press, 2000.

The Civil War

Barnes, Kenneth C. *Who Killed John Clayton? Political Violence and the Emergence of the New South 1861–1893.* Durham: Duke University Press, 1998.

Christ, Mark, ed. *All Cut to Pieces and Gone to Hell: The Civil War, Race Relations and the Battle of Poison Spring.* Little Rock: August House, 2003.

DeBlack, Tom. *With Fire and Sword: Arkansas 1861–1874.* Fayetteville: University of Arkansas Press, 2003.

Finley, Randy. *From Slavery to Uncertain Freedom: the Freedmen's Bureau in Arkansas, 1865–1969.* Fayetteville: University of Arkansas Press, 1996.

Lovett, Bobby L. "African Americans, Civil War, and Aftermath in Arkansas." *Arkansas Historical Quarterly* 45 (1995).

Moneyhon, Carl. *Impact of the Civil War.*

Reconstruction

Barnes. *Who Killed John Clayton?*

DeBlack. *With Fire and Sword.*

Foner, Eric. *Forever Free: The Story of Emancipation and Reconstruction.* New York: Alfred A. Knopf, 2005.

Graves, John. *Town and Country: Race Relations and Urban Development in Arkansas 1865–1905.* Fayetteville: University of Arkansas Press, 1990.

Moneyhon. *Impact of the Civil War.*

Singletary, Otis A. "Militia Disturbances in Arkansas During Reconstruction." *Arkansas Historical Quarterly* 15 (1956).

St. Hilaire, Joseph M. "The Negro Delegates in the Arkansas

Constitutional Convention of 1868: A Group Profile." *Arkansas Historical Quarterly* 33 (1974).
Wintory, Blake J. "African-American Legislators in the Arkansas General Assembly, 1868–1893." *Arkansas Historical Quarterly* 65 (2006).
———. "Environmental and Social Change in Lee County Arkansas and the St. Francis River Basin, 1865–1905. Dissertation, University of Arkansas, 2005.

The Redeemer Era

Barnes, Kenneth C. *Journey of Hope: The Back-to-Africa Movement in Arkansas in the Late 1800s.* Chapel Hill: University of North Carolina Press, 2004.
———. *Who Killed John Clayton?*
Giggie, John. "Disband Him from the Church: African Americans and the Spiritual Politics of Disfranchisement in Post-Reconstruction Arkansas." *Arkansas Historical Quarterly* 60 (2001).
Gordon, Fon. *Caste & Class: The Black Experience in Arkansas, 1880–1920.* Athens: University of Georgia, 1995.
Graves. *Town and Country.*
Hahn, Steven. *A Nation under Our Feet: Black Political Struggles in the Rural South from Slavery to the Great Migration.* Cambridge, MA: Belknap Press of Harvard University Press, 2003.
Hoguet, Helen. "Protecting the Perfect Africa: The Politics of Race and Property in Post-Reconstruction Arkansas." Master's thesis, University of Wisconsin, 2004.
Lloyd, Peggy. "The Howard County Race Riots of 1883." *Arkansas Historical Quarterly* 59 (2000).
Patterson. *The Seed of Sally Good'n.*
Pickens, William. *Bursting Bonds: The Autobiography of a "New Negro."* Bloomington: Indiana University Press, 1991.
Welch, Melanie. "Violence and the Decline of Black Politics in St. Francis County." *Arkansas Historical Quarterly* 60 (2001).
Wintory, Blake. Dissertation, University of Arkansas, 2005.
Woodward, C. Vann. *The Strange Career of Jim Crow.* New York: Oxford University Press, 1966.

Jim Crow, Lynching, Disfranchisement, and Racial Cleansing

Arsenault, Raymond. *The Wild Ass of the Ozarks: Jeff Davis and the Social Basis of Southern Politics.* Philadelphia: Temple University Press, 1984.
Barnes. *Who Killed John Clayton, Journey of Hope.*
Bolsterli, Margaret Jones. *Born in the Delta: Reflections on the Making of a*

Southern White Sensibility. Fayetteville: University of Arkansas Press, 2000.

Buckelew, Richard. "Racial Violence in Arkansas: Lynchings and Mob Rule, 1860–1930." Dissertation, University of Arkansas, 1999.

Cook, Charles Orson. "Arkansas's Charles Hillman Brough, 1876–1935: An Interpretation." Dissertation, University of Houston, 1980.

Cortner, Richard. *A Mob Intent on Death: The NAACP and the Arkansas Riot Cases*. Middleton, CT: Wesleyan University Press, 1988.

Dillard, Tom. "Madness With a Past: An Overview of Race Violence in Arkansas History." *Arkansas Review* 32 (2001).

———. "Scipio A. Jones." *Arkansas Historical Quarterly* 31 (1972).

Finley, Randy. "Black Arkansans and World War One." *Arkansas Historical Quarterly* 49 (1990).

Froelich, Jacqueline and David Zimmerman. "Total Eclipse: The Destruction of the African American Community of Harrison, Arkansas in 1905 and 1909." *Arkansas Historical Quarterly* 58 (1999).

Gatewood, Willard B. *Aristocrats of Color: The Black Elite, 1880–1920*. Bloomington: Indiana University Press, 1990.

Gordon. *Caste & Class*.

Graves. *Town and Country*.

Holmes, William F. "The Arkansas Cotton Pickers Strike of 1891 and the Demise of the Colored Farmers Alliance." *Arkansas Historical Quarterly* 32 (1973).

Kirk, John A. "Dr. J. M. Robinson, the Arkansas Negro Democratic Association and Black Politics in Little Rock, Arkansas 1928–1952." *Pulaski County Historical Review* 41 (Spring 1993).

Lewis, Todd. "Race Relations in Arkansas, 1910–1919." Dissertation, University of Arkansas, 1995.

Loewen, James. *Sundown Towns: A Hidden Dimension of American Racism*. New York: New Press, 2005.

Moneyhon, Carl. *Arkansas and the New South, 1874–1929*. Fayetteville: University of Arkansas Press, 1997.

Patterson. *The Seed of Sally Good'n*.

Rolinson, Mary Gambrell. *Grass Roots Garveyism: The Universal Negro Improvement Association in the Rural South, 1920–1927*. Chapel Hill: University of North Carolina Press, 2007.

Stockley, Grif. *Blood in Their Eyes: The Elaine Race Massacres of 1919*. Fayetteville: University of Arkansas Press, 2000.

Taylor, Kieran. "We Have Just Begun: Black Organizing and White Response in the Arkansas Delta, 1919." *Arkansas Historical Quarterly* 58 (1999).

Vinikas, Vincent. "Specters in the Past: The St. Charles, Arkansas Lynching of 1904 and the Limits of Historical Inquiry." *Journal of Southern History* 55 (1999).

Wells-Barnett, Ida B. *The Arkansas Race Riot*. Chicago: Hume Job Print, 1920.

Whayne, Jeannie M. "Low Villains and Wickedness in High Places: Race and Class in Elaine Race Riots." *Arkansas Historical Quarterly* 58 (1999).

Whitaker, Robert. *On the Laps of Gods: The Red Summer of 1919 and the Struggle for Justice that Remade a Nation.* New York: Crown Publishers, 2008.

Williamson, Joel. *The Crucible of Race Black White Relations in the American South since Emancipation.* New York: Oxford University Press, 1984.

Woodruff, Nan. *American Congo: The African American Freedom Struggle in the Delta.* Cambridge, MA: Harvard University Press, 2003.

Race Relations in the Great Depression and the Beginning Challenges to Jim Crow in the Forties

Angelou, Maya. *The Collected Autobiographies.* New York: Modern Library, 2004.

Bolsterli. *Born in the Delta.*

Clemons, James T., ed. *Crisis of Conscience: Arkansas Methodists and the Civil Rights Struggle.* Little Rock: Butler Center for Arkansas Studies, 2007.

Grubbs, Donald. *Cry from the Cotton: The Southern Tenant Farmers Union and the New Deal.* Chapel Hill: University of North Carolina Press, 1971.

Holley, Donald. *The Second Great Emancipation: The Mechanical Cotton picker, Black Migration, and How They Shaped the Modern South.* Fayetteville: University of Arkansas Press, 2000.

Johnson, Ben III. *Arkansas in Modern America 1930–1999.* Fayetteville: University of Arkansas Press, 2000.

Kilpatrick, Judith. *There When We Needed Him: Wiley Austin Branton Civil Rights Warrior.* Fayetteville: University of Arkansas Press, 2007.

Kirk, John A. "A Study in Second Class Citizenship: Race, Urban Development, and Little Rock's Gillam Park, 1934–2004." *Arkansas Historical Quarterly* 64 (2005).

———. *Redefining the Color Line: Black Activism in Little Rock, Arkansas, 1940–1970.* Gainesville: University Press of Florida, 2002.

Love, Berna J. *The End of the Line: A History of Little Rock's West Ninth Street.* Little Rock: Center for Arkansas Studies, UALR, 2003.

Nichols, Guerdon D. "Breaking the Color Barrier at the University of Arkansas." *Arkansas Historical Quarterly* 27 (1968).

Smith, Griffin, Jr. "Localism and Segregation: Racial Patterns in Little Rock, Arkansas, 1945–1954." Master's thesis, Columbia University, 1965.

Smith, C. Calvin. *War and Wartime Changes: The Transformation of*

Arkansas, 1940–1945. Fayetteville: University of Arkansas Press, 1996.
Stockley. *Daisy Bates.*
Woodruff. *American Congo.*

Brown v. Board of Education and the 1957 Little Rock School Desegregation Crisis

Beals, Melba. *Warriors Don't Cry: A Searing Memoir of the Battle to Integrate Little Rock Central High*. New York: Pocket Books, 1994.
Bradburn, Gary. *On the Opposite Shore: The Making of North Little Rock*. Marceline, MO: Walsworth, 2004.
Brodie, Ralph and Marvin Swartz. *Central in Our Lives: Voices from Little Rock Central High School, 1957–1959*. Little Rock: Butler Center for Arkansas Studies, 2007.
Chappell, David. *A Stone of Hope: Prophetic Religion and the Death of Jim Crow*. Chapel Hill: University of North Carolina Press, 2001.
Clemons. *Crisis of Conscience*.
Freyer, Tony. *Little Rock on Trial:* Cooper v. Aaron *and School Desegregation*. Lawrence: University of Kansas, 2007.
———. *The Little Rock Crisis: A Constitutional Interpretation*. Westport, CT: Greenwood Press, 1984.
Godfrey, Phoebe. "Bayonets, Brainwashing, and Bathrooms: The Discourse of Race, Gender, and Sexuality in the Desegregation of Little Rock's Central High." *Arkansas Historical Quarterly* 62 (2001).
Jacoway, Elizabeth. *Turn Away Thy Son: Little Rock, The Crisis That Shocked the Nation*. Free Press: New York, 2007.
Johnson, Ben III "After 1957: Resisting Integration in Little Rock." *Arkansas Historical Quarterly* 66 (2007).
———. *Arkansas in Modern America*.
Kirk, John A. "The Little Rock Crisis and Postwar Black Activism in Arkansas." *Arkansas Historical Quarterly* 66 (2007).
———. *Beyond Little Rock: The Origins and Legacies of the Central High Crisis*. Fayetteville: University of Arkansas Press, 2007.
———. *Redefining the Color Line*.
McDowell, Linda and Samuel S. Taylor. "Arkansas Federal Writers' Project Interviewer." *Pulaski Historical Review* 5 (Spring 2007).
Miller, Laura A. *Fearless: Irene Gaston Samuel and the Life of a Southern Liberal*. Little Rock: Center for Arkansas Studies, 2002.
Morgan, Gordon. "The Arkansas Negro Boys' Industrial School, A Case Study in Institutional Organization." Master's thesis, University of Arkansas, 1956.
Nichols, David A. *A Matter of Justice Eisenhower and the Beginning of the Civil Rights Revolution*. New York: Simon & Schuster, 2007.

Ogden, Dunbar H. *My Father Said Yes: A White Pastor in Little Rock School Integration.* Nashville: Vanderbilt University Press, 2008.

Reed, Roy. " Out of Socialism into Realism." *Arkansas Historical Quarterly* 66 (2007).

———. *Orval Faubus: The Life and Times of an American Prodigal.* Fayetteville: University of Arkansas Press, 1997.

Spitzberg, Irving J., Jr., *Racial Politics in Little Rock, 1954–1954.* New York: Garland, 1987.

Stockley. *Daisy Bates.*

Vinzant, Gene. "The Pupil Placement Law and the Little Rock Crisis." Unp. paper presented to Arkansas Historical Association, April 27, 2007.

Williams, C. Fred. "Class, The Central Issue in the 1957 Little Rock School Crisis." *Arkansas Historical Quarterly* 56 (1997).

Wynn, Xavier. "The Development of African American Schools in Arkansas, 1863–1963: A Historical Comparison of Black and White Schools with Regards to Funding and Quality of Education." Dissertation, University of Mississippi, 1995.

The Modern Civil Rights Movement in Arkansas

Adler, William. *Land of Opportunity: One Family's Quest for the American Dream in the Age of Crack.* New York: Atlantic Monthly Press, 1995.

Blair, Diane and Jay Barth. *Arkansas Politics and Government.* Lincoln: University Press of Nebraska, 2005.

Finley, Randy. "Crossing the White Line: SNCC in Arkansas 1960–1967." Unpub., Grif Stockley Papers, Butler Center for Arkansas Studies.

———. "Crossing the White Line: SNCC in Three Delta Towns, 1963–1967." *Arkansas Historical Quarterly* 65 (2006).

Frei, Terry. *Horns, Hogs, & Nixon Coming: Texas v. Arkansas in Dixie's Last Stand.* New York: Simon & Schuster, 2002.

Gaillard, Frye. *The Dream Long Deferred: The Landmark Struggle for Desegregation in Charlotte, North Carolina.* Columbia: The University of South Carolina Press, 2006.

Greenberg, Paul. *Entirely Personal.* Jackson: University Press of Mississippi, 1992.

Harris, E. Lynn. *What Becomes of the Brokenhearted.* New York: Doubleday, 2003.

Kearney, Janis. *Cotton Field of Dreams.* Chicago: Writing Our World Press, 2004.

Kirk. *Redefining the Color Line.*

Kotz, Nick. *Judgment Days Lyndon Johnson, Martin Luther King, Jr., and the Laws that Changed America.* New York: Houghton Mifflin, 2005.

"Many Voices." Grif Stockley Papers, Butler Center for Arkansas Studies.

Mathis, Deborah. *Yet A Stranger, Why Black Americans Still Don't Feel at Home.* New York: Warner Books, 2002.

McGee, Holly Y. "It was the Wrong Time, and They Just Weren't Ready: Direct Action Protest in Pine Bluff, 1963." *Arkansas Historical Quarterly* 66 (2007).

Morgan, Gordon. *Marianna: A Sociological Essay on an Eastern Arkansas Town.* Jefferson City: New Scholars Press, 1973.

———. *The Edge of Campus: A Journal of the Black Experience at the University of Arkansas.* Fayetteville: University of Arkansas Press, 1990.

Ranchino, Jim. *Faubus to Bumpers: Arkansas Votes, 1960–70.* Arkadelphia, AR: Action Research, Inc. 1972.

Riffel, Brent. "In the Storm: William Hansen and the Student Non-violent Coordinating Committee in Arkansas, 1962–1967." *Arkansas Historical Quarterly* 63 (2004).

Roy, Beth. *Bitters in the Honey: Tales of Hope and Disappointment across Divides of Race and Time.* Fayetteville: University of Arkansas Press, 1999.

Schwartz, Marvin. *In Service to America: A History of VISTA in Arkansas 1965–1985.* Fayetteville: University of Arkansas Press, 1988.

Stockley. *Daisy Bates.*

Stone, Jayme. "The 1960s Civil Rights Work of Carrie Dilworth: Militant, Organized, and Willing to Catch Hell." Unpub., Grif Stockley Papers, Butler Center for Arkansas Studies.

———. "The ARKSNCC Freedom Summer Project: The Civil Rights Movement's Other Freedom Summer." Unpub., Grif Stockley Papers, Butler Center for Arkansas Studies.

———. "Women of the Arkansas Delta: Grassroots Activism and the Student Nonviolent Coordinating Committee (SNCC, 1963–1967)." Unpub., Grif Stockley Papers, Butler Center for Arkansas Studies.

Zinn, Howard. *SNCC: The New Abolitionists.* Boston: Beacon Press, 1964.

INDEX

A

C

E

F

I

J

K

L

M

N

GRIF STOCKLEY is the author of three nonfiction books, including *Race Relations in the Natural State; Daisy Bates: Civil Rights Crusader from Arkansas,* winner of the J. G. Ragsdale Award from the Arkansas Historical Association and the Arkansiana Award from the Arkansas Library Association; and *Blood in Their Eyes: The Elaine Race Massacres of 1919,* winner of the Booker Worthen Prize from the Central Arkansas Library System and recipient of a certificate of commendation from the American Association for State and Local History. In 1999 Stockley was awarded the Porter Prize for his fiction and in 2000 was inducted into the Arkansas Writers Hall of Fame. An attorney who has worked with the Center for Arkansas Legal Services, the Disability Rights Center, and the Arkansas branch of the American Civil Liberties Union, Stockley is also the author of six legal mysteries and is currently a historian with the Butler Center for Arkansas Studies in Little Rock.